KT-489-785

A Critical and Cultural Theory Reader

WITHDRAWN

1 1 JUN 2024
York St John University

3 8025 00592544 4

A Critical and Cultural Theory Reader

2nd Edition

edited by Antony Easthope and Kate McGowan

YORK ST. JOHN
LIBRARY & INFORMATION
SERVICES

Open University Press

Second edition first published in
North America in 2004 by
University of Toronto Press
Toronto and Buffalo

First published 1992. Reprinted 1993, 1994 (twice), 1996, 1997, 1998, 2003.
First published in this second edition, 2004.
Reprinted 2009, 2012

Editorial material and selection © Antony Easthope and Kate McGowan, 1992. The estate
of Antony Easthope, and Kate McGowan, 2004.
Individual chapters © The contributors.

Permission for this edition was arranged through McGraw-Hill International (UK) Limited

ISBN 978-0-8020-3859-3(cloth)
ISBN 978-0-8020-3800-5(paper)

All rights reserved. No part of this publication may be reproduced, stored in a retrieval
system or transmitted in any form or by any means, without written permission from the
publisher.

National Library of Canada Cataloguing in Publication

   A Critical and cultural theory reader/edited by Antony Easthope and
Kate McGowan – 2nd ed.

Includes bibliographical references and index.
ISBN 978-0-8020-3859-3(bound). – ISBN 978-0-8020-3800-5(pbk)

   1. Culture. 2. Popular culture. 3. Critical theory. I. Easthope,
Antony II. McGowan, Kate

PN81.C74 2004   306   C2004–901733–0

Typeset by YHT Ltd, London
Printed in the U.S.A.

∞

Printed on Acid-free paper.

Contents

SECTION 6
Postmodernism

Foreword

Antony Easthope died on 14 December 1999. We had been discussing the second edition of this Reader for several years, but our progress towards completing it had been hampered by serious illness on both sides. While we worried and fretted about each other, the writing we had embarked upon together took something of a back seat. At the time that Antony died, I think he believed a second edition would never make it to press. I probably thought the same way. However, spurred by the knowledge of how deeply committed to the project he was, and in something of a spurious effort to continue my intellectual conversations with him beyond the grave, I felt it important to finish on my own what we had started together. What results is an effect of many joint decisions and many playful, yet robust, conversations about theory undertaken when he was alive. In his absence I have had to make some of my own decisions about new materials to include, and I have been afforded the liberty of summarizing and introducing them on my own terms. But, wherever possible, I have attempted to take account of the positions Antony so eloquently articulated in the many books about theory and culture he has left us to plunder. I can only hope that what I have selected and described maintains the spirit and integrity of his thinking.

This book is most definitely for him, and it would never have been possible without him. However, I would also like to thank Diane Easthope for her encouragement of the project when I was ready to resume it, and Catherine Belsey for the enthusiasm with which she supported my proposal after Antony's death, as well as the intellectual inspiration she has provided for my thinking over many, many years.

Kate McGowan

Acknowledgements

In compiling this collection we have profited greatly from discussion with many people, from whom we have learned through both agreement and sometimes constructive disagreement: Barry Atkins, Margaret Beetham, Linnie Blake, Rob Lapsley, Shafqat Nasir, Jacqueline Roy and Michael Westlake. We are also grateful to Simon Malpas, Catherine Belsey and Scott Wilson, for their specific advice and criticisms, to Justin Vaughan at the Open University Press for allowing me to continue on my own and to Chris Cudmore for seeing the project through.

The editors and publishers are grateful to the following for permission to reprint copyright material. All possible care has been taken to trace ownership of the selections included, and to make full acknowledgement of their use. Peter Owen Ltd, London for the extract from *Course in General Linguistics* by Ferdinand de Saussure, edited by Charles Bally and Albert Sechehaye, translated by Wade Baskin. 'The Great Family of Man' from *Mythologies* by Roland Barthes is used by permission of the Estate of Roland Barthes, the translator Annette Lavers, Jonathan Cape as publishers, The Random House Group Limited. (*Mythologies* was first published in French by Editions du Seuil in 1957.) Pierre Macherey and Taylor & Francis for an extract from *A Theory of Literary Production*, translated by Geoffrey Wall. Umberto Eco and Indiana University Press for an extract from *The Role of The Reader*. The editorial board of *Screen* and Manchester University Press for an extract from *Theoretical Essays* by Colin MacCabe. Lawrence and Wishart Ltd, London, for extracts from Karl Marx, *The Critique of Political Economy* and Marx and Friedrich Engels, *The German Ideology* from the *Collected Works*. Verso for an extract from *Lenin* and *Philosophy* by Louis Althusser, translated by Ben Brewster. The extract from *The Second Sex* by Simone de Beauvoir, translated by H. M. Parshley, copyright 1952 and renewed 1980 by Alfred A. Knopf, a division of Random House, Inc., is used by permission of Alfred A. Knopf, a division of Random House, Inc. Pantheon for an extract from *Orientalism* by Edward Said. Homi K. Bhabha and *Screen*, vol. 24, no. 6 (1983) for the extract from 'The "Other" Question'. Verso for an extract from *The Sublime Object of Ideology* by Slavoj Žižek. The extract from *Beyond The Pleasure Principle* is reprinted by permission of the Random House Group Limited. Sigmund Freud © Copyrights, The Institute of Psychoanalysis and The Hogarth Press for permission to quote from *The Standard*

Edition of the Complete Psychological Works of Sigmund Freud, translated and edited by James Strachey. For an extract from *Écrits, A Selection* by Jacques Lacan, translated by Alan Sheridan, © 1977, Taylor and Francis Books Ltd (Tavistock). Editions du Seuil and Grove Atlantic for the extract from *Black Skin/White Masks* by Frantz Fanon. Julia Kristeva and *The Times Literary Supplement* of 12 October 1973 for an extract from 'The system and the speaking subject'. The six pages from *The History of Sexuality; Volume 1, An Introduction* by Michel Foucault, translated by Robert Hurley, are reproduced by permission of Penguin Books Ltd (Allen Lane 1979, first published as 'La Volonte de Savoir' 1976) copyright © Editions Gallimard 1976, translation copyright © Random House Inc. 1977. The eight pages from *Discipline and Punish: The Birth of the Prison* by Michel Foucault, translated by Alan Sheridan, are reproduced by permission of Penguin (first published as *Surveiller et Punir; Naissance de le prison* by Éditions Gallimard 1975, Allen Lane, 1975), copyright © Alan Sheridan, 1977. For an excerpt from *The Pleasure of the Text* by Roland Barthes, translation copyright © 1975 by Farrar, Straus & Giroux, Inc., original © 1973 by Editions du Seuil, reprinted by permission of Hill and Wang, a division of Farrar, Straus and Giroux, LLC. Northwestern University Press for the essay 'Differance' from *Speech and Phenomena and Other Essays on Husserl's Theory of Signs*, by Jacques Derrida, translated by David B. Allison (the essay first appeared in French as 'La Différance' in the *Bulletin de la société français de philosophie*, vol. LXII (1968)). For an extract from 'On the Universal Tendency to Debasement in the Sphere of Love', Sigmund Freud, © copyrights, The Institute of Psychoanalysis and The Hogarth Press for permission to quote from *The Standard Edition of the Complete Psychological Works of Sigmund Freud*, translated and edited by James Strachey, reprinted by permission of the Random House Group Limited. Hélène Cixous for an extract from 'Sorties'. The editorial board of *Screen* for an extract from 'Visual pleasure and narrative cinema' by Laura Mulvey. Taylor & Francis for the extract from *Welcome to the Jungle* by Kobena Mercer, Routledge, 1994. Taylor & Francis for an extract from *Real and Imagined Women*, by Rajeswari Sunder Rajan, 1993, Routledge. Copyright © 1990 from *Gender Trouble: Feminism and the Subversion of Identity* by Judith Butler, reproduced by permission of Routledge/Taylor & Francis Books, Inc. Homi K. Bhabha and Taylor & Francis for the extract from *The location of culture*, 1994, Routledge (Methuen). For an extract from *The Postmodern Condition*, translation of the French by Geoff Bennington and Brian Massumi, 1979, Manchester University Press, Manchester, UK and University of Minnesota Press. Jean Baudrillard and Semiotext(e) Inc. for an extract from *Simulations*, translated by Paul Foss, Paul Patton and Philip Beitchman. Polity Press Ltd for the extract from *The Inhuman* by Jean-François Lyotard. The University of Chicago Press, Chicago and London, for the extract from *The Gift of Death* by Jacques Derrida, translated by David Wills, Religion and Postmodernism: A Series Edited by Mark C. Taylor. Verso for an extract from *The Spirit of Terrorism* by Jean Baudrillard. Verso for an extract from *Welcome to the Desert of the Real* by Slavoj Žižek.

Finally, special thanks go to Shafqat Nasir for putting up with the stress of producing the volume, and for rescuing my hard drive when it crashed right at the end of the whole process. .

Introduction

In the gap between the first edition and the second updated edition of this Reader, critical and cultural theory has undergone something of a transformation. Initially regarded with suspicion, many of the ideas that constitute the discipline have filtered through the academy and have now become required reading in subjects ranging from English literature, cultural studies and art history to the humanities generally. It is no longer the job of this Reader, then, simply to insist on putting critical and cultural theory 'out there' into the Anglo-American domain. However, this in itself poses a special kind of problem, which must be addressed. Whenever initially disturbing ideas become accepted within a mainstream that has resisted them, there is invariably an issue as to how, why and in what terms that acceptance has been possible. While some of the terms of critical and cultural theory have undoubtedly provided 'buzz-words' for English and cultural studies over the years, it is less certain that the concepts they establish have been as readily embraced. If the acceptance of some of the work in critical and cultural theory has been possible without a rigorous regard for the full implications of the ideas they offer, then the radical potential of such ideas to challenge and disturb the disciplines within which they operate is lost. Perhaps the job of this Reader now is to continue to insist upon the full spectrum of those ideas encountered in their original contexts and without the inevitable dilution of easy 'how to' guides or reductive readings that make unfamiliar ideas appear more palatable. This means an insistence on reading Saussure, Derrida, Lyotard *et al.* first hand, and on tracing the logic through which ideas in the contemporary can be placed and understood.

We are conscious at the same time, of course, that the very selection of material for this Reader has its own consequences. It does, unashamedly, proffer a *particular* pathway through critical and cultural theory. It privileges a particular set of ideas that start from an attention to language as the seat of meaning. It deals, then, very specifically with poststructuralist and postmodern ideas, and it focuses specifically on issues of textuality. One attraction of this paradigm of study is that it breaks with the supremacy of the canon of traditional English literature, and with the idea of the literary work as a supposedly self-defining object. Within its terms, the work comes to be seen as *transitive*, an effect of the relation between text and the reader, and as culturally constituted in much the same way as other kinds of text less venerated than literature. To this end, we have included a range of work, influenced variously by psychoanalysis and theories of the subject, which explores how texts can become effects in and for their readers, and which actively encourage the study of the texts of high and popular culture together. In doing this, this selection of readings also marks itself off from the more sociological aspects of cultural studies, which focus on analyses of reception, audiences and the ways in which groups and classes have reproduced and used cultural texts. To have done justice to this, and to the writings of Mikhail Bakhtin, Claude Lévi-Strauss, Jürgen Habermas, Pierre Bourdieu and Clifford Geertz (among others), would have required a second, companion volume. Perhaps this is a starting point for another kind of project.

In the meantime, however, no selection is natural, no anthology perfect. We are conscious that this one traces a particular history of the reception of continental ideas into the Anglophone world. And while the collection of readings for this second edition represents something of an 'updating', it is interesting to note how much of the content of the original Reader remains crucial to an understanding of the 'new'. The readings selected are grouped into six sections. Five consist of 'Semiology', 'Ideology', 'Subjectivity', 'Difference' and 'Gender and Race'. Another is used to indicate the crucial importance of understanding the present, a question acutely posed by the issue of postmodernism. One special problem for this new domain of critical and cultural theory is posed by the fact that the medium of popular culture is frequently visual – film, television, advertising, journalistic photography. In response to this, we include a number of essays which address the analysis of specifically visual material. Finally, with regard to the ideological effect of language, we have taken the liberty of noting its operation in some of the original text. On the first occasion a writer has assumed everyone is male, we have written [sic] but not subsequently.

Much of the work collected here was written in France, particularly after the 'events' of May 1968, and has had to be translated into English. Some of it is difficult to follow, partly because it is written in general theoretical terms, but often because it argues for views that are, as we have claimed, disturbingly unfamiliar. For this reason, as well as an 'Introduction' to each section, every text is given an outline 'Summary' at the end of the book. In writing these, we have been guided by our experience of teaching students at Manchester Metropolitan University, though these summaries represent only a version of each text, another voice in the discussion the texts themselves should provoke.

Section 1
SEMIOLOGY

Introduction

A sign is something that stands for something. In his foundational work, *Course in General Linguistics* (1916), Saussure (see 'Biographical notes') presciently anticipates a new kind of human science:

> *A science that studies the life of signs within society* is conceivable; it would be a part of social psychology and consequently of general psychology; I shall call it *semiology* (from the Greek *semeion*, 'sign'). Semiology would show what constitutes signs, what laws govern them.
>
> (Saussure 1974: 16)

Semiology (or semiotics) would be based on the model of linguistics drawing on several of the distinctions Saussure introduced: 'signifier/signified', 'synchronic/diachronic', '*langue/parole*' (see Section 1.1).

Through the work of the Russian Formalists between 1915 and 1930 (see Bennett 1979) and the structuralism of the 1960s (see Hawkes 1977) semiology has developed as the study of signs, though it owes less to psychology (as Saussure thought) than to its association with theories of ideology and of subjectivity. Its basic principle is that where there is signification and a text, there must be a knowable underlying system giving rise to meaning. That methodological assumption rests on Saussure's distinction between *langue* and *parole*, between the synchronic system of a given language and anything anyone might actually say or write in that language. Obviously we are writing this and you are following it because both parties share in a familiarity with modern English, its sound patterns and rules for making sentences. On this model texts can be analysed in terms of shared features in an attempt to describe the rules that would generate such texts as instances of these rules.

For example, in Britain inns or public houses have names, often with signs outside giving the name. Although knowing the name of a pub seems the most natural activity in the world, it can be asked whether there is in fact a sign system at work in pub names. If we knew the rules we could prove it by inventing some plausible names. Clearly one set of names is emblematic, often taking a title from a natural object, 'The Sun', 'The Moon', 'The White Horse'. Equally another set of names is heraldic, 'The King's Arms', 'The Royal Oak', or takes the name of a famous individual, 'The Duke of Wellington', 'The Nelson'. But another large group has doubled names, such as 'The Pig and Whistle', 'The Dog and Partridge', 'The Coach and Horses', 'The Lamb and Flag', 'The Rose and Crown', 'The Elephant and Castle'. Two systems seem to be at play here, one generating names by coupling a natural object with a human artefact ('Pig and Whistle', 'Lamb and Flag', 'Rose and Crown', 'Elephant and Castle'), another coupling two objects by causal association (dogs hunt partridges), though 'Coach and Horses' seems to embody both rules (horses pull coaches).

'Signs can only arise on inter-individual territory' and therefore the sign is always ideological, writes Voloshinov (1973: 12). Semiology remains merely formalist if it fails to recognize that the sign is not autonomous and self-sufficient but always determined within ideology and in relation to subjectivity. Each of the examples collected here applies semiology to different sign systems. Barthes in *Mythologies* summarizes a way to analyse the specific operation of the sign in popular culture, particularly with instances of visual signification (photography, advertising). Macherey argues that traditional notions of the literary text as unified must yield to awareness of the actual decentredness of any text. Leaning on the work of Macherey, Eco provides a discussion of the ideological implications of the narrating structures of a populist set of texts in order to account for the systems of form that simply confirm for the reader a common-sense notion of the 'real'. And in an account theorizing realism in both the novel and classic Hollywood cinema, Colin MacCabe explores the limits of semiology in an attempt to make it cohere with conceptions of ideology and of the position accorded to the reading subject by the realist text.

Working impartially on literary and popular texts, these examples, taken together, imply the need to acknowledge:

1 That texts must be understood in terms of their specificity as forms of sign, and so their difference.

2 That signs are always ideological but that ideology is a matter not just of the signified meaning but also of the *operation* of the signifier.

1.1

Ferdinand de Saussure, from *Course in General Linguistics* (1916)

1 Language as organized thought coupled with sound

To prove that language is only a system of pure values, it is enough to consider the two elements involved in its functioning: ideas and sounds.

Psychologically our thought – apart from its expression in words – is only a shapeless and indistinct mass. Philosophers and linguists have always agreed in recognizing that without the help of signs we would be unable to make a clear-cut, consistent distinction between two ideas. Without language, thought is a vague, uncharted nebula. There are no pre-existing ideas, and nothing is distinct before the appearance of language.

Against the floating realm of thought, would sounds by themselves yield pre-delimited entities? No more so than ideas. Phonic substance is neither more fixed nor more rigid than thought; it is not a mould into which thought must of necessity fit but a plastic substance divided in turn into distinct parts to furnish the signifiers needed by thought. The linguistic fact can therefore be pictured in its totality – i.e. language – as a series of contiguous subdivisions marked off on both the indefinite plane of jumbled ideas (*A*) and the equally vague plane of sounds (*B*). The following diagram gives a rough idea of it:

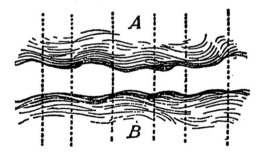

The characteristic role of language with respect to thought is not to create a material phonic means for expressing ideas but to serve as a link between thought and sound, under conditions that of necessity bring about the reciprocal delimitations of units. Thought, chaotic by nature, has to become ordered in the process of its decomposition. Neither are thoughts given material form nor are sounds transformed into mental entities; the somewhat mysterious fact is rather that 'thought-sound' implies division, and that language works out its units while taking shape between two shapeless masses. Visualize the air in contact with a sheet of water; if the atmospheric pressure changes, the surface of the water will be broken up into a series of divisions, waves; the waves resemble the union or coupling of thought with phonic substance.

Language might be called the domain of articulations, using the word as it was defined earlier. Each linguistic term is a member, an *articulus* in which an idea is fixed in a sound and a sound becomes the sign of an idea.

Language can also be compared with a sheet of paper: thought is the front and the sound the back; one cannot cut the front without cutting the back at the same time; likewise in language, one can neither divide sound from thought nor thought from sound; the division could be accomplished only abstractedly, and the result would be either pure psychology or pure phonology.

Linguistics then works in the borderland where the elements of sound and thought combine; *their combination produces a form, not a substance.*

These views give a better understanding of what was said before about the arbitrariness of signs. Not only are the two domains that are linked by the linguistic fact shapeless and confused, but the choice of a given slice of sound to name a given idea is completely arbitrary. If this were not true, the notion of value would be compromised, for it would include an externally imposed element. But actually values remain entirely relative, and that is why the bond between the sound and the idea is radically arbitrary.

The arbitrary nature of the sign explains in turn why the social fact alone can create a linguistic system. The community is necessary if values that owe their existence solely to usage and general acceptance are to be set up; by himself the individual is incapable of fixing a single value.

In addition, the idea of value, as defined, shows that to consider a term as simply the union of a certain sound with a certain concept is grossly misleading. To define it in this way would isolate the term from its system; it would mean assuming that one can start from the terms and construct the system by adding them together when, on the contrary, it is from the interdependent whole that one must start and through analysis obtain its elements.

To develop this thesis, we shall study value successively from the viewpoint of the signified or concept (Section 2), the signifier (Section 3), and the complete sign (Section 4).

Being unable to seize the concrete entities or units of language directly, we shall work with words. While the word does not conform exactly to the definition of the linguistic unit, it at least bears a rough resemblance to the unit and has the advantage of being concrete; consequently, we shall use words as specimens equivalent to real terms in a synchronic system, and the principles that we evolve with respect to words will be valid for entities in general.

2 Linguistic value from a conceptual viewpoint

When we speak of the value of a word, we generally think first of its property of standing for an idea, and this is in fact one side of linguistic value. But if this is true, how does *value* differ from *signification*? Might the two words be synonyms? I think not, although it is easy to confuse them, since the confusion results not so much from their similarity as from the subtlety of the distinction that they mark.

From a conceptual viewpoint, value is doubtless one element in signification, and it is difficult to see how signification can be dependent upon value and still be distinct from it. But we must clear up the issue or risk reducing language to a simple naming-process.

Let us first take signification as it is generally understood. As the arrows in the drawing show, it is only the counterpart of the sound-image. Everything that occurs concerns only the sound-image and the concept when we look upon the word as independent and self-contained.

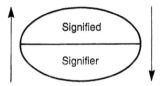

But here is the paradox: on the one hand the concept seems to be the counterpart of the sound-image, and on the other hand the sign itself is in turn the counterpart of the other signs of language.

Language is a system of interdependent terms in which the value of each term results solely from the simultaneous presence of the others, as in the diagram:

How, then, can value be confused with signification, i.e. the counterpart of the sound-image? It seems impossible to liken the relations represented here by horizontal arrows to those represented above by vertical arrows. Putting it another way – and again taking up the example of the sheet of paper that is cut in two (see p. 8) – it is clear that the observable relation between the different pieces A, B, C, D, etc. is distinct from the relation between the front and back of the same piece as in A/A′, B/B′, etc.

To resolve the issue, let us observe from the outset that even outside language all values are apparently governed by the same paradoxical principle. They are always composed:

(1) of a *dissimilar* thing that can be *exchanged* for the thing of which the value is to be determined; and

(2) of *similar* things that can be *compared* with the thing of which the value is to be determined.

Both factors are necessary for the existence of a value. To determine what a five-franc piece is worth one must therefore know: (1) that it can be exchanged for a fixed quantity of a different thing, e.g. bread; and (2) that it can be compared with a similar value of the same system, e.g. a one-franc piece, or with coins of another system (a dollar, etc.). In the same way a word can be exchanged for something dissimilar, an idea; besides, it can be compared with something of the same nature, another word. Its value is therefore not fixed so long as one simply states that it can be 'exchanged' for a given concept, i.e. that it has this or that signification: one must also compare it with similar values, with other words that stand in opposition to it. Its content is really fixed only by the concurrence of everything that exists outside it. Being part of a system, it is endowed not only with a signification but also and especially with a value, and this is something quite different.

A few examples will show clearly that this is true. Modern French *mouton* can have the same signification as English *sheep* but not the same value, and this for several reasons, particularly because in speaking of a piece of meat ready to be served on the table, English uses *mutton* and not *sheep*. The difference in value between *sheep* and *mouton* is due to the fact that *sheep* has beside it a second term while the French word does not.

Within the same language, all words used to express related ideas limit each other reciprocally; synonyms like French *redouter* 'dread', *craindre* 'fear,' and *avoir peur* 'be afraid' have value only through their opposition: if *redouter* did not exist, all its content would go to its competitors. Conversely, some words are enriched through contact with others: e.g. the new element introduced in *décrépit* (un vieillard *décrépit*) results from the co-existence of *décrépi* (un mur *décrépi*). The value of just any term is accordingly determined by its environment; it is impossible to fix even the value of the word signifying 'sun' without first considering its surroundings: in some languages it is not possible to say 'sit in the *sun*.'

Everything said about words applies to any term of language, e.g. to grammatical entities. The value of a French plural does not coincide with that of a Sanskrit plural even though their signification is usually identical; Sanskrit has three numbers instead of two (*my eyes, my ears, my arms, my legs*, etc. are dual),[1] it would be wrong to attribute the same value to the plural in Sanskrit and in French; its value clearly depends on what is outside and around it.

If words stood for pre-existing concepts, they would all have exact equivalents in meaning from one language to the next; but this is not true. French uses *louer* (*une maison*) 'let (a house)' indifferently to mean both 'pay for' and 'receive payment for,' whereas German uses two words, *mieten* and *vermieten*; there is obviously no exact correspondence of values. The German verbs *schätzen* and *urteilen* share a number of significations, but that correspondence does not hold at several points.

Inflection offers some particularly striking examples. Distinctions of time, which are so familiar to us, are unknown in certain languages. Hebrew does not recognize even the fundamental distinctions between the past, present, and future. Proto-Germanic has no special form for the future; to say that the future is expressed by the present is wrong, for the value of the present is not the same in Germanic as in languages that have a future along with the present. The Slavic languages regularly single out two aspects of the verb: the perfective represents action as a point, complete in its totality; the imperfective represents it as taking place, and on the line of time. The categories are difficult for a Frenchman to understand, for they are unknown in French; if they were predetermined, this would not be true. Instead of pre-existing ideas then, we find in all the foregoing examples *values* emanating from the system. When they are said to correspond to concepts, it is understood that the concepts are purely differential and defined not by their positive content but negatively by their relations with the other terms of the system. Their most precise characteristic is in being what the others are not.

Now the real interpretation of the diagram of the signal becomes apparent. Thus

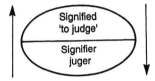

means that in French the concept 'to judge' is linked to the sound-image *juger*; in short, it symbolizes signification. But it is quite clear that initially the concept is nothing, that is only a value determined by its relations with other similar values, and that without them the signification would not exist. If I state simply that a word signifies something when I have in mind the associating of a sound-image with a concept, I am making a statement that may suggest what actually happens, but by no means am I expressing the linguistic fact in its essence and fullness.

3 Linguistic value from a material viewpoint

The conceptual side of value is made up solely of relations and differences with respect to the other terms of language, and the same can be said of its material side. The important thing in the word is not the sound alone but the phonic differences that make it possible to distinguish this word from all others, for differences carry signification.

This may seem surprising, but how indeed could the reverse be possible? Since one vocal image is no better suited than the next for what it is commissioned to express, it is evident, even *a priori*, that a segment of language can never in the final analysis be based on anything except its noncoincidence with the rest. *Arbitrary* and *differential* are two correlative qualities.

The alteration of linguistic signs clearly illustrates this. It is precisely because the terms *a* and *b* as such are radically incapable of reaching the level of consciousness – one is always conscious of only the *a/b* difference – that each term is free to change according to laws that are unrelated to its signifying function. No positive sign characterizes the genitive plural in Czech *žen*; still the two forms *žena*:

žen function as well as the earlier forms *žena*: *ženb*; *žen* has value only because it is different.

Here is another example that shows even more clearly the systematic role of phonic differences: in Greek, *éphēn* is an imperfect and *éstēn* an aorist although both words are formed in the same way; the first belongs to the system of the present indicative of *phēmí* 'I say,' whereas there is no present **stēmi*; now it is precisely the relation *phēmí*: *éphēn* that corresponds to the relation between the present and the imperfect (cf. *déiknūmi*: *edéiknūn*, etc.). Signs function, then, not through their intrinsic value but through their relative position.

In addition, it is impossible for sound alone, a material element, to belong to language. It is only a secondary thing, substance to be put to use. All our conventional values have the characteristic of not being confused with the tangible element which supports them. For instance, it is not the metal in a piece of money that fixes its value. A coin nominally worth five francs may contain less than half its worth of silver. Its value will vary according to the amount stamped upon it and according to its use inside or outside a political boundary. This is even more true of the linguistic signifier, which is not phonic but incorporeal – constituted not by its material substance but by the differences that separate its sound-image from all others.

The foregoing principle is so basic that it applies to all the material elements of language, including phonemes. Every language forms its words on the basis of a system of sonorous elements, each element being a clearly delimited unit and one of a fixed number of units. Phonemes are characterized not, as one might think, by their own positive quality but simply by the fact that they are distinct. Phonemes are above all else opposing, relative, and negative entities.

Proof of this is the latitude that speakers have between points of convergence in the pronunciation of distinct sounds. In French, for instance, general use of a dorsal *r* does not prevent many speakers from using a tongue-tip trill; language is not in the least disturbed by it; language requires only that the sound be different and not, as one might imagine, that it have an invariable quality. I can even pronounce the French *r* like German *ch* in *Bach*, *doch*, etc., but in German I could not use *r* instead of *ch*, for German gives recognition to both elements and must keep them apart.

4 The sign considered in its totality

Everything that has been said up to this point boils down to this: in language there are only differences. Even more important: a difference generally implies positive terms between which the difference is set up; but in language there are only differences *without positive terms*. Whether we take the signified or the signifier, language has neither ideas nor sounds that existed before the linguistic system, but only conceptual and phonic differences that have issued from the system. The idea or phonic substance that a sign contains is of less importance than the other signs that surround it. Proof of this is that the value of a term may be modified without either its meaning or its sound being affected, solely because a neighboring term has been modified (see p. 10).

But the statement that everything in language is negative is true only if the signified and the signifier are considered separately; when we consider the sign in its totality, we have something that is positive in its own class. A linguistic system is a series of differences of sound combined with a series of differences of ideas; but the pairing of a certain number of acoustical signs with as many cuts made from the mass of thought engenders a system of values; and this system serves as the effective link between the phonic and psychological elements within each sign. Although both the signified and the signifier are purely differential and negative when considered separately, their combination is a positive fact; it is even the sole type of facts that language, has, for maintaining the parallelism between the two classes of differences is the distinctive function of the linguistic institution.

Note

1   The use of the comparative form for two and the superlative for more than two in English (e.g. *may the* better *boxer win*: *the* best *boxer in the world*) is probably a remnant of the old distinction between the dual and the plural number. (Tr.)

1.2

Roland Barthes, from *Mythologies* (1957)
'The Great Family of Man'

A big exhibition of photographs has been held in Paris, the aim of which was to show the universality of human actions in the daily life of all the countries of the world: birth, death, work, knowledge, play, always impose the same types of behaviour; there is a family of Man.

The Family of Man, such at any rate was the original title of the exhibition which came here from the United States. The French have translated it as: *The Great Family of Man*. So what could originally pass for a phrase belonging to zoology, keeping only the similarity in behaviour, the unity of a species, is here amply moralized and sentimentalized. We are at the outset directed to this ambiguous myth of the human 'community', which serves as an alibi to a large part of our humanism.

This myth functions in two stages: first the difference between human morphologies is asserted, exoticism is insistently stressed, the infinite variations of the species, the diversity in skins, skulls and customs are made manifest, the image of Babel is complacently projected over that of the world. Then, from this pluralism, a type of unity is magically produced: man is born, works, laughs and dies everywhere in the same way; and if there still remains in these actions some ethnic peculiarity, at least one hints that there is underlying each one an identical 'nature', that their diversity is only formal and does not belie the existence of a common mould. Of course this means postulating a human essence, and here is God re-introduced into our Exhibition: the diversity of men proclaims his power, his richness; the unity of their gestures demonstrates his will. This is what the intro-ductory leaflet confides to us when it states, by the pen of M. André Chamson, that *'this look over the human condition must somewhat resemble the benevolent gaze of God on our absurd and sublime ant-hill'*. The pietistic intention is underlined by the quotations which accompany each chapter of the Exhibition: these quotations often are 'primitive' proverbs or verses from the Old Testament. They all define an eternal wisdom, a class of assertions which escape History: '*The Earth is a Mother who never dies, Eat bread and salt and speak the truth*, etc.' This is the reign of gnomic truths, the meeting of all the ages of humanity at the most neutral point of their nature, the point where the obviousness of the truism has no longer any value except in the realm of a purely 'poetic' language. Everything here, the content and appeal of the pictures, the discourse which justifies them, aims to suppress the determining weight of History: we are held back at the surface of an identity, prevented precisely by sentimentality from penetrating into this ulterior zone of human behaviour where historical alienation introduces some 'differences' which we shall here quite simply call 'injustices'.

This myth of the human 'condition' rests on a very old mystification, which always consists in placing Nature at the bottom of History. Any classic humanism postulates that in scratching the history of men a little, the relativity of their institutions or the superficial diversity of their skins (but why not ask the parents of Emmet Till, the young Negro assassinated by the Whites what *they* think of *The Great Family of Man?*), one very quickly reaches the solid rock of a universal human nature. Progressive humanism, on the contrary, must always remember to reverse the terms of this very old imposture, constantly to scour nature, its 'laws' and its 'limits' in order to discover History there, and at last to establish Nature itself as historical.

Examples? Here they are: those of our Exhibition. Birth, death? Yes, these are facts of nature, universal facts. But if one removes History from them, there is nothing more to be said about them; any comment about them becomes purely tautological. The failure of photography seems to me to be flagrant in this connection: to reproduce death or birth tells us, literally, nothing. For these natural facts to gain access to a true language, they must be inserted into a category of knowledge which means postulating that one can transform them, and precisely subject their naturalness to our human criticism. For however universal, they are the signs of an historical writing. True, children are *always* born: but in the whole mass of the human problem, what does the 'essence' of this process matter to us, compared to its modes which, as for them, are perfectly historical? Whether or not the child is born with ease or difficulty, whether or not his birth causes suffering to his mother, whether or not he is threatened by a high mortality rate, whether or not such and such a type of future is open to him: this is what your Exhibitions should be telling people, instead of an eternal lyricism of birth. The same goes for death: must we really celebrate its essence once more, and thus risk forgetting that there is still so much we can do to fight it? It is this very young, far too young power that we must exalt, and not the sterile identity of 'natural' death.

And what can be said about work, which the Exhibition places among great universal facts, putting it on the same plane as birth and death, as if it was quite evident that it belongs to the same order of fate? That work is an age-old fact does not in the least prevent it from remaining a perfectly historical fact. Firstly, and evidently, because of its modes, its motivations, its ends and its benefits, which matter to such an extent that it will never be fair to confuse in a purely gestural identity the colonial and the Western worker (let us also ask the North African workers of the Goutte d'Or district in Paris what they think of *The Great Family of Man*). Secondly, because of the very differences in its inevitability: we know very well that work is 'natural' just as long as it is 'profitable', and that in modifying the inevitability of the profit, we shall perhaps one day modify the inevitability of labour. It is this entirely historified work which we should be told about, instead of an eternal aesthetics of laborious gestures.

So that I rather fear that the final justification of all this Adamism is to give to the immobility of the world the alibi of a 'wisdom' and a 'lyricism' which only make the gestures of man look eternal the better to defuse them.

1.3

Pierre Macherey, from *A Theory of Literary Production* (1978)

Implicit and explicit

In order to ascertain their real opinions, I ought to take cognisance of what they practised rather than of what they said, not only because, in the corruption of our manners, there are few disposed to speak exactly as they believe, but also because very many are not aware of what it is that they really believe, for as the act of mind by which a thing is believed is different from that by which we know we believe it, the one act is often found without the other.

(Descartes, *Discourse on Method*, III)

For there to be a critical discourse which is more than a superficial and futile *reprise* of the work, the speech stored in the book must be incomplete; because it has not said everything, there remains the possibility of saying something else, *after another fashion*. The recognition of the area of shadow in or around the work is the initial moment of criticism. But we must examine the nature of this shadow: does it denote a true absence, or is it the extension of a half-presence? This can be reformulated in terms of a previous question: Will it be the pillar of an explanation or the pretext for an interpretation?

Initially, we will be inclined to say that criticism, in relation to its object, is its *explication*. What, then, is involved in making-explicit? Explicit is to implicit as explication is to implication: these oppositions derive from the distinction between the manifest and the latent, the discovered and the concealed. That which is formally accounted for, expressed, and even concluded, is explicit: the 'explicit' at the end of a book echoes the 'incipit' at the beginning, and indicates that 'all is (has been) said'. To explicate comes from *explicare*: to display and unfold. 'Spread eagle', a heraldic term: one with wings outstretched. And thus the critic, opening the book – whether he intends to find buried treasure there, or whether he wants to see it flying with its own wings – means to give it a different status, or even a different appearance. It might be said that the aim of criticism is to *speak the truth*, a truth not unrelated to the book, but not as the content of its expression. In the book, then, not everything is said, and for everything to be said we must await the critical 'explicit', which may actually be interminable. Nevertheless, although the critical discourse is not spoken by the book, it is in some way the property of the book, constantly alluded to, though never announced openly. What is this silence – an accidental hesitation, or a statutory necessity? Whence the problem: are there books which say what they mean, without being critical books, that is to say, without *depending directly* on other books?

Here we recognise the classic problem of the interpretation of latent meaning. But, in this new instance, the problem tends to take a new form: in fact, the language of the book claims to be a language complete in itself, the source and measure of all 'diction'. The conclusion is inscribed even in its initial moments. Unwinding *within a closed circle*, this language reveals only ... itself; it has only its *own* content and its *own* limits, and the 'explicit' is imprinted on each of these terms. Yet it is not perfect: under close scrutiny the speech inscribed by the book appears interminable; but it takes this absence of a conclusion as its ending. In the space in which the work unfolds, everything is to be said, and is therefore never said, but this does not suffer being altered by any other discourse, enclosed as it is within the definitive limits which constitute its imperfection. This seems to be the origin of criticism's inability to add anything to the discourse of the work: at most, it might extend the work – either in a reduction or in a pursuit of its discourse.

Yet it remains obvious that although the work is self-sufficient it does not contain or engender its own theory; it does not *know* itself. When the critic speaks he is not repeating, reproducing or remaking it; neither is he illuminating its dark corners, filling its margins with annotation, specifying that which was never specific. When the critical discourse begins from the hypothesis that the work speaks falteringly, it is not with the aim of *completing* it, reducing its deficiencies, as though the book were too small for the space it occupied. We have seen that a knowledge of the work is not elaborated within the work, but supposes a distance between knowledge and its object; to know what the writer is saying, it is not enough to *let him speak*, for his speech is hollow and can never be completed at its own level. Theoretical inquiry rejects the notion of the *space* or *site* of the work. Critical discourse does not attempt to complete the book, for theory begins from that incompleteness which is so radical that it cannot be located.

Thus, the silence of the book is not a lack to be remedied, an inadequacy to be made up for. It is not a temporary silence that could be finally abolished. We must distinguish the necessity of this silence. For example, it can be shown that it is the juxtaposition and conflict of several meanings which produces the radical otherness which shapes the work: this conflict it not resolved or absorbed, but simply *displayed*.

Thus the work cannot speak of the more or less complex opposition which structures it; though it is its expression and embodiment. In its every particle, the work *manifests*, uncovers, what it cannot say. This silence gives it life.

The spoken and the unspoken

The speech of the book comes from a certain silence, a matter which it endows with form, a ground on which it traces a figure. Thus, the book is not self-sufficient; it is necessarily accompanied by a *certain absence*, without which it would not exist. A knowledge of the book must include a consideration of this absence.

This is why it seems useful and legitimate to ask of every production what it tacitly implies, what it does not say. Either all around or in its wake the explicit requires the implicit: for in order to say anything, there are other things *which must not be said*. Freud relegated this *absence of certain words* to a new place which he was the first to explore, and which he paradoxically *named*: the unconscious. To reach utterance, all speech envelops itself in the unspoken. We must ask why it does not speak of this interdict: can it be identified before one might wish to acknowledge it? There is not even the slightest hint of the absence of what it does not, perhaps cannot, say: the disavowal (*dénégation*) extends even to the act that banished the forbidden term; its absence is unacknowledged.

This moment of absence founds the speech of the work. Silences shape all speech. Banality?

Can we say that this silence is hidden? What is it? A condition of existence – point of departure, methodical beginning – essential foundation – ideal culmination – absolute origin which lends meaning to the endeavour? Means or form of connection?

Can we make this silence speak? What is the unspoken saying? What does it mean? To what extent is dissimulation a way of speaking? Can something that has hidden *itself* be recalled to our presence? Silence as the source of expression. Is what I am really saying what I am not saying? Hence the main risk run by those who would say everything. After all, perhaps the work is not hiding what it does not say; this is simply *missing*.

Yet the unspoken has many other resources: it assigns speech to its exact position, designating its domain. By speech, silence becomes the centre and principle of expression, its vanishing point. Speech eventually has nothing more to tell us: we investigate the silence, for it is the silence that is doing the speaking.

Silence reveals speech – unless it is speech that reveals the silence.

These two methods of explanation by recourse to the latent or concealed are not equivalent: it is the second which allows least value to the latent, since there appears an absence of speech through the absent speech, that is to say, a certain presence which it is enough to extricate. There is agreement to relate speech to its contrary, figure and ground. But there is a reluctance to leave these terms in equilibrium, an urge to resolve them: figure or ground? Here, once again, we encounter all the ambiguities of the notions of origin and creation. The unacknowledged co-existence of the visible and the hidden: the visible is merely the hidden in a different guise. The problem is merely to *pass across* from the one to the other.

The first image is the more profound, in so far as it enables us to recuperate the form of the second without becoming trapped in a mechanical problematic of transition: in being a necessary medium of expression, this ground of silence does not lose its significance. It is not the sole meaning, but that which endows meaning with a meaning: it is this silence which tells us – not just anything, since it exists to say nothing – which informs us of the precise conditions for the appearance of an utterance, and thus its limits, giving its real significance, without, for all that, speaking in its place. The latent is an intermediate means: this does not amount to pushing it into the background; it simply means that the latent is not another meaning which ultimately and miraculously *dispels* the first (manifest) meaning. Thus, we can see that meaning is in the *relation* between the implicit and the explicit, not on one or the other side of that fence: for in the latter case, we should be obliged to choose, in other words, as ever, translation or commentary.

What is important in the work is what it does not say. This is not the same as the careless notation 'what it refuses to say', although that would in itself be interesting: a method might be built on it, with the task of *measuring silences*, whether acknowledged or unacknowledged. But rather than this, what the work *cannot say* is important, because there the elaboration of the utterance is acted out, in a sort of journey to silence.

The basic issue, then, is to know whether we can examine that absence of speech which is the prior condition of all speech.

> Insidious Questions: When we are confronted with any manifestation which someone has permitted us to see, we may ask: what is it meant to conceal? What is it meant to draw our attention from? What prejudice does it seek to raise? and again, how far does the subtlety of the dissimulation go? and in what respect is the man mistaken?
>
> (*The Dawn of Day*, section 523)

For Nietzsche, these are insidious questions, *Hinterfrage*, questions which come from behind, held in reserve, lying in wait, snares.

'It might be asked': thus Nietzsche inquires, and even before showing how to put questions, he points out the necessity of *asking* questions; for there are several. The object or target of these questions is 'all that a man allows to appear'. Everything: that is to say that the Nietzschean interrogation – which is the precise opposite of an examination, since, as we shall see, it reaches the point of calling itself into question – is of such theoretical generality that we may wonder if it is legitimate to apply it to the specific domain of literary production. What in fact 'becomes visible' is the work, all the works. We shall try to apply this general proposition to a specific domain.

'All that a man allows to appear': obviously the German words say more than the English. *Lassen*: this is both to do, to allow, and to oblige. This word, better than any other, designates the act of literary production. It reveals it – on condition that we do not search there for the shapes of some evocative magic: inspiration, visitation or creation. Production: to show and to reveal. The question 'What does he mean?' proves that it is not a matter of dispossession. Also 'to reveal' is an affirmation rather than a decision: the expression of an active force, which yet does not exclude a certain autonomous actualisation of the visible.

Interrogation penetrates certain actions: 'hiding', 'diverting attention', and, further on, 'cheating'. Obviously, linking all these, there is a single impulse: 'hiding' is to keep from sight; 'diverting attention' is to show without being seen, to prevent what is visible from being seen; which also expresses the image of 'dissimulation': to dissimulate requires action. Therefore everything happens as though the accent had been shifted: the work is revealed to itself and to others on two different levels: it makes visible, and it makes invisible. Not because something has to be hidden in order to show something else; but because attention is diverted from the very thing which is shown. This is the superposition of utterance and statement (*du parler et du dire*): if the author does not always say what he states, he does not necessarily state what he says.

In the text from Nietzsche, then, it is a question of a prejudice, a mystification, a deception. Not by virtue of this or that particular word, but because of speech itself, all speech. A prejudice is that which is not judged in language but before it, but which is nevertheless offered as a judgment. Prejudice, the pseudo-judgment, is the utterance which remains imperceptibly beyond language.

Yet this proposition has two meanings: speech evokes a prejudice as a judgment; but equally, by the *fact of evocation*, it holds it up as a prejudice. It creates an allegory of judgment. And speech exists because it wishes for this allegory whose appearance it prepares for. This is the portion of the visible and the invisible, the revealed and the concealed, of language and silence.

Then we arrive at the meaning of the last questions. '*And yet*': we move to a new level of the systematic order, in what is almost an inversion. It could be said that there is a question directed at the first questions. This question which completes the construction of the trap challenges the first question, setting off the structure of the work and the structure of the criticism of it.

$$\left.\begin{array}{l} \text{utterance} \\[2ex] \text{question 1} \end{array}\right\} \text{question 2}$$

We can then ask to what extent the first question was based on an error: because this dissimulation applies to everything it must not be thought that it is total and unlimited. Since it is a relative silence which depends on an even more silent margin, it is impossible to dissemble the truth of language.

Naturally it is incorrect to see in this equivocation of speech its division into the spoken and the unspoken; a division which is only possible because it makes speech depend on a fundamental veracity, a plenitude of expression, a reflection of the Hegelian dialectic – that dialectic which Nietzsche (like Marx, an enemy of idols) could only contemplate in its inverted form. If it is insisted that we find references to these questions in poetic form, we would do better to take them from the work of Spinoza. The transition from dissimulation to error, with the essential moment of 'and yet', is also the movement to the third kind of knowledge. In a famous book, Spinoza has posed Nietzsche's questions, posed them concerning Scripture, which could once have seemed to be the model of all books.

So the real trap of language is its tacit positiveness which makes it into a truly active insistence: the error belongs as much with the one who reveals it as it does with the one who asks the first questions, the critic.

The ordinary critic (the one who stops at the first question) and the author are equally remote from a true appreciation of the work: but there is another kind of critic who asks the second question.

The labyrinth of the two questions – a labyrinth in reverse, because it leads to a way out – endlessly proposes a choice between a false and a true subtlety: the one views the author from the critic's point of view, as a critic; the other only judges him when it has taken up position in the expressive veracity of language, and his language. Torn from the false limits of its empirical presence, the work then begins to acquire a significance.

The two questions

Thus the critical task is not simple: it necessarily implies the superposition of two questions. To know the work, we must move outside it. Then, in the second moment, we question the work in its alleged plenitude; not from a different point of view, a different side – by translating it into a different language, or by applying a different standard – but not entirely from within, from what it says and asserts that it says. Conjecturally, the work has its *margins*, an area of incompleteness from which we can observe its birth and its production.

The critical problem will be in the conjunction of the two questions; not in a choice between them, but in the point from which they appear to become differentiated. The complexity of the critical problem will be the articulation between the two questions. To grasp this *articulation* is to accept a discontinuity, to establish a discontinuity: the questions are not spontaneously given in their specificity. Initially, the questions must be asked – asked simultaneously, in a way that amounts to allowing them an equal status.

The recognition of this simultaneity, which precludes any notion of priority, is fundamental because it makes possible – from the beginning – an exorcism of the ghosts of aesthetic legality: by the fact that the question which is supposed to inhabit the mind of the writer is not simple, but divided by its reference to another question, the problem to be explicitly resolved will not be merely the realisation of a project according to the rules of validity (beauty) and conformity (fidelity). Even the question of the formal limits imposed on expression will no longer form part of the problem: it will be completely eliminated as a distinct element of the problematic. In so far as a conscious intention to realise a project of writing begins inevitably by taking the form of an ideological imperative – something *to say* (not the acceptance of rules), in other words something that must not be said – it will have to adopt the conditions of the possibility of such an undertaking: the implements, the actual means of this practice; and the rules will play their part in so far as they are *directly* useful.

The real problem is not that of being restricted by rules – or the absence of such a restriction – but the necessity of inventing forms of expression, or merely finding them: not ideal forms, or forms derived from a principle which transcends the enterprise itself, but forms which can be used immediately as the means of expression for a determinate content; likewise, the question of the value of these forms cannot reach beyond this immediate issue. However, these forms do not exist just in the mode of an immediate presence: they can survive beyond the moment of their usefulness, and it will be seen that this poses a very serious problem; they can be revived, in which case they will have undergone a slight but crucial change in value which must be determined. In fact, these forms do not appear instantaneously but at the end of a long history – a history of the elaboration of ideological themes. The history of forms – which will subsequently be designated as *themes*, in the strict sense of the word – corresponds to the history of ideological themes; indeed, they are exactly parallel, as can easily be demonstrated with the history of any idea: that of Robinson Crusoe, for example. The form takes shape or changes in response to new imperatives of the idea: but it is also capable of independent transformations, or of an inertia, which bends the path of ideological history. But, whatever the mode of its realisation, there is always a correspondence, which could thus be considered automatic: refuting the conception of these two histories as the expression of a superficial question – which is not self-sufficient, because it is based on a parallelism – the question of the work. The level of interpretation determined by this parallelism will only acquire meaning from the elucidation of another level, with which it will have a determining relationship: the question of this question.

The investigation into the conditions of the possibility of the work is accomplished in the answer to an explicit question, but it will not be able to seek the conditions of those conditions, nor will it be able to see that this answer constitutes a question. Nevertheless, the second question will necessarily be posed within the first question, or even through it. It is this second question which, for us, defines the space of history: it reveals the work in so far as it entertains a specific but undisguised (which does not mean innocent) relation with history. We must show, through the study of an effort of expression, how it is possible to render visible the conditions of this effort – conditions of which it has no awareness, though this does not mean that it does not apprehend them: the work encounters the question of questions as an obstacle; it is only aware of the conditions which it adopts or utilises. We could account for this latent knowledge (which necessarily exists, since without it the work would be accomplished no further than if the explicit conditions were not realised) by recourse to *the unconscious of the work* (not of the author). But this unconscious does not perform as an understudy – on the contrary, it arises in the interior of the labour itself: there it is at work – nor as an extension of the explicit purpose, since it derives from a completely different principle. Neither is it a question of another consciousness: the consciousness of another or others, or the other consciousness of the same thing. There is no understudy creative-unconscious to the creative pseudo-consciousness: if there is an unconscious it cannot be creative, in so far as it precedes all production as its condition. It is a question of something other than consciousness: what we are seeking is analogous to that relationship which Marx acknowledges when he insists on seeing material relations as being derived from the social infrastructure behind all ideological phenomena, not in order to explain these phenomena as emanations from the infrastructure, which would amount to saying that the ideological is the economic in another form: whence the possibility of reducing the ideological to the economic.

For Marx and Engels, the study of an ideological phenomenon – that is to say, a conflict at the level of ideology – cannot be isolated from the movement at the economic level: not because it is a different conflict, a different form of the conflict, but because it is the conflict of this conflict. The composition of *an* ideology implies the relation of the ideological to the economic.

The problem of the work, if it exists, is now squarely posed in and by the work, but it is something altogether different from the awareness of a problem. This is why an authentic explanation must attend to several levels at once, though never failing to consider them separately, in their specificity:

1   The first question, properly interior to the work, in the sense of an intimacy, remains diffuse: indeed, it is there and not there, divided between several determinations which give it the status of a quasi-presence. Materially scattered, it must be reconstituted, recalled, recognised. But it would be incorrect to present this task as a deciphering: the secret is not hidden, and in any case *does not conceal itself*, does not resist this census which is a simple classification, changing at most its form; it loses nothing of its nature, its vividness, its mystery.

This first procedure is a question, if you will, of structures. But we have gone far beyond that formulation: to conclude with structures is merely to gather the scattered limbs. It would not be correct to believe that one had thus established a system. What system? In what relation to other systems? In what relation to that which is not part of the system?

2   Once the question has emerged from its half-light, we must find its meaning and its importance. It might be suggested: inscribe it in ideological history, the history which generates the succession of questions and the thread of problematics. But this inscription is not calculated by the simple situation of the question in relation to other questions, or by the presence of history outside this particular work, in so far as it gives it both its domain and its place. This history is not in a simple external relation to the work: it is present in the work, in so far as the emergence of the work required this history, which is its only principle of reality and also supplies its means of expression. This history, which is not merely the history of works of the same nature, entirely determines the work: gives the work its reality, but also that which it is not, and this is the most important. To anticipate an example which will subsequently be analysed, if Jules Verne chose to be the spokesman of a certain ideological condition, he could not choose to be what he in fact became. He chose to be the spokesman for a certain condition; he expressed that choice. These are two different operations, the conjuncture of which constitutes a specific enterprise: in this case, the production of a certain number of books. These are the two 'choices'; the gap between them measures the absence within the work, but they cannot be judged by the same standards, because they are not of the same nature.

It must then be possible to examine a work from an accurate description which respects the specificity of this work, but which is more than just a new exposition of its content, in the form of a systematisation, for example. For as we quickly come to realise, we can only describe, only remain within the work, if we also decide to go beyond it: to bring out, for example, what the work is *compelled* to say in order to say what it *wants* to say, because not only would the work have wanted not to say it (which is another question), but certainly the work did not want to say it. Thus, it is not a question of introducing a historical explanation which is stuck on to the work from the outside. On the contrary, we must show a sort of splitting within the work: this division is *its* unconscious, in so far as it possesses one – the unconscious which is history, the play of history beyond its edges, encroaching on those edges this is why it is possible to trace the path which leads from the haunted work to that which haunts it. Once again it is not a question of redoubling the work with an unconscious, but a question of revealing in the very gestures of expression that which it is not. Then, the reverse side of what is written will be history itself.

Moreover, we shall be looking within the work itself for reasons for moving beyond it: from the explicit question, and from the reply which it actually elicits – the form of the question being legible in this answer – we shall certainly be able to put the question of the question, and not the one apart from the other. This endeavour is full of surprises: we realise that in seeking the meaning of the work – not the meaning that it gives itself but the meaning that seizes hold of it – we have at our disposal, in turning to the work itself, material that is already prepared, already invested by the question which we are going to ask. The real resistances are elsewhere, in the reader we might say: but they do not hinder this unforeseen inquiry, for the work – it is absurd to repeat this – does not say what it does not say. This is precisely the opposite of an interpretation or a commentary: an interpretation seeks *pretexts*, but the explanation proposed here finds its object wholly prepared and is content to give a true idea of it.

To take a specific example which will later be studied in detail: the 'problem' of Jules Verne breaks down into *two questions*. The important thing is that this dissociation itself remains *within* the problem, that the coherence of the problem should survive: we shall not, for example, be trying to find two Jules Vernes, or to establish a preference for a particular Jules Verne at the expense of all the other possible Jules Vernes. This problem, because it concerns a literary object, is crystallised in what we can call a theme, which is, in its abstract form, the conquest of nature; in the ideological realisation which gives it the form of *a motif*: the voyage, or Robinson Crusoe (a veritable ideological obsession with Verne, and present in all his books, even if only as an allusion). This theme can be studied at two different levels:

1   The utilisation of the theme: initially the adventures of its form, which moreover contain (even though the collocation of the words is casual) the form of the adventure. This raises the question of the writer at work.

2   The meaning of the theme: not a meaning which exists independently of the work, but the meaning that the theme actually acquires within the work.

First question: the work originates in a secret to be *explained*.

Second question: the work is realised in the revelation of its secret. The simultaneity of the two questions defines a minute rupture, minutely distinct from a continuity. It is this rupture which must be studied.

1.4

Umberto Eco, from 'The Narrative Structure in Fleming' (1966)

In 1953 Ian Fleming published the first novel in the 007 series, *Casino Royale*. Being a first work, it is subject to the then current literary influence, and in the fifties, which had abandoned the traditional detective whodunit trail in favour of violent action, it was impossible to ignore the presence of Spillane.

To Spillane, *Casino Royale* owes, beyond doubt, at least two characteristic elements. First of all the girl Vesper Lynd, who arouses the confident love of Bond, in the end is revealed as an enemy agent. In a novel by Spillane the hero would have killed her, while in Fleming the woman had the grace to commit suicide; but Bond's reaction when it happens has the Spillane characteristic of transforming love into hatred and tenderness to ferocity: 'She's dead, the bitch' Bond telephones to his London office, and so ends his romance.

In the second place Bond is obsessed by an image: that of a Japanese expert in codes whom he had killed in cold blood on the thirty-sixth floor of the R.C.A. Skyscraper at Rockefeller Centre – with a bullet – from a window on the fortieth floor of the skyscraper opposite. By an analogy that is surely not accidental, Mike Hammer seemed to be consistently haunted by the memory of a small Japanese he killed in the jungle during the war, though with greater emotive participation (while Bond's homicide, authorised officially by the double-zero, is more ascetic and bureaucratic). The memory of the Japanese was the beginning of the undoubted nervous disorder of Mike Hammer (of his sadistic masochism, of his arguable impotence); the memory of his first homicide could have been the origin of the neurosis of James Bond, except that, within the ambit of *Casino Royale*, either the character or his author solves the problem by non-therapeutic means: that is by excluding the neurosis from the narrative. This decision was to influence the structure of the following eleven novels by Fleming and presumably forms the basis for their success.

After having helped to dispose of two Bulgarians who had tried to get rid of him, after having suffered torture in the form of a cruel abuse of his testicles, having been present at the elimination of Le Chiffre by the action of a Soviet agent, having received from him a scar on the hand, cold-bloodedly carved while he was conscious, and after having risked the effect on his love life, Bond, enjoying his well-earned convalescence on a hospital bed, confided a chilling doubt to his French colleague, Mathis. Have they been fighting for a just cause? Le Chiffre, who had financed Communist spies among the French workers, was he not 'serving a wonderful purpose, a really vital purpose, perhaps the best and highest purpose of all'? The difference between good and evil, is it really something neat, recognisable, as the hagiography of counter-espionage would like us to believe? At this point Bond is ripe for the crisis, for the salutary recognition of universal ambiguity, and he sets off along the route traversed by the protagonist of le Carré. But in the very moment when he questions himself about the appearance of the devil and, sympathising with the Enemy, is inclined to recognise him as a 'lost brother', James Bond is treated to a salve from Mathis: 'When you get back to London you will find there are other Le Chiffres seeking to destroy you and your friends and your country. M will tell you about them. And now that you have seen a really evil man, you will know how evil they can be and you will go after them to destroy them in order to protect yourself and the people you love. You know what they look like now and what they can do to people ... Surround yourself with human beings, my dear James. They are easier to fight for than principles. But don't let me down and become human yourself. We could lose such a wonderful machine.'

With this lapidary phrase Fleming defines the character of James Bond for the novels to come. From *Casino Royale* there remained the scar on his cheek, the slightly cruel smile, the taste for good food, together with a number of subsidiary characteristics minutely documented in the course of this first volume: but convinced by Mathis's words, Bond was to abandon the treacherous life of moral meditation and of psychological anger, with all the neurotic dangers that they entail. Bond ceased to be a subject of psychiatry and remained at the most a physiological object (except for a return to the subject of the psyche in the last, untypical novel in the series, *The Man with the Golden Gun*), a magnificent machine, as the author and the public, as well as Mathis, had wished. From that moment Bond did not meditate upon truth and upon justice, upon life and death, except in rare moments of boredom, usually in the bar of an airport, but always in the form of a casual daydream, never allowing himself to be infected by doubt (at least in novels – he did indulge in such intimate luxuries in the short stories).

From the psychological point of view a conversion has taken place quite suddenly, on the base of four conventional phrases pronounced by Mathis, but the conversion was not really justified on a psychological level. In the last pages of *Casino Royale* Fleming, in fact, renounces all psychology as the motive of narrative and decides to transfer characters and situations to the level of an objective and conventional structural strategy. Without knowing it, Fleming makes a choice familiar to many contemporary disciplines: he passes from the psychological method to that of the formula.

In *Casino Royale* there are already all the elements for the building of a machine that would function basically as a unit along very simple, straight lines, conforming to the strict rules of combination. This machine, which was to function without deviation of fortune in the novels that followed, lies at the basis of the success of the '007 saga' – a success which, singularly, has been due both to the adulation of the masses and to the appreciation of more sophisticated readers. We intend here to examine in detail this narrating machine in order to identify the reasons for its success. It is our plan to devise a descriptive table of the narrative structure in Ian Fleming while seeking to evaluate for each structural element the probable incidence upon the reader's sensitivity. We shall try, therefore, to distinguish such a narrative structure at five levels:

(1) The juxtaposition of the characters and of values.
(2) Play situations and the plot as a 'game'.
(3) A Manichean ideology.
(4) Literary techniques.
(5) Literature as montage.

Our enquiry covers the range of the following novels listed in order of publication (the date of composition was presumably a year earlier in each case):

Casino Royale, 1953
Live and Let Die, 1954
Moonraker, 1955
Diamonds are Forever, 1956
From Russia with Love, 1957
Dr. No, 1958
Goldfinger, 1959
Thunderball, 1961
On Her Majesty's Secret Service, 1963
You Only Live Twice, 1964

We shall refer also to the stories in *For Your Eyes Only* (1960), and to *The Man with the Golden Gun* published in 1965. But we shall not take into consideration *The Spy who Loved Me* (1962), which seems quite untypical.

1 The Juxtaposition of the Characters and of Values

The novels of Fleming seem to be built on a series of 'oppositions' which allow a limited number of permutation and reactions. These dichotomies constitute a constant feature around which minor couples rotate and they form, from novel to novel, variations on them. We have here singled out fourteen couples, four of which are contrasted to four actual characters, while the others form a conflict of values, variously personified by the four basic characters. The fourteen couples are:

(a) Bond – M
(b) Bond – Villain
(c) Villain – Woman
(d) Woman – Bond
(e) Free World – Soviet Union

(f) Great Britain – Countries not Anglo-Saxon

(g) Duty – Sacrifice

(h) Cupidity   Ideals

(i) Love – Death

(j) Chance – Planning

(k) Luxury – Discomfort

(l) Excess – Moderation

(m) Perversion – Innocence

(n) Loyalty – Disloyalty

These pairs do not represent 'vague' elements but 'simple' ones that are immediate and universal, and if we consider the range of each pair we see that the variants allowed cover a vast field and in fact include all the narrative ideas of Fleming.

1.5

Colin MacCabe, from 'Realism and the Cinema' (1974)

The classic realist text

> Criticism, at least Marxist criticism, must proceed methodically and concretely
> in each case, in short scientifically. Loose talk is of no help here, whatever its
> vocabulary. In no circumstances can the necessary guide-lines for a practical
> definition of realism be derived from literary works alone. (Be like Tolstoy – but
> without his weaknesses! Be like Balzac – only up-to-date!) Realism is an issue
> not only for literature: it is a major political, philosophical and practical issue
> and must be handled and explained as such – as a matter of general human
> interest.[1]

One of the difficulties of any discussion about realism is the lack of any really
effective vocabulary with which to discuss the topic. Most discussions turn on the
problems of the production of discourse which will fully adequate the real. This
notion of adequacy is accepted both by the realists and indeed by the anti-realists
whose main argument is that no discourse can ever be adequate to the multifarious
nature of the real. This notion of the real is, however, I wish to suggest, a notion
which is tied to a particular type of literary production – the nineteenth-century
realist novel. The dominance of this novel form is such that people still tend to
confuse the general question of realism with the particular forms of the nineteenth-
century realist novel. In order to make the discussion clearer I want therefore to
attempt to define the structure which typifies the nineteenth-century realist novel
and to show how that structure can also be used to describe a great number of films.
The detour through literature is necessary because, in many ways, the structure is
much more obvious there and also because of the historical dominance of the
classic realist novel over much film production. What to a large extent will be
lacking in this article is the specific nature of the film form but this does not seem to
me to invalidate the setting up of certain essential categories from which further
discussion must progress. The structure I will attempt to disengage I shall call the
classic realist text and I shall apply it to novels and films.

A classic realist text may be defined as one in which there is a hierarchy amongst the discourses which compose the text and this hierarchy is defined in terms of an empirical notion of truth. Perhaps the easiest way to understand this is through a reflection on the use of inverted commas within the classic realist novel. While those sections in the text which are contained in inverted commas may cause a certain difficulty for the reader – a certain confusion vis-à-vis what really is the case – this difficulty is abolished by the unspoken (or more accurately the unwritten) prose that surrounds them. In the classical realist novel the narrative prose functions as a metalanguage that can state all the truths in the object language – those words held in inverted commas – and can also explain the relation of this object language to the real. The metalanguage can thereby explain the relation of this object language to the world and the strange methods by which the object languages attempt to express truths which are straightforwardly conveyed in the metalanguage. What I have called an unwritten prose (or a metalanguage) is exactly that language, which while placing other languages between inverted commas and regarding them as certain material expressions which express certain meanings, regards those same meanings as finding transparent expression within the metalanguage itself. Transparent in the sense that the metalanguage is not regarded as material; it is dematerialised to achieve perfect representation – to let the identity of things shine through the window of words. For insofar as the metalanguage is treated itself as material – it, too, can be reinterpreted; new meanings can be found for it in a further metalanguage. The problem is the problem that has troubled western thought since the pre-Socratics recognised the separation between what was said and the act of saying. This separation must be thought both as time and space – as the space, which in the distance from page to eye or mouth to ear allows the possibility of misunderstanding – as the time taken to traverse the page or listen to an utterance which ensures the deferred interpretation of words which are always only defined by what follows. The problem is that in the moment that we say a sentence the meaning (what is said) seems fixed and evident but what is said does not exist solely for the moment and is open to further interpretations. Even in this formulation of the problem I have presupposed an original moment when there is strict contemporaneity between the saying and what is said, but the difficulty is more radical for there is no such original moment. The separation is always already there as we cannot locate the presence of what is said – distributed as it is through space – nor the present of what is said – distributed as it is through time.

This separation bears witness to the real as articulated. The thing represented does not appear in a moment of pure identity as it tears itself out of the world and presents itself, but rather is caught in an articulation in which each object is defined in a set of differences and oppositions.

It is this separation that the unwritten text attempts to *anneal*, to make whole, through denying its own status as writing – as marks of material difference distributed through time and space. Whereas other discourses within the text are considered as material which are open to re-interpretation, the narrative discourse simply allows reality to appear and denies its own status as articulation. This relationship between discourses can be clearly seen in the work of such a writer as George Eliot. In the scene in *Middlemarch* where Mr Brooke goes to visit the Dagley's farm we read two different languages. One is the educated, well-meaning, but not very intelligent discourse of Mr Brooke and the other is the uneducated, violent and very nearly unintelligible discourse of the drunken Dagley. But the whole dialogue is surrounded by a metalanguage, which being unspoken is also unwritten, and which places these discourses in inverted commas and can thus discuss these discourses' relation to truth – a truth which is illuminatingly revealed in the metalanguage. The metalanguage reduces the object languages into a simple division between form and content and extracts the meaningful content from the useless form. One can see this process at work in the following passage which ends the scene:

> He [Mr Brooke] had never been insulted on his own land before, and had been inclined to regard himself as a general favourite (we are all apt to do so, when we think of our own amiability more than what other people are likely to want of us). When he had quarrelled with Caleb Garth twelve years before he had thought that the tenants would be pleased at the landlord's taking everything into his own hands.
>
> Some who follow the narrative of this experience may wonder at the midnight darkness of Mr Dagley; but nothing was easier in those times than for a hereditary farmer of his grade to be ignorant, in spite somehow of having a rector in the twin parish who was a gentleman to the backbone, a curate nearer at hand who preached more learnedly than the rector, a landlord who had gone into everything, especially fine art and social improvement and all the lights of Middlemarch only three miles off.[2]

This passage provides the necessary interpretations for the discourses that we have read earlier in the chapter. Both the discourses of Dagley and Mr Brooke are revealed as springing from two types of ignorance which the metalanguage can expose and reveal. So we have Mr Brooke's attitude to what his tenants thought of him contrasted with the reality which is available through the narrative prose. No discourse is allowed to speak for itself but rather it must be placed in a context which will reduce it to a simple explicable content. And in the claim that the narrative prose has direct access to a final reality we can find the claim of the classic realist novel to present us with the truths of human nature. The ability to reveal the truth about Mr Brooke is the ability that guarantees the generalisations of human nature.

Thus then a first definition of the classic realist text – but does this definition carry over into films where it is certainly less evident where to locate the dominant discourse? It seems to me that it does and in the following fashion. The narrative prose achieves its position of dominance because it is in the position of knowledge and this function of knowledge is taken up in the cinema by the narration of events. Through the knowledge we gain from the narrative we can split the discourses of the various characters from their situation and compare what is said in these discourses with what has been revealed to us through narration. The camera shows us what happens – it tells the truth against which we can measure the discourses. A good example of this classical realist structure is to be found in Pakula's film *Klute*. This film is of particular interest because it was widely praised for its realism on its release. Perhaps even more significantly it tended to be praised for its realistic presentation of the leading woman, Bree (played by Jane Fonda).

In *Klute* the relationship of dominance between discourses is peculiarly accentuated by the fact that the film is interspersed with fragments of Bree talking to her psychiatrist. This subjective discourse can be exactly measured against the reality provided by the unfolding of the story. Thus all her talk of independence is portrayed as finally an illusion as we discover, to no great surprise but to our immense relief, what she really wants is to settle down in the mid-West with John Klute (the detective played by Donald Sutherland) and have a family. The final sequence of the film is particularly telling in this respect. While Klute and Bree pack their bags to leave, the soundtrack records Bree at her last meeting with her psychiatrist. Her own estimation of the situation is that it most probably won't work but the reality of the image ensures us that this is the way it will really be. Indeed Bree's monologue is even more interesting – for in relation to the reality of the image it marks a definite advance on her previous statements. She has gained insight through the plot development and like many good heroines of classic realist texts her discourse is more nearly adequate to the truth at the end of the film than at the beginning. But if a progression towards knowledge is what marks Bree, it is possession of knowledge which marks the narrative, the reader of the film and John Klute himself. For Klute is privileged by the narrative as the one character whose discourse is also a discourse of knowledge. Not only is Klute a detective and thus can solve the problem of his friend's disappearance – he is also a man, and a man who because he has not come into contact with the city has not had his virility undermined. And it is as a full-blooded man that he can know not only the truth of the mystery of the murders but also the truth of the woman Bree. Far from being a film which goes any way to portraying a woman liberated from male definition (a common critical response), *Klute* exactly guarantees that the real essence of woman can only be discovered and defined by a man.

The analysis sketched here is obviously very schematic but what, hopefully, it does show is that the structure of the classic realist text can be found in film as well. That narrative of events – the knowledge which the film provides of how things really are – is the metalanguage in which we can talk of the various characters in the film. What would still remain to be done in the elaboration of the structure of the classic realist text in cinema is a more detailed account of the actual mechanisms by which the narrative is privileged (and the way in which one or more of the characters within the narrative can be equally privileged) and also a history of the development of this dominant narrative. On the synchronic level it would be necessary to attempt an analysis of the relationship between the various types of shot and their combination into sequences – are there for example certain types of shot which are coded as subjective and therefore subordinate to others which are guaranteed as objective? In addition how does music work as the guarantee or otherwise of truth? On the diachronic level it would be necessary to study how this form was produced – what relationship obtains between the classic realist text and technical advances such as the development of the talkie? What ideological factors were at work in the production and dominance of the classic realist text?

To return, however, to the narrative discourse. It is necessary to attempt to understand the type of relations that this dominant discourse produces. The narrative discourse cannot be mistaken in its identifications because the narrative discourse is not present as discourse – as articulation. The unquestioned nature of the narrative discourse entails that the only problem that reality poses is to go and look and see what *Things* there *are*. The relationship between the reading subject and the real is placed as one of pure specularity. The real is not articulated – it is. These features imply two essential features of the classic realist text:

1   The classic realist text cannot deal with the real as contradictory.
2   In a reciprocal movement the classic realist text ensures the position of the subject in a relation of dominant specularity.

Notes

1   Bertholt Brecht, *Gesammelte Werke*, 20 vols (Frankfurt: Suhrkamp Verlag, 1967).
2   George Eliot, *Middlemarch* (Harmondsworth, Middlesex: Penguin, 1965), pp. 432–3.

Section 2

IDEOLOGY

Introduction

Every sign is ideological. Yet it is hard to give a relatively objective and impartial account of the concept of ideology, one that is not tendentious, because the question of ideology is so deeply bound up with politics, domination and issues of power. In introducing the topic for this collection a sense of our own position cannot be entirely withheld. There is a politics of ideology, one that in the West has taken the form of a particular history. When Marx and Engels were working on the foundational text *The German Ideology* in 1846 they were writing in a historical situation in which the control of ideas was relatively unimportant to the maintenance of the existing social order, and the exercise of force by the ruling class was relatively overt and un-ashamed. Since then, with the development of mass education, forms of parlia-mentary democracy and, in the twentieth and twenty-first centuries, the mass media, the social control of thought has become of major political importance, and with it, the question of ideology. Definitions of ideology have spread in widening circles, from a local concern with the ideologies of groups in a conjuncture, to those of a period, an epoch and, especially since the success of the great post-war movements against European imperialism, a sense of ideology as perhaps characterizing the whole of Western culture since Ancient Greece. To give a preliminary map of this intellectual terrain it is useful to follow a rough but by no means comprehensive chronology, one that, significantly, begins with a sense of ideology as conscious and deliberate but develops increasingly to regard ideology as permeating lived experience, subjectivity and even the unconscious.

A baseline definition of ideology would contrast it with the notion of ideas. While the term ideas, in the general usage, envisages meanings as something individuals think up for themselves, ideology specifies meanings in so far as they are social and collective. 'It is not', writes Marx, 'the consciousness of people that determines their being, but, on the contrary, their social being that determines their consciousness' (p. 37). Of course, how to draw a line between ideas originating with the individual and ideology constituted socially is a matter of continuing debate. Terry Eagleton, in his fine book, *Ideology: An Introduction* (1991: 8) suggests that a breakfast-time quarrel between husband and wife over who burned the toast need not be ideological but becomes so when, for example, 'it begins to engage questions of sexual power, beliefs about gender roles and so on' (though it is hard to imagine such a quarrel *not* engaging with those questions today).

Ideology as expression of class interests

Outside the academy, in journalism and on television, the word ideology is used with a precise meaning as the conscious political programme of a political party: for example, in Britain with references to the ideology of the Labour Party (promoting the welfare state) or the Conservative Party (fostering entrepreneurship and 'private enterprise'). Originating in fact with Napoleon Bonaparte, this usage continues to be widely dominant. In *The German Ideology* and elsewhere (Sections 2.1 and 2.2) Marx and Engels developed an account of ideology in terms of 'economic base' and 'ideological superstructure'. If a person's class position is determined by his or her economic position in relation to the mode of production, then this individual will share an ideology representing the economic interests of the class they belong to.

In one of the clearest and most striking illustrations of ideology in this sense, Marx in *The Eighteenth Brumaire of Louis Napoleon*, writing of the events surrounding the failed revolution of 1848 in France, gives a sardonic and sweeping analysis of how ideology works. To win power for itself the revolutionary class of capitalism, the bourgeoisie, had to overthrow the feudal order (as it did in France with the Revolution of 1789). Since, 'the tradition of all the dead generations weighs like a nightmare on the brain of the living' (Marx and Engels 1950, vol. 1: 225), the bourgeoisie needed also to win a battle of ideas, and did so by performing two manoeuvres. One was to represent its own sectarian, class interests as universal and of democratic value, the other was to step aside from the religious ideology of the feudal epoch. Both of these were achieved through neo-Classicism, reviving the discourses, styles and outward institutions of the ancient Roman imperialism. At a stroke the bourgeoisie claimed a post-medieval originality for itself *and* aligned itself with a universal ideal compre-hending ancient civilization. In the 'resurrected Romance' of the French Revolution the bourgeoisie found 'the self-deceptions that they needed' (*ibid.*: 226). In this example two things come through strongly: that ideology consists of ideas in the service of class interests, and that ideology is a gigantic masquerade.

This second issue, the falseness of ideology, has provided another topic for continuing debate. Is ideology simply 'false consciousness', an illusion, albeit one its proponents share in through self-deception, and so possibly opposed to the true knowledge objectively obtained by science? If so, what does this 'false conscious-ness' consist of, since far from sounding like a material effect, it appears to be somehow not real at all? How does ideology gain credence, and what are the mechanisms by which it works?

Ideology as hegemony and subjectivity

In Britain in 1867 the Second Reform Bill was passed, vastly extending the franchise, and in 1870 an Act introducing state education. A cynic might say that having got the vote the working class had to be taught who to vote for – in the 1890s Engels observed that many newly enfranchised members of the working class voted Tory, not even for the Liberals. In the twentieth century, with the extraordinary growth of the modern state and the development of parliamentary democracy, the question of whether ideology was 'false consciousness' became ever more crucial.

The Italian Marxist Antonio Gramsci (see 'Biographical notes') addressed these changed circumstances by exploring a concept he borrowed from Lenin, that of hegemony. Enormously impressed by the traditional power of the Catholic Church in Italy to hold allegiance in the hearts and minds of the people, Gramsci theorized that a ruling group, whether of the left or the right, must now govern through a balance of force and persuasion:

> The methodological criterion on which our own study must be based is the fol-lowing: that the supremacy of a social group manifests itself in two ways, as 'domination' and as 'intellectual and moral leadership'. A social group dominates antagonistic groups, which it tends to 'liquidate', or to subjugate perhaps even by armed force; it leads kindred and allied groups. A social group can, and indeed must, already exercise 'leadership' before winning governmental power (this indeed is one of the principle [sic] conditions for the winning of such power); it subsequently becomes dominant when it exercises power, but even if it holds it firmly in its grasp, it must continue to 'lead' as well.
>
> (Gramsci 1971: 57–8)

Comprehending ideology, institutions and practices (such as education), the concept of hegemony (not represented elsewhere in this Reader) is at once suggestively flexible in detail and, at root, very simple. Essentially it repeats the Chartist aim, summed up in the slogan 'peaceably if we can, forcibly if we must'. Hegemony specifies ideology as ways a ruling group, bloc or class must rule by winning consent *in conjunction with* the threat of force, the effectiveness of hegemony depending on how rarely force, always present, actually has to be used.

A problem with the notion of hegemony inheres in the question of how exactly one defines consent. For the question of consent is predicated on a conception of the subject: does the subject agree to be led through explicit, active and conscious choice or is a less premeditated and conscious acquiescence or non-resistance sufficient? Enormously influenced by Gramsci, Louis Althusser (see 'Biographical notes' and Section 2.3) analyses ideology as functioning across a range of state institutions to reproduce subjects who 'work by themselves' and live out their sub-ordination unconsciously.

A false consciousness that reaches far into the subject, even hoping (with Althusser) to include the process of the unconscious, hardly qualifies any more as in any useful sense 'false' or 'conscious'. It also poses acutely the question of where exactly the analysts of ideology stand in relation to what they analyse. For Althusser in principle this is not a difficulty since 'ideological practice' is opposed to 'theoretical practice' (or science) in such a way that the application of theory can know ideology as it does not know itself. But in the writings of Michel Foucault that opposition is seen as untenable: ideology and science combine into a single conceptualization of discursive and social practices as the operation of 'power/knowledge' (see 'Bio-graphical notes' and Sections 3.5 and 3.6). It would not be an excessive prejudge-ment to say that Foucault's procedure has the advantage of making visible the work of ideology at intimately lived levels of human experience previously unnoticed and unchallenged (talking to your doctor about your backache, for instance); but it achieves this at a price, for there now appears to be no absolutely exterior point from which the prevailing and all-pervading operation of power can be made subject to critique so that it may be consciously and explicitly *resisted.*

Now extended to become so all-embracing, the concept of ideology risks vacuity and loss of substantial content. Three other problems compound that difficulty. One is that the concept of ideology, in having to work across so many different cultural discourses, tends to treat each of these as though it was merely a transparent vehicle for ideology, tending therefore to ignore the signifier and what is specific in the operation of different signifying practices. Another is that, in the prevailing tradition, the concept of ideology can be accused of ignoring issues of gender or subsuming them in traditionally masculine concerns such as the economy and the outward institutions of political power. A third, as briefly, is that ideology does not so obviously address the exercise of discursive power in the arenas of empire and race. The work of Simone de Beauvoir challenges the concept of ideology in its traditionally masculine concerns by insisting on the questions both of gender and of the operation of the signifier in constituting gender (see 'Biographical notes' and Section 2.4). Since the works of Edward Said on 'Orientalism' and Homi K. Bhabha on the racial subject as 'other' (see 'Biographical notes' and Sections 2.5 and 2.6) are directed at social critiques of forms of ideology in the area of race, they have also been included in the section on ideology. Finally, Slavoj Žižek's work specifically on ideology (Section 2.7) points more insistently towards the precariousness of the unconscious work of ideology, and urges us to read all cultural texts as symptoms of a variety of resistant positions.

Overlapping definitions of ideology have come to exceed what is usefully dis-criminated as ideology, posing questions about the power of particular signifying practices in reproducing conceptions of gender, of race and indeed of Western culture itself in its continuity from Athens. This is recognized in the present collection by the marking out of separate sections on subjectivity, on gender and race and on differ-ence. In one respect, however, these are all concerned with ideology in its particu-larities and difference.

2.1

Karl Marx, from 'Preface', *A Contribution to the Critique of Political Economy* (1859)

The general result at which I arrived and which, once won, served as a guiding thread for my studies, can be briefly formulated as follows: In the social production of their life, men enter into definite relations that are indispensable and independent of their will, relations of production which correspond to a definite stage of development of their material productive forces. The sum total of these relations of production constitutes the economic structure of society, the real foundation, on which rises a legal and political superstructure and to which correspond definite forms of social consciousness. The mode of production of material life conditions the social, political and intellectual life process in general. It is not the consciousness of men that determines their being, but, on the contrary, their social being that determines their consciousness. At a certain stage of their development, the material productive forces of society come in conflict with the existing relations of production, or – what is but a legal expression for the same thing – with the property relations within which they have been at work hitherto. From forms of development of the productive forces these relations turn into their fetters. Then begins an epoch of social revolution. With the change of the economic foundation the entire immense superstructure is more or less rapidly transformed. In considering such transformations a distinction should always be made between the material transformation of the economic conditions of production, which can be determined with the precision of natural science, and the legal, political, religious, aesthetic or philosophic – in short, ideological forms in which men become conscious of this conflict and fight it out. Just as our opinion of an individual is not based on what he thinks of himself, so can we not judge of such a period of transformation by its own consciousness; on the contrary, this consciousness must be explained rather from the contradictions of material life, from the existing conflict between the social productive forces and the relations of production. No social order ever perishes before all the productive forces for which there is room in it have developed; and new, higher relations of production never appear before the material conditions of their existence have matured in the womb of the old society itself. Therefore mankind always sets itself only such tasks as it can solve; since, looking at the matter more closely, it will always be found that the task itself arises only when the material conditions for its solution already exist or are at least in the process of formation. In broad outlines Asiatic, ancient, feudal, and modern bourgeois modes of production can be designated as progressive epochs in the economic formation of society. The bourgeois relations of production are the last antagonistic form of the social process of production – antagonistic not in the sense of individual antagonism, but of one arising from the social conditions of life of the individuals; at the same time the productive forces developing in the womb of bourgeois society create the material conditions for the solution of that antagonism. This social formation brings, therefore, the prehistory of human society to a close.

2.2

Karl Marx and Friedrich Engels, from *The German Ideology* (1846)

The ruling class and the ruling ideas. How the Hegelian conception of the domination of the spirit in history arose

The ideas of the ruling class are in every epoch the ruling ideas: i.e., the class which is the ruling *material* force of society is at the same time its ruling *intellectual* force. The class which has the means of material production at its disposal, consequently also controls the means of mental production, so that the ideas of those who lack the means of mental production are on the whole subject to it. The ruling ideas are nothing more than the ideal expression of the dominant material relations, the dominant material relations grasped as ideas; hence of the relations which make the one class the ruling one, therefore, the ideas of its dominance. The individuals composing the ruling class possess among other things consciousness, and therefore think. Insofar, therefore, as they rule as a class and determine the extent and compass of an historical epoch, it is self-evident that they do this in its whole range, hence among other things rule also as thinkers, as producers of ideas, and regulate the production and distribution of the ideas of their age: thus their ideas are the ruling ideas of the epoch. For instance, in an age and in a country where royal power, aristocracy and bourgeoisie are contending for domination and where, therefore, domination is shared, the doctrine of the separation of powers proves to be the dominant idea and is expressed as an 'eternal law'.

The division of labour, which we already saw above as one of the chief forces of history up till now, manifests itself also in the ruling class as the division of mental and material labour, so that inside this class one part appears as the thinkers of the class (its active, conceptive ideologists, who make the formation of the illusions of the class about itself their chief source of livelihood), while the others' attitude to these ideas and illusions is more passive and receptive, because they are in reality the active members of this class and have less time to make up illusions and ideas about themselves. Within this class this cleavage can even develop into a certain opposition and hostility between the two parts, but whenever a practical collision occurs in which the class itself is endangered they automatically vanish, in which case there also vanishes the appearance of the ruling ideas being not the ideas of the ruling class and having a power distinct from the power of this class. The existence of revolutionary ideas in a particular period presupposes the existence of a revolutionary class; about the premises of the latter sufficient has already been said above.

If now in considering the course of history we detach the ideas of the ruling class from the ruling class itself and attribute to them an independent existence, if we confine ourselves to saying that these or those ideas were dominant at a given time, without bothering ourselves about the conditions of production and the producers of these ideas, if we thus ignore the individuals and world conditions which are the source of the ideas, then we can say, for instance, that during the time the aristocracy was dominant, the concepts honour, loyalty, etc., were dominant, during the dominance of the bourgeoisie the concepts freedom, equality, etc. The ruling class itself on the whole imagines this to be so. This conception of history, which is common to all historians, particularly since the eighteenth century, will necessarily come up against the phenomenon that ever more abstract ideas hold sway, i.e., ideas which increasingly take on the form of universality. For each new class which puts itself in the place of one ruling before it is compelled, merely in order to carry through its aim, to present its interest as the common interest of all the members of society, that is, expressed in ideal form: it has to give its ideas the form of universality, and present them as the only rational, universally valid ones. The class making a revolution comes forward from the very start, if only because it is opposed to a *class*, not as a class but as the representative of the whole of society, as the whole mass of society confronting the one ruling class.[1] It can do this because initially its interest really is as yet mostly connected with the common interest of all other non-ruling classes, because under the pressure of hitherto existing conditions its interest has not yet been able to develop as the particular interest of a particular class. Its victory, therefore, benefits also many individuals of other classes which are not winning a dominant position, but only insofar as it now enables these individuals to raise themselves into the ruling class. When the French bourgeoisie overthrew the rule of the aristocracy, it thereby made it possible for many proletarians to raise themselves above the proletariat, but only insofar as they became bourgeois. Every new class, therefore, achieves domination only on a broader basis than that of the class ruling previously; on the other hand the opposition of the non-ruling class to the new ruling class then develops all the more sharply and profoundly. Both these things determine the fact that the struggle to be waged against this new ruling class, in its turn, has as its aim a more decisive and more radical negation of the previous conditions of society than all previous classes which sought to rule could have.

This whole appearance, that the rule of a certain class is only the rule of certain ideas, comes to a natural end, of course, as soon as class rule in general ceases to be the form in which society is organised, that is to say, as soon as it is no longer necessary to represent a particular interest as general or the 'general interest' as ruling.

Note

1   Universality corresponds to: (1) the class versus the estate; (2) the competition, world intercourse etc.; (3) the great numerical strength of the ruling class; (4) the illusion of the *common* interests (in the beginning this illusion is true); (5) the delusion of the ideologists and the division of labour.

2.3

Louis Althusser, from 'Ideology and Ideological State Apparatuses' (1970)

What are the ideological State apparatuses (ISAs)?

They must not be confused with the (repressive) State apparatus. Remember that in Marxist theory, the State Apparatus (SA) contains: the Government, the Administration, the Army, the Police, the Courts, the Prisons, etc., which constitute what I shall in future call the Repressive State Apparatus. Repressive suggests that the State Apparatus in question 'functions by violence' – at least ultimately (since repression, e.g. administrative repression, may take non-physical forms).

I shall call Ideological State Apparatuses a certain number of realities which present themselves to the immediate observer in the form of distinct and specialized institutions. I propose an empirical list of these which obviously have to be examined in detail, tested, corrected and reorganized. With all the reservations implied by this requirement, we can for the moment regard the following in situations as Ideological State Apparatuses (the order in which I have listed them has no particular significance):

- the religious ISA (the system of the different Churches),
- the educational ISA (the system of the different public and private 'Schools'),
- the family ISA,[1]
- the legal ISA,[2]
- the political ISA (the political system, including the different Parties),
- the trade-union ISA,
- the communications ISA (press, radio and television, etc.),
- the cultural ISA (Literature, the Arts, sports, etc.).

I have said that the ISAs must not be confused with the (Repressive) State Apparatus. What constitutes the difference?

As a first moment, it is clear that while there is *one* (Repressive) State Apparatus, there is a *plurality* of Ideological State Apparatuses. Even pre-supposing that it exists, the unity that constitutes this plurality of ISAs as a body is not immediately visible.

As a second moment, it is clear that whereas the – unified – (Repressive) State Apparatus belongs entirely to the *public* domain, much the larger part of the Ideological State Apparatuses (in their apparent dispersion) are part, on the contrary, of the *private* domain. Churches, Parties, Trade Unions, families, some schools, most newspapers, cultural ventures, etc., etc., are private.

We can ignore the first observation for the moment. But someone is bound to question the second, asking me by what right I regard as Ideological *State* Apparatuses, institutions which for the most part do not possess public status, but are quite simply *private* institutions. As a conscious Marxist, Gramsci already forestalled this objection in one sentence. The distinction between the public and the private is a distinction internal to bourgeois law, and valid in the (subordinate) domains in which bourgeois law exercises its 'authority'. The domain of the State escapes it because the latter is 'above the law': the State, which is the State of the ruling class is neither public nor private; on the contrary, it is the precondition for any distinction between public and private. The same thing can be said from the starting-point of our State Ideological Apparatuses. It is unimportant whether the institutions in which they are realized are 'public' or 'private'. What matters is how they function. Private institutions can perfectly well 'function' as Ideological State Apparatuses. A reasonably thorough analysis of any one of the ISAs proves it.

But now for what is essential. What distinguishes the ISAs from the (Repressive) State Apparatus is the following basic difference: the Repressive State Apparatus functions 'by violence', whereas the Ideological State Apparatuses *function 'by ideology'*.

I can clarify matters by correcting this distinction. I shall say rather that every State Apparatus, whether Repressive or Ideological, 'functions' both by violence and by ideology, but with one very important distinction which makes it imperative not to confuse the Ideological State Apparatuses with the (Repressive) State Apparatus.

This is the fact that the (Repressive) State Apparatus functions massively and predominantly *by repression* (including physical repression), while functioning secondarily by ideology. (There is no such thing as a purely repressive apparatus.) For example, the Army and the Police also function by ideology both to ensure their own cohesion and reproduction, and in the 'values' they propound externally.

In the same way, but inversely, it is essential to say that for their part the Ideological State Apparatuses function massively and predominantly *by ideology*, but they also function secondarily by repression, even if ultimately, but only ultimately, this is very attenuated and concealed, even symbolic. (There is no such thing as purely ideological apparatus.) Thus Schools and Churches use suitable methods of punishment, expulsion, selection, etc., to 'discipline' not only their shepherds, but also their flocks. The same is true of the Family ... The same is true of the cultural IS Apparatus (censorship, among other things), etc.

Ideology is a 'representation' of the imaginary relationship of individuals to their real conditions of existence

In order to approach my central thesis on the structure and functioning of ideology, I shall first present two theses, one negative, the other positive. The first concerns the object which is 'represented' in the imaginary form of ideology, the second concerns the materiality of ideology.

THESIS I   Ideology represents the imaginary relationship of individuals to their real conditions of existence.

We commonly call religious ideology, ethical ideology, legal ideology, political ideology, etc., so many 'world outlooks'. Of course, assuming that we do not live one of these ideologies as the truth (e.g. 'believe' in God, Duty, Justice, etc. . . . .), we admit that the ideology we are discussing from a critical point of view, examining it as the ethnologist examines the myths of a 'primitive society', that these 'world outlooks' are largely imaginary, i.e. do not 'correspond to reality'.

However, while admitting that they do not correspond to reality, i.e. that they constitute an illusion, we admit that they do make allusion to reality, and that they need only be 'interpreted' to discover the reality of the world behind their imaginary representation of that world (ideology = *illusion/allusion*).

Now I can return to a thesis which I have already advanced: it is not their real conditions of existence, their real world, that 'men' 'represent to themselves' in ideology, but above all it is their relation to those conditions of existence which is represented to them there. It is this relation which is at the centre of every ideological, i.e. imaginary, representation of the real world. It is this relation that contains the 'cause' which has to explain the imaginary distortion of the ideological representation of the real world. Or rather, to leave aside the language of causality it is necessary to advance the thesis that it is the *imaginary nature of this relation* which underlies all the imaginary distortion that we can observe (if we do not live in its truth) in all ideology.

To speak in a Marxist language, if it is true that the representation of the real conditions of existence of the individuals occupying the posts of agents of production, exploitation, repression, ideologization and scientific practice, does in the last analysis arise from the relations of production, and from relations deriving from the relations of production, we can say the following: all ideology represents in its necessarily imaginary distortion not the existing relations of production (and the other relations that derive from them), but above all the (imaginary) relationship of individuals to the relations of production and the relations that derive from them. What is represented in ideology is therefore not the system of the real relations which govern the existence of individuals, but the imaginary relation of those individuals to the real relations in which they live.

If this is the case, the question of the 'cause' of the imaginary distortion of the real relations in ideology disappears and must be replaced by a different question: why is the representation given to individuals of their (individual) relation to the social relations which govern their conditions of existence and their collective and individual life necessarily an imaginary relation? And what is the nature of this imaginariness? Posed in this way, the question explodes the solution by a 'clique',[3] by a group of individuals (Priests or Despots) who are the authors of the great ideological mystification, just as it explodes the solution by the alienated character of the real world. We shall see why later in my exposition. For the moment I shall go no further.

THESIS II   Ideology has a material existence.

I have already touched on this thesis by saying that the 'ideas' or 'representations', etc., which seem to make up ideology do not have an ideal (*idéale* or *idéelle*) or spiritual existence, but a material existence. I even suggested that the ideal (*idéale, idéelle*) and spiritual existence of 'ideas' arises exclusively in an ideology of the 'idea' and of ideology, and let me add, in an ideology of what seems to have 'founded' this conception since the emergence of the science, i.e. what the practitioners of the sciences represent to themselves in their spontaneous ideology as 'ideas', true or false. Of course, presented in affirmative form, this thesis is unproven. I simply ask that the reader be favourably disposed towards it, say, in the name of materialism. A long series of arguments would be necessary to prove it.

This hypothetical thesis of the not spiritual but material existence of 'ideas' or other 'representations' is indeed necessary if we are to advance in our analysis of the nature of ideology. Or rather, it is merely useful to us in order the better to reveal what every at all serious analysis of any ideology will immediately and empirically show to every observer, however critical.

While discussing the ideological State apparatuses and their practices, I said that each of them was the realization of an ideology (the unity of these different regional ideologies – religious, ethical, legal, political, aesthetic, etc. – being assured by their subjection to the ruling ideology). I now return to this thesis: an ideology always exists in an apparatus, and its practice, or practices. This existence is material.

Of course, the material existence of the ideology in an apparatus and its practices does not have the same modality as the material existence of a paving-stone or a rifle. But, at the risk of being taken for a Neo-Aristotelian (NB Marx had a very high regard for Aristotle), I shall say that 'matter is discussed in many senses', or rather that it exists in different modalities, all rooted in the last instance in 'physical' matter.

And I shall immediately set down two conjoint theses:

1   there is no practice except by and in an ideology;
2   there is no ideology except by the subject and for subjects.

I can now come to my central thesis.

Ideology interpellates individuals as subjects

This thesis is simply a matter of making my last proposition explicit: there is no ideology except by the subject and for subjects. Meaning, there is no ideology except for concrete subjects, and this destination for ideology is only made possible by the subject: meaning, *by the category of the subject* and its functioning.

By this I mean that, even if it only appears under this name (the subject) with the rise of bourgeois ideology, above all with the rise of legal ideology,[4] the category of the subject (which may function under other names: e.g., as the soul in Plato, as God, etc.) is the constitutive category of all ideology, whatever its determination (regional or class) and whatever its historical date – since ideology has no history.

I say: the category of the subject is constitutive of all ideology, but at the same time and immediately I add that *the category of the subject is only constitutive of all ideology insofar as all ideology has the function (which defines it) of 'constituting' concrete individuals as subjects*. In the interaction of this double constitution exists the functioning of all ideology, ideology being nothing but its functioning in the material forms of existence of that functioning.

In order to grasp what follows, it is essential to realize that both he who is writing these lines and the reader who reads them are themselves subjects, and therefore ideological subjects (a tautological proposition), i.e. that the author and the reader of these lines both live 'spontaneously' or 'naturally' in ideology in the sense in which I have said that 'man is an ideological animal by nature'.

That the author, insofar as he writes the lines of a discourse which claims to be scientific, is completely absent as a 'subject' from 'his' scientific discourse (for all scientific discourse is by definition a subject-less discourse, there is no 'Subject of science' except in an ideology of science) is a different question which I shall leave on one side for the moment.

As St Paul admirably put it, it is in the 'Logos', meaning in ideology, that we 'live, move and have our being'. It follows that, for you and for me, the category of the subject is a primary 'obviousness' (obviousnesses are always primary): it is clear that you and I are subjects (free, ethical, etc. ...). Like all obviousnesses, including those that make a word 'name a thing' or 'have a meaning' (therefore including the obviousness of the 'transparency' of language), the 'obviousness' that you and I are subjects – and that that does not cause any problems – is an ideological effect, the elementary ideological effect.[5] It is indeed a peculiarity of ideology that it imposes (without appearing to do so, since these are 'obviousnesses') obviousnesses as obviousnesses, which we cannot *fail to recognize* and before which we have the inevitable and natural reaction of crying out (aloud or in the 'still, small voice of conscience'): 'That's obvious! That's right! That's true!'

At work in this reaction is the ideological *recognition* function which is one of the two functions of ideology as such (its inverse being the function of *misrecognition – méconnaissance*).

To take a highly 'concrete' example, we all have friends who, when they knock on our door and we ask, through the door, the question 'Who's there?', answer (since 'it's obvious') 'It's me'. And we recognize that 'it is him', or 'her'. We open the door, and 'it's true, it really was she who was there'. To take another example, when we recognize somebody of our (previous) acquaintance ((*re*)-*connaissance*) in the street, we show him that we have recognized him (and have recognized that he has recognized us) by saying to him 'Hello, my friend', and shaking his hand (a material ritual practice of ideological recognition in everyday life – in France, at least; elsewhere, there are other rituals).

In this preliminary remark and these concrete illustrations, I only wish to point out that you and I are *always already* subjects, and as such constantly practice the rituals of ideological recognition, which guarantee for us that we are indeed concrete, individual, distinguishable and (naturally) irreplaceable subjects. The writing I am currently executing and the reading you are currently[6] performing are also in this respect rituals of ideological recognition, including the 'obviousness' with which the 'truth' or 'error' of my reflections may impose itself on you.

But to recognize that we are subjects and that we function in the practical rituals of the most elementary everyday life (the hand-shake, the fact of calling you by your name, the fact of knowing, even if I do not know what it is, that you 'have' a name of your own, which means that you are recognized as a unique subject, etc.) – this recognition only gives us the 'consciousness' of our incessant (eternal) practice of ideological recognition – its consciousness, i.e. its *recognition* – but in no sense does it give us the (scientific) *knowledge* of the mechanism of this recognition. Now it is this knowledge that we have to reach, if you will, while speaking in ideology, and from within ideology we have to outline a discourse which tries to break with ideology, in order to dare to be the beginning of a scientific (i.e. subjectless) discourse on ideology.

Thus in order to represent why the category of the 'subject' is constitutive of ideology, which only exists by constituting concrete subjects as subjects, I shall employ a special mode of exposition: 'concrete' enough to be recognized, but abstract enough to be thinkable and thought, giving rise to a knowledge.

As a first formulation I shall say: *all ideology hails or interpellates concrete individuals as concrete subjects*, by the functioning of the category of the subject.

This is a proposition which entails that we distinguish for the moment between concrete individuals on the one hand and concrete subjects on the other, although at this level concrete subjects only exist insofar as they are supported by a concrete individual.

I shall then suggest that ideology 'acts' or 'functions' in such a way that it 'recruits' subjects among the individuals (it recruits them all), or 'transforms' the individuals into subjects (it transforms them all) by that very precise operation which I have called *interpellation* or hailing, and which can be imagined along the lines of the most commonplace everyday police (or other) hailing: 'Hey, you there!'[7]

Assuming that the theoretical scene I have imagined takes place in the street, the hailed individual will turn round. By this mere one-hundred-and-eighty-degree physical conversion, he becomes a *subject*. Why? Because he has recognized that the hail was 'really' addressed to him, and that 'it was *really him* who was hailed' (and not someone else). Experience shows that the practical telecommunication of hailings is such that they hardly ever miss their man: verbal call or whistle, the one hailed always recognizes that it is really him who is being hailed. And yet it is a strange phenomenon, and one which cannot be explained solely by 'guilt feelings', despite the large numbers who 'have something on their consciences'.

Naturally for the convenience and clarity of my little theoretical theatre I have had to present things in the form of a sequence, with a before and an after, and thus in the form of a temporal succession. There are individuals walking along. Somewhere (usually behind them) the hail rings out: 'Hey, you there!' One individual (nine times out of ten it is the right one) turns round, believing/suspecting/knowing that it is for him, i.e. recognizing that 'it really is he' who is meant by the hailing. But in reality these things happen without any succession. The existence of ideology and the hailing or interpellation of individuals as subjects are one and the same thing.

I might add: what thus seems to take place outside ideology (to be precise, in the street), in reality takes place in ideology. What really takes place in ideology seems therefore to take place outside it. That is why those who are in ideology believe themselves by definition outside ideology: one of the effects of ideology is the practical *denegation* of the ideological character of ideology by ideology: ideology never says, 'I am ideological'. It is necessary to be outside ideology, i.e. in scientific knowledge, to be able to say: I am in ideology (a quite exceptional case) or (the general case): I was in ideology. As is well known, the accusation of being in ideology only applies to others, never to oneself (unless one is really a Spinozist or a Marxist, which, in this matter, is to be exactly the same thing). Which amounts to saying that ideology *has no outside* (for itself), but at the same time *that it is nothing but outside* (for science and reality).

Let me summarize what we have discovered about ideology in general.

The duplicate mirror-structure of ideology ensures simultaneously:

1   the interpellation of 'individuals' as subjects;

2   their subjection to the Subject;

3   the mutual recognition of subjects and Subject, the subjects' recognition of each other, and finally the subject's recognition of himself;[8]

4   the absolute guarantee that everything really is so, and that on condition that the subjects recognize what they are and behave accordingly, everything will be all right: Amen – '*So be it*'.

Result: caught in this quadruple system of interpellation as subjects, of subjection to the Subject, of universal recognition and of absolute guarantee, the subjects 'work', they 'work by themselves' in the vast majority of cases, with the exception of the 'bad subjects' who on occasion provoke the intervention of one of the detachments of the (repressive) State apparatus. But the vast majority of (good) subjects work all right 'all by themselves', i.e. by ideology (whose concrete forms are realized in the Ideological State Apparatuses). They are inserted into practices governed by the rituals of the ISAs. They 'recognize' the existing state of affairs (*das Bestehende*), that 'it really is true that it is so and not otherwise', and that they must be obedient to God, to their conscience, to the priest, to de Gaulle, to the boss, to the engineer, that thou shalt 'love thy neighbour as thyself', etc. Their concrete, material behaviour is simply the inscription in life of the admirable words of the prayer: '*Amen – So be it*'.

Yes, the subjects 'work by themselves'. The whole mystery of this effect lies in the first two moments of the quadruple system I have just discussed, or, if you prefer, in the ambiguity of the term *subject*. In the ordinary use of the term, subject in fact means: (1) a free subjectivity, a centre of initiatives, author of and responsible for its actions; (2) a subjected being, who submits to a higher authority, and is therefore stripped of all freedom except that of freely accepting his submission. This last note gives us the meaning of this ambiguity, which is merely a reflection of the effect which produces it: the individual *is interpellated as a (free) subject in order that he shall submit freely to the commandments of the Subject, i.e. in order that he shall (freely) accept his subjection*, i.e. in order that he shall make the gestures and actions of his subjection 'all by himself'. *There are no subjects except by and for their subjection*. That is why they 'work all by themselves'.

'*So be it!* . . .' This phrase which registers the effect to be obtained proves that it is not 'naturally' so ('naturally': outside the prayer, i.e. outside the ideological intervention). This phrase proves that it *has* to be so if things are to be what they must be, and let us let the words slip: if the reproduction of the relations of production is to be assured, even in the processes of production and circulation, every day, in the 'consciousness', i.e. in the attitudes of the individual-subjects occupying the posts which the sociotechnical division of labour assigns to them in production, exploitation, repression, ideologization, scientific practice, etc. Indeed, what is really in question in this mechanism of the mirror recognition of the Subject and of the individuals interpellated as subjects, and of the guarantee given by the Subject to the subjects if they freely accept their subjection to the Subject's 'commandments'? The reality in question in this mechanism, the reality which is necessarily *ignored* (*méconnue*) in the very forms of recognition (ideology = misrecognition/ ignorance) is indeed, in the last resort, the reproduction of the relations of production and of the relations deriving from them.

January–April 1969

Notes

1   The family obviously has other 'functions' than that of an ISA. It intervenes in the reproduction of labour power. In different modes of production it is the unit of production and/or the unit of consumption.

2   The 'Law' belongs both to the (Repressive) State Apparatuses and to the system of the ISAs.

3   I use this very modern term deliberately. For even in Communist circles, unfortunately, it is a commonplace to 'explain' some political deviation (left or right opportunism) by the action of a 'clique'.

4   Which borrowed the legal category of 'subject in law' to make an ideological notion: man is by nature a subject.

5   Linguists and those who appeal to linguistics for various purposes often run up against difficulties which arise because they ignore the action of the ideological effects in all discourses – including even scientific discourse.

6   NB This double 'currently' is one more proof of the fact that ideology is 'eternal', since these two 'currentlys' are separated by an indefinite interval; I am writing these lines on April 1969, you may read them at any subsequent time.

7   Hailing as an everyday practice subject to a precise ritual takes a quite 'special' form in the policeman's practice of 'hailing' which concerns the hailing of 'suspects'.

8   Hegel is (unknowingly) an admirable 'theoretician' of ideology insofar as he is a 'theoretician' of Universal Recognition who unfortunately ends up in the ideology of Absolute Knowledge. Feurbach is an astonishing 'theoretician' of the mirror connection, who unfortunately ends up in the ideology of the Human Essence. To find the material with which to construct a theory of the guarantee, we must turn to Spinoza.

2.4

Simone de Beauvoir, from *The Second Sex* (1953)

If her functioning as a female is not enough to define woman, if we decline also to explain her through 'the eternal feminine', and if nevertheless we admit, provisionally, that women do exist, then we must face the question: what is a woman?

To state the question is, to me, to suggest, at once, a preliminary answer. The fact that I ask it is in itself significant. A man would never set out to write a book on the peculiar situation of the human male. But if I wish to define myself, I must first of all say: 'I am a woman'; on this truth must be based all further discussion. A man never begins by presenting himself as an individual of a certain sex; it goes without saying that he is a man. The terms *masculine* and *feminine* are used symmetrically only as a matter of form, as on legal papers. In actuality the relation of the two sexes is not quite like that of two electrical poles, for man represents both the positive and the neutral, as is indicated by the common use of *man* to designate human beings in general; whereas woman represents only the negative, defined by limiting criteria, without reciprocity. In the midst of an abstract discussion it is vexing to hear a man say: 'You think thus and so because you are a woman'; but I know that my only defence is to reply: 'I think thus and so because it is true,' thereby removing my subjective self from the argument. It would be out of the question to reply: 'And you think the contrary because you are a man', for it is understood that the fact of being a man is no peculiarity. A man is in the right in being a man; it is the woman who is in the wrong. It amounts to this: just as for the ancients there was an absolute vertical with reference to which the oblique was defined, so there is an absolute human type, the masculine. Woman has ovaries, a uterus: these peculiarities imprison her in her subjectivity, circumscribe her within the limits of her own nature. It is often said that she thinks with her glands. Man superbly ignores the fact that his anatomy also includes glands, such as the testicles, and that they secrete hormones. He thinks of his body as a direct and normal connection with the world, which he believes he apprehends objectively, whereas he regards the body of woman as a hindrance, a prison, weighed down by everything peculiar to it. 'The female is a female by virtue of a certain *lack* of qualities,' said Aristotle; 'we should regard the female nature as afflicted with a natural defectiveness.' And St Thomas for his part pronounced woman to be an 'imperfect man', an 'incidental' being.

This is symbolized in Genesis where Eve is depicted as made from what Bossuet called 'a supernumerary bone' of Adam.

Thus humanity is male and man defines woman not in herself but as relative to him; she is not regarded as an autonomous being. Michelet writes: 'Woman, the relative being ...' And Benda is most positive in his *Rapport d'Uriel*: 'The body of man makes sense in itself quite apart from that of woman, whereas the latter seems wanting in significance by itself ... Man can think of himself without woman. She cannot think of herself without man.' And she is simply what man decrees; thus she is called 'the sex', by which is meant that she appears essentially to the male as a sexual being. For him she is sex – absolute sex, no less. She is defined and differentiated with reference to man and not he with reference to her; she is the incidental, the inessential as opposed to the essential. He is the Subject, he is the Absolute – she is the Other.

The category of the *Other* is as primordial as consciousness itself. In the most primitive societies, in the most ancient mythologies, one finds the expression of a duality – that of the Self and the Other. This duality was not originally attached to the division of the sexes; it was not dependent upon any empirical facts. It is revealed in such works as that of Granet on Chinese thought and those of Dumézil on the East Indies and Rome. The feminine element was at first no more involved in such pairs as Varuna-Mitra, Uranus-Zeus, Sun-Moon, and Day-Night than it was in the contrasts between Good and Evil, lucky and unlucky auspices, right and left, God and Lucifer. Otherness is a fundamental category of human thought.

Thus it is that no group ever sets itself up as the One without at once setting up the Other over against itself. If three travellers chance to occupy the same compartment, that is enough to make vaguely hostile 'others' out of all the rest of the passengers on the train. In small-town eyes all persons not belonging to the village are 'strangers' and suspect; to the native of a country all who inhabit other countries are 'foreigners'; Jews are 'different' for the anti-Semite. Negroes are 'inferior' for American racists, aborigines are 'natives' for colonists, proletarians are the 'lower class' for the privileged.

Lévi-Strauss, at the end of a profound work on the various forms of primitive societies, reaches the following conclusion: 'Passage from the state of Nature to the state of Culture is marked by man's ability to view biological relations as a series of contrasts; duality, alternation, opposition, and symmetry. whether under definite or vague forms, constitute not so much phenomena to be explained as fundamental and immediately given data of social reality.' These phenomena would be incomprehensible if in fact human society were simply a *Mitsein* or fellowship based on solidarity and friendliness. Things become clear, on the contrary, if, following Hegel, we find in consciousness itself a fundamental hostility towards every other consciousness: the subject can be posed only in being opposed – he sets himself up as the essential, as opposed to the other, the inessential, the object.

But the other consciousness, the other ego, sets up a reciprocal claim. The native travelling abroad is shocked to find himself in turn regarded as a 'stranger' by the natives of neighbouring countries. As a matter of fact, wars, festivals, trading, treaties, and contests among tribes, nations, and classes tend to deprive the concept *Other* of its absolute sense and to make manifest its relativity: willy-nilly, individuals and groups are forced to realize the reciprocity of their relations. How is it, then, that this reciprocity has not been recognized between the sexes, that one of the contrasting terms is set up as the sole essential, denying any relativity in regard to its correlative and defining the latter as pure otherness? Why is it that women do not dispute male sovereignty? No subject will readily volunteer to become the object, the inessential: it is not the Other who, in defining himself as the Other, establishes the One. The Other is posed as such by the One in defining himself as the One. But if the Other is not to regain the status of being the One, he must be submissive enough to accept this alien point of view. Whence comes this submission in the case of woman?

There are, to be sure, other cases in which a certain category has been able to dominate another completely for a time. Very often this privilege depends upon inequality of numbers – the majority imposes its rule upon the minority or perse-cutes it. But women are not a minority, like the American Negroes or the Jews; there are as many women as men on earth. Again, the two groups concerned have often been originally independent; they may have been formerly unaware of each other's existence, or perhaps they recognized each other's autonomy. But a his-torical event has resulted in the subjugation of the weaker by the stronger. The scattering of the Jews, the introduction of slavery into America, the conquests of imperialism are examples in point. In these cases the oppressed retained at least the memory of former days; they possessed in common a past, a tradition, sometimes a religion or a culture.

The parallel drawn by Bebel between women and the proletariat is valid in that neither ever formed a minority or a separate collective unit of mankind. And instead of a single historical event it is in both cases a historical development that explains their status as a class and accounts for the membership of *particular individuals* in that class. But proletarians have not always existed, whereas there have always been women. They are women in virtue of their anatomy and physiology. Throughout history they have always been subordinated to men and hence their dependency is not the result of a historical event or a social change – it was not something that *occurred*. The reason why otherness in this case seems to be an absolute is in part that it lacks the contingent or incidental nature of historical facts. A condition brought about at a certain time can be abolished at some other time, as the Negroes of Haiti and others have proved; but it might seem that a natural condition is beyond the possibility of change. In truth, however, the nature of things is no more immutably given, once for all, than is historical reality. If woman seems to be the inessential which never becomes the essential, it is because she herself fails to bring about this change. Proletarians say 'We'; Negroes also. Regarding themselves as subjects, they transform the bourgeois, the whites, into 'others'. But women do not say 'We', except at some congress of feminists or similar formal demonstration; men say 'women', and women use the same word in referring to themselves. They do not authentically assume a subjective attitude. The proletarians have accomplished the revolution in Russia, the Negroes in Haiti, the Indo-Chinese are battling for it in Indo-China; but the women's effort has never been anything more than a symbolic agitation. They have gained only what men have been willing to grant; they have taken nothing, they have only received. . . .

In proving woman's inferiority, the anti-feminists then began to draw not only upon religion, philosophy, and theology, as before, but also upon science – biology, experimental psychology, etc. At most they were willing to grant 'equality in difference' to the *other* sex. That profitable formula is most significant; it is precisely like the 'equal but separate' formula of the Jim Crow laws aimed at the North American Negroes. As is well known, this so-called equalitarian segregation has resulted only in the most extreme discrimination. The similarity just noted is in no way due to chance, for whether it is a race, a caste, a class, or a sex that is reduced to a position of inferiority, the methods of justification are the same. 'The eternal feminine' corresponds to 'the black soul' and to 'the Jewish character'. True, the Jewish problem is on the whole very different from the other two – to the anti-Semite the Jew is not so much an inferior as he is an enemy for whom there is to be granted no place on earth, for whom annihilation is the fate desired. But there are deep similarities between the situation of woman and that of the Negro. Both are being emancipated today from a like paternalism, and the former master class wishes to 'keep them in their place' – that is, the place chosen for them. In both cases the former masters lavish more or less sincere eulogies, either on the virtues of 'the good Negro' with his dormant, childish, merry soul – the submissive Negro – or on the merits of the woman who is 'truly feminine' – that is, frivolous, infantile, irresponsible – the submissive woman. In both cases the dominant class bases its argument on a state of affairs that it has itself created. As George Bernard Shaw puts it, in substance. 'The American white relegates the black to the rank of shoeshine boy; and he concludes from this that the black is good for nothing but shining shoes.' This vicious circle is met with in all analogous circumstances: when an individual (or a group of individuals) is kept in a situation of inferiority, the fact is that he is inferior. But the significance of the verb to *be* must be rightly understood here; it is in bad faith to give it a static value when it really has the dynamic Hegelian sense of 'to have become'. Yes, women on the whole *are* today inferior to men; that is, their situation affords them fewer possibilities. The question is: should that state of affairs continue?

2.5

Edward Said, from *Orientalism* (1978)

My principal operating assumptions were – and continue to be – that fields of learning, as much as the works of even the most eccentric artist, are constrained and acted upon by society, by cultural traditions, by worldly circumstance, and by stabilizing influences like schools, libraries, and governments; moreover, that both learned and imaginative writing are never free, but are limited in their imagery, assumptions, and intentions; and finally, that the advances made by a 'science' like Orientalism in its academic form are less objectively true than we often like to think. In short, my study hitherto has tried to describe the *economy* that makes Orientalism a coherent subject matter, even while allowing that as an idea, concept, or image the word *Orient* has a considerable and interesting cultural resonance in the West.

I realize that such assumptions are not without their controversial side. Most of us assume in a general way that learning and scholarship move forward; they get better, we feel, as time passes and as more information is accumulated, methods are refined, and later generations of scholars improve upon earlier ones. In addition, we entertain a mythology of creation, in which it is believed that artistic genius, an original talent, or a powerful intellect can leap beyond the confines of its own time and place in order to put before the world a new work. It would be pointless to deny that such ideas as these carry some truth. Nevertheless the possibilities for work present in the culture to a great and original mind are never unlimited, just as it is also true that a great talent has a very healthy respect for what others have done before it and for what the field already contains. The work of predecessors, the institutional life of a scholarly field, the collective nature of any learned enterprise: these, to say nothing of economic and social circumstances, tend to diminish the effects of the individual scholar's production. A field like Orientalism has a cumulative and corporate identity, one that is particularly strong given its associations with traditional learning (the classics, the Bible, philology), public institutions (governments, trading companies; geographical societies, universities), and generically determined writing (travel books, books of exploration, fantasy, exotic description). The result for Orientalism has been a sort of consensus: certain things, certain types of statement, certain types of work have seemed for the Orientalist correct. He has built his work and research upon them, and they in turn have pressed hard upon new writers and scholars. Orientalism can thus be regarded as a manner of regularized (or Orientalized) writing, vision, and study, dominated by imperatives, perspectives, and ideological biases ostensibly suited to the Orient. The Orient is taught, researched, administered, and pronounced upon in certain discrete ways.

The Orient that appears in Orientalism, then, is a system of representations framed by a whole set of forces that brought the Orient into Western learning, Western consciousness, and later, Western empire. If this definition of Orientalism seems more political than not, that is simply because I think Orientalism was itself a product of certain political forces and activities. Orientalism is a school of interpretation whose material happens to be the Orient, its civilizations, peoples, and localities. Its objective discoveries – the work of innumerable devoted scholars who edited texts and translated them, codified grammars, wrote dictionaries, reconstructed dead epochs, produced positivistically verifiable learning – are and always have been conditioned by the fact that its truths, like any truths delivered by language, are embodied in language, and what is the truth of language, Nietzsche once said, but

> a mobile army of metaphors, metonyms, and anthropomorphisms – in short, a sum of human relations, which have been enhanced, transposed, and embellished poetically and rhetorically, and which after long use seem firm, canonical, and obligatory to a people: truths are illusions about which one has forgotten that this is what they are.[1]

Perhaps such a view as Nietzsche's will strike us as too nihilistic, but at least it will draw attention to the fact that so far as it existed in the West's awareness, the Orient was a word which later accrued to it a wide field of meanings, associations, and connotations, and that these did not necessarily refer to the real Orient but to the field surrounding the word.

Thus Orientalism is not only a positive doctrine about the Orient that exists at any one time in the West; it is also an influential academic tradition (when one refers to an academic specialist who is called an Orientalist), as well as an area of concern defined by travelers, commercial enterprises, governments, military expeditions, readers of novels and accounts of exotic adventure, natural historians, and pilgrims to whom the Orient is a specific kind of knowledge about specific places, peoples, and civilizations. For the Orient idioms became frequent, and these idioms took firm hold in European discourse. Beneath the idioms there was a layer of doctrine about the Orient; this doctrine was fashioned out of the experiences of many Europeans, all of them converging upon such essential aspects of the Orient as the Oriental character, Oriental despotism, Oriental sensuality, and the like. For any European during the nineteenth century – and I think one can say this almost without qualification – Orientalism was such a system of truths, truths in Nietzsche's sense of the word. It is therefore correct that every European, in what he could say about the Orient, was consequently a racist, an imperialist, and almost totally ethnocentric. Some of the immediate sting will be taken out of these labels if we recall additionally that human societies, at least the more advanced cultures, have rarely offered the individual anything but imperialism, racism, and ethno-centrism for dealing with 'other' cultures. So orientalism aided and was aided by general cultural pressures that tended to make more rigid the sense of difference between the European and Asiatic parts of the world. My contention is that Orientalism is fundamentally a political doctrine willed over the Orient because the Orient was weaker than the West, which elided the Orient's difference with its weakness.

Style, expertise, vision: Orientalism's worldliness

As he appears in several poems, in novels like *Kim*, and in too many catchphrases to be an ironic fiction, Kipling's White Man, as an idea, a persona, a style of being, seems to have served many Britishers while they were abroad. The actual color of their skin set them off dramatically and reassuringly from the sea of natives, but for the Britisher who circulated amongst Indians, Africans, or Arabs there was also the certain knowledge that he belonged to, and could draw upon the empirical and spiritual reserves of, a long tradition of executive responsibility towards the colored races. It was of this tradition, its glories and difficulties, that Kipling wrote when he celebrated the 'road' taken by White Men in the colonies:

> Now, this is the road that the White Men tread
> When they go to clean a land –
> Iron underfoot and the vine overhead
> And the deep on either hand.
> We have trod that road – and a wet and windy road –
> Our chosen star for guide.
> Oh, well for the world when the White Men tread
> Their highway side by side![2]

'Cleaning a land' is best done by White Men in delicate concert with each other, an allusion to the present dangers of European rivalry in the colonies; for failing in the attempt to coordinate policy, Kipling's White Men are quite prepared to go to war: 'Freedom for ourselves and freedom for our sons/And, failing freedom, War.' Behind the White Man's mask of amiable leadership there is always the express willingness to use force, to kill and be killed. What dignifies his mission is some sense of intellectual dedication; he is a White Man, but not for mere profit, since his 'chosen star' presumably sits far above earthly gain. Certainly many White Men often wondered what it was they fought for on that 'wet and windy road,' and certainly a great number of them must have been puzzled as to how the color of their skins gave them superior ontological status plus great power over much of the inhabited world. Yet in the end, being a White Man, for Kipling and for those whose perceptions and rhetoric he influenced, was a self-confirming business. One became a White Man because one *was* a White Man; more important, 'drinking that cup,' living that unalterable destiny in 'the White Man's day,' left one little time for idle speculation on origins, causes, historical logic.

Being a White Man was therefore an idea and a reality. It involved a reasoned position towards both the white and the non-white worlds. It meant – in the colonies – speaking in a certain way, behaving according to a code of regulations, and even feeling certain things and not others. It meant specific judgments, evaluations, gestures. It was a form of authority before which nonwhites, and even whites themselves, were expected to bend. In the institutional forms it took (colonial governments, consular corps, commercial establishments) it was an agency for the expression, diffusion, and implementation of policy towards the world, and within this agency, although a certain personal latitude was allowed, the impersonal communal idea of being a White Man ruled. Being a White Man, in short, was a very concrete manner of being-in-the-world, a way of taking hold of reality, language, and thought. It made a specific style possible.

Kipling himself could not merely have happened; the same is true of his White Man. Such ideas and their authors emerge out of complex historical and cultural circumstances, at least two of which have much in common with the history of Orientalism in the nineteenth century. One of them is the culturally sanctioned habit of deploying large generalizations by which reality is divided into various collectives: languages, races, types, colors, mentalities, each category being not so much a neutral designation as an evaluative interpretation. Underlying these categories is the rigidly binomial opposition of 'ours' and 'theirs,' with the former always encroaching upon the latter (even to the point of making 'theirs' exclusively a function of 'ours'). This opposition was reinforced not only by anthropology, linguistics, and history but also, of course, by the Darwinian theses on survival and natural selection, and – no less decisive – by the rhetoric of high cultural humanism. What gave writers like Renan and Arnold the right to generalities about race was the official character of their formed cultural literacy. 'Our' values were (let us say) liberal, humane, correct; they were supported by the tradition of belles-lettres, informed scholarship, rational inquiry; as Europeans (and white men) 'we' shared in them every time their virtues were extolled. Nevertheless, the human partnerships formed by reiterated cultural values excluded as much as they included. For every idea about 'our' art spoken for by Arnold, Ruskin, Mill, Newman, Carlyle, Renan, Gobineau, or Comte, another link in the chain binding 'us' together was formed while another outsider was banished. Even if this is always the result of such rhetoric, wherever and whenever it occurs, we must remember that for nineteenth-century Europe an imposing edifice of learning and culture was built, so to speak, in the face of actual outsiders (the colonies, the poor, the delinquent), whose role in the culture was to give definition to what *they* were constitutionally unsuited for.[3]

The other circumstance common to the creation of the White Man and Orientalism is the 'field' commanded by each, as well as the sense that such a field entails peculiar modes, even rituals, of behavior, learning, and possession. Only an Occidental could speak of Orientals, for example, just as it was the White Man who could designate and name the coloreds, or nonwhites. Every statement made by Orientalists or White Men (who were usually interchangeable) conveyed a sense of the irreducible distance separating white from colored, or Occidental from Oriental; moreover, behind each statement there resonated the tradition of experience, learning, and education that kept the Oriental-colored to his position of *object studied by the Occidental-white*, instead of vice versa. Where one was in a position of power – as Cromer was, for example – the Oriental belonged to the system of rule whose principle was simply to make sure that no Oriental was ever allowed to be independent and rule himself. The premise there was that since the Orientals were ignorant of self-government, they had better be kept that way for their own good.

Since the White Man, like the Orientalist, lived very close to the line of tension keeping the coloreds at bay, he felt it incumbent on him readily to define and redefine the domain he surveyed. Passages of narrative description regularly alternate with passages of rearticulated definition and judgment that disrupt the narrative; this is a characteristic style of the writing produced by Oriental experts who operated using Kipling's White Man as a mask. Here is T. E. Lawrence, writing to V. W. Richards in 1918.

> ... the Arab appealed to my imagination. It is the old, old civilisation, which has refined itself clear of household gods, and half the trappings which ours hastens to assume. The gospel of bareness in materials is a good one, and it involves apparently a sort of moral bareness too. They think for the moment, and endeavour to slip through life without turning corners or climbing hills. In part it is a mental and moral fatigue, a race trained out, and to avoid difficulties they have to jettison so much that we think honorable and grave: and yet without in any way sharing their point of view, I think I can understand it enough to look at myself and other foreigners from their direction, and without condemning it. I know I am a stranger to them, and always will be; but I cannot believe them worse, any more than I could change to their ways.[4]

A similar perspective, however different the subject under discussion may seem to be, is found in these remarks by Gertrude Bell:

> How many thousand years this state of things has lasted [namely, that Arabs live in 'a state of war'], those who shall read the earliest records of the inner desert will tell us, for it goes back to the first of them, but in all the centuries the Arab has bought no wisdom from experience. He is never safe, and yet he behaves as though security were his daily bread.[5]

To which, as a gloss, we should add her further observation, this time about life in Damascus:

> I begin to see dimly what the civilisation of a great Eastern city means, how they live, what they think; and I have got on to terms with them. I believe the fact of my being English is a great help ... We have gone up in the world since five years ago. The difference is very marked. I think it is due to the success of our government in Egypt to a great extent ... The defeat of Russia stands for a great deal, and my impression is that the vigorous policy of Lord Curzon in the Persian Gulf and on the India frontier stands for a great deal more. No one who does not know the East can realise how it all hangs together. It is scarcely an exaggeration to say that if the English mission had been turned back from the

gates of Kabul, the English tourist would be frowned upon in the streets of Damascus.[6]

In such statements as these, we note immediately that 'the Arab' or 'Arabs' have an aura of apartness, definiteness, and collective self-consistency such as to wipe out any traces of individual Arabs with narratable life histories. What appealed to Lawrence's imagination was the clarity of the Arab, both as an image and as a supposed philosophy (or attitude) towards life: in both cases what Lawrence fastens on is the Arab as if seen from the cleansing perspective of one not an Arab, and one for whom such un-self-conscious primitive simplicity as the Arab possesses is something defined by the observer, in this case the White Man. Yet Arab refinement, which in its essentials corresponds to Yeats's visions of Byzantium where

Flames that no faggot feeds, flint nor steel has lit,
Nor storm disturbs, flames begotten of flame,
Where blood-begotten spirits come
And all complexities of fury leave[7]

is associated with Arab perdurability, as if the Arab had not been subject to the ordinary processes of history. Paradoxically, the Arab seems to Lawrence to have exhausted himself in his very temporal persistence. The enormous age of Arab civilization has thus served to refine the Arab down to his quintessential attributes, and to tire him out morally in the process. What we are left with is Bell's Arab: centuries of experience and no wisdom. As a collective entity, then, the Arab accumulates no existential or even semantical thickness. He remains the same, except for the exhausting refinements mentioned by Lawrence, from one end to the other of 'the records of the inner desert.' We are to assume that if *an* Arab feels joy, if he is sad at the death of his child or parent, if he has a sense of the injustices of political tyranny, then those experiences are necessarily subordinate to the sheer, unadorned, and persistent fact of being an Arab.

The primitiveness of such a state exists simultaneously on at least two levels: one, *in the definition*, which is reductive; and two (according to Lawrence and Bell), *in reality*. This absolute coincidence was itself no simple coincidence. For one, it could only have been made from the outside by virtue of a vocabulary and epistemological instruments designed both to get to the heart of things and to avoid the distractions of accident, circumstance, or experience. For another, the coincidence was a fact uniquely the result of method, tradition, and politics all working together. Each in a sense obliterated the distinctions between the type – *the* Oriental, *the* Semite, *the* Arab, *the* Orient – and ordinary human reality, Yeats's 'uncontrollable mystery on the bestial floor,' in which all human beings live. The scholarly investigator took a type marked 'Oriental' for the same thing as any individual Oriental he might encounter. Years of tradition had encrusted discourse about such matters as the Semitic or Oriental spirit with some legitimacy. And political good sense taught, in Bell's marvelous phrase, that in the East 'it all hangs together.' Primitiveness therefore inhered in the Orient, *was* the Orient, an idea to which anyone dealing with or writing about the Orient had to return, as if to a touchstone outlasting time or experience.

Notes

1   Friedrich Nietzsche, 'On Truth and lie in an extra-moral sense,' in *The Portable Nietzsche*, ed. and trans. Walter Kaufmann (New York: Viking Press, 1954), pp. 46–7.
2   Rudyard Kipling, *Verse* (Garden City, N.Y.: Doubleday and Co., 1954), p. 280.
3   The themes of exclusion and confinement in nineteenth-century culture have played an important role in Michel Foucault's work, most recently in his *Discipline and Punish: The Birth of the Prison* (New York: Pantheon Books, 1977), and *The History of Sexuality, Volume 1: An Introduction* (New York: Pantheon Books, 1978).
4   *The Letters of T.E. Lawrence*, ed. David Garnett (1938; reprint ed., London: Spring Books, 1964), p. 244.
5   Gertrude Bell, *The Desert and the Sown* (London: William Heinemann, 1907), p. 244.
6   Gertrude Bell, *From Her Personal Papers, 1889–1914*, ed. Elizabeth Burgoyne (London: Ernest Benn, 1958), p. 204.
7   William Butler Yeats, 'Byzantium', *The Collected Poems* (New York: Macmillan and Co., 1959), p. 244.

2.6

Homi K. Bhabha, from 'The "Other" Question' (1983)

> To concern oneself with the founding concepts of the entire history of philo-
> sophy, to deconstitute them, is not to undertake the work of the philologist or
> of the classic historian of philosophy. Despite appearances, it is probably the
> most daring way of making the beginnings of a step outside of philosophy.
>
> Jacques Derrida, 'Structure, sign and play'[1]

An important feature of colonial discourse is its dependence on the concept of
'fixity' in the ideological construction of otherness. Fixity, as the sign of cultural/
historical/racial difference in the discourse of colonialism, is a paradoxical mode of
representation: it connotes rigidity and an unchanging order as well as disorder,
degeneracy and daemonic repetition. Likewise the stereotype, which is its major
discursive strategy, is a form of knowledge and identification that vacillates between
what is always 'in place', already known, and something that must be anxiously
repeated ... as if the essential duplicity of the Asiatic or the bestial sexual licence of
the African that needs no proof, can never really, in discourse, be proved. It is this
process of *ambivalence*, central to the stereotype, that this chapter explores as it
constructs a theory of colonial discourse. For it is the force of ambivalence that
gives the colonial stereotype its currency: ensures its repeatability in changing
historical and discursive conjunctures; informs its strategies of individuation and
marginalization; produces that effect of probabilistic truth and predictability which,
for the stereotype, must always be in *excess* of what can be empirically proved or
logically construed. Yet the function of ambivalence as one of the most significant
discursive and psychical strategies of discriminatory power – whether racist or
sexist, peripheral or metropolitan – remains to be charted.

The absence of such a perspective has its own history of political expediency.
To recognize the stereotype as an ambivalent mode of knowledge and power
demands a theoretical and political response that challenges deterministic or
functionalist modes of conceiving of the relationship between discourse and politics. The analytic of ambivalence questions dogmatic and moralistic positions on
the meaning of oppression and discrimination. My reading of colonial discourse
suggests that the point of intervention should shift from the ready recognition of

images as positive or negative, to an understanding of the *processes of subjectification* made possible (and plausible) through stereotypical discourse. To judge the stereo-typed image on the basis of a prior political normativity is to dismiss it, not to displace it, which is only possible by engaging with its *effectivity*; with the repertoire of positions of power and resistance, domination and dependence that constructs colonial identification subject (both colonizer and colonized). I do not intend to deconstruct the colonial discourse to reveal its ideological misconceptions or repressions, to exult in its self-reflexivity, or to indulge its liberatory 'excess'. In order to understand the productivity of colonial power it is crucial to construct its regime of truth, not to subject its representations to a normalizing judgement. Only then does it become possible to understand the *productive* ambivalence of the object of colonial discourse – that 'otherness' which is at once an object of desire and derision, an articulation of difference contained within the fantasy of origin and identity. What such a reading reveals are the boundaries of colonial discourse and it enables a transgression of these limits from the space of that otherness.

The construction of the colonial subject in discourse, and the exercise of colonial power through discourse, demands an articulation of forms of difference – racial and sexual. Such an articulation becomes crucial if it is held that the body is always simultaneously (if conflictually) inscribed in both the economy of pleasure and desire and the economy of discourse, domination and power. I do not wish to conflate, unproblematically, two forms of the marking – and splitting – of the subject nor to globalize two forms of representation. I want to suggest, however, that there is a theoretical space and a political place for such an *articulation* – in the sense in which that word itself denies an 'original' identity or a 'singularity' to objects of difference – sexual or racial. If such a view is taken, as Feuchtwang argues in a different context,[2] it follows that the epithets racial or sexual come to be seen as modes of differentiation, realized as multiple, cross-cutting determinations, poly-morphous and perverse, always demanding a specific and strategic calculation of their effects. Such is, I believe, the moment of colonial discourse. It is a form of discourse crucial to the binding of a range of differences and discriminations that inform the discursive and political practices of racial and cultural hierarchization.

Before turning to the construction of colonial discourse, I want to discuss briefly the process by which forms of racial/cultural/historical otherness have been marginalized in theoretical texts committed to the articulation of 'difference', or 'contradiction', in order, it is claimed, to reveal the limits of Western representa-tionalist discourse. In facilitating the passage 'from work to text' and stressing the arbitrary, differential and systemic construction of social and cultural signs, these critical strategies unsettle the idealist quest for meanings that are, most often, intentionalist and nationalist. So much is not in question. What does need to be questioned, however, is the *mode of representation of otherness*.

Where better to raise the question of the subject of racial and cultural difference than in Stephen Heath's masterly analysis of the chiaroscuro world of Welles's classic, *A Touch of Evil*? I refer to an area of its analysis which has generated the least comment, that is, Heath's attention to the structuration of the Mexican/US border that circulates through the text affirming and exchanging some notion of 'limited being'. Heath's work departs from the traditional analysis of racial and cultural differences, which identify stereotype and image and elaborate them in a moralistic or nationalistic discourse that affirms the *origin* and *unity* of national identity. Heath's attentiveness to the contradictory and diverse sites within the textual system, which *construct* national/cultural differences in their deployment of the semes of 'foreignness', 'mixedness', 'impurity', as transgressive and corrupting, is extremely relevant. His attention to the turnings of this much neglected subject as sign (not symbol or stereotype) disseminated in the codes (as 'partition', 'exchange', 'naming', 'character', etc.), gives us a useful sense of the circulation and proliferation of racial and cultural otherness. Despite the awareness of the multiple or cross-cutting determinations in the construction of modes of sexual and racial differentiation there is a sense in which Heath's analysis marginalizes otherness. Although I shall argue that the problem of the Mexican/US border is read too singularly, too exclusively under the sign of sexuality, it is not that I am not aware of the many proper and relevant reasons for that 'feminist' focus. The 'entertainment' operated by the realist Hollywood film of the 1950s was always also a containment of the subject in a narrative economy of voyeurism and fetishism. Moreover, the displacement that organizes any textual system, within which the display of difference circulates, demands that the play of 'nationalities' should participate in the sexual positioning, troubling the Law and desire. There is, nevertheless, a singularity and reductiveness in concluding that:

> Vargas is the position of desire, its admission and its prohibition. Not surprisingly he has two names: the name of desire is Mexican, Miguel ... that of the Law American – Mike. ... The film uses the border, the play between American and Mexican ... at the same time it seeks to hold that play finally in the opposition of purity and mixture which in turn is a version of Law and desire.[3]

However liberatory it is from one position to see the logic of the text traced ceaselessly between the Ideal Father and the Phallic Mother, in another sense, seeing only one possible articulation of the differential complex 'race–sex', it half colludes with the proffered images of marginality. For if the naming of Vargas is crucially mixed and split in the economy of desire, then there are other mixed economies which make naming and positioning equally problematic 'across the border'. To identify the 'play' on the border as purity and mixture and to see it as an allegory of Law and desire reduces the articulation of racial and sexual difference to what is dangerously close to becoming a circle rather than a spiral of difference. On that basis, it is not possible to construct the polymorphous and perverse collusion between racism and sexism as a *mixed economy* – for instance, the discourses of American cultural colonialism and Mexican dependency, the fear/desire of miscegenation, the American border as cultural signifier of a pioneering, male 'American' spirit always under threat from races and cultures beyond the border or frontier. If the death of the Father is the interruption on which the narrative is initiated, it is through that death that miscegenation is both possible and deferred; if, again, it is the purpose of the narrative to restore Susan as 'good object', it also becomes its project to deliver Vargas from his racial 'mixedness'.

* * *

II

The difference of colonial discourse as an apparatus of power[4] will emerge more fully as this chapter develops. At this stage, however, I shall provide what I take to be the minimum conditions and specifications of such a discourse. It is an apparatus that turns on the recognition and disavowal of racial/cultural/historical differences. Its predominant strategic function is the creation of a space for a 'subject peoples' through the production of knowledges in terms of which surveillance is exercised and a complex form of pleasure/unpleasure is incited. It seeks authorization for its strategies by the production of knowledges of colonizer and colonized which are stereotypical but antithetically evaluated. The objective of colonial discourse is to construe the colonized as a population of degenerate types on the basis of racial origin, in order to justify conquest and to establish systems of administration and instruction. Despite the play of power within colonial discourse and the shifting positionalities of its subjects (for example, effects of class, gender, ideology, different social formations, varied systems of colonization and so on), I am referring to a form of governmentality that in marking out a 'subject nation', appropriates, directs and dominates its various spheres of activity. Therefore, despite the 'play' in the colonial system which is crucial to its exercise of power, colonial discourse produces the colonized as a social reality which is at once an 'other' and yet entirely knowable and visible. It resembles a form of narrative whereby the productivity and circulation of subjects and signs are bound in a reformed and recognizable totality. It employs a system of representation, a regime of truth, that is structurally similar to realism. And it is in order to intervene within that system of representation that Edward Said proposes a semiotic of 'Orientalist' power, examining the varied European discourses which constitute 'the Orient' as a unified racial, geographical, political and cultural zone of the world. Said's analysis is revealing of, and relevant to, colonial discourse:

> Philosophically, then, the kind of language, thought, and vision that I have been calling orientalism very generally is a form or *radical realism*; anyone employing orientalism, which is the habit for dealing with questions, objects, qualities and regions deemed Oriental, will designate, name, point to, fix, what he is talking or thinking about with a word or phrase, which then is considered either to have acquired, or more simply to be, reality. ... The tense they employ is the timeless eternal; they convey an impression of repetition and strength. ... For all these functions it is frequently enough to use the simple copula *is*.[5]

For Said, the copula seems to be the point at which western rationalism preserves the boundaries of sense for itself. Of this, too, Said is aware when he hints continually at a polarity or division at the very centre of Orientalism.[6] It is, on the one hand, a topic of learning, discovery, practice; on the other, it is the site of dreams, images, fantasies, myths, obsessions and requirements. It is a static system of 'synchronic essentialism', a knowledge of 'signifiers of stability' such as the lexicographic and the encyclopaedic. However, this site is continually under threat from diachronic forms of history and narrative, signs of instability. And, finally, this line of thinking is given a shape analogical to the dreamwork, when Said refers explicitly to a distinction between 'an unconscious positivity' which he terms *latent* Orientalism, and the stated knowledges and views about the Orient which he calls *manifest* Orientalism.

The originality of this pioneering theory could be extended to engage with the alterity and ambivalence of Orientalist discourse. Said contains this threat by introducing a binarism within the argument which, in initially setting up an opposition between these two discursive scenes, finally allows them to be correlated as a congruent system of representation that is unified through a political-ideological *intention* which, in his words, enables Europe to advance securely and *un-metaphorically* upon the Orient. Said identifies the *content* of Orientalism as the unconscious repository of fantasy, imaginative writings and essential ideas; and the *form* of manifest Orientalism as the historically and discursively determined, diachronic aspect. This division/correlation structure of manifest and latent Orientalism leads to the effectivity of the concept of discourse being undermined by what could be called the polarities of intentionality.

This produces a problem with Said's use of Foucault's concepts of power and discourse. The productivity of Foucault's concept of power/knowledge lies in its refusal of an epistemology which opposes essence/appearance, ideology/science. '*Pouvoir/Savoir*' places subjects in a relation of power and recognition that is not part of a symmetrical or dialectical relation – self/other, master/slave – which can then be subverted by being inverted. Subjects are always disproportionately placed in opposition or domination through the symbolic decentring of multiple power relations which play the role of support as well as target or adversary. It becomes difficult, then, to conceive of the *historical* enunciations of colonial discourse without them being either functionally overdetermined or strategically elaborated or displaced by the *unconscious* scene of latent Orientalism. Equally, it is difficult to conceive of the process of subjectification as a placing *within* Orientalist or colonial discourse for the dominated subject without the dominant being strategically placed within it too. The terms in which Said's Orientalism is unified – the intentionality and unidirectionality of colonial power – also unify the subject of colonial enunciation.

This results in Said's inadequate attention to representation as a concept that articulates the historical and fantasy (as the scene of desire) in the production of the 'political' effects of discourse. He rightly rejects a notion of Orientalism as the misrepresentation of an Oriental essence. However, having introduced the concept of 'discourse' he does not face up to the problems it creates for an instrumentalist notion of power/knowledge that he seems to require. This problem is summed up by his ready acceptance of the view that, 'Representations are formations, or as Roland Barthes has said of all the operations of language, they are deformations.'[7]

This brings me to my second point. The closure and coherence attributed to the unconscious pole of colonial discourse and the unproblematized notion of the subject, restrict the effectivity of both power and knowledge. It is not possible to see how power functions productively as incitement and interdiction. Nor would it be possible, without the attribution of ambivalence to relations of power/knowledge, to calculate the traumatic impact of the return of the oppressed – those terrifying stereotypes of savagery, cannibalism, lust and anarchy which are the signal points of identification and alienation, scenes of fear and desire, in colonial texts. It is precisely this function of the stereotype as phobia and fetish that, according to Fanon, threatens the closure of the racial/epidermal schema for the colonial subject and opens the royal road to colonial fantasy.

* * *

My argument relies upon a particular reading of the problematic of representation which, Fanon suggests, is specific to the colonial situation. He writes:

> the originality of the colonial context is that the economic substructure is also a superstructure ... you are rich because you are white, you are white because you are rich. This is why Marxist analysis should always be slightly stretched every time we have to do with the colonial problem.[8]

Fanon could either be seen to be adhering to a simple reflectionist or determinist notion of cultural/social signification or, more interestingly, he could be read as taking an 'anti-repressionist' position (attacking the notion that ideology as miscognition, or misrepresentation, is the repression of the real). For our purposes I tend towards the latter reading which then provides a 'visibility' to the exercise of power; gives force to the argument that skin, as a signifier of discrimination, must be produced or processed as visible.

* * *

This is precisely the kind of recognition, as spontaneous and visible, that is attributed to the stereotype. The difference of the object of discrimination is at once visible and natural – colour as the cultural/political *sign* of inferiority or degeneracy, skin as its natural '*identity*'.

* * *

The problem of origin as the problematic of racist, stereotypical knowledge is a complex one and what I have said about its construction will come clear in this illustration from Fanon. Stereotyping is not the setting up of a false image which becomes the scapegoat of discriminatory practices. It is a much more ambivalent text of projection and introjection, metaphoric and metonymic strategies, displacement, overdetermination, guilt, aggressivity; the masking and splitting of 'official' and phantasmatic knowledges to construct the positionalities and oppositionalities of racist discourse:

> My body was given back to me sprawled out, distorted, recoloured, clad in mourning in that white winter day. The Negro is an animal, the Negro is bad, the Negro is mean, the Negro is ugly; look, a nigger, it's cold, the nigger is shivering, the nigger is shivering because he is cold, the little boy is trembling

because he is afraid of the nigger, the nigger is shivering with cold, that cold that goes through your bones, the handsome little boy is trembling because he thinks that the nigger is quivering with rage, the little white boy throws himself into his mother's arms: Mama, the nigger's going to eat me up.[9]

It is the scenario of colonial fantasy which, in staging the ambivalence of desire, articulates the demand for the Negro which the Negro disrupts. For the stereotype is at once a substitute and a shadow. By acceding to the wildest fantasies (in the popular sense) of the colonizer, the stereotyped Other reveals something of the 'fantasy' (as desire, defence) of that position of mastery. For if 'skin' in racist discourse is the visibility of darkness, and a prime signifier of the body and its social and cultural correlates, then we are bound to remember what Karl Abrahams says in his seminal work on the scopic drive.[10] The pleasure-value of darkness is a withdrawal in order to know nothing of the external world. Its symbolic meaning, however, is thoroughly ambivalent. Darkness signifies at once both birth and death; it is in all cases a desire to return to the fullness of the mother, a desire for an unbroken and undifferentiated line of vision and origin.

But surely there is another scene of colonial discourse in which the native or Negro meets the demand of colonial discourse; where the subverting 'split' is recuperable within a strategy of social and political control. It is recognizably true that the chain of stereotypical signification is curiously mixed and split, poly-morphous and perverse, an articulation of multiple belief. The black is both savage (cannibal) and yet the most obedient and dignified of servants (the bearer of food); he is the embodiment of rampant sexuality and yet innocent as a child; he is mystical, primitive, simple-minded and yet the most worldly and accomplished liar, and manipulator of social forces. In each case what is being dramatized is a separation – *between* races, cultures, histories, *within* histories – a separation between *before* and *after* that repeats obsessively the mythical moment or disjunc-tion.

Despite the structural similarities with the play of need and desire in primal fantasies, the colonial fantasy does not try to cover up that moment of separation. It is more ambivalent. On the one hand, it proposes a teleology – under certain conditions of colonial domination and control the native is progressively reform-able. On the other, however, it effectively displays the 'separation', makes it more visible. It is the visibility of this separation which, in denying the colonized the capacities of self-government, independence, Western modes of civility, lends authority to the official version and mission of colonial power.

Racist stereotypical discourse, in its colonial moment, inscribes a form of governmentality that is informed by a productive splitting in its constitution of knowledge and exercise of power. Some of its practices recognize the difference of race, culture and history as elaborated by stereotypical knowledges, racial theories, administrative colonial experience, and on that basis institutionalize a range of political and cultural ideologies that are prejudicial, discriminatory, vestigial, archaic, 'mythical', and, crucially, are recognized as being so. By 'knowing' the native population in these terms, discriminatory and authoritarian forms of political control are considered appropriate. The colonized population is then deemed to be both the cause and effect of the system, imprisoned in the circle of interpretation. What is visible is the *necessity* of such rule which is justified by those moralistic and normative ideologies of amelioration recognized as the Civilizing Mission or the White Man's Burden. However, there coexist within the same apparatus of colonial power, modern systems and sciences of government, progressive 'Western' forms of social and economic organization which provide the manifest justification for the project of colonialism – an argument which, in part, impressed Karl Marx. It is on the site of this coexistence that strategies of hierarchization and marginalization are employed in the management of colonial societies. And if my deduction from Fanon about the peculiar visibility of colonial power is justified, then I would extend that to say that it is a form of governmentality in which the 'ideological' space functions in more openly collaborative ways with political and economic exigencies. The barracks stands by the church which stands by the schoolroom; the cantonment stands hard by the 'civil lines'. Such visibility of the institutions and apparatuses of power is possible because the exercise of colonial power makes their *relationship* obscure, produces them as fetishes, spectacles of a 'natural'/racial pre-eminence. Only the seat of government is always elsewhere – alien and separate by that distance upon which surveillance depends for its strategies of objectification, normalization and discipline.

Notes

1   J. Derrida, 'Structure, sign and play in the discourse of the human sciences', in his *Writing and Difference*, Alan Bass (trans.) (Chicago: Chicago University Press, 1978), p. 284.
2   S. Feuchtwang, 'Socialist, feminist and anti-racist struggles', *m/f*, no. 4 (1980), p. 41.
3   S. Heath, 'Film and system, terms of analysis', Part 11, *Screen*, vol. 16, no. 2 (summer 1975), p. 93.
4   This concept is further developed in Chapter 6, pp. 108–17.
5   E. Said, *Orientalism* (London: Routledge & Kegan Paul, 1978), p. 72; emphasis added.
6   Ibid., p. 206.
7   Ibid., p. 273.
8   F. Fanon, *The Wretched of the Earth* (Harmondsworth: Penguin Books, 1969).
9   Fanon, *Black Skins, White Masks*, p. 80.
10 See K. Abraham, 'Transformations of scopophilia', in his *Selected Papers in Psychoanalysis* (London: Hogarth Press, 1978).

2.7

Slavoj Žižek, from *The Sublime Object of Ideology* (1989)

Fantasy as a Support of Reality

This problem must be approached from the Lacanian thesis that it is only in the dream that we come close to the real awakening – that is, to the Real of our desire. When Lacan says that the last support of what we call 'reality' is a fantasy, this is definitely not to be understood in the sense of 'life is just a dream', 'what we call reality is just an illusion', and so forth. We find such a theme in many science-fiction stories: reality as a generalized dream or illusion. The story is usually told from the perspective of a hero who gradually makes the horrifying discovery that all the people around him are not really human beings but some kind of automatons, robots, who only look and act like real human beings; the final point of these stories is of course the hero's discovery that he himself is also such an automaton and not a real human being. Such a generalized illusion is impossible: we find the same paradox in a well-known drawing by Escher of two hands drawing each other.

The Lacanian thesis is, on the contrary, that there is always a hard kernel, a leftover which persists and cannot be reduced to a universal play of illusory mir-roring. The difference between Lacan and 'naïve realism' is that for Lacan, *the only point at which we approach this hard kernel of the Real is indeed the dream*. When we awaken into reality after a dream, we usually say to ourselves 'it was just a dream', thereby blinding ourselves to the fact that in our everyday, wakening reality we are *nothing but a consciousness of this dream*. It was only in the dream that we approached the fantasy-framework which determines our activity, our mode of acting in reality itself.

It is the same with the ideological dream, with the determination of ideology as a dreamlike construction hindering us from seeing the real state of things, reality as such. In vain do we try to break out of the ideological dream by 'opening our eyes and trying to see reality as it is', by throwing away the ideological spectacles: as the subjects of such a post-ideological, objective, sober look, free of so-called ideolo-gical prejudices, as the subjects of a look which views the facts as they are, we remain throughout 'the consciousness of our ideological dream'. The only way to break the power of our ideological dream is to confront the Real of our desire which announces itself in this dream.

Let us examine anti-Semitism. It is not enough to say that we must liberate ourselves of so-called 'anti-Semitic prejudices' and learn to see Jews as they really are – in this way we will certainly remain victims of these so-called prejudices. We must confront ourselves with how the ideological figure of the 'Jew' is invested with our unconscious desire, with how we have constructed this figure to escape a certain deadlock of our desire.

Let us suppose, for example, that an objective look would confirm – why not? – that Jews really do financially exploit the rest of the population, that they do sometimes seduce our young daughters, that some of them do not wash regularly. Is it not clear that this has nothing to do with the real roots of our anti-Semitism? Here, we have only to remember the Lacanian proposition concerning the pathologically jealous husband: even if all the facts he quotes in support of his jealousy are true, even if his wife really is sleeping around with other men, this does not change one bit the fact that his jealousy is a pathological, paranoid construction.

Let us ask ourselves a simple question: In the Germany of the late 1930s, what would be the result of such a non-ideological, objective approach? Probably something like: 'The Nazis are condemning the Jews too hastily, without proper argument, so let us take a cool, sober look and see if they are really guilty or not; let us see if there is some truth in the accusations against them.' Is it really necessary to add that such an approach would merely confirm our so-called 'unconscious prejudices' with additional rationalizations? The proper answer to anti-Semitism is therefore not 'Jews are really not like that' but 'the anti-Semitic idea of Jew has nothing to do with Jews; the ideological figure of a Jew is a way to stitch up the inconsistency of our own ideological system.'

That is why we are also unable to shake so-called ideological prejudices by taking into account the pre-ideological level of everyday experience. The basis of this argument is that the ideological construction always finds its limits in the field of everyday experience – that it is unable to reduce, to contain, to absorb and annihilate this level. Let us again take a typical individual in Germany in the late 1930s. He is bombarded by anti-Semitic propaganda depicting a Jew as a monstrous incarnation of Evil, the great wire-puller, and so on. But when he returns home he encounters Mr Stern, his neighbour: a good man to chat with in the evenings, whose children play with his. Does not this everyday experience offer an irreducible resistance to the ideological construction?

The answer is, of course, no. If everyday experience offers such a resistance, then the anti-Semitic ideology has not yet really grasped us. An ideology is really 'holding us' only when we do not feel any opposition between it and reality – that is, when the ideology succeeds in determining the mode of our everyday experience of reality itself. How then would our poor German, if he were a good anti-Semite, react to this gap between the ideological figure of the Jew (schemer, wire-puller, exploiting our brave men and so on) and the common everyday experience of his good neighbour, Mr Stern? His answer would be to turn this gap, this discrepancy itself, into an argument for anti-Semitism: 'You see how dangerous they really are? It is difficult to recognize their real nature. They hide it behind the mask of everyday appearance – and it is exactly this hiding of one's real nature, this duplicity, that is a basic feature of the Jewish nature.' An ideology really succeeds when even the facts which at first sight contradict it start to function as arguments in its favour.

Section 3
SUBJECTIVITY

Introduction

The sign is always in address to someone. When Descartes proclaimed 'I think, therefore I am', he was drawing upon the humanist notion that identity and being are mutually dependent factors of individual existence. Common sense tells us that human nature determines identity, that as human beings we are the authors of all that we think and speak, and that as such we shape the world around us and the knowledges that structure that world. Common sense, then, assumes that the nature of human 'being' is given in some way – that it exists *prior* to language simply to label the world of its own experience. Within this framework, the human individual is conceived as a unified centre of control from which meaning emanates.

Against this humanist notion, the concept of subjectivity decentres the individual by problematizing the simplistic relationship between language and the individual that common sense presumes. It replaces human nature with concepts of history, society and culture as determining factors in the *construction* of individual identity, and destabilizes the coherence of that identity by making it an *effect* rather than simply an origin of linguistic practice. Instead of being confirmed by recourse to a universalizing principle, 'humanity' (which then in turn confirms the world which surrounds it), the subject is seen as *made* and so open to transformation. In other words, the theory of the subject proposes a notion of identity as precariously constituted in the discourses of the social, whereby it is both determined and regulated by the forces of power inherent in a given social formation, but capable also of undermining them.

The unstable I

Sigmund Freud was one of the first to introduce the notion of the unstable subject, radically and uncertainly divided between the conscious and unconscious. For Freud, this division comes about as a result of the movement of the individual from being into meaning, whereby the raw material of human subjectivity (the infant) encounters the laws of culture and the demand to take up a position within the symbolic structures of that culture (meaning). This means giving up original anarchic and asocial drives and desires in favour of those acceptable to the social order. In doing so, the individual is required to repress those drives and desires into the space that at that moment opens up for them, that of the unconscious. Thus, the movement from being into meaning inevitably involves the founding principle of loss. Falling victim to loss in the earliest stages of becoming social subjects, we are then compelled to rehearse a fantasy of mastering that loss, and are destined to seek to recuperate it in substitutes that seem to promise a restoration of the plenitude we have surrendered. Freud records one instance of this in observations of his young grandson at play (Section 3.1). In what has become known as the 'fort-da' game, Freud advances an analysis of this experience of loss and the attempt to overcome it, by reading the meaning of the child's game of throwing something out of reach in order to retrieve it. While this reiterates the principle of loss, it also provides the illusion of mastery over it.

Within the analysis that Jacques Lacan offers, the subject is formed through a series of stages. In an initial stage the infant exists as an amorphous mass of uncoordinated limbs and sounds, and its experience of itself is continuous, since it draws no distinction between self and other. In a second stage (the mirror stage, see Section 3.2) a distinction is introduced between the self and the other. As the infant sees its reflection in the mirror it becomes aware of a split between the 'I' that looks and the 'I' that is seen, though this split is immediately recuperated – for the reflected other *appears* to have the unity and control of itself that the perceiving 'I' lacks. Although such control is *imaginary*, the infant none the less desires and identifies with that which it does not have in the image of the other. With the entry into language (the final stage) comes the insertion of the subject into a position within the symbolic order in which it is both *produced* in language and *subjected* to the laws of the symbolic that pre-exist it. Produced from within language, identity depends upon both difference (between the self and the other realized at the mirror stage) and accession to the position of an 'I' within discourse, a position that (only provisionally) constructs meaning. (All of this is hard to explain because it must avoid the conventional humanist terms – 'I experience', 'I know' – which suppose the 'I' is there *from the very start*. What is at issue is how the 'I' gets to be able to say 'I experience', 'I know', 'I think that . . .')

Although the subject may speak, it does so only within the terms that the laws of language allow. Just as Saussure had argued that language does not simply name a reality that pre-exists it, but *produces* the concept of reality through the system of differences that *is* language (see Section 1.1), so Lacan argues that the position of the 'I' within language does not simply represent the presence of a subject that pre-exists it, but produces the concept of the subject through a process of differentiation between the 'I' and 'not I' of discourse. This concept of difference, expanded by Jacques Derrida (see Section 4.1), is important, since it removes the subject from the fixed position of presence and puts it into a process dependent upon the exchange between presence and absence. Based on difference, both subjectivity and the language that produces it constitute a process in which meaning is never fully present in any individual utterance (of the 'I') but is always deferred and always only ever provisional.

Lacan's analysis has provided a foundation upon which many subsequent theories of subjectivity are based, but it has also been critiqued from a variety of positions inscribed in difference for what is perceived as its tendency to universalize
subjectivity. Frantz Fanon's work on 'blackness' (see Section 3.3) has subsequently
provided one basis from which to begin such a critique in relation to issues of race. In
the extract reprinted here, the implications of the significations of skin colour within
the context of colonialism are explored in relation to their impact upon the possibilities for subjectivity of the racialized other. Similarly, the work of many feminist writers
has taken up the issue of the privileging of the phallus (even though it is imaginary, as
we must insist it is for Lacan) as the governing signifier in the law of the symbolic
organizing lack into an order of coherence. Julia Kristeva, for example, takes up the
notion of language as the constituent of subjectivity, but focuses her analysis upon
the transgressions of the law of the symbolic in the form of the semiotic, which, she
argues, is an integral and revolutionary part of symbolic language (see Section 3.4).
Much of the work of French feminist writers like Hélène Cixous (see Section 5.2) and
Luce Irigaray (see Irigaray 1985a, b) also serves to challenge the authority of the
phallus as the governing principle of gendered subjectivity, asserting instead various
claims to the 'feminine' aspects of pre-Oedipal language, maintained by the poly-
morphous qualities of female sexuality, the bisexually charged body and the body of
the mother.

Power/knowledge

While the work of these theorists focuses upon the constitution of subjectivity in
terms of a kind of psycho-linguistics, there is yet another strand within contemporary
theory, which turns more towards history and the structures of society in order to
understand the material circumstances and implications of subjective construction.
The foundation of much of this work – on the *discursive* construction of subjectivity –
has been provided by the work of Michel Foucault. This has suggested that many
modern sciences, particularly social sciences, exercise power while claiming to be
objective knowledge.

For Foucault the subject is constituted in discourse through the specific vocabulary of knowledges that circulate in society. In particular, his work explores the
institutional effects of discourse and the ways in which it operates to produce and
govern individual subjects. *Discipline and Punish* (see Section 3.5), *The History of
Sexuality* (Section 3.6) and *Madness and Civilisation* (1971), for example, provide
detailed analyses of the ways in which power is exercised to produce and to police
individual subjects through the production of detailed knowledges of 'the criminal',
'the pervert' and 'the lunatic' within the discourses of criminality, sexuality and psychiatry and the institutions (particularly state institutions) that guarantee them. That
the individual is the site of this regime is crucial to the formulation of the social order,
but the regime is also crucial to the formulation of the subject. It is not that the
innocent and unsuspecting individual pre-exists the knowledges that are produced
and is then somehow cruelly shaped into a subject by the power they wield, but that

the individual is 'carefully fabricated' within them. Within the discourse of science, for example, 'the pervert' does not pre-exist a simple scientific labelling, but is *produced* (comes into existence) in and through discursive constructions of 'the pervert'.

Like the psycho-linguistic theories of subject construction, discursive theories also maintain that plurality and constant deferral of meaning are inherent in the structuring of the subject so that it remains precarious, open to change. Within any given social and historical moment a variety of discourses exist and compete for control of subjectivity. The subject thus becomes the site of a discursive battle for the meaning of their identity; their interpellation (see Section 2.3) as subjects within any single discourse can never be final. Although most forms of discourse deny their own partiality by laying claim to the 'truth' of individual existence, the contradictions brought about by the plurality of discursive fields ensure that the individual is constantly subjected to a range of possible meanings, and is therefore an unstable site of constructions and reconstructions, which often overlap; see, for example, Foucault's, *Herculine Barbin* (1980) and *I, Pierre Riviere* (1978b).

In addition, while most discourses work to produce particular forms of subjectivity, their very organization also implies the possibility of other subject positions and with them the possibilities of resistance to meanings that may be dominant. Meanings also change over time, and although particular knowledges may initially serve the interests of specific forms of power, the relationship between them can never be guaranteed. Within the discourse of sexology in the late nineteenth and early twentieth centuries, for example, a whole medical language and knowledge of classifications emerged and a whole technology of power was exercised in the production of the 'homosexual' subject. While this initially served the interests of policing the norm of reproductive 'heterosexuality', the language that sexology provided has subsequently served the causes of gay liberation and a variety of resistances to the notion of the homosexual as either 'sick' or 'sorry'. In sum, then, through recent work represented in this section, the concept of ideology has been widened to include not just how we think but ways in which we are constituted as thinking, experiencing, gendered and racialized individuals in the first place.

3.1

Sigmund Freud, from *Beyond the Pleasure Principle* (1920)

The study of dreams may be considered the most trustworthy method of investigating deep mental processes. Now dreams occurring in traumatic neuroses have the characteristic of repeatedly bringing the patient back into the situation of his accident, a situation from which he wakes up in another fright. This astonishes people far too little. They think the fact that the traumatic experience is constantly forcing itself upon the patient even in his sleep is a proof of the strength of that experience: the patient is, as one might say, fixated to his trauma. Fixations to the experience which started the illness have long been familiar to us in hysteria. Breuer and Freud declared in 1893[1] that 'hysterics suffer mainly from reminiscences'. In the war neuroses, too, observers like Ferenczi and Simmel have been able to explain certain motor symptoms by fixation to the moment at which the trauma occurred.

I am not aware, however, that patients suffering from traumatic neurosis are much occupied in their waking lives with memories of their accident. Perhaps they are more concerned with *not* thinking of it. Anyone who accepts it as something self-evident that their dreams should put them back at night into the situation that caused them to fall ill has misunderstood the nature of dreams. It would be more in harmony with their nature if they showed the patient pictures from his healthy past or of the cure for which he hopes. If we are not to be shaken in our belief in the wish-fulfilling tenor of dreams by the dreams of traumatic neurotics, we still have one resource open to us: we may argue that the function of dreaming, like so much else, is upset in this condition and diverted from its purposes, or we may be driven to reflect on the mysterious masochistic trends of the ego.[2]

At this point I propose to leave the dark and dismal subject of the traumatic neurosis and pass on to examine the method of working employed by the mental apparatus in one of its earliest *normal* activities – I mean in children's play.

The different theories of children's play have only recently been summarized and discussed from the psychoanalytic point of view by Pfeifer (1919), to whose paper I would refer my readers. These theories attempt to discover the motives which lead children to play, but they fail to bring into the foreground the *economic* motive, the consideration of the yield of pleasure involved. Without wishing to include the whole field covered by these phenomena, I have been able, through a chance opportunity which presented itself, to throw some light upon the first game played by a little boy of one and a half and invented by himself. It was more than a mere fleeting observation, for I lived under the same roof as the child and his parents for some weeks, and it was some time before I discovered the meaning of the puzzling activity which he constantly repeated.

The child was not at all precocious in his intellectual development. At the age of one and a half he could say only a few comprehensible words; he could also make use of a number of sounds which expressed a meaning intelligible to those around him. He was, however, on good terms with his parents and their one servant-girl, and tributes were paid to his being a 'good boy'. He did not disturb his parents at night, he conscientiously obeyed orders not to touch certain things or go into certain rooms, and above all he never cried when his mother left him for a few hours. At the same time, he was greatly attached to his mother, who had not only fed him herself but had also looked after him without any outside help. This good little boy, however, had an occasional disturbing habit of taking any small objects he could get hold of and throwing them away from him into a corner, under the bed, and so on, so that hunting for his toys and picking them up was often quite a business. As he did this he gave vent to a loud, long-drawn-out 'o-o-o-o', accompanied by an expression of interest and satisfaction. His mother and the writer of the present account were agreed in thinking that this was not a mere interjection but represented the German word 'fort' ['gone']. I eventually realized that it was a game and that the only use he made of any of his toys was to play 'gone' with them. One day I made an observation which confirmed my view. The child had a wooden reel with a piece of string tied round it. It never occurred to him to pull it along the floor behind him, for instance, and play at its being a carriage. What he did was to hold the reel by the string and very skilfully throw it over the edge of his curtained cot, so that it disappeared into it, at the same time uttering his expressive 'o-o-o-o'. He then pulled the reel out of the cot again by the string and hailed its reappearance with a joyful 'da' ['there']. This, then, was the complete game – disappearance and return. As a rule one only witnessed its first act, which was repeated untiringly as a game in itself, though there is no doubt that the greater pleasure was attached to the second act.[3]

The interpretation of the game then became obvious. It was related to the child's great cultural achievement – the instinctual renunciation (that is, the renunciation of instinctual satisfaction) which he had made in allowing his mother to go away without protesting. He compensated himself for this, as it were, by himself staging the disappearance and return of the objects within his reach. It is of course a matter of indifference from the point of view of judging the effective nature of the game whether the child invented it himself or took it over on some outside suggestion. Our interest is directed to another point. The child cannot possibly have felt his mother's departure as something agreeable or even indifferent. How then does his repetition of this distressing experience as a game fit in with the pleasure principle? It may perhaps be said in reply that her departure had to be enacted as a necessary preliminary to her joyful return, and that it was in the latter that lay the true purpose of the game. But against this must be counted the observed fact that the first act, that of departure, was staged as a game in itself and far more frequently than the episode in its entirety, with its pleasurable ending.

No certain decision can be reached from the analysis of a single case like this. On an unprejudiced view one gets an impression that the child turned his experience into a game from another motive. At the outset he was in a *passive* situation – he was overpowered by the experience; but, by repeating it, unpleasurable though it was, as a game, he took on an *active* part. These efforts might be put down to an instinct for mastery that was acting independently of whether the memory was in itself pleasurable or not. But still another interpretation may be attempted. Throwing away the object so that it was 'gone' might satisfy an impulse of the child's, which was suppressed in his actual life, to revenge himself on his mother for going away from him. In that case it would have a defiant meaning: 'All right, then, go away! I don't need you. I'm sending you away myself.' A year later, the same boy whom I had observed at his first game used to take a toy, if he was angry with it, and throw it on the floor, exclaiming: 'Go to the fwont!' He had heard at that time that his absent father was 'at the front', and was far from regretting his absence; on the contrary he made it quite clear that he had no desire to be disturbed in his sole possession of his mother.[4] We know of other children who liked to express similar hostile impulses by throwing away objects instead of persons.[5] We are therefore left in doubt as to whether the impulse to work over in the mind some overpowering experience so as to make oneself master of it can find expression as a primary event, and independently of the pleasure principle. For, in the case we have been discussing, the child may, after all, only have been able to repeat his unpleasant experience in play because the repetition carried along with it a yield of pleasure of another sort but none the less a direct one.

Nor shall we be helped in our hesitation between these two views by further considering children's play. It is clear that in their play children repeat everything that has made a great impression on them in real life, and that in doing so they abreact the strength of the impression and, as one might put it, make themselves master of the situation. But on the other hand it is obvious that all their play is influenced by a wish that dominates them the whole time – the wish to be grown-up and to be able to do what grown-up people do. It can also be observed that the unpleasurable nature of an experience does not always unsuit it for play. If the doctor looks down a child's throat or carries out some small operation on him, we may be quite sure that these frightening experiences will be the subject of the next game; but we must not in that connection overlook the fact that there is a yield of pleasure from another source. As the child passes over from the passivity of the experience to the activity of the game, he hands on the disagreeable experience to one of his playmates and in this way revenges himself on a substitute.[6]

Nevertheless, it emerges from this discussion that there is no need to assume the existence of a special imitative instinct in order to provide a motive for play. Finally, a reminder may be added that the artistic play and artistic imitation carried out by adults, which, unlike children's, are aimed at an audience, do not spare the spectators (for instance, in tragedy) the most painful experiences and can yet be felt by them as highly enjoyable. This is convincing proof that, even under the dominance of the pleasure principle, there are ways and means enough of making what is in itself unpleasurable into a subject to be recollected and worked over in the mind. The consideration of these cases and situations, which have a yield of pleasure as their final outcome, should be undertaken by some system of aesthetics with an economic approach to its subject-matter. They are of no use for *our* purposes, since they presuppose the existence and dominance of the pleasure principle; they give no evidence of the operation of tendencies *beyond* the pleasure principle, that is, of tendencies more primitive than it and independent of it.[7]

Notes

1   ['On the Psychical Mechanism of Hysterical Phenomena' (1893a), end of Section 1, *P.F.L.*, 3 58]
2   [The last 15 words of this sentence were added in 1921. For all this see *The Interpretation of Dreams* (1900a), *P.F.L.*, 4, 701ff.]
3   A further observation subsequently confirmed this interpretation fully. One day the child's mother had been away for several hours and on her return was met with the words 'Baby o-o-o-o!' which was at first incomprehensible. It soon turned out, however, that during this long period of solitude the child had found a method of making *himself* disappear. He had discovered his reflection in a full-length mirror which did not quite reach to the ground, so that by crouching down he could make his mirror-image 'gone'. [A further reference to this story will be found in *The Interpretation of Dreams*, *P.F.L.*, 4, 596 *n*.]
4   When this child was five and three-quarters, his mother died. Now that she was really 'gone' (o-o-o), the little boy showed no signs of grief. It is true that in the interval a second child had been born and had roused him to violent jealousy.
5   Cf. my note on a childhood memory of Goethe's (1917b).
6   [This observation is repeated in Section III of 'Female Sexuality' (1931b), *P.F.L.*, 7, 383–4.]
7   [Freud had made a tentative study of this point in his posthumously published paper on 'Psychopathic Characters on the Stage' (1942a) which was probably written in 1905 or 1906.]

3.2

Jacques Lacan, from 'The Mirror Stage' (1949)

The conception of the mirror stage that I introduced at our last congress, thirteen years ago, has since become more or less established in the practice of the French group. However, I think it worthwhile to bring it again to your attention, especially today, for the light it sheds on the formation of the *I* as we experience it in psychoanalysis. It is an experience that leads us to oppose any philosophy directly issuing from the *Cogito*.

Some of you may recall that this conception originated in a feature of human behaviour illuminated by a fact of comparative psychology. The child, at an age when he is for a time, however short, outdone by the chimpanzee in instrumental intelligence, can nevertheless already recognize as such his own image in a mirror. This recognition is indicated in the illuminative mimicry of the *Aha-Erlebnis*, which Köhler sees as the expression of situational apperception, an essential stage of the act of intelligence.

This act, far from exhausting itself, as in the case of the monkey, once the image has been mastered and found empty, immediately rebounds in the case of the child in a series of gestures in which he experiences in play the relation between the movements assumed in the image and the reflected environment, and between this virtual complex and the reality it reduplicates – the child's own body, and the persons and things, around him.

This event can take place, as we have known since Baldwin, from the age of six months, and its repetition has often made me reflect upon the startling spectacle of the infant in front of the mirror. Unable as yet to walk, or even to stand up, and held tightly as he is by some support, human or artificial (what, in France, we call a '*trotte-bébé*'), he nevertheless overcomes, in a flutter of jubilant activity, the obstructions of his support and, fixing his attitude in a slightly leaning-forward position, in order to hold it in his gaze, brings back an instantaneous aspect of the image.

For me, this activity retains the meaning I have given it up to the age of eighteen months. This meaning discloses a libidinal dynamism, which has hitherto remained problematic, as well as an ontological structure of the human world that accords with my reflections on paranoiac knowledge.

We have only to understand the mirror stage as *an identification*, in the full sense that analysis gives to the term: namely, the transformation that takes place in the subject when he assumes an image – whose predestination to this phase-effect is sufficiently indicated by the use, in analytic theory, of the ancient term *imago*.

This jubilant assumption of his specular image by the child at the *infans* stage, still sunk in his motor incapacity and nursling dependence, would seem to exhibit in an exemplary situation the symbolic matrix in which the *I* is precipitated in a primordial form, before it is objectified in the dialectic of identification with the other, and before language restores to it, in the universal, its function as subject.

This form would have to be called the Ideal-I,[1] if we wished to incorporate it into our usual register, in the sense that it will also be the source of secondary identifications, under which term I would place the functions of libidinal normalization. But the important point is that this form situates the agency of the ego, before its social determination, in a fictional direction, which will always remain irreducible for the individual alone, or rather, which will only rejoin the coming-into-being (*le devenir*) of the subject asymptotically, whatever the success of the dialectical syntheses by which he must resolve as *I* his discordance with his own reality.

The fact is that the total form of the body by which the subject anticipates in a mirage the maturation of his power is given to him only as *Gestalt*, that is to say, in an exteriority in which this form is certainly more constituent than constituted, but in which it appears to him above all in a contrasting size (*un relief de stature*) that fixes it and in a symmetry that inverts it, in contrast with the turbulent movements that the subject feels are animating him. Thus, this *Gestalt* – whose pregnancy should be regarded as bound up with the species, though its motor style remains scarcely recognizable – by these two aspects of its appearance, symbolizes the mental permanence of the *I* at the same time as it prefigures its alienating destination; it is still pregnant with the correspondences that unite the *I* with the statue in which man projects himself, with the phantoms that dominate him, or with the automaton in which, in an ambiguous relation, the world of his own making tends to find completion.

Indeed, for the *imagos* – whose veiled faces it is our privilege to see in outline in our daily experience and in the penumbra of symbolic efficacity[2] – the mirror-image would seem to be the threshold of the visible world, if we go by the mirror disposition that the *imago of one's own body* presents in hallucinations or dreams, whether it concerns its individual features, or even its infirmities, or its object-projections; or if we observe the role of the mirror apparatus in the appearances of the *double*, in which psychical realities, however heterogeneous, are manifested.

That a *Gestalt* should be capable of formative effects in the organism is attested by a piece of biological experimentation that is itself so alien to the idea of psychical causality that it cannot bring itself to formulate its results in these terms. It nevertheless recognizes that it is a necessary condition for the maturation of the gonad of the female pigeon that it should see another member of its species, of either sex; so sufficient in itself is this condition that the desired effect may be obtained merely by placing the individual within reach of the field of reflection of a mirror. Similarly, in the case of the migratory locust, the transition within a generation from the solitary to the gregarious form can be obtained by exposing the individual, at a certain stage, to the exclusively visual action of a similar image, provided it is animated by movements of a style sufficiently close to that characteristic of the species. Such facts are inscribed in an order of homeomorphic identification that would itself fall within the larger question of the meaning of beauty as both formative and erogenic.

But the facts of mimicry are no less instructive when conceived as cases of heteromorphic identification, in as much as they raise the problem of the signification of space for the living organism – psychological concepts hardly seem less appropriate for shedding light on these matters than ridiculous attempts to reduce them to the supposedly supreme law of adaptation. We have only to recall how Roger Caillois (who was then very young, and still fresh from his breach with the sociological school in which he was trained) illuminated the subject by using the term *'legendary psychasthenia'* to classify morphological mimicry as an obsession with space in its derealizing effect.

I have myself shown in the social dialectic that structures human knowledge as paranoiac[3] why human knowledge has greater autonomy than animal knowledge in relation to the field of force of desire, but also why human knowledge is determined in that 'little reality' (*ce peu de réalité*), which the Surrealists, in their restless way, saw as its limitation. These reflections lead me to recognize in the spatial captation manifested in the mirror-stage, even before the social dialectic, the effect in man of an organic insufficiency in his natural reality – in so far as any meaning can be given to the word 'nature'.

I am led, therefore, to regard the function of the mirror-stage as a particular case of the function of the *imago*, which is to establish a relation between the organism and its reality – or, as they say, between the *Innenwelt* and the *Umwelt*.

In man, however, this relation to nature is altered by a certain dehiscence at the heart of the organism, a primordial Discord betrayed by the signs of uneasiness and motor unco-ordination of the neo-natal months. The objective notion of the anatomical incompleteness of the pyramidal system and likewise the presence of certain humoral residues of the maternal organism confirm the view I have formulated as the fact of a real *specific prematurity of birth* in man.

It is worth noting, incidentally, that this is a fact recognized as such by embryologists, by the term *foetalization*, which determines the prevalence of the so-called superior apparatus of the neurax, and especially of the cortex, which psycho-surgical operations lead us to regard as the intra-organic mirror.

This development is experienced as a temporal dialectic that decisively projects the formation of the individual into history. The *mirror stage* is a drama whose internal thrust is precipitated from insufficiency to anticipation – and which manufactures for the subject, caught up in the lure of spatial identification, the succession of phantasies that extends from a fragmented body-image to a form of its totality that I shall call orthopaedic – and, lastly, to the assumption of the armour of an alienating identity, which will mark with its rigid structure the subject's entire mental development. Thus, to break out of the circle of the *Innenwelt* into the *Umwelt* generates the inexhaustible quadrature of the ego's verifications.

This fragmented body – which term I have also introduced into our system of theoretical references – usually manifests itself in dreams when the movement of the analysis encounters a certain level of aggressive disintegration in the individual. It then appears in the form of disjointed limbs, or of those organs represented in exoscopy, growing wings and taking up arms for intestinal persecutions – the very same that the visionary Hieronymus Bosch has fixed, for all time, in painting, in their ascent from the fifteenth century to the imaginary zenith of modern man. But this form is even tangibly revealed at the organic level, in the lines of 'fragilization' that define the anatomy of phantasy, as exhibited in the schizoid and spasmodic symptoms of hysteria.

Correlatively, the formation of the *I* is symbolized in dreams by a fortress, or a stadium – its inner arena and enclosure, surrounded by marshes and rubbish-tips, dividing it into two opposed fields of contest where the subject flounders in quest of the lofty, remote inner castle whose form (sometimes juxtaposed in the same scenario) symbolizes the id in a quite startling way. Similarly, on the mental plane, we find realized the structures of fortified works, the metaphor of which arises spontaneously, as if issuing from the symptoms themselves, to designate the mechanisms of obsessional neurosis – inversion, isolation, reduplication, cancellation and displacement.

But if we were to build on these subjective givens alone – however little we free them from the condition of experience that makes us see them as partaking of the nature of a linguistic technique – our theoretical attempts would remain exposed to the charge of projecting themselves into the unthinkable of an absolute subject. This is why I have sought in the present hypothesis, grounded in a conjunction of objective data, the guiding grid for a *method of symbolic reduction.*

It establishes in the *defences of the ego* a genetic order, in accordance with the wish formulated by Miss Anna Freud, in the first part of her great work, and situates (as against a frequently expressed prejudice) hysterical repression and its returns at a more archaic stage than obsessional inversion and its isolating processes, and the latter in turn as preliminary to paranoic alienation, which dates from the deflection of the specular *I* into the social *I.*

This moment in which the mirror-stage comes to an end inaugurates, by the identification with the *imago* of the counterpart and the drama of primordial jealousy (so well brought out by the school of Charlotte Bühler in the phenomenon of infantile *transitivism*), the dialectic that will henceforth link the *I* to socially elaborated situations.

It is this moment that decisively tips the whole of human knowledge into mediatization through the desire of the other, constitutes its objects in an abstract equivalence by the co-operation of others, and turns the I into that apparatus for which every instinctual thrust constitutes a danger, even though it should correspond to a natural maturation – the very normalization of this maturation being henceforth dependent, in man, on a cultural mediation as exemplified, in the case of the sexual object, by the Oedipus complex.

In the light of this conception, the term primary narcissism, by which analytic doctrine designates the libidinal investment characteristic of that moment, reveals in those who invented it the most profound awareness of semantic latencies. But it also throws light on the dynamic opposition between this libido and the sexual libido, which the first analysts tried to define when they invoked destructive and, indeed, death instincts, in order to explain the evident connection between the narcissistic libido and the alienating function of the *I*, the aggressivity it releases in any relation to the other, even in a relation involving the most Samaritan of aid.

In fact, they were encountering that existential negativity whose reality is so vigorously proclaimed by the contemporary philosophy of being and nothingness.

But unfortunately that philosophy grasps negativity only within the limits of a self-sufficiency of consciousness, which, as one of its premises, links to the *méconnaissances* that constitute the ego, the illusion of autonomy to which it entrusts itself. This flight of fancy, for all that it draws, to an unusual extent, on borrowings from psychoanalytic experience, culminates in the pretention of providing an existential psychoanalysis.

At the culmination of the historical effort of a society to refuse to recognize that it has any function other than the utilitarian one, and in the anxiety of the individual confronting the 'concentrational'[4] form of the social bond that seems to arise to crown this effort, existentialism must be judged by the explanations it gives of the subjective impasses that have indeed resulted from it; a freedom that is never more authentic than when it is within the walls of a prison; a demand for commitment, expressing the impotence of a pure consciousness to master any situation; a voyeuristic-sadistic idealization of the sexual relation; a personality that realizes itself only in suicide; a consciousness of the other that can be satisfied only by Hegelian murder.

These propositions are opposed by all our experience, in so far as it teaches us not to regard the ego as centred on the *perception-consciousness system*, or as organized by the 'reality principle' – a principle that is the expression of a scientific prejudice most hostile to the dialectic of knowledge. Our experience shows that we should start instead from the *function of méconnaissance* that characterizes the ego in all its structures, so markedly articulated by Miss Anna Freud. For, if the *Verneinung* represents the patent form of that function, its effects will, for the most part, remain latent, so long as they are not illuminated by some light reflected on to the level of fatality, which is where the id manifests itself.

We can thus understand the inertia characteristic of the formations of the *I*, and find there the most extensive definition of neurosis – just as the captation of the subject by the situation gives us the most general formula for madness, not only the madness that lies behind the walls of asylums, but also the madness that deafens the world with its sound and fury.

The sufferings of neurosis and psychosis are for us a schooling in the passions of the soul, just as the beam of the psychoanalytic scales, when we calculate the tilt of its threat to entire communities, provides us with an indication of the deadening of the passions in society.

At this junction of nature and culture, so persistently examined by modern anthropology, psychoanalysis alone recognizes this knot of imaginary servitude that love must always undo again, or sever.

For such a task, we place no trust in altruistic feeling, we who lay bare the aggressivity that underlies the activity of the philanthropist, the idealist, the pedagogue, and even the reformer.

In the recourse of subject to subject that we preserve, psychoanalysis may accompany the patient to the ecstatic limit of the '*Thou art that*', in which is revealed to him the cipher of his mortal destiny, but it is not in our mere power as practitioners to bring him to that point where the real journey begins.

Notes

1   Throughout this article I leave in its peculiarity the translation I have adopted for Freud's *Ideal-Ich* (i.e., 'je-idéal'), without further comment, other than to say I have not maintained it since.

2   Cf. Claude Lévi-Strauss, *Structural Anthropology*, chapter X.

3   Cf. 'Aggressivity in psychoanalysis' (another paper collected in *Écrits*).

4   '*Concentrationnaire*', an adjective coined after World War II (this article was written in 1949) to describe the life of the concentration-camp. In the hands of certain writers it became, by extension, applicable to many aspects of 'modern' life (Tr.).

3.3

Frantz Fanon, from *Black Skin/White Masks* (1952)

The fact of blackness

'Dirty nigger!' Or simply, 'Look, a Negro!'

I came into the world imbued with the will to find a meaning in things, my spirit filled with the desire to attain to the source of the world, and then I found that I was an object in the midst of other objects.

Sealed into that crushing objecthood, I turned beseechingly to others. Their attention was a liberation, running over my body suddenly abraded into nonbeing, endowing me once more with an agility that I had thought lost, and by taking me out of the world, restoring me to it. But just as I reached the other side, I stumbled, and the movements, the attitudes, the glances of the other fixed me there, in the sense in which a chemical solution is fixed by a dye. I was indignant; I demanded an explanation. Nothing happened. I burst apart. Now the fragments have been put together again by another self.

As long as the black man is among his own, he will have no occasion, except in minor internal conflicts, to experience his being through others. There is of course the moment of 'being for others,' of which Hegel speaks, but every ontology is made unattainable in a colonized and civilized society. It would seem that this fact has not been given sufficient attention by those who have discussed the question. In the *Weltanschauung* of a colonized people there is an impurity, a flaw that outlaws any ontological explanation. Someone may object that this is the case with every individual, but such an objection merely conceals a basic problem. Ontology – once it is finally admitted as leaving existence by the wayside – does not permit us to understand the being of the black man. For not only must the black man be black; he must be black in relation to the white man. Some critics will take it on themselves to remind us that this proposition has a converse. I say that this is false. The black man has no ontological resistance in the eyes of the white man. Overnight the Negro has been given two frames of reference within which he has had to place himself. His metaphysics, or, less pretentiously, his customs and the sources on which they were based, were wiped out because they were in conflict with a civilization that he did not know and that imposed itself on him.

The black man among his own in the twentieth century does not know at what moment his inferiority comes into being through the other. Of course I have talked about the black problem with friends, or, more rarely, with American Negroes. Together we protested, we asserted the equality of all men in the world. In the Antilles there was also that little gulf that exists among the almost-white, the mulatto, and the nigger. But I was satisfied with an intellectual understanding of these differences. It was not really dramatic. And then . . .

And then the occasion arose when I had to meet the white man's eyes. An unfamiliar weight burdened me. The real world challenged my claims. In the white world the man of color encounters difficulties in the development of his bodily schema. Consciousness of the body is solely a negating activity. It is a third-person consciousness. The body is surrounded by an atmosphere of certain uncertainty. I know that if I want to smoke, I shall have to reach out my right arm and take the pack of cigarettes lying at the other end of the table. The matches, however, are in the drawer on the left, and I shall have to lean back slightly. And all these movements are made not out of habit but out of implicit knowledge. A slow composition of my *self* as a body in the middle of a spatial and temporal world – such seems to be the schema. It does not impose itself on me; it is rather, a definitive structuring of the self and of the world – definitive because it creates a real dialectic between my body and the world.

For several years certain laboratories have been trying to produce a serum for 'denegrification'; with all the earnestness in the world, laboratories have sterilized their test tubes, checked their scales, and embarked on researches that might make it possible for the miserable Negro to whiten himself and thus to throw off the burden of that corporeal malediction. Below the corporeal schema I had sketched a historico-racial schema. The elements that I used had been provided for me not by 'residual sensations and perceptions primarily of a tactile, vestibular, kinesthetic, and visual character,'[1] but by the other, the white man, who had woven me out of a thousand details, anecdotes, stories. I thought that what I had in hand was to construct a physiological self, to balance space, to localize sensations, and here I was called on for more.

'Look, a Negro!' It was an external stimulus that flicked over me as I passed by. I made a tight smile.

'Look, a Negro!' It was true. It amused me.

'Look, a Negro!' The circle was drawing a bit tighter. I made no secret of my amusement.

'Mama, see the Negro! I'm frightened!' Frightened! Frightened! Now they were beginning to be afraid of me. I made up my mind to laugh myself to tears, but laughter had become impossible.

I could no longer laugh, because I already knew that there were legends, stories, history, and above all *historicity*, which I had learned about from Jaspers. Then, assailed at various points, the corporeal schema crumbled, its place taken by a racial epidermal schema. In the train it was no longer a question of being aware of my body in the third person but in a triple person. In the train I was given not one but two, three places. I had already stopped being amused. It was not that I was finding febrile coordinates in the world. I existed triply: I occupied space. I moved toward the other . . . and the evanescent other, hostile but not opaque, transparent, not there, disappeared. Nausea . . .

I was responsible at the same time for my body, for my race, for my ancestors. I subjected myself to an objective examination, I discovered my blackness, my ethnic characteristics; and I was battered down by tom-toms, cannibalism, intellectual deficiency, fetichism, racial defects, slave-ships, and above all else, above all: 'Sho' good eatin'.'

On that day, completely dislocated, unable to be abroad with the other, the white man, who unmercifully imprisoned me, I took myself far off from my own presence, far indeed, and made myself an object. What else could it be for me but an amputation, an excision, a hemorrhage that spattered my whole body with black blood? But I did not want this revision, this thematization. All I wanted was to be a man among other men. I wanted to come lithe and young into a world that was ours and to help to build it together.

Note

1   Jean Lhremitte, *L'Image de notre corps* (Paris: Nouvelle Revue critique, 1939), p. 17.

3.4

Julia Kristeva, from 'The System and the Speaking Subject' (1973)

In my view, a critique of this 'semiology of systems' and of its phenomenological foundations is possible only if it starts from a theory of meaning which must necessarily be a theory of the speaking subject. It is common knowledge that the linguistic revival which goes by the name of Generative Grammar – whatever its variants and mutations – is based on the rehabilitation of the Cartesian conception of language as an *act* carried out by a *subject*. On close inspection, as certain linguists (from Jakobson to Kuroda) have shown in recent years, this 'speaking subject' turns out in fact to be that *transcendental ego* which, in Husserl's view, underlies any and every predicative synthesis, if we 'put in brackets' logical or linguistic externality. Generative Grammar, based firmly on this subject, not only expresses the truth of language which structuralism describes as a system – namely that it is the act of an *ego* which has momentarily broken off its connection with that externality, which may be social, natural or unconscious – but creates for itself the opportunity of describing, better than its predecessors, the logic of this thetic act, starting out from an infinity of predication which each national language subjects to strict systems of rules. Yet this transcendental subject is not the essential concern of the semiological revival, and if it bases itself on the conception of language proper to Generative Grammar, semiology will not get beyond the reduction – still commonly characteristic of it – of signifying *practices* to their systematic aspect.

In respect of the subject and of signifying, it is the Freudian revolution which seems to me to have achieved the definitive displacement of the Western *épistémé* from its presumed centrality. But although the effects of that revolution have been superbly and authoritatively worked out in the writings of Jacques Lacan in France, or, in a rather different way, in the English anti-psychiatry of R. D. Laing and David Cooper, it has by no means reached far enough yet to affect the semiotic conception of language and of practices. The theory of meaning now stands at a crossroad: either it will remain an attempt at formalizing meaning-systems by increasing sophistication of the logico-mathematical tools which enable it to formulate models on the basis of a conception (already rather dated) of meaning as the act of a *transcendental ego*, cut off from its body, its unconscious and also its history; or else it will attune itself to the theory of the speaking subject as a divided subject (conscious/unconscious) and go on to attempt to specify the types of operation characteristic of the two sides of this split, thereby exposing them to those forces extraneous to the logic of the systematic; exposing them, that is to say, on the one hand, to bio-physiological processes (themselves already inescapably part of signifying processes, what Freud labelled 'drives'); and, on the other hand, to social constraints (family structures, modes of production, etc.).

In following this latter path, semiology, or, as I have suggested calling it, *semanalysis*, conceives of meaning not as a sign-system but as a *signifying process*. Within this process one might see the release and subsequent articulation of the drives as constrained by the social code yet not reducible to the language system as a *genotext* and the signifying system as it presents itself to phenomenological intuition as a *phenotext*; describable in terms of structure, or of competence/performance, or according to other models. The presence of the *genotext* within the *phenotext* is indicated by what I have called a *semiotic disposition*. In the case, for example, of a signifying practice such as 'poetic language', the *semiotic disposition* will be the various deviations from the grammatical rules of the language: articulatory effects which shift the phonematic system back towards its articulatory, phonetic base and consequently towards the drive-governed bases of sound-production; the over-determination of a lexeme by multiple meanings which it does not carry in ordinary usage but which accure to it as a result of its occurrence in other texts; syntactic irregularities such as ellipses, non-recoverable deletions, indefinite embeddings, etc.; the replacement of the relationship between the protagonists of any enunciation as they function in a locutory act – see here the work of J. L. Austin and John Searle – by a system of relations based on fantasy; and so forth.

These variations may be partly described by way of what are called the *primary* processes (displacement, condensation – or metonymy, metaphor), transversal to the logico-symbolic processes that function in the predicative synthesis towards establishing the language system. They had already been discovered by the structuralists, following Freud, at the 'lower', phonological, level of the linguistic synthesis. To them must be added the compulsion to repetition, but also 'operations' characteristic of topologies and capable of establishing *functions* between the signifying code and the fragmented body of the speaking subject as well as the bodies of his familial and social partners. All functions which suppose a *frontier* (in this case the fissure created by the act of naming and the logico-linguistic synthesis which it sets off) and the transgression of that frontier (the sudden appearance of new signifying chains) are relevant to any account of signifying *practice*, where practice is taken as meaning the acceptance of a symbolic law together with the transgression of that law for the purpose of renovating it.

The moment of transgression is the key moment in practice: we can speak of practice wherever there is a transgression of systematicity, i.e., a transgression of the unity proper to the *transcendental ego*. The subject of the practice cannot be the transcendental subject, who lacks the shift, the split in logical unity brought about by language which separates out, within the signifying body, the symbolic order from the workings of the libido (this last revealing itself by the *semiotic disposition*). Identifying the semiotic disposition means in fact identifying the shift in the speaking subject, his capacity for renewing the order in which he is inescapably caught up; and that capacity is, for the *subject*, the capacity for enjoyment.

It must, however, be remembered that although it can be described in terms of operations and concepts, this logic of shifts, splits and the infinitization of the symbolic limit leads us towards operations heterogeneous to meaning and its system. By that I mean that these 'operations' are *pre-meaning* and *pre-sign* (or *trans-meaning, trans-sign*), and that they bring us back to processes of division in the living matter of an organism subject to biological constraints as well as social norms. Here it seems indispensable that Melanie Klein's theory of drives should be refined and extended, together with the psycholinguistic study of the acquisition of language (provided that this study is conceived as something more than the mere reiteration of what is amply demonstrated in and by the linguistic system of the *transcendental ego*).

The point is not to replace the semiotics of signifying systems by considerations on the biological code appropriate to the nature of those employing them – a tautological exercise, after all, since the biological code has been modelled on the language system. It is rather to postulate the *heterogeneity* of biological operations in respect of signifying operations, and to study the dialectics of the former (that is, the fact that, though invariably subject to the signifying and/or social codes, they infringe the code in the direction of allowing the subject to get pleasure from it, renew it, even endanger it; where, that is, the processes are not blocked by him in repression or 'mental illness').

But since it is itself a metalanguage, semiotics can do no more than postulate this heterogeneity: as soon as it speaks about it, it homogenizes the phenomenon, links it with a system, loses hold of it. Its specificity can be preserved only in the signifying practices which set off the heterogeneity at issue: thus poetic language making free with the language code; music, dancing, painting, reordering the psychic drives which have not been harnessed by the dominant symbolization systems and thus renewing their own tradition; and (in a different mode) experiences with drugs – all seek out and make use of this heterogeneity and the ensuing fracture of a symbolic code which can no longer 'hold' its (speaking) subjects.

But if semiotics thus openly recognizes its inability to apprehend the heterogeneity of the signifying process other than by reducing it to a systematicity, does it thereby declare its own intellectual bankruptcy? Everything in current research that is solid and intellectually adequate impels those pursuing it to stress the limits of their own metalanguage in relation to the signifying process; their own metalanguage can apprehend only that part of the signifying process belonging to the domain of the general metalanguage to which their own efforts are tributary; the (vast) *remainder* has had, historically, to find a home in religion (notoriously, if more or less marginally, associated with semiotic reflection since the Stoics), moving up through medieval theories of the *modi significandi*, Leibniz's *Art of Combinations*, to phenomenology or positivism. It is only now, and only on the basis of a theory of the speaking subject as subject of a heterogeneous process, that semiotics can show that what lies outside its metalinguistic mode of operation – the 'remainder', the 'waste' – is what, in the process of the speaking subject, represents the moment in which it is set in action, put on trial, put to death: a heterogeneity with respect to system, operating within the practice and one which is liable, if not seen for what it is, to be reified into a transcendence.

3.5

Michel Foucault, from *Discipline and Punish* (1977)

The following, according to an order published at the end of the seventeenth century, were the measures to be taken when the plague appeared in a town.[1]

First, a strict spatial partitioning: the closing of the town and its outlying districts, a prohibition to leave the town on pain of death, the killing of all stray animals; the division of the town into distinct quarters, each governed by an intendant. Each street is placed under the authority of a syndic, who keeps it under surveillance; if he leaves the street, he will be condemned to death. On the appointed day, everyone is ordered to stay indoors: it is forbidden to leave on pain of death. The syndic himself comes to lock the door of each house from the outside; he takes the key with him and hands it over to the intendant of the quarter; the intendant keeps it until the end of the quarantine. Each family will have made its own provisions; but, for bread and wine, small wooden canals are set up between the street and the interior of the houses, thus allowing each person to receive his ration without communicating with the suppliers and other residents; meat, fish and herbs will be hoisted up into the houses with pulleys and baskets. If it is absolutely necessary to leave the house, it will be done in turn, avoiding any meeting. Only the intendants, syndics and guards will move about the streets and also, between the infected houses, from one corpse to another, the 'crows', who can be left to die: these are 'people of little substance who carry the sick, bury the dead, clean and do many vile and abject offices'. It is a segmented, immobile, frozen space. Each individual is fixed in his place. And, if he moves, he does so at the risk of his life, contagion or punishment.

Inspection functions ceaselessly. The gaze is alert everywhere: 'A considerable body of militia, commanded by good officers and men of substance', guards at the gates, at the town hall and in every quarter to ensure the prompt obedience of the people and the most absolute authority of the magistrates, 'as also to observe all disorder, theft and extortion'. At each of the town gates there will be an observation post; at the end of each street sentinels. Every day, the intendant visits the quarter in his charge, inquires whether the syndics have carried out their tasks, whether the inhabitants have anything to complain of; they 'observe their actions'. Every day, too, the syndic goes into the street for which he is responsible; stops before each house: gets all the inhabitants to appear at the windows (those who live overlooking the courtyard will be allocated a window looking onto the street at which no one but they may show themselves); he calls each of them by name; informs himself as to the state of each and every one of them – 'in which respect the inhabitants will be compelled to speak the truth under pain of death'; if someone does not appear at the window, the syndic must ask why: 'In this way he will find out easily enough whether dead or sick are being concealed.' Everyone locked up in his cage, everyone at his window, answering to his name and showing himself when asked – it is the great review of the living and the dead.

This surveillance is based on a system of permanent registration: reports from the syndics to the intendants, from the intendants to the magistrates or mayor. At the beginning of the 'lock up', the role of each of the inhabitants present in the town is laid down, one by one; this document bears 'the name, age, sex of everyone, notwithstanding his condition': a copy is sent to the intendant of the quarter, another to the office of the town hall, another to enable the syndic to make his daily roll call. Everything that may be observed during the course of the visits – deaths, illnesses, complaints, irregularities – is noted down and transmitted to the intendants and magistrates. The magistrates have complete control over medical treatment; they have appointed a physician in charge; no other practitioner may treat, no apothecary prepare medicine, no confessor visit a sick person without having received from him a written note 'to prevent anyone from concealing and dealing with those sick of the contagion, unknown to the magistrates'. The registration of the pathological must be constantly centralized. The relation of each individual to his disease and to his death passes through the representatives of power, the registration they make of it, the decisions they take on it.

Five or six days after the beginning of the quarantine, the process of purifying the houses one by one is begun. All the inhabitants are made to leave; in each room 'the furniture and goods' are raised from the ground or suspended from the air; perfume is poured around the room; after carefully sealing the windows, doors and even the keyholes with wax, the perfume is set alight. Finally, the entire house is closed while the perfume is consumed; those who have carried out the work are searched, as they were on entry, 'in the presence of the residents of the house, to see that they did not have something on their persons as they left that they did not have on entering'. Four hours later, the residents are allowed to re-enter their homes.

This enclosed, segmented space, observed at every point, in which the individuals are inserted in a fixed place, in which the slightest movements are supervised, in which all events are recorded, in which an uninterrupted work of writing links the centre and periphery, in which power is exercised without division, according to a continuous hierarchical figure, in which each individual is constantly located, examined and distributed among the living beings, the sick and the dead – all this constitutes a compact model of the disciplinary mechanism. The plague is met by order; its function is to sort out every possible confusion: that of the disease, which is transmitted when bodies are mixed together; that of the evil, which is increased when fear and death overcome prohibitions. It lays down for each individual his place, his body, his disease and his death, his well-being, by means of an omnipresent and omniscient power that subdivides itself in a regular, uninterrupted way even to the ultimate determination of the individual, of what characterizes him, of what belongs to him, of what happens to him. Against the plague, which is a mixture, discipline brings into play its power, which is one of analysis. A whole literary fiction of the festival grew up around the plague: suspended laws, lifted prohibitions, the frenzy of passing time, bodies mingling together without respect, individuals unmasked, abandoning their statutory identity and the figure under which they had been recognized, allowing a quite different truth to appear. But there was also a political dream of the plague, which was exactly its reverse: not the collective festival, but strict divisions; not laws transgressed, but the penetration of regulation into even the smallest details of everyday life through the mediation of the complete hierarchy that assured the capillary functioning of power; not masks that were put on and taken off, but the assignment to each individual of his 'true' name, his 'true' place, his 'true' body, his 'true' disease. The plague as a form, at once real and imaginary, of disorder had as its medical and political correlative discipline. Behind the disciplinary mechanisms can be read the haunting memory of 'contagions', of the plague, of rebellions, crimes, vagabondage, desertions, people who appear and disappear, live and die in disorder.

If it is true that the leper gave rise to rituals of exclusion, which to a certain extent provided the model for and general form of the great Confinement, then the plague gave rise to disciplinary projects. Rather than the massive, binary division between one set of people and another, it called for multiple separations, individualizing distributions, an organization in depth of surveillance and control, an intensification and a ramification of power. The leper was caught up in a practice of rejection, of exile-enclosure; he was left to his doom in a mass among which it was useless to differentiate; those sick of the plague were caught up in a meticulous tactical partitioning in which individual differentiations were the constricting effects of a power that multiplied, articulated and subdivided itself; the great confinement on the one hand; the correct training on the other. The leper and his separation; the plague and its segmentations. The first is marked; the second analysed and distributed. The exile of the leper and the arrest of the plague do not bring with them the same political dream. The first is that of a pure community, the second that of a disciplined society. Two ways of exercising power over men, of controlling their relations, of separating out their dangerous mixtures. The plague-stricken town, traversed throughout with hierarchy, surveillance, observation, writing; the town immobilized by the functioning of an extensive power that bears in a distinct way over all individual bodies – this is the utopia of the perfectly governed city. The plague (envisaged as a possibility at least) is the trial in the course of which one may define ideally the exercise of disciplinary power. In order to make rights and laws function according to pure theory, the jurists place themselves in imagination in the state of nature; in order to see perfect disciplines functioning, rulers dreamt of the state of plague. Underlying disciplinary projects the image of the plague stands for all forms of confusion and disorder; just as the image of the leper, cut off from all human contact, underlies projects of exclusion.

They are different projects, then, but not incompatible ones. We see them coming slowly together, and it is the peculiarity of the nineteenth century that it applied to the space of exclusion of which the leper was the symbolic inhabitant (beggars, vagabonds, madmen and the disorderly formed the real population) the technique of power proper to disciplinary partitioning. Treat 'lepers' as 'plague victims', project the subtle segmentations of discipline onto the confused space of internment, combine it with the methods of analytical distribution proper to power, individualize the excluded, but use procedures of individualization to mark exclusion – this is what was operated regularly by disciplinary power from the beginning of the nineteenth century in the psychiatric asylum, the penitentiary, the reformatory, the approved school and, to some extent, the hospital. Generally speaking, all the authorities exercising individual control function according to a double mode; that of binary division and branding (mad/sane; dangerous/harmless; normal/abnormal); and that of coercive assignment, of different distribution (who he is; where he must be; how he is to be characterized; how he is to be recognized; how a constant surveillance is to be exercised over him in an individual way, etc.). On the one hand, the lepers are treated as plague victims; the tactics of individualizing disciplines are imposed on the excluded; and, on the other hand, the universality of disciplinary controls makes it possible to brand the 'leper' and to bring into play against him the dualistic mechanisms of exclusion. The constant division between the normal and the abnormal, to which every individual is subjected, brings us back to our own time, by applying the binary branding and exile of the leper to quite different objects; the existence of a whole set of techniques and institutions for measuring, supervising and correcting the abnormal brings into play the disciplinary mechanisms to which the fear of the plague gave rise. All the mechanisms of power which, even today, are disposed around the abnormal individual, to brand him and to alter him, are composed of those two forms from which they distantly derive.

Bentham's *Panopticon* is the architectural figure of this composition. We know the principle on which it was based: at the periphery, an annular building; at the centre, a tower; this tower is pierced with wide windows that open onto the inner side of the ring; the peripheric building is divided into cells, each of which extends the whole width of the building; they have two windows, one on the inside, corresponding to the windows of the tower; the other, on the outside, allows the light to cross the cell from one end to the other. All that is needed, then, is to place a supervisor in a central tower and to shut up in each cell a madman, a patient, a condemned man, a worker or a schoolboy. By the effect of backlighting, one can observe from the tower, standing out precisely against the light, the small captive shadows in the cells of the periphery. They are like so many cages, so many small theatres, in which each actor is alone, perfectly individualized and constantly visible. The panoptic mechanism arranges spatial unities that make it possible to see constantly and to recognize immediately. In short, it reverses the principle of the dungeon; or rather of its three functions – to enclose, to deprive of light and to hide – it preserves only the first and eliminates the other two. Full lighting and the eye of a supervisor capture better than darkness, which ultimately protected. Visibility is a trap.

To begin with, this made it possible – as a negative effect – to avoid those compact, swarming, howling masses that were to be found in places of confinement, those painted by Goya or described by Howard. Each individual, in his place, is securely confined to a cell from which he is seen from the front by the supervisor; but the side walls prevent him from coming into contact with his companions. He is seen, but he does not see; he is the object of information, never a subject in communication. The arrangement of his room, opposite the central tower, imposes on him an axial visibility; but the divisions of the ring, those separated cells, imply a lateral invisibility. And this invisibility is a guarantee of order. If the inmates are convicts, there is no danger of a plot, an attempt at collective escape, the planning of new crimes for the future, bad reciprocal influences; if they are patients, there is no danger of contagion; if they are madmen there is no risk of their committing violence upon one another; if they are schoolchildren, there is no copying, no noise, no chatter, no waste of time; if they are workers, there are no disorders, no theft, no coalitions, none of those distractions that slow down the rate of work, make it less perfect or cause accidents. The crowd, a compact mass, a locus of multiple exchanges, individualities merging together, a collective effect, is abolished and replaced by a collection of separated individualities. From the point of view of the guardian, it is replaced by a multiplicity that can be numbered and supervised; from the point of view of the inmates, by a sequestered and observed solitude.

Hence the major effect of the Panopticon: to induce in the inmate a state of conscious and permanent visibility that assures the automatic functioning of power. So to arrange things that the surveillance is permanent in its effects, even if it is discontinuous in its action; that the perfection of power should tend to render its actual exercise unnecessary; that this architectural apparatus should be a machine for creating and sustaining a power relation independent of the person who exercises it; in short, that the inmates should be caught up in a power situation of which they are themselves the bearers. To achieve this, it is at once too much and too little that the prisoner should be constantly observed by an inspector: too little, for what matters is that he knows himself to be observed; too much, because he has no need in fact of being so. In view of this, Bentham laid down the principle that power should be visible and unverifiable. Visible: the inmate will constantly have before his eyes the tall outline of the central tower from which he is spied upon. Unverifiable: the inmate must never know whether he is being looked at at any one moment; but he must be sure that he may always be so. In order to make the presence or absence of the inspector unverifiable, so that the prisoners, in their cells, cannot even see a shadow, Bentham envisaged not only venetian blinds on the windows of the central observation hall, but, on the inside, partitions that intersected the hall at right angles and, in order to pass from one quarter to the other, not doors but zig-zag openings; for the slightest noise, a gleam of light, a brightness in a half-opened door would betray the presence of the guardian.[2] The Panopticon is a machine for dissociating the see/being seen dyad: in the peripheric ring, one is totally seen, without ever seeing; in the central tower, one sees everything without ever being seen.[3]

It is an important mechanism, for it automatizes and disindividualizes power. Power has its principle not so much in a person as in a certain concerted distribution of bodies, surfaces, lights, gazes; in an arrangement whose internal mechanisms produce the relation in which individuals are caught up. The ceremonies, the rituals, the marks by which the sovereign's surplus power was manifested are useless. There is a machinery that assures dissymmetry, disequilibrium, difference. Consequently, it does not matter who exercises power. Any individual, taken almost at random, can operate the machine: in the absence of the director, his family, his friends, his visitors, even his servants (Bentham, 45). Similarly, it does not matter what motive animates him: the curiosity of the indiscreet, the malice of a child, the thirst for knowledge of a philosopher who wishes to visit this museum of human nature, or the perversity of those who take pleasure in spying and punishing. The more numerous those anonymous and temporary observers are, the greater the risk for the inmate of being surprised and the greater his anxious awareness of being observed. The Panopticon is a marvellous machine which, whatever use one may wish to put it to, produces homogeneous effects of power.

A real subjection is born mechanically from a fictitious relation. So it is not necessary to use force to constrain the convict to good behaviour, the madman to calm, the worker to work, the schoolboy to application, the patient to the observation of the regulations. Bentham was surprised that panoptic institutions could be so light: there were no more bars, no more chains, no more heavy locks; all that was needed was that the separations should be clear and the openings well arranged. The heaviness of the old 'houses of security', with their fortress-like architecture, could be replaced by the simple, economic geometry of a 'house of certainty'. The efficiency of power, its constraining force have, in a sense, passed over to the other side – to the side of its surface of application. He who is subjected to a field of visibility, and who knows it, assumes responsibility for the constraints of power; he makes them play spontaneously upon himself; he inscribes in himself the power relation in which he simultaneously plays both roles; he becomes the principle of his own subjection. By this very fact, the external power may throw off its physical weight; it tends to the non-corporal; and, the more it approaches this limit, the more constant, profound and permanent are its effects: it is a perpetual victory that avoids any physical confrontation and which is always decided in advance.

* * *

The plague-stricken town, the panoptic establishment – the differences are important. They mark, at a distance of a century and a half, the transformations of the disciplinary programme. In the first case, there is an exceptional situation: against an extraordinary evil, power is mobilized; it makes itself everywhere present and visible; it invents new mechanisms; it separates, it immobilizes, it partitions; it constructs for a time what is both a counter-city and the perfect society; it imposes an ideal functioning, but one that is reduced, in the final analysis, like the evil that it combats, to a simple dualism of life and death: that which moves brings death, and one kills that which moves. The Panopticon, on the other hand, must be understood as a generalizable model of functioning; a way of defining power relations in terms of the everyday life of men ... But the Panopticon must not be understood as a dream building: it is the diagram of a mechanism of power reduced to its ideal form; its functioning, abstracted from any obstacle, resistance or friction, must be represented as a pure architectural and optical system: it is in fact a figure of political technology that may and must be detached from any specific use.

* * *

'Discipline' may be identified neither with an institution nor with an apparatus; it is a type of power, a modality for its exercise, comprising a whole set of instruments, techniques, procedures, levels of application, targets; it is a 'physics' or an 'anatomy' of power, a technology. And it may be taken over either by 'specialized' institutions (the penitentiaries or 'houses of correction' of the nineteenth century), or by institutions that use it as an essential instrument for a particular end (schools, hospitals), or by pre-existing authorities that find in it a means of reinforcing or reorganizing their internal mechanisms of power (one day we should show how intra-familial relations, essentially in the parents–children cell, have become 'disciplined', absorbing since the classical age external schemata, first educational and military, then medical, psychiatric, psychological, which have made the family the privileged locus of emergence for the disciplinary question of the normal and the abnormal); or by apparatuses that have made discipline their principle of internal functioning (the disciplinarization of the administrative apparatus from the Napoleonic period), or finally by state apparatuses whose major, if not exclusive, function is to assure that discipline reigns over society as a whole (the police).

On the whole, therefore, one can speak of the formation of a disciplinary society in this movement that stretches from the enclosed disciplines, a sort of social 'quarantine', to an indefinitely generalizable mechanism of 'panopticism'. Not because the disciplinary modality of power has replaced all the others; but because it has infiltrated the others, sometimes undermining them, but serving as an intermediary between them, linking them together, extending them and above all making it possible to bring the effects of power to the most minute and distant elements. It assures an infinitesimal distribution of the power relations.

A few years after Bentham, Julius gave this society its birth certificate. Speaking of the panoptic principle, he said that there was much more there than architectural ingenuity: it was an event in the 'history of the human mind'. In appearance, it is merely the solution of a technical problem; but, through it, a whole type of society emerges. Antiquity had been a civilization of spectacle. 'To render accessible to a multitude of men the inspection of a small number of objects': this was the problem to which the architecture of temples, theatres and circuses responded. With spectacle, there was a predominance of public life, the intensity of festivals, sensual proximity. In these rituals in which blood flowed, society found new vigour and formed for a moment a single great body. The modern age poses the opposite problem: 'To procure for a small number, or even for a single individual, the instantaneous view of a great multitude.' In a society in which the principal elements are no longer the community and public life, but, on the one hand, private individuals and, on the other, the state, relations can be regulated only in a form that is the exact reverse of the spectacle: 'It was to the modern age, to the ever-growing influence of the state, to its ever more profound intervention in all the details and all the relations of social life, that was reserved the task of increasing and perfecting its guarantees, by using and directing towards that great aim the building and distribution of buildings intended to observe a great multitude of men at the same time.'

Julius saw as a fulfilled historical process that which Bentham had described as a technical programme. Our society is one not of spectacle, but of surveillance; under the surface of images, one invests bodies in depth; behind the great abstraction of exchange, there continues the meticulous, concrete training of useful forces; the circuits of communication are the supports of an accumulation and a centralization of knowledge; the play of signs defines the anchorages of power; it is not that the beautiful totality of the individual is amputated, repressed, altered by our social order, it is rather that the individual is carefully fabricated in it, according to a whole technique of forces and bodies. We are much less Greeks than we believe. We are neither in the amphitheatre, nor on the stage, but in the panoptic machine, invested by its effects of power, which we bring to ourselves since we are part of its mechanism. The importance, in historical mythology, of the Napoleonic character probably derives from the fact that it is at the point of junction of the monarchical, ritual exercise of sovereignty and the hierarchical, permanent exercise of indefinite discipline. He is the individual who looms over everything with a single gaze which no detail, however minute, can escape: 'You may consider that no part of the Empire is without surveillance, no crime, no offence, no contravention that remains unpunished, and that the eye of the genius who can enlighten all embraces the whole of this vast machine, without, however, the slightest detail escaping his attention'.

Notes

1   Archives militaires de Vincennes, A 1,516 91 sc. Pièce. This regulation is broadly similar to a whole series of others that date from the same period and earlier.

2   In the *Postscript to the Panopticon*, 1791, Bentham adds dark inspection galleries painted in black around the inspector's lodge, each making it possible to observe two storeys of cells.

3   In his first version of the *Panopticon*, Bentham had also imagined an acoustic surveillance, operated by means of pipes leading from the cells to the central tower. In the *Postscript* he abandoned the idea, perhaps because he could not introduce into it the principle of dissymmetry and prevent the prisoners from hearing the inspector as well as the inspectors hearing them. Julius tried to develop a system of dissymmetrical listening Julius, N.H., *Leçons sur les prisons*, I, 1831 (Fr. trans.), p. 18.

3.6

Michel Foucault, from *The History of Sexuality* (1978)

Those who believe that sex was more rigorously elided in the nineteenth century than ever before, through a formidable mechanism of blockage and a deficiency of discourse, can say what they please. There was no deficiency, but rather an excess, a redoubling, too much rather than not enough discourse, in any case an interference between two modes of production of truth: procedures of confession, and scientific discursivity.

And instead of adding up the errors, naïvetés, and moralisms that plagued the nineteenth-century discourse of truth concerning sex, we would do better to locate the procedures by which that will to knowledge regarding sex, which characterizes the modern Occident, caused the rituals of confession to function within the norms of scientific regularity: how did this immense and traditional extortion of the sexual confession come to be constituted in scientific terms?

1 *Through a clinical codification of the inducement to speak.* Combining confession with examination, the personal history with the deployment of a set of decipherable signs and symptoms; the interrogation, the exacting questionnaire, and hypnosis, with the recollection of memories and free association: all were ways of reinscribing the procedure of confession in a field of scientifically acceptable observations.

2 *Through the postulate of a general and diffuse causality.* Having to tell everything, being able to pose questions about everything, found their justification in the principle that endowed sex with an inexhaustible and polymorphous causal power. The most discrete event in one's sexual behavior – whether an accident or a deviation, a deficit or an excess – was deemed capable of entailing the most varied consequences throughout one's existence; there was scarcely a malady or physical disturbance to which the nineteenth century did not impute at least some degree of sexual etiology. From the bad habits of children to the phthises of adults, the apoplexies of old people, nervous maladies, and the degenerations of the race, the medicine of that era wove an entire network of sexual causality to explain them. This may well appear fantastic to us, but the principle of sex as a 'cause of any and everything' was the theoretical underside of a confession that had to be thorough,

meticulous, and constant, and at the same time operate within a scientific type of practice. The limitless dangers that sex carried with it justified the exhaustive character of the inquisition to which it was subjected.

3   *Through the principle of a latency intrinsic to sexuality.* If it was necessary to extract the truth of sex through the technique of confession, this was not simply because it was difficult to tell, or stricken by the taboos of decency, but because the ways of sex were obscure; it was elusive by nature; its energy and its mechanisms escaped observation, and its causal power was partly clandestine. By integrating it into the beginnings of a scientific discourse, the nineteenth century altered the scope of the confession; it tended no longer to be concerned solely with what the subject wished to hide, but with what was hidden from himself, being incapable of coming to light except gradually and through the labor of a confession in which the questioner and the questioned each had a part to play. The principle of a latency essential to sexuality made it possible to link the forcing of a difficult confession to a scientific practice. It had to be exacted, by force, since it involved something that tried to stay hidden.

4   *Through the method of interpretation.* If one had to confess, this was not merely because the person to whom one confessed had the power to forgive, console, and direct, but because the work of producing the truth was obliged to pass through this relationship if it was to be scientifically validated. The truth did not reside solely in the subject who, by confessing, would reveal it wholly formed. It was constituted in two stages: present but incomplete, blind to itself, in the one who spoke, it could only reach completion in the one who assimilated and recorded it. It was the latter's function to verify this obscure truth: the revelation of confession had to be coupled with the decipherment of what it said. The one who listened was not simply the forgiving master, the judge who condemned or acquitted; he was the master of truth. His was a hermeneutic function. With regard to the confession, his power was not only to demand it before it was made, or decide what was to follow after it, but also to constitute a discourse of truth on the basis of its decipherment. By no longer making the confession a test, but rather a sign, and by making sexuality something to be interpreted, the nineteenth century gave itself the possibility of causing the procedures of confession to operate within the regular formation of a scientific discourse.

5   *Through the medicalization of the effects of confession.* The obtaining of the confession and its effects were recodified as therapeutic operations. Which meant first of all that the sexual domain was no longer accounted for simply by the notions of error or sin, excess or transgression, but was placed under the rule of the normal and the pathological (which, for that matter, were the transposition of the former categories); a characteristic sexual morbidity was defined for the first time; sex appeared as an extremely unstable pathological field: a surface of repercussion for other ailments, but also the focus of a specific nosography, that of instincts, tendencies, images, pleasure, and conduct. This implied furthermore that sex would derive its meaning and its necessity from medical interventions: it would be

required by the doctor, necessary for diagnosis, and effective by nature in the cure. Spoken in time, to the proper party, and by the person who was both the bearer of it and the one responsible for it, the truth healed.

Let us consider things in broad historical perspective: breaking with the traditions of the *ars erotica*, our society has equipped itself with a *scientia sexualis*. To be more precise, it has pursued the task of producing true discourses concerning sex, and this by adapting – not without difficulty – the ancient procedure of confession to the rules of scientific discourse. Paradoxically, the *scientia sexualis* that emerged in the nineteenth century kept as its nucleus the singular ritual of obligatory and exhaustive confession, which in the Christian West was the first technique for producing the truth of sex. Beginning in the sixteenth century, this rite gradually detached itself from the sacrament of penance, and via the guidance of souls and the direction of conscience – the *ars artium* – emigrated toward pedagogy, relationships between adults and children, family relations, medicine, and psychiatry. In any case, nearly one hundred and fifty years have gone into the making of a complex machinery for producing true discourses on sex: a deployment that spans a wide segment of history in that it connects the ancient injunction of confession to clinical listening methods. It is this deployment that enables something called 'sexuality' to embody the truth of sex and its pleasures.

'Sexuality': the correlative of that slowly developed discursive practice which constitutes the *scientia sexualis*. The essential features of this sexuality are not the expression of a representation that is more or less distorted by ideology, or of a misunderstanding caused by taboos; they correspond to the functional requirements of a discourse that must produce its truth. Situated at the point of intersection of a technique of confession and a scientific discursivity, where certain major mechanisms had to be found for adapting them to one another (the listening technique, the postulate of causality, the principle of latency, the rule of interpretation, the imperative of medicalization), sexuality was defined as being 'by nature': a domain susceptible to pathological processes, and hence one calling for therapeutic or normalizing interventions; a field of meanings to decipher; the site of processes concealed by specific mechanisms; a focus of indefinite causal relations; and an obscure speech (*parole*) that had to be ferreted out and listened to. The 'economy' of discourses – their intrinsic technology, the necessities of their operation, the tactics they employ, the effects of power which underlie them and which they transmit – this, and not a system of representations, is what determines the essential features of what they have to say. The history of sexuality – that is, the history of what functioned in the nineteenth century as a specific field of truth – must first be written from the viewpoint of a history of discourses.

Let us put forward a general working hypothesis. The society that emerged in the nineteenth century – bourgeois, capitalist, or industrial society, call it what you will – did not confront sex with a fundamental refusal of recognition. On the contrary, it put into operation an entire machinery for producing true discourses concerning it. Not only did it speak of sex and compel everyone to do so; it also set out to formulate the uniform truth of sex. As if it suspected sex of harboring a fundamental secret. As if it needed this production of truth. As if it was essential that sex be inscribed not only in an economy of pleasure but in an ordered system of knowledge. Thus sex gradually became an object of great suspicion; the general and disquieting meaning that pervades our conduct and our existence, in spite of ourselves; the point of weakness where evil portents reach through to us; the fragment of darkness that we each carry within us: a general signification, a universal secret, an omnipresent cause, a fear that never ends. And so, in this 'question' of sex (in both senses: as interrogation and problematization, and as the need for confession and integration into a field of rationality), two processes emerge, the one always conditioning the other: we demand that sex speak the truth (but, since it is the secret and is oblivious to its own nature, we reserve for ourselves the function of telling the truth of its truth, revealed and deciphered at last), and we demand that it tell us our truth, or rather, the deeply buried truth of that truth about ourselves which we think we possess in our immediate consciousness. We tell it its truth by deciphering what it tells us about that truth; it tells us our own by delivering up that part of it that escaped us. From this interplay there has evolved, over several centuries, a knowledge of the subject; a knowledge not so much of his form, but of that which divides him, determines him perhaps, but above all causes him to be ignorant of himself. As unlikely as this may seem, it should not surprise us when we think of the long history of the Christian and juridical confession, of the shifts and transformations this form of knowledge-power, so important in the West, has undergone: the project of a science of the subject has gravitated, in ever narrowing circles, around the question of sex. Causality in the subject, the unconscious of the subject, the truth of the subject in the other who knows, the knowledge he holds unbeknown to him, all this found an opportunity to deploy itself in the discourse of sex. Not, however, by reason of some natural property inherent in sex itself, but by virtue of the tactics of power immanent in this discourse.

Scientia sexualis versus *ars erotica*, no doubt. But it should be noted that the *ars erotica* did not disappear altogether from Western civilization; nor has it always been absent from the movement by which one sought to produce a science of sexuality. In the Christian confession, but especially in the direction and examination of conscience, in the search for spiritual union and the love of God, there was a whole series of methods that had much in common with an erotic art: guidance by the master along a path of initiation, the intensification of experiences extending down to their physical components, the optimization of effects by the discourse that accompanied them. The phenomena of possession and ecstasy, which were quite frequent in the Catholicism of the Counter Reformation, were undoubtedly effects that had got outside the control of the erotic technique immanent in this subtle science of the flesh. And we must ask whether, since the nineteenth century, the *scientia sexualis* – under the guise of its decent positivism – has not functioned, at least to a certain extent, as an *ars erotica*. Perhaps this production of truth, intimidated though it was by the scientific model, multiplied, intensified, and even created its own intrinsic pleasures. It is often said that we have been incapable of imagining any new pleasures. We have at least invented a different kind of pleasure: pleasure in the truth of pleasure, the pleasure of knowing that truth, of discovering and exposing it, the fascination of seeing it and telling it, of captivating and capturing others by it, of confiding it in secret, of luring it out in the open – the specific pleasure of the true discourse on pleasure.

The most important elements of an erotic art linked to our knowledge about sexuality are not to be sought in the ideal, promised to us by medicine, of a healthy sexuality, nor in the humanist dream of a complete and flourishing sexuality, and certainly not in the lyricism of orgasm and the good feelings of bio-energy (these are but aspects of its normalizing utilization), but in this multiplication and intensification of pleasures connected to the production of the truth about sex. The learned volumes, written and read; the consultations and examinations; the anguish of answering questions and the delights of having one's words interpreted; all the stories told to oneself and to others, so much curiosity, so many confidences offered in the face of scandal, sustained – but not without trembling a little – by the obligation of truth; the profusion of secret fantasies and the dearly paid right to whisper them to whoever is able to hear them; in short, the formidable 'pleasure of analysis' (in the widest sense of the latter term) which the West has cleverly been fostering for several centuries: all this constitutes something like the errant fragments of an erotic art that is secretly transmitted by confession and the science of sex. Must we conclude that our *scientia sexualis* is but an extraordinarily subtle form of *ars erotica*, and that it is the Western, sublimated version of that seemingly lost tradition? Or must we suppose that all these pleasures are only the by-products of a sexual science, a bonus that compensates for its many stresses and strains?

In any case, the hypothesis of a power of repression exerted by our society on sex for economic reasons appears to me quite inadequate if we are to explain this whole series of reinforcements and intensifications that our preliminary inquiry has discovered: a proliferation of discourses, carefully tailored to the requirements of power; the solidification of the sexual mosaic and the construction of devices capable not only of isolating it but of stimulating and provoking it, of forming it into focuses of attention, discourse, and pleasure; the mandatory production of confessions and the subsequent establishment of a system of legitimate knowledge and of an economy of manifold pleasures. We are dealing not nearly so much with a negative mechanism of exclusion as with the operation of a subtle network of discourses, special knowledges, pleasures, and powers. At issue is not a movement bent on pushing rude sex back into some obscure and inaccessible region, but on the contrary, a process that spreads it over the surface of things and bodies, arouses it, draws it out and bids it speak, implants it in reality and enjoins it to tell the truth: an entire glittering sexual array, reflected in a myriad of discourses, the obstination of powers, and the interplay of knowledge and pleasure.

All this is an illusion, it will be said, a hasty impression behind which a more discerning gaze will surely discover the same great machinery of repression. Beyond these few phosphorescences, are we not sure to find once more the somber law that always says no? The answer will have to come out of a historical inquiry. An inquiry concerning the manner in which a knowledge of sex has been forming over the last three centuries; the manner in which the discourses that take it as their object have multiplied, and the reasons for which we have come to attach a nearly fabulous price to the truth they claimed to produce. Perhaps these historical analyses will end by dissipating what this cursory survey seems to suggest. But the postulate I started out with, and would like to hold to as long as possible, is that these deployments of power and knowledge, of truth and pleasures, so unlike those of repression, are not necessarily secondary and derivative; and further, that repression is not in any case fundamental and overriding. We need to take these mechanisms seriously, therefore, and reverse the direction of our analysis: rather than assuming a generally acknowledged repression, and an ignorance measured against what we are supposed to know, we must begin with these positive mechanisms, insofar as they produce knowledge, multiply discourse, induce pleasure, and generate power; we must investigate the conditions of their emergence and operation, and try to discover how the related facts of interdiction or concealment are distributed with respect to them. In short, we must define the strategies of power that are immanent in this will to knowledge. As far as sexuality is concerned, we shall attempt to constitute the 'political economy' of a will to knowledge.

3.7

Roland Barthes, from *The Pleasure of the Text* (1973)

Is not the most erotic portion of a body *where the garment gapes*? In perversion (which is the realm of textual pleasure) there are no 'erogenous zones' (a foolish expression, besides); it is intermittence, as psychoanalysis has so rightly stated, which is erotic: the intermittence of skin flashing between two articles of clothing (trousers and sweater), between two edges (the open-necked shirt, the glove and the sleeve); it is this flash itself which seduces, or rather: the staging of an appearance-as-disappearance.

The pleasure of the text is not the pleasure of the corporeal striptease or of narrative suspense. In these cases, there is no tear, no edges: a gradual unveiling: the entire excitation takes refuge in the *hope* of seeing the sexual organ (schoolboy's dream) or in knowing the end of the story (novelistic satisfaction). Paradoxically (since it is mass-consumed), this is a far more intellectual pleasure than the other: an Oedipal pleasure (to denude, to know, to learn the origin and the end), if it is true that every narrative (every unveiling of the truth) is a staging of the (absent, hidden, or hypostatized) father – which would explain the solidarity of narrative forms, of family structures, and of prohibitions of nudity, all collected in our culture in the myth of Noah's sons covering his nakedness.

Yet the most classical narrative (a novel by Zola or Balzac or Dickens or Tolstoy) bears within it a sort of diluted tmesis: we do not read everything with the same intensity of reading; a rhythm is established, casual, unconcerned with the *integrity* of the text; our very avidity for knowledge impels us to skim or to skip certain passages (anticipated as 'boring') in order to get more quickly to the warmer parts of the anecdote (which are always its articulations: whatever furthers the solution of the riddle, the revelation of fate): we boldly skip (no one is watching) descriptions, explanations, analyses, conversations; doing so, we resemble a spectator in a nightclub who climbs onto the stage and speeds up the dancer's striptease, tearing off her clothing, *but in the same order*, that is: on the one hand respecting and on the other hastening the episodes of the ritual (like a priest *gulping down* his Mass). Tmesis, source or figure of pleasure, here confronts two prosaic edges with one another; it sets what is useful to a knowledge of the secret against what is useless to such knowledge; tmesis is a seam or flaw resulting from a simple principle of functionality; it does not occur at the level of the structure of languages but only at the moment of their consumption; the author cannot predict tmesis: he cannot choose to write *what will not be read*. And yet, it is the very rhythm of what is read and what is not read that creates the pleasure of the great narratives: has anyone ever read Proust, Balzac, *War and Peace*, word for word? (Proust's good fortune: from one reading to the next, we never skip the same passages.)

Thus, what I enjoy in a narrative is not directly its content or even its structure, but rather the abrasions I impose upon the fine surface: I read on, I skip, I look up, I dip in again. Which has nothing to do with the deep laceration the text of bliss inflicts upon language itself, and not upon the simple temporality of its reading.

Whence two systems of reading: one goes straight to the articulations of the anecdote, it considers the extent of the text, ignores the play of language (if I read Jules Verne, I go fast: I lose discourse, and yet my reading is not hampered by any verbal *loss* – in the speleological sense of that word); the other reading skips nothing; it weighs, it sticks to the text, it reads, so to speak, with application and transport, grasps at every point in the text the asyndeton which cuts the various languages – and not the anecdote: it is not (logical) extension that captivates it, the winnowing out of truths, but the layering of significance; as in the children's game of topping hands, the excitement comes not from a processive haste but from a kind of vertical din (the verticality of language and of its destruction); it is at the moment when each (different) hand skips over the next (and not one *after* the other) that the hole, the gap, is created and carries off the subject of the game – the subject of the text. Now paradoxically (so strong is the belief that one need merely *go fast* in order not to be bored), this second, *applied* reading (in the real sense of the word 'application') is the one suited to the modern text, the limit-text. Read slowly, read *all* of a novel by Zola, and the book will drop from your hands; read fast, in snatches, some modern text, and it becomes opaque, inaccessible to your pleasure: you want something to happen and nothing does, for *what happens to the language does not happen to the discourse:* what 'happens,' what 'goes away,' the seam of the two edges, the interstice of bliss, occurs in the volume of the languages, in the uttering, not in the sequence of utterances: not to devour, to gobble, but to graze, to browse scrupulously, to rediscover – in order to read today's writers – the leisure of bygone readings: to be *aristocratic* readers.

* * *

If I agree to judge a text according to pleasure, I cannot go on to say: this one is good, that bad. No awards, no 'critique,' for this always implies a tactical aim, a social usage, and frequently an extenuating image-reservoir. I cannot apportion, imagine that the text is perfectible, ready to enter into a play of normative predicates: it is too much *this*, not enough *that*; the text (the same is true of the singing voice) can wring from me only this judgment, in no way adjectival: *that's it!* And further still: *that's it for me!* This 'for me' is neither subjective nor existential, but Nietzschean ('. . . basically, it is always the same question: What is it *for me?* . . .').

The *brio* of the text (without which, after all, there is no text) is its *will to bliss:* just where it exceeds demand, transcends prattle, and whereby it attempts to overflow, to break through the constraint of adjectives – which are those doors of language through which the ideological and the imaginary come flowing in.

* * *

Text of pleasure: the text that contents, fills, grants euphoria; the text that comes from culture and does not break with it, is linked to a *comfortable* practice of reading. Text of bliss: the text that imposes a state of loss, the text that discomforts (perhaps to the point of a certain boredom), unsettles the reader's historical, cultural, psychological assumptions, the consistency of his tastes, values, memories, brings to a crisis his relation with language.

Now the subject who keeps the two texts in his field and in his hands the reins of pleasure and bliss is an anachronic subject, for he simultaneously and contradictorily participates in the profound hedonism of all culture (which permeates him quietly under cover of an *art de vivre* shared by the old books) and in the destruction of that culture: he enjoys the consistency of his selfhood (that is his pleasure) and seeks its loss (that is his bliss). He is a subject split twice over, doubly perverse.

* * *

Society of the Friends of the Text: its members would have nothing in common (for there is no necessary agreement on the texts of pleasure) but their enemies: fools of all kinds, who decree foreclosure of the text and of its pleasure, either by cultural conformism or by intransigent rationalism (suspecting a 'mystique' of literature) or by political moralism or by criticism of the signifier or by stupid pragmatism or by snide vacuity or by destruction of the discourse, loss of verbal desire. Such a society would have no site, could function only in total atopia; yet it would be a kind of phalanstery, for in it contradictions would be acknowledged (and the risks of ideological imposture thereby restricted), difference would be observed and conflict rendered insignificant (being unproductive of pleasure).

'Let difference surreptitiously replace conflict.' Difference is not what makes or sweetens conflict: it is achieved over and above conflict, it is *beyond and alongside* conflict. Conflict is nothing but the moral state of difference; whenever (and this is becoming frequent) conflict is not tactical (aimed at transforming a real situation), one can distinguish in it the failure-to-attain-bliss, the debacle of a perversion crushed by its own code and no longer able to invent itself: conflict is always coded, aggression is merely the most worn-out of languages. Forgoing violence, I forgo the code itself (in Sade's texts, outside all codes because they continually invent their own, appropriate only to themselves, there are no conflicts: only triumphs). I love the text because for me it is that rare locus of language from which any 'scene' (in the household, conjugal sense of the term), any logomachy is absent. The text is never a 'dialogue': no risk of feint, of aggression, of blackmail, no rivalry of ideolects; the text establishes a sort of islet within the human – the common – relation, manifests the asocial nature of pleasure (only leisure is social), grants a glimpse of the scandalous truth about bliss: that it may well be, once the image-reservoir of speech is abolished, *neuter*.

* * *

On the stage of the text, no footlights: there is not, behind the text, someone active (the writer) and out front someone passive (the reader): there is not a subject and an object. The text supersedes grammatical attitudes: it is the undifferentiated eye which an excessive author (Angelus Silesius) describes: 'The eye by which I see God is the same eye by which He sees me.'

Apparently Arab scholars, when speaking of the text, use this admirable expression: *the certain body*. What body? We have several of them; the body of anatomists and physiologists, the one science sees or discusses: this is the text of grammarians, critics, commentators, philologists (the pheno-text). But we also have a body of bliss consisting solely of erotic relations, utterly distinct from the first body: it is another contour, another nomination; thus with the text: it is no more than the open list of the fires of language (those living fires, intermittent lights, wandering features strewn in the text like seeds and which for us advantageously replace the '*semina aeternitatis*,' the '*zopyra*,' the common notions, the fundamental assumptions of ancient philosophy). Does the text have human form, is it a figure, an anagram of the body? Yes, but of our erotic body. The pleasure of the text is irreducible to physiological need.

The pleasure of the text is that moment when my body pursues its own ideas – for my body does not have the same ideas I do.

*   *   *

How can we take pleasure in a *reported* pleasure (boredom of all narratives of dreams, of parties)? How can we read criticism? Only one way: since I am here a second-degree reader, I must shift my position: instead of agreeing to be the confidant of this critical pleasure – a sure way to miss it – I can make myself its voyeur: I observe clandestinely the pleasure of others, I enter perversion; the commentary then becomes in my eyes a text, a fiction, a fissured envelope. The writer's perversity (his pleasure in writing is *without function*), the doubled, the trebled, the infinite perversity of the critic and of his reader.

Section 4

DIFFERENCE

Introduction

> What therefore is truth? A mobile army of metaphors, metonymies, anthro-
> pomorphisms ... truths are illusions of which one has forgotten that they are
> illusions.
>
> (Nietzsche, cited in the 'Preface' by Gayatri Spivak
> to *Of Grammatology*, Derrida 1976: xxii)

Every sign is different

'What is difference? Difference is ...' To us, situated as inheritors of a rational
tradition stretching back to Plato and ancient Greek philosophy, it seems obvious and
natural that such questions should have clear and definite answers. Why bother with
a writer such as Derrida, who appears unable or unwilling to give a straight answer, to
begin at the beginning, go on to the middle and end with the conclusion, explaining
what he really means? Yet Derrida's work renders each of these terms problematic
when applied to modes of writing: 'straight', 'beginning', 'middle', 'end', 'means',
'really', 'really means', even (especially) 'is'. His writing and his account of difference
touch on so many of the texts gathered in this present collection that it becomes
inescapable, represented here by the whole of the essay 'Differance'. Again, because
Derrida's writing, without fitting into any one category or discipline, breaches and runs
across traditional boundaries (between culture and philosophy, linguistics and theories of the subject, between all of these and issues of gender), it requires its own
separate section under 'Difference'.

The foregoing means that there can be no mastering 'introduction' to difference
or concluding 'summary' of the essay 'Differance'. An analogy and two matters for
reflection may help to frame some of the issues over which the essay intervenes
(intervening to promote the question of difference in February 1968, when the
'events' of that year were just starting to get under way on the streets of Paris).

There is a helpful analogy with the work of Jacques Lacan (see Section 3.2). It could be argued that Lacan, sharing with Derrida the philosophical inheritance of Heidegger's challenge to the tradition of Western metaphysics, turns Plato on his head. If Plato posited an ideal world of Forms in which Being was perfectly and timelessly present to itself and of which this mortal world is an unhappy copy, the effect of Lacan is to regard *manque à être* (lack in being) as originary and foundational; emerging from being into meaning, the human subject is constituted by its failed attempt to make good the lack it discovers as it enters language and the 'defiles' of the signifier. Within and on the grounds of the pre-existing intersubjective order of the Symbolic, the I becomes present and substantial only in so far as it wins over from there an Imaginary identity for itself. There is, then, an analogy between Lacan's account of lack and identity and Derrida's account of difference and presence. But it is an analogy only, for Derrida offers no comparable theory of the subject and has, moreover, differed fiercely with Lacan on the question of mastery and truth (see 'Le facteur de la vérité', in *The Post Card* 1987b; see also note 2, p. 141).

Speech/writing

One line of reflection on the writing of Derrida would take *Of Grammatology* (1976) as its point of departure. There Derrida cites a number of texts that show how often and unreflectingly the Western tradition takes a very partial and common-sense view of the nature of writing and particularly of the relation between speech and writing. Consistently, writers including Aquinas, Hegel, Rousseau and, more recently, Saussure and Lévi-Strauss (see 'Biographical notes'), have privileged speech over writing on the grounds that it is closer to inwardness and thought, and so treated writing as merely a technical derivation from speech, a writing down of what is already there. Speech has been placed as inside with writing outside, in similar terms to the presumed relation of mind and body. For example, Derrida (1976: 11) quotes Aristotle from *De Interpretatione* to the effect that 'spoken words (*ta en tē phonē*) are the symbols of mental experience (*pathēmata tēs psychēs*) and written words are the symbols of spoken words'. Writing is disparaged because it stands for something else of which it is a trace. There is a strong tendency, therefore, to equate being with mind and thought as though thought were fully present to itself, and writing had nothing to do with making meaning possible. This tendency or disposition Derrida names *logocentrism* and regards as forming the very basis for metaphysics, because it thus prioritizes presence. He hopes to see logocentrism yield to something else, a concern with 'archiwriting': that is, in the widest sense, the very *possibility* of writing. To give full weight to writing would be to recognize the dependence of presence on a trace.

Speech/writing stands as a binary opposition, which Derrida offers to *deconstruct* when he argues (among other things) that thought, speech and writing all depend upon representation and the signifier. So it would be possible to begin at the other end, as it were, and propose that 'Writing precedes and follows speech, it comprehends it' (Derrida 1976: 238). But it is not so much writing itself Derrida is concerned with as the condition at work 'inside' writing, which makes it possible, the graphematic. (You might see a neon sign for SHELL with a faulty circuit for the S so that it reads HELL, though a similar chance occurrence might have made it read SHE or HE or S ELL; now, what produced those meanings, the reader or the material system on which the sign relied?)

The method of deconstruction is as important as its consequences. For to deconstruct (in this strict, Derridean sense) is to attend to a traditionally empowered binary hierarchy in which the first term is privileged over the second needed to define it, and then to breach or unsettle that opposition in one way or another (*not* all binary oppositions but those whose hierarchy supports – and is supported by – power). Simply to invert the opposition by privileging the *second* term would retain the power relations exercised in the binary already in place. In *Dissemination* Derrida (1981: 85) lists some oppositions that have sustained the metaphysics of presence in the Western tradition: 'speech/writing, life/death, father/son, master/servant, first/second, legitimate son/orphan-bastard, soul/body, inside/outside, seriousness/play'. And in the essay 'White mythology' (*Margins of Philosophy* (Derrida 1982)) he adds the binary literal/figurative (associated with philosophy/literature), though it would be easy to extend the list as binary oppositions saturate the texts of contemporary culture, high and popular.

Is the most forceful and encompassing binary represented by the hierarchy masculine/feminine, linking all the others? Derrida has certainly encouraged this conclusion, identifying logocentrism with *phallogocentrism* and claiming that 'it is one and the same system: the erection of a paternal logos ... and of the phallus as "privileged signifier"' (Derrida 1973a: 311). If so, 'speech', 'life', 'master', 'first', 'soul', 'inside', 'seriousness' would make up a series that has been qualified as 'masculine', while 'writing', 'death', 'second', 'body', 'outside', 'play' would form another denoted as 'feminine' (a possibility whose implications have been explored by Cixous; see Section 5.2).

Different times

Speech/writing opens one approach to 'Differance'; the question of time broaches another and may help to focus a little what Derrida is writing against (though the very terms 'for' and 'against' suppose a fixed opposition between inside and outside that tempts deconstruction, and in any case it is hard to know how anyone nurtured in the Western tradition today could yet find themselves sufficiently apart from it to be genuinely *against* it). Nevertheless, there is a respect in which the post-Socratic tradition begins with a certain conception of time.

Until recently a watch was a large object carried on a chain slung across the waist, but since the 1920s almost every adult in the West carries time on their wrist, marking off seconds, minutes, hours, days, months in remorseless accumulation. Such a conception of time as an absolute, even, continuous and homogeneous *linearity* has been dominant in the West since Ancient Greece. Implicit in commonplace metaphors of 'the stream of time' or 'the passage of time', this kind of time is thought of as spacelike, as though the now were either a stake driven into the bed of a river (the future flowing by the stake and into the past) or a train crossing the prairies (the lines in front leading to an invisible horizon in the future and those behind to one in the past). Aristotle in his foundational account (*Physics* 217b–224a) envisages the now as a spatio-temporal succession of units, the now always the same but in a different position, for it is the present. Intersected, absolute linear time makes it possible to make confident divisions into points of origin and points of completion in which a potential, already present in the beginning, is realized by the end, with only a middle to separate them: 'My beginning is my end' as T. S. Eliot says in *Four Quartets*.

But if, as Derrida argues (in '*Ousia* and *Gramme*' in *Margins of Philosophy* (1982)), time is thought of (as it should be) not as a kind of space but as time, then the now can no longer be considered as a *point* on a *line*. The now can be defined only by its difference from another now which this now is not. A conception of time as the present must give way to another sense of time as multidimensional, time not as a single line but as something like an uneven bundle of swerves. And further, in that the apparently punctual and present now is a necessary condition for the I to appear to be present to itself as a pure self-consciousness, this view of the subject must also be surrendered.

Differance

In French, as in English, *difference* and *differance* are both pronounced the same, so that, looking almost like a Freudian slip (or lapse), the difference represents what is at issue between speech and writing. 'An interval must separate the present from what it is not in order for the present to be itself, but this interval that constitutes it as present must, by the same token, divide the present in and of itself, thereby also dividing, along with the present, everything that is thought on the basis of the present' (p. 128). An interval separates two things in space as well as two in time; differance presides over such an interval, combining as it does both difference in space and deferral in time. It cannot be defined as 'a concept' because that would commit it in advance to a 'theology of being' ('ontotheology', p. 123), to a metaphysics of pre-sence ('difference is . . .'). Of differance the essay provides three main instances.

The first is Saussurian linguistics, developed as it is from the notion of linguistic value. Whereas we may usually think of value as the property of a thing (and are always disappointed), the value of terms in linguistics, whether one takes signifier or signified, is purely relational, as Saussure explains in a passage Derrida quotes (and see pp. 10–11). Signification supposes both difference and deferral: that meaning is never present (fully formed) in individual signifiers but is produced through a series of differences; that meaning is always temporally deferred, sliding under a chain of signifiers that has no end. (With reference to Saussure, Derrida (1976: 44–73) also recalls his criticism that even Saussure privileges speech over writing.)

If Saussure tends to suggest that the presence of the subject in consciousness is, because of the nature of the differences within the sign, an effect, that view is confirmed by psychoanalysis. In the work of Freud (see Section 5.1) the subject can never be present to itself because drive is always deferred or deflected; for instance, in the way that sexual drive becomes necessarily turned aside into human activities as divergent from a manifestly sexual aim as smoking cigarettes and editing anthologies of cultural criticism. It does so because 'the finding of an object is in fact a refinding of it' (*Standard Edition*, vol. 7: 222): because (for example) through the demands of the Oedipus complex the mother has to be refound in another adult man or woman; because of the split between unconscious and conscious such that (in the same example) the incestuous drive towards the mother becomes repressed, even though it motivates adult love of which an individual will not be fully aware. Insisting on this detour of the pleasure principle, which seeks pleasure and avoids unpleasure, is the reality principle, which modifies the demands of the pleasure principle, postponing impossible satisfactions now in order to achieve more limited pleasures later. But finding/refinding, conscious/unconscious, reality/pleasure principle are not *opposites*, for each is defined dynamically in relation to the other, as are *Eros* and *Thanatos*, the life drives and the death drives in *Beyond the Pleasure Principle* (*Standard Edition*, vol. 18).

In Freud's concept of *Nachträglichkeit* or deferral the sense in which drives consist only of detours and differences appears particularly unsettling. Weaning and the loss of the breast happen at an earlier stage in the infant's physical development than the threat of castration; but once reached, Freud suggests, the earlier experience is reinterpreted retrospectively as an anticipation of the later experience. Deferral defines the way memories are reinterpreted in the light of subsequent experiences so that the subject is constantly and unendingly rearranging its past by retranscribing it in the present. Such examples imply that for the unconscious there can be no absolute point of origin or conclusion, that each origin and conclusion exists only in relation to another and in the difference between them.

The 'ontico-ontological difference' is the distinction Heidegger in *Being and Time* (1962: 10) marks between entities or 'real things' (the 'ontic') and Being (or the 'ontological'). Being is the process, mode or condition of existence that makes entities possible. The first sentence of *Being and Time* says that the question of Being 'has today been forgotten' (p. 2), and the rest of the work seeks to rethink Being in contrast to the logocentric tradition, which, according to Heidegger, since the time of pre-Socratic philosophers such as Heraclitus and Parmenides has disregarded the importance of Being. At the opening of *An Introduction to Metaphysics* Heidegger (1959: 1) tries to reinstate a sense of Being by asking as a fundamental question (borrowed from Leibniz): 'Why are there essents rather than nothing?' ('essents' = 'existents', 'things that are').

Logocentrism admits but seeks to recuperate the difference between Being and beings; for example, in the way that for Plato entities fallen away from the perfected Being of the world of Forms re-aspire to that state. For Heidegger the distinction between Being and beings is like that between 'presencing' and what is present. Being appears as 'presencing' if the now is assumed to be a self-identical spot or point in which consciousness can be present to itself. But since time is not like that, human existence (*Dasein*, 'Being There') can never be present to itself and remains incomplete across a past continuous with a future: thrown by the past into a world it cannot master, Being There projects itself from a present in which it is always contingent and dependent into a future that is only a possibility. Entities are to be defined not by their participation in Being but in their difference from it and from each other (*Differenz* is in fact a Heideggerian term; see Heidegger 1962: 481, fn.). But since Being is not actually present, what can be said about it? If in *Being and Time* Heidegger seems to think he can address Being, in his later work he is clear that he can't, writing Being with a cross through it so that it appears only 'under erasure'.

Derrida's instances – from the order of the sign, the order of the subject and the order of being – may not make his radical import as readily grasped as it might be if thought of in terms of traditional ideas of divinity. Logocentrism and the metaphysics of presence are certainly at work in the Platonism of the Hellenic tradition and in the idea of God in the Judaeo-Christian inheritance. After the visible natural signs (wind, earthquake, fire) and transcending these, God appears to Elijah as 'a still small voice' (1 Kings 19: 12). Or again there is the repeated claim that God is *alpha* and *omega*, absolute origin terminating in a correspondingly absolute end, another reason why Derrida welcomes the insertion of an 'a' into *differance*, which is ' "older" than Being itself' (p. 139). Derrida's task has been to suggest how a transcendental signified is at work, underground, in the post-Renaissance and Enlightenment tradition precisely because it felt so secure that it had purified itself of the idea of God.

A transcendental signified may appear not only in rationalist forms of philosophy but also in its negation. Thus Derrida is concerned to show he is not practising a negative theology (see note 2, p. 141). Cataphatic or positive theology describes what God is (inevitably in terms of human experience: God is love etc.), while apophatic or negative theology says what God is not, and so in the mystical tradition terms such as *emptiness* and *void* have a positive force. For Derrida there is a dilemma here: if he defines *differance* positively (difference is ...) he betrays its nature; if he says it is not presence and Being, he risks attributing to the absence of Being a comparable function to its presence. He is scrupulous, therefore, in working through the writings of Saussure, Freud and Heidegger, to resist the possibility of a nostalgia through which we might think of ourselves as lost or alienated from a sense of Being (which, negatively, would thus continue to be affirmed).

It is fair to ask what might be the consequences of taking on board something of Derrida's philosophically complex argument. What is at stake politically over *differance*?

> It governs nothing, reigns over nothing, and nowhere exercises any authority. It is not announced by any capital letter. Not only is there no kingdom of *differance*, but *differance* instigates the subversion of every kingdom. Which makes it obviously threatening and infallibly dreaded by everything within us that desires a kingdom, the past or future presence of a kingdom (p. 135).

Wherever, within the cultural matrix, power claims privilege for itself in the name of Being, presence, authoritative speech, essential nature, absolute Truth, in sum as pure identity and sameness, then *differance* can be called on to instigate a relativization and subversion of that power. Three domains may particularly invite those strategies. One would be that of gender, whenever masculine and feminine are posed as opposites, self-identical and so the same all the way through. Another would be that of the social formation, particularly nationhood, if it is advanced as pure, not made up of differences. And a third is familiar already, for it is that by which, as Edward Said has shown, Europe ascribes to itself a oneness and fixity in opposition to the differences of 'the Orient'. As someone born in Algeria and writing in Paris in 1968, Derrida is aware of the politics of *differance*.

4.1

Jacques Derrida, 'Differance' (1968)

The verb 'to differ' [*différer*] seems to differ from itself. On the one hand, it indicates difference as distinction, inequality, or discernibility; on the other, it expresses the interposition of delay, the interval of a *spacing* and *temporalizing* that puts off until 'later' what is presently denied, the possible that is presently impossible. Sometimes the *different* and sometimes the *deferred* correspond [in French] to the verb 'to differ.' This correlation, however, is not simply one between act and object, cause and effect, or primordial and derived.

In the one case 'to differ' signifies nonidentity; in the other case it signifies the order of the *same*. Yet there must be a common, although entirely differant[1] [*différante*], root within the sphere that relates the two movements of differing to one another. We provisionally give the name *differance* to this *sameness* which is not *identical*: by the silent writing of its *a*, it has the desired advantage of referring to differing, *both* as spacing/temporalizing and as the movement that structures every dissociation.

As distinct from difference, differance thus points out the irreducibility of temporalizing (which is also temporalization – in transcendental language which is no longer adequate here, this would be called the constitution of primordial temporality – just as the term 'spacing' also includes the constitution of primordial spatiality). Differance is not simply active (any more than it is a subjective accomplishment); it rather indicates the middle voice, it precedes and sets up the opposition between passivity and activity. With its *a*, differance more properly refers to what in classical language would be called the origin or production of differences and the differences between differences, the *play* [*jeu*] of differences. Its locus and operation will therefore be seen wherever speech appeals to difference.

Differance is neither a *word* nor a *concept*. In it, however, we shall see the juncture – rather than the summation – of what has been most decisively inscribed in the thought of what is conveniently called our 'epoch': the difference of forces in Nietzsche, Saussure's principle of semiological difference, differing as the possibility of [neurone] facilitation,[2] impression and delayed effect in Freud, difference as the irreducibility of the trace of the other in Levinas, and the ontic-ontological difference in Heidegger.

Reflection on this last determination of difference will lead us to consider differance as the *strategic* note or connection – relatively or provisionally *privileged* – which indicates the closure of presence, together with the closure of the conceptual order and denomination, a closure that is effected in the functioning of traces.

I SHALL SPEAK, THEN, OF A LETTER – the first one, if we are to believe the alphabet and most of the speculations that have concerned themselves with it.

I shall speak then of the letter *a*, this first letter which it seemed necessary to introduce now and then in writing the word 'difference.' This seemed necessary in the course of writing about writing, and of writing within a writing whose different strokes all pass, in certain respects, through a gross spelling mistake, through a violation of the rules governing writing, violating the law that governs writing and regulates its conventions of propriety. In fact or theory we can always erase or lessen this spelling mistake, and, in each case, while these are analytically different from one another but for practical purposes the same, find it grave, unseemly, or, indeed, supposing the greatest ingenuousness, amusing. Whether or not we care to quietly overlook this infraction, the attention we give it beforehand will allow us to recognize, as though prescribed by some mute irony, the inaudible but displaced character of this literal permutation. We can always act as though this makes no difference. I must say from the start that my account serves less to justify this silent spelling mistake, or still less to excuse it, than to aggravate its obtrusive character.

On the other hand, I must be excused if I refer, at least implicitly, to one or another of the texts that I have ventured to publish. Precisely what I would like to attempt to some extent (although this is in principle and in its highest degree impossible, due to essential *de jure* reasons) is to bring together an *assemblage* of the different ways I have been able to utilize – or, rather, have allowed to be imposed on me – what I will provisionally call the word or concept of differance in its new spelling. It is literally neither a word nor a concept, as we shall see. I insist on the word 'assemblage' here for two reasons: on the one hand, it is not a matter of describing a history, of recounting the steps, text by text, context by context, each time showing which scheme has been able to impose this graphic disorder, although this could have been done as well; rather, we are concerned with the *general system of all these schemata*. On the other hand, the word 'assemblage' seems more apt for suggesting that the kind of bringing-together proposed here has the structure of an interlacing, a weaving, or a web, which would allow the different threads and different lines of sense or force to separate again, as well as being ready to bind others together.

In a quite preliminary way, we now recall that this particular graphic intervention was conceived in the writing-up of a question about writing; it was not made simply to shock the reader or grammarian. Now, in point of fact, it happens that this graphic difference (the *a* instead of the *e*), this marked difference between two apparently vocalic notations, between vowels, remains purely graphic: it is written or read, but it is not heard. It cannot be heard, and we shall see in what respects it is also beyond the order of understanding. It is put forward by a silent mark, by a tacit monument, or, one might even say, by a pyramid – keeping in mind not only the capital form of the printed letter but also that passage from Hegel's *Encyclopaedia*

where he compares the body of the sign to an Egyptian pyramid. The *a* of differance, therefore, is not heard; it remains silent, secret, and discreet, like a tomb.[3]

It is a tomb that (provided one knows how to decipher its legend) is not far
from signaling the death of the king.

It is a tomb that cannot even be made to resonate. For I cannot even let you
know, by my talk, now being spoken before the Société Française de Philosophie,
which difference I am talking about at the very moment I speak of it. I can only talk
about this graphic difference by keeping to a very indirect speech about writing, and
on the condition that I specify each time that I am referring to difference with an *e*
or difference with an *a*. All of which is not going to simplify matters today, and will
give us all a great deal of trouble when we want to understand one another. In any
event, when I do specify which difference I mean – when I say 'with an *e*' or 'with an
a' – this will refer irreducibly to a *written text*, a text governing my talk, a text that I
keep in front of me, that I will read, and toward which I shall have to try to lead
your hands and eyes. We cannot refrain here from going by way of a written text,
from ordering ourselves by the disorder that is produced therein – and this is what
matters to me first of all.

Doubtless this pyramidal silence of the graphic difference between the *e* and the
a can function only within the system of phonetic writing and within a language or
grammar historically tied to phonetic writing and to the whole culture which is
inseparable from it. But I will say that it is just this – this silence that functions only
within what is called phonetic writing – that points out or reminds us in a very
opportune way that, contrary to an enormous prejudice, there is no phonetic
writing. There is no purely and strictly phonetic writing. What is called phonetic
writing can only function – in principle and *de jure*, and not due to some factual and
technical inadequacy – by incorporating nonphonetic 'signs' (punctuation, spacing,
etc.); but when we examine their structure and necessity, we will quickly see that
they are ill described by the concept of signs. Saussure had only to remind us that
the play of difference was the functional condition, the condition of possibility, for
every sign; and it is itself silent. The difference between two phonemes, which
enables them to exist and to operate, is inaudible. The inaudible opens the two
present phonemes to hearing, as they present themselves. If, then, there is no purely
phonetic writing, it is because there is no purely phonetic phone. The difference
that brings out phonemes and lets them be heard and understood [*entendre*] itself
remains inaudible.

It will perhaps be objected that, for the same reasons, the graphic difference
itself sinks into darkness, that it never constitutes the fullness of a sensible term, but
draws out an invisible connection, the mark of an inapparent relation between two
spectacles. That is no doubt true. Indeed, since from this point of view the difference between the *e* and the *a* marked in 'differance' eludes vision and hearing,
this happily suggests that we must here let ourselves be referred to an order that no
longer refers to sensibility. But we are not referred to intelligibility either, to an
ideality not fortuitously associated with the objectivity of *theōrein* or understanding.
We must be referred to an order, then, that resists philosophy's founding opposition between the sensible and the intelligible. The order that resists this opposition,
that resists it because it sustains it, is designated in a movement of differance (with

an *a*) between two differences or between two letters. This differance belongs neither to the voice nor to writing in the ordinary sense, and it takes place, like the strange space that will assemble us here for the course of an hour, *between* speech and writing and beyond the tranquil familiarity that binds us to one and to the other, reassuring us sometimes in the illusion that they are two separate things.

NOW, HOW AM I TO SPEAK OF the *a* of differance? It is clear that it cannot be *exposed*. We can expose only what, at a certain moment, can become *present*, manifest; what can be shown, presented as a present, a being-present in its truth, the truth of a present or the presence of a present. However, if differance [is] (I also cross out the 'is') what makes the presentation of being-present possible, it never presents itself as such. It is never given in the present or to anyone. Holding back and not exposing itself, it goes beyond the order of truth on this specific point and in this determined way, yet is not itself concealed, as if it were something, a mysterious being, in the occult zone of a nonknowing. Any exposition would expose it to disappearing as a disappearance. It would risk appearing, thus disappearing.

Thus, the detours, phrases, and syntax that I shall often have to resort to will resemble – will sometimes be practically indiscernible from – those of negative theology. Already we had to note *that* differance *is not*, does not exist, and is not any sort of being-present (*on*). And we will have to point out everything *that* it *is not*, and, consequently, that it has neither existence nor essence. It belongs to no category of being, present or absent. And yet what is thus denoted as differance is not theological, not even in the most negative order of negative theology. The latter, as we know, is always occupied with letting a supraessential reality go beyond the finite categories of essence and existence, that is, of presence, and always hastens to remind us that, if we deny the predicate of existence to God, it is in order to recognize him as a superior, inconceivable, and ineffable mode of being. Here there is no question of such a move, as will be confirmed as we go along. Not only is differance irreducible to every ontological or theological – onto-theological – reappropriation, but it opens up the very space in which onto-theology – philosophy – produces its system and its history. It thus encompasses and irrevocably surpasses onto-theology or philosophy.

For the same reason, I do not know where *to begin* to mark out this assemblage, this graph, of differance. Precisely what is in question here is the requirement that there be a *de jure* commencement, an absolute point of departure, a responsibility arising from a principle. The problem of writing opens by questioning the *archē*. Thus what I put forth here will not be developed simply as a philosophical discourse that operates on the basis of a principle, of postulates, axioms, and definitions and that moves according to the discursive line of a rational order. In marking out differance, everything is a matter of strategy and risk. It is a question of strategy because no transcendent truth present outside the sphere of writing can theologically command the totality of this field. It is hazardous because this strategy is not simply one in the sense that we say that strategy orients the tactics according to a final aim, a *telos* or the theme of a domination, a mastery or an ultimate reappropriation of movement and field. In the end, it is a strategy without finality. We might call it blind tactics or empirical errance, if the value of empiricism did not itself derive all its meaning from its opposition to philosophical responsibility. If there is a certain errance in the tracing-out of differance, it no longer follows the line of logico-philosophical speech or that of its integral and symmetrical opposite, logico-empirical speech. The concept of *play* [*jeu*] remains beyond this opposition; on the eve and aftermath of philosophy, it designates the unity of chance and necessity in an endless calculus.

By decision and, as it were, by the rules of the game, then, turning this thought around, let us introduce ourselves to the thought of differance by way of the theme of strategy or strategem. By this merely strategic justification, I want to emphasize that the efficacy of this thematics of differance very well may, and even one day must, be sublated, i.e., lend itself, if not to its own replacement, at least to its involvement in a series of events which in fact it never commanded. This also means that it is not a theological thematics.

I will say, first of all, that differance, which is neither a word nor a concept, seemed to me to be strategically the theme most proper to think out, if not master (thought being here, perhaps, held in a certain necessary relation with the structional limits of mastery), in what is most characteristic of our 'epoch.' I start off, then, strategically, from the place and time in which 'we' are, even though my opening is not justifiable in the final account, and though it is always on the basis of differance and its 'history' that we can claim to know who and where 'we' are and what the limits of an 'epoch' can be.

Although 'differance' is neither a word nor a concept, let us nonetheless attempt a simple and approximative semantic analysis which will bring us in view of what is at stake [*en vue de l'enjeu*].

We do know that the verb 'to differ' [*différer*] (the Latin verb *differre*) has two seemingly quite distinct meanings; in the *Littré* dictionary, for example, they are the subject of two separate articles. In this sense, the Latin *differre* is not the simple translation of the Greek *diapherein*; this fact will not be without consequence for us in tying our discussion to a particular language, one that passes for being less philosophical, less primordially philosophical, than the other. For the distribution of sense in the Greek *diapherein* does not carry one of the two themes of the Latin *differre*, namely, the action of postponing until later, of taking into account, the taking-account of time and forces in an operation that implies an economic reckoning, a detour, a respite, a delay, a reserve, a representation – all the concepts that I will sum up here in a word I have never used but which could be added to this series: *temporalizing*. 'To differ' in this sense is to temporalize, to resort, consciously or unconsciously, to the temporal and temporalizing mediation of a detour that suspends the accomplishment or fulfillment of 'desire' or 'will,' or carries desire or will out in a way that annuls or tempers their effect. We shall see, later, in what respects this temporalizing is also a temporalization and spacing, is space's becoming-temporal and time's becoming-spatial, is 'primordial constitution' of space and time, as metaphysics or transcendental phenomenology would call it in the language that is here criticized and displaced.

The other sense of 'to differ' [*différer*] is the most common and most identifiable, the sense of not being identical, of being other, of being discernible, etc. And in 'differents,' whether referring to the alterity of dissimilarity or the alterity of allergy or of polemics, it is necessary that interval, distance, *spacing* occur among the different elements and occur actively, dynamically, and with a certain perseverence in repetition.

But the word 'difference' (with an *e*) could never refer to differing as temporalizing or to difference as *polemos*. It is this loss of sense that the word differance (with an *a*) will have to schematically compensate for. Differance can refer to the whole complex of its meanings at once, for it is immediately and irreducibly multivalent, something which will be important for the discourse I am trying to develop. It refers to this whole complex of meanings not only when it is supported by a language or interpretive context (like any signification), but it already does so somehow of itself. Or at least it does so more easily by itself than does any other word: here the *a* comes more immediately from the present participle [*différant*] and brings us closer to the action of 'differing' that is in progress, even before it has produced the effect that is constituted as different or resulted in difference (with an *e*). Within a conceptual system and in terms of classical requirements, differance could be said to designate the productive and primordial constituting causality, the process of scission and division whose differings and differences would be the constituted products or effects. But while bringing us closer to the infinitive and active core of differing, 'differance' with an *a* neutralizes what the infinitive denotes as simply active, in the same way that 'parlance' does not signify the simple fact of speaking, of speaking to or being spoken to. Nor is resonance the act of resonating. Here in the usage of our language we must consider that the ending *-ance* is undecided between active and passive. And we shall see why what is designated by 'differance' is neither simply active nor simply passive, that it announces or rather recalls something like the middle voice, that it speaks of an operation which is not an operation, which cannot be thought of either as a passion or as an action of a subject upon an object, as starting from an agent or from a patient, or on the basis of, or in view of, any of these *terms*. But philosophy has perhaps commenced by distributing the middle voice, expressing a certain intransitiveness, into the active and the passive voice, and has itself been constituted in this repression.

How are differance as temporalizing and differance as spacing conjoined?

Let us begin with the problem of signs and writing – since we are already in the midst of it. We ordinarily say that a sign is put in place of the thing itself, the present thing – 'thing' holding here for the sense as well as the referent. Signs represent the present in its absence; they take the place of the present. When we cannot take hold of or show the thing, let us say the present, the being-present, when the present does not present itself, then we signify, we go through the detour of signs. We take up or give signs; we make signs. The sign would thus be a deferred presence. Whether it is a question of verbal or written signs, monetary signs, electoral delegates, or political representatives, the movement of signs defers the moment of encountering the thing itself, the moment at which we could lay hold of it, consume or expend it, touch it, see it, have a present intuition of it. What I am describing here is the structure of signs as classically determined, in order to define – through a commonplace characterization of its traits – signification as the differance of temporalizing. Now this classical determination presupposes that the sign (which defers presence) is conceivable only *on the basis of* the presence that it defers and *in view of* the deferred presence one intends to reappropriate. Following this classical semiology, the substitution of the sign for the thing itself is both *secondary* and *provisional:* it is second in order after an original and lost presence, a presence from which the sign would be derived. It is provisional with respect to this final and missing presence, in view of which the sign would serve as a movement of mediation.

In attempting to examine these secondary and provisional aspects of the substitute, we shall no doubt catch sight of something like a primordial differance. Yet we could no longer even call it primordial or final, inasmuch as the characteristics of origin, beginning, *telos, eschaton,* etc., have always denoted presence – *ousia, parousia,* etc. To question the secondary and provisional character of the sign, to oppose it to a 'primordial' differance, would thus have the following consequences:

1   Differance can no longer be understood according to the concept of 'sign,' which has always been taken to mean the representation of a presence and has been constituted in a system (of thought or language) determined on the basis of and in view of presence.

2   In this way we question the authority of presence or its simple symmetrical contrary, absence or lack. We thus interrogate the limit that has always constrained us, that always constrains us – we who inhabit a language and a system of thought – to form the sense of being in general as presence or absence, in the categories of being or beingness (*ousia*). It already appears that the kind of questioning we are thus led back to is, let us say, the Heideggerian kind, and that differance *seems* to lead us back to the ontic-ontological difference. But permit me to postpone this reference. I shall only note that between differance as temporalizing-temporalization (which we can no longer conceive within the horizon of the present) and what Heidegger says about temporalization in *Sein und Zeit* (namely, that as the transcendental horizon of the question of being it must be freed from the traditional and metaphysical domination by the present or the now) – between these two there is a close, if not exhaustive and irreducibly necessary, interconnection.

But first of all, let us remain with the semiological aspects of the problem to see how differance as temporalizing is conjoined with differance as spacing. Most of the semiological or linguistic research currently dominating the field of thought (whether due to the results of its own investigations or due to its role as a generally recognized regulative model) traces its genealogy, rightly or wrongly, to Saussure as its common founder. It was Saussure who first of all set forth the *arbitrariness of signs* and the *differential character* of signs as principles of general semiology and particularly of linguistics. And, as we know, these two themes – the arbitrary and the differential – are in his view inseparable. Arbitrariness can occur only because the system of signs is constituted by the differences between the terms, and not by their fullness. The elements of signification function not by virtue of the compact force of their cores but by the network of oppositions that distinguish them and relate them to one another. 'Arbitrary and differential' says Saussure 'are two correlative qualities.'

As the condition for signification, this principle of difference affects the *whole sign,* that is, both the signified and the signifying aspects. The signified aspect is the concept, the ideal sense. The signifying aspect is what Saussure calls the material or physical (e.g., acoustical) 'image.' We do not here have to enter into all the problems these definitions pose. Let us only cite Saussure where it interests us:

> The conceptual side of value is made up solely of relations and differences with respect to the other terms of language, and the same can be said of its material side. ... Everything that has been said up to this point boils down to this: in language there are only differences. Even more important: a difference generally implies positive terms between which the difference is set up; but in language there are only differences *without positive terms*. Whether we take the signified or the signifier, language has neither ideas nor sounds that existed before the linguistic system, but only conceptual and phonic differences that have issued from the system. The idea or phonic substance that a sign contains is of less importance than the other signs that surround it.[4]

The first consequence to be drawn from this is that the signified concept is never present in itself, in an adequate presence that would refer only to itself. Every concept is necessarily and essentially inscribed in a chain or a system, within which it refers to another and to other concepts, by the systematic play of differences. Such a play, then – differance – is no longer simply a concept, but the possibility of conceptuality, of the conceptual system and process in general. For the same reason, differance, which is not a concept, is not a mere word; that is, it is not what we represent to ourselves as the calm and present self-referential unity of a concept and sound [*phonie*]. We shall later discuss the consequences of this for the notion of a word.

The difference that Saussure speaks about, therefore, is neither itself a concept nor one word among others. We can say this *a fortiori* for differance. Thus we are brought to make the relation between the one and the other explicit.

Within a language, within the *system* of language, there are only differences. A taxonomic operation can accordingly undertake its systematic, statistical, and classificatory inventory. But, on the one hand, these differences *play a role* in language, in speech as well, and in the exchange between language and speech. On the other hand, these differences are themselves *effects*. They have not fallen from the sky ready made; they are no more inscribed in a *topos noētos* than they are prescribed in the wax of the brain. If the word 'history' did not carry with it the theme of a final repression of differance, we could say that differences alone could be 'historical' through and through and from the start.

What we note as *differance* will thus be the movement of play that 'produces' (and not by something that is simply an activity) these differences, these effects of difference. This does not mean that the differance which produces differences is before them in a simple and in itself unmodified and indifferent present. Differance is the nonfull, nonsimple 'origin'; it is the structured and differing origin of differences.

Since language (which Saussure says is a classification) has not fallen from the sky, it is clear that the differences have been produced; they are the effects produced, but effects that do not have as their cause a subject or substance, a thing in general, or a being that is somewhere present and itself escapes the play of difference. If such a presence were implied (quite classically) in the general concept of cause, we would therefore have to talk about an effect without a cause, something that would very quickly lead to no longer talking about effects. I have tried to indicate a way out of the closure imposed by this system, namely, by means of the 'trace.' No more an effect than a cause, the 'trace' cannot of itself, taken outside its context, suffice to bring about the required transgression.

As there is no presence before the semiological difference or outside it, we can extend what Saussure writes about language to signs in general: 'Language is necessary in order for speech to be intelligible and to produce all of its effects; but the latter is necessary in order for language to be established; historically, the fact of speech always comes first.'[5]

Retaining at least the schema, if not the content, of the demand formulated by Saussure, we shall designate by the term *differance* the movement by which language, or any code, any system of reference in general, becomes 'historically' constituted as a fabric of differences. Here, the terms 'constituted,' 'produced,' 'created,' 'movement,' 'historically,' etc., with all they imply, are not to be understood only in terms of the language of metaphysics, from which they are taken. It would have to be shown why the concepts of production, like those of constitution and history, remain accessories in this respect to what is here being questioned; this, however, would draw us too far away today, toward the theory of the representation of the 'circle' in which we seem to be enclosed. I only use these terms here, like many other concepts, out of strategic convenience and in order to prepare the deconstruction of the system they form at the point which is now most decisive. In any event, we will have understood, by virtue of the very circle we appear to be caught up in, that differance, as it is written here, is no more static than genetic, no more structural than historical. Nor is it any less so. And it is completely to miss the point of this orthographical impropriety to want to object to it on the basis of the oldest of metaphysical oppositions – for example, by opposing some generative point of view to a structuralist-taxonomic point of view, or conversely. These oppositions do not pertain in the least to differance; and this, no doubt, is what makes thinking about it difficult and uncomfortable.

If we now consider the chain to which 'differance' gets subjected, according to the context, to a certain number of nonsynonymic substitutions, one will ask why we resorted to such concepts as 'reserve,' 'protowriting,' 'prototrace,' 'spacing,' indeed to 'supplement' or '*pharmakon*,' and, before long, to 'hymen,' etc.[6]

Let us begin again. Differance is what makes the movement of signification possible only if each element that is said to be 'present,' appearing on the stage of presence, is related to something other than itself but retains the mark of a past element and already lets itself be hollowed out by the mark of its relation to a future element. This trace relates no less to what is called the future than to what is called the past, and it constitutes what is called the present by this very relation to what it is not, to what it absolutely is not; that is, not even to a past or future considered as a modified present. In order for it to be, an interval must separate it from what it is not; but the interval that constitutes it in the present must also, and by the same token, divide the present in itself, thus dividing, along with the present, everything that can be conceived on its basis, that is, every being – in particular, for our metaphysical language, the substance or subject. Constituting itself, dynamically dividing itself, this interval is what could be called *spacing*; time's becoming-spatial or space's becoming-temporal (*temporalizing*). And it is this constitution of the present as a 'primordial' and irreducibly nonsimple, and, therefore, in the strict sense nonprimordial, synthesis of traces, retentions, and protentions (to reproduce here, analogically and provisionally, a phenomenological and transcendental language that will presently be revealed as inadequate) that I propose to call proto-writing, prototrace, or differance. The latter (is) (both) spacing (and) temporalizing.[7]

Given this (active) movement of the (production of) differance without origin, could we not, quite simply and without any neographism, call it *differentiation*? Among other confusions, such a word would suggest some organic unity, some primordial and homogeneous unity, that would eventually come to be divided up and take on difference as an event. Above all, formed on the verb 'to differentiate,' this word would annul the economic signification of detour, temporalizing delay, 'deferring.' I owe a remark in passing to a recent reading of one of Koyré's texts entitled 'Hegel at Jena.'[8] In that text, Koyré cites long passages from the Jena *Logic* in German and gives his own translation. On two occasions in Hegel's text he encounters the expression '*differente Beziehung.*' This word (*different*), whose root is Latin, is extremely rare in German and also, I believe, in Hegel, who instead uses *verschieden* or *ungleich*, calling difference *Unterschied* and qualitative variety *Verschiedenheit*. In the Jena *Logic*, he uses the word *different* precisely at the point where he deals with time and the present. Before coming to Koyré's valuable remark, here are some passages from Hegel, as rendered by Koyré:

> The infinite, in this simplicity is – as a moment opposed to the self-identical –
> the negative. In its moments, while the infinite presents the totality to (itself)
> and in itself, (it is) excluding in general, the point or limit; but in this, its own
> (action of) negating, it relates itself immediately to the other and negates itself.
> The limit or moment of the present (*der Gegen-wart*), the absolute 'this' of time
> or the now, is an absolutely negative simplicity, absolutely excluding all mul-
> tiplicity from itself, and by this very fact is absolutely determined; it is not an
> extended whole or *quantum* within itself (and) which would in itself also have
> an undetermined aspect or qualitative variety, which of itself would be related,
> indifferently (*gleichgültig*) or externally to another, but on the contrary, this is an
> absolutely different relation of the simple.[9]

And Koyré specifies in a striking note: 'Different relation: *differente Beziehung*. We could say: differentiating relation.' And on the following page, from another text of Hegel, we can read: '*Diese Beziehung ist Gegenwart, als eine differente Beziehung*' (This relation is [the] present, as a different relation). There is another note by Koyré: 'The term "*different*" is taken here in an active sense.'

Writing 'differing' or 'differance' (with an *a*) would have had the utility of making it possible to translate Hegel on precisely this point with no further quali-fications – and it is a quite decisive point in his text. The translation would be, as it always should be, the transformation of one language by another. Naturally, I maintain that the word 'differance' can be used in other ways, too; first of all, because it denotes not only the activity of primordial difference but also the temporalizing detour of deferring. It has, however, an even more important usage. Despite the very profound affinities that differance thus written has with Hegelian speech (as it should be read), it can, at a certain point, not exactly break with it, but rather work a sort of displacement with regard to it. A definite rupture with Hegelian language would make no sense, nor would it be at all likely; but this displacement is both infinitesimal and radical. I have tried to indicate the extent of this displacement elsewhere; it would be difficult to talk about it with any brevity at this point.

Differences are thus 'produced' – differed – by differance. But *what* differs, or *who* differs? In other words, *what is* differance? With this question we attain another stage and another source of the problem.

What differs? Who differs? What is differance?

If we answered these questions even before examining them as questions, even before going back over them and questioning their form (even what seems to be most natural and necessary about them), we would fall below the level we have now reached. For if we accepted the form of the question in its own sense and syntax ('What?,' 'What is?,' 'Who is?'), we would have to admit that differance is derived, supervenient, controlled, and ordered from the starting point of a being-present, one capable of being something, a force, a state, or power in the world, to which we could give all kinds of names: a *what*, or being-present as a *subject*, a *who*. In the latter case, notably, we would implicitly admit that the being-present (for example, as a self-present being or consciousness) would eventually result in differing: in delaying or in diverting the fulfillment of a 'need' or 'desire,' or in differing from itself. But in none of these cases would such a being-present be 'constituted' by this differance.

Now if we once again refer to the semiological difference, what was it that Saussure in particular reminded us of? That 'language [which consists only of differences] is not a function of the speaking subject.' This implies that the subject (self-identical or even conscious of self-identity, self-conscious) is inscribed in the language, that he is a 'function' of the language. He becomes a *speaking* subject only by conforming his speech – even in the aforesaid 'creation,' even in the aforesaid 'transgression' – to the system of linguistic prescriptions taken as the system of differences, or at least to the general law of differance, by conforming to that law of language which Saussure calls 'language without speech.' 'Language is necessary for the spoken word to be intelligible and so that it can produce all of its effects.'[10]

If, by hypothesis, we maintain the strict opposition between speech and language, then differance will be not only the play of differences within the language but the relation of speech to language, the detour by which I must also pass in order to speak, the silent token I must give, which holds just as well for linguistics in the strict sense as it does for general semiology; it dictates all the relations between usage and the formal schema, between the message and the particular code, etc. Elsewhere I have tried to suggest that this differance within language, and in the relation between speech and language, forbids the essential dissociation between speech and writing that Saussure, in keeping with tradition, wanted to draw at another level of his presentation. The use of language or the employment of any code which implies a play of forms – with no determined or invariable substratum – also presupposes a retention and protention of differences, a spacing and temporalizing, a play of traces. This play must be a sort of inscription prior to writing, a protowriting without a present origin, without an *archē*. From this comes the systematic crossing-out of the *archē* and the transformation of general semiology into a grammatology, the latter performing a critical work upon everything within semiology – right down to its matrical concept of signs – that retains any metaphysical presuppositions incompatible with the theme of differance.

We might be tempted by an objection: to be sure, the subject becomes a *speaking* subject only by dealing with the system of linguistic differences; or again, he becomes a *signifying* subject (generally by speech or other signs) only by entering into the system of differences. In this sense, certainly, the speaking or signifying subject would not be self-present, insofar as he speaks or signifies, except for the play of linguistic or semiological differance. But can we not conceive of a presence and self-presence of the subject before speech or its signs, a subject's self-presence in a silent and intuitive consciousness?

Such a question therefore supposes that prior to signs and outside them, and excluding every trace and differance, something such as consciousness is possible. It supposes, moreover, that, even before the distribution of its signs in space and in the world, consciousness can gather itself up in its own presence. What then is consciousness? What does 'consciousness' mean? Most often in the very form of 'meaning' ['*vouloir-dire*'], consciousness in all its modifications is conceivable only as self-presence, a self-perception of presence. And what holds for consciousness also holds here for what is called subjective existence in general. Just as the category of subject is not and never has been conceivable without reference to presence as *hypokeimenon* or *ousia*, etc., so the subject as consciousness has never been able to be evinced otherwise than as self-presence. The privilege accorded to consciousness thus means a privilege accorded to the present; and even if the transcendental temporality of consciousness is described in depth, as Husserl described it, the power of synthesis and of the incessant gathering-up of traces is always accorded to the 'living present.'

This privilege is the ether of metaphysics, the very element of our thought insofar as it is caught up in the language of metaphysics. We can only de-limit such a closure today by evoking this import of presence, which Heidegger has shown to be the onto-theological determination of being. Therefore, in evoking this import of presence, by an examination which would have to be of a quite peculiar nature, we question the absolute privilege of this form or epoch of presence in general, that is, consciousness as meaning [*vouloir-dire*] in self-presence.

We thus come to posit presence – and, in particular, consciousness, the being-next-to-itself of consciousness – no longer as the absolutely matrical form of being but as a 'determination' and an 'effect.' Presence is a determination and effect within a system which is no longer that of presence but that of differance; it no more allows the opposition between activity and passivity than that between cause and effect or in-determination and determination, etc. This system is of such a kind that even to designate consciousness as an effect or determination – for strategic reasons, reasons that can be more or less clearly considered and systematically ascertained – is to continue to operate according to the vocabulary of that very thing to be de-limited.

Before being so radically and expressly Heideggerian, this was also Nietzsche's and Freud's move, both of whom, as we know, and often in a very similar way, questioned the self-assured certitude of consciousness. And is it not remarkable that both of them did this by starting out with the theme of differance?

This theme appears almost literally in their work, at the most crucial places. I shall not expand on this here; I shall only recall that for Nietzsche 'the important main activity is unconscious' and that consciousness is the effect of forces whose essence, ways, and modalities are not peculiar to it. Now force itself is never present; it is only a play of differences and quantities. There would be no force in general without the difference between forces; and here the difference in quantity counts more than the content of quantity, more than the absolute magnitude itself.

> Quantity itself therefore is not separable from the difference in quantity. The difference in quantity is the essence of force, the relation of force with force. To fancy two equal forces, even if we grant them opposing directions, is an approximate and crude illusion, a statistical dream in which life is immersed, but which chemistry dispels.[11]

Is not the whole thought of Nietzsche a critique of philosophy as active indifference to difference, as a system of reduction or adiaphoristic repression? Following the same logic – logic itself – this does not exclude the fact that philosophy lives *in* and *from* differance, that it thereby blinds itself to the *same*, which is not the identical. The same is precisely differance (with an *a*), as the diverted and equivocal passage from one difference to another, from one term of the opposition to the other. We could thus take up all the coupled oppositions on which philosophy is constructed, and from which our language lives, not in order to see opposition vanish but to see the emergence of a necessity such that one of the terms appears as the differance of the other, the other as 'differed' within the systematic ordering of the same (e.g., the intelligible as differing from the sensible, as sensible differed; the concept as differed-differing intuition, life as differing-differed matter; mind as differed-differing life; culture as differed-differing nature; and all the terms designating what is other than *physis* – *technē, nomos*, society, freedom, history, spirit, etc. – as *physis* differed or *physis* differing: *physis in differance*). It is out of the unfolding of this 'same' as differance that the sameness of difference and of repetition is presented in the eternal return.

In Nietzsche, these are so many themes that can be related with the kind of symptomatology that always serves to diagnose the evasions and ruses of anything disguised in its differance. Or again, these terms can be related with the entire thematics of active interpretation, which substitutes an incessant deciphering for the disclosure of truth as a presentation of the thing itself in its presence, etc. What results is a cipher without truth, or at least a system of ciphers that is not dominated by truth value, which only then becomes a function that is understood, inscribed, and circumscribed.

We shall therefore call differance this 'active' (in movement) discord of the different forces and of the differences between forces which Nietzsche opposes to the entire system of metaphysical grammar, wherever that system controls culture, philosophy, and science.

It is historically significant that this diaphoristics, understood as an energetics or an economy of forces, set up to question the primacy of presence qua consciousness, is also the major theme of Freud's thought; in his work we find another diaphoristics, both in the form of a theory of ciphers or traces and an energetics. The questioning of the authority of consciousness is first and always differential.

The two apparently different meanings of differance are tied together in Freudian theory: differing [*le différer*] as discernibility, distinction, deviation, diastem, *spacing*; and deferring [*le différer*] as detour, delay, relay, reserve, *temporalizing*. I shall recall only that:

1   The concept of trace (*Spur*), of facilitation (*Bahnung*), of forces of facilitation are, as early as the composition of the *Entwurf*, inseparable from the concept of difference. The origin of memory and of the psyche as a memory in general (conscious or unconscious) can only be described by taking into account the difference between the facilitation thresholds, as Freud says explicitly. There is no facilitation [*Bahnung*] without difference and no difference without a trace.

2   All the differences involved in the production of unconscious traces and in the process of inscription (*Niederschrift*) can also be interpreted as moments of differance, in the sense of 'placing on reserve.' Following a schema that continually guides Freud's thinking, the movement of the trace is described as an effort of life to protect itself *by deferring* the dangerous investment, by constituting a reserve (*Vorrat*). And all the conceptual oppositions that furrow Freudian thought relate each concept to the other like movements of a detour, within the economy of differance. The one is only the other deferred, the one differing from the other. The one is the other in differance, the one is the differance from the other. Every apparently rigorous and irreducible opposition (for example, that between the secondary and primary) is thus said to be, at one time or another, a 'theoretical fiction.' In this way again, for example (but such an example covers everything or communicates with everything), the difference between the pleasure principle and the reality principle is only differance as detour (*Aufschieben, Aufschub*). In *Beyond the Pleasure Principle*, Freud writes:

Under the influence of the ego's instincts of self-preservation, the pleasure principle is replaced by the reality principle. This latter principle does not abandon the intention of ultimately obtaining pleasure, but it nevertheless demands and carries into effect the postponement of satisfaction, the abandonment of a number of possibilities of gaining satisfaction and the temporary toleration of unpleasure as a step on the long indirect road (*Aufschub*) to pleasure.[12]

Here we touch on the point of greatest obscurity, on the very enigma of differance, on how the concept we have of it is divided by a strange separation. We must not hasten to make a decision too quickly. How can we conceive of differance as a systematic detour which, within the element of the same, always aims at either finding again the pleasure or the presence that had been deferred by (conscious or unconscious) calculation, and, *at the same time,* how can we, on the other hand, conceive of differance as the relation to an impossible presence, as an expenditure without reserve, as an irreparable loss of presence, an irreversible wearing-down of energy, or indeed as a death instinct and a relation to the absolutely other that apparently breaks up any economy? It is evident – it is evidence itself – that system and nonsystem, the same and the absolutely other, etc., cannot be conceived *together.*

If differance is this inconceivable factor, must we not perhaps hasten to make it evident, to bring it into the philosophical element of evidence, and thus quickly dissipate its mirage character and illogicality, dissipate it with the infallibility of the calculus we know well – since we have recognized its place, necessity, and function within the structure of differance? What would be accounted for philosophically here has already been taken into account in the system of differance as it is here being calculated. I have tried elsewhere, in a reading of Bataille,[13] to indicate what might be the establishment of a rigorous, and in a new sense 'scientific,' *relating* of a 'restricted economy' – one having nothing to do with an unreserved expenditure, with death, with being exposed to nonsense, etc. – to a 'general economy' or system that, so to speak, *takes account of* what is unreserved. It is a relation between a difference that is accounted for and a difference that fails to be accounted for, where the establishment of a pure presence, without loss, is one with the occurrence of absolute loss, with death. By establishing this relation between a restricted and a general system, we shift and recommence the very project of philosophy under the privileged heading of Hegelianism.

The economic character of differance in no way implies that the deferred presence can always be recovered, that it simply amounts to an investment that only temporarily and without loss delays the presentation of presence, that is, the per-ception of gain or the gain of perception. Contrary to the metaphysical, dialectical, and 'Hegelian' interpretation of the economic movement of differance, we must admit a game where whoever loses wins and where one wins and loses each time. If the diverted presentation continues to be somehow definitively and irreducibly withheld, this is not because a particular present remains hidden or absent, but because differance holds us in a relation with what exceeds (though we necessarily fail to recognize this) the alternative of presence or absence. A certain alterity – Freud gives it a metaphysical name, the unconscious – is definitively taken away from every process of presentation in which we would demand for it to be shown forth in person. In this context and under this heading, the unconscious is not, as we know, a hidden, virtual, and potential self-presence. It is differed – which no doubt means that it is woven out of differences, but also that it sends out, that it delegates, representatives or proxies; but there is no chance that the mandating subject 'exists' somewhere, that it is present or is 'itself,' and still less chance that it will become conscious. In this sense, contrary to the terms of an old debate, strongly symptomatic of the metaphysical investments it has always assumed, the 'unconscious' can no more be classed as a 'thing' than as anything else; it is no more of a thing than an implicit or masked consciousness. This radical alterity, removed from every possible mode of presence, is characterized by irreducible aftereffects, by delayed effects. In order to describe them, in order to read the traces of the 'unconscious' traces (there are no 'conscious' traces), the language of presence or absence, the metaphysical speech of phenomenology, is in principle inadequate.

The structure of delay (*retardement: Nachträglichkeit*) that Freud talks about indeed prohibits our taking temporalization (temporalizing) to be a simple dialectical complication of the present; rather, this is the style of transcendental phenomenology. It describes the living present as a primordial and incessant synthesis that is constantly led back upon itself, back upon its assembled and assembling self, by retentional traces and protentional openings. With the alterity of the 'unconscious,' we have to deal not with the horizons of modified presents – past or future – but with a 'past' that has never been nor will ever be present, whose 'future' will never be produced or reproduced in the form of presence. The concept of trace is therefore incommensurate with that of retention, that of the becoming-past of what had been present. The trace cannot be conceived – nor, therefore, can differance – on the basis of either the present or the presence of the present.

A past that has never been present: with this formula Emmanuel Levinas designates (in ways that are, to be sure, not those of psychoanalysis) the trace and the enigma of absolute alterity, that is, the Other [*autrui*]. At least within these limits, and from this point of view, the thought of differance implies the whole critique of classical ontology undertaken by Levinas. And the concept of trace, like that of differance, forms – across these different traces and through these differences between traces, as understood by Nietzsche, Freud, and Levinas (these 'authors' names' serve only as indications) – the network that sums up and permeates our 'epoch' as the de-limitation of ontology (of presence).

The ontology of presence is the ontology of beings and beingness. Everywhere, the dominance of beings is solicited by differance – in the sense that *sollicitare* means, in old Latin, to shake all over, to make the whole tremble. What is questioned by the thought of differance, therefore, is the determination of being in presence, or in beingness. Such a question could not arise and be understood without the difference between Being and beings opening up somewhere. The first consequence of this is that differance is not. It is not a being-present, however excellent, unique, principal, or transcendent one makes it. It commands nothing, rules over nothing, and nowhere does it exercise any authority. It is not marked by a capital letter. Not only is there no realm of differance, but differance is even the subversion of every realm. This is obviously what makes it threatening and necessarily dreaded by everything in us that desires a realm, the past or future presence of a realm. And it is always in the name of a realm that, believing one sees it ascend to the capital letter, one can reproach it for wanting to rule.

Does this mean, then, that differance finds its place within the spread of the ontic-ontological difference, as it is conceived, as the 'epoch' conceives itself within it, and particularly 'across' the Heideggerian meditation, which cannot be gotten around?

There is no simple answer to such a question.

In one particular respect, differance is, to be sure, but the historical and epochal *deployment* of Being or of the ontological difference. The *a* of differance marks the *movement* of this deployment.

And yet, is not the thought that conceives the *sense* or *truth* of Being, the determination of differance as ontic-ontological difference – difference conceived within the horizon of the question of *Being* – still an intrametaphysical effect of differance? Perhaps the deployment of differance is not only the truth or the epochality of Being. Perhaps we must try to think this *unheard-of* thought, this silent tracing, namely, that the history of Being (the thought of which is committed to the Greco-Western logos), as it is itself produced across the ontological difference, is only one epoch of the *diapherein*. Then we could no longer even call it an 'epoch,' for the concept of epochality belongs within history understood as the history of Being. Being has always made 'sense,' has always been conceived or spoken of as such, only by dissimulating itself in beings; thus, in a particular and very strange way, differance (is) 'older' than the ontological difference or the truth of Being. In this age it can be called the play of traces. It is a trace that no longer belongs to the horizon of Being but one whose sense of Being is borne and bound by this play; it is a play of traces or differance that has no sense and is not, a play that does not belong. There is no support to be found and no depth to be had for this bottomless chessboard where being is set in play.

It is perhaps in this way that the Heraclitean play of the *hen diapheron heautōi*, of the one differing from itself, of what is in difference with itself, already becomes lost as a trace in determining the *diapherein* as ontological difference.

To think through the ontological difference doubtless remains a difficult task, a task whose statement has remained nearly inaudible. And to prepare ourselves for venturing beyond our own logos, that is, for a differance so violent that it refuses to be stopped and examined as the epochality of Being and ontological difference, is neither to give up this passage through the truth of Being, nor is it in any way to 'criticize,' 'contest,' or fail to recognize the incessant necessity for it. On the contrary, we must stay within the difficulty of this passage; we must repeat this passage in a rigorous reading of metaphysics, wherever metaphysics serves as the norm of Western speech, and not only in the texts of 'the history of philosophy.' Here we must allow the trace of whatever goes beyond the truth of Being to appear/disappear in its fully rigorous way. It is a trace of something that can never present itself; it is itself a trace that can never be presented, that is, can never appear and manifest itself as such in its phenomenon. It is a trace that lies beyond what profoundly ties fundamental ontology to phenomenology. Like differance, the trace is never presented as such. In presenting itself it becomes effaced; in being sounded it dies away, like the writing of the *a*, inscribing its pyramid in differance.

We can always reveal the precursive and secretive traces of this movement in metaphysical speech, especially in the contemporary talk about the closure of ontology, i.e., through the various attempts we have looked at (Nietzsche, Freud, Levinas) – and particularly in Heidegger's work.

The latter provokes us to question the essence of the present, the presence of the present.

What is the present? What is it to conceive the present in its presence?

Let us consider, for example, the 1946 text entitled 'Der Spruch des Anaximander.' Heidegger there recalls that the forgetting of Being forgets about the difference between Being and beings:

> But the point of Being (*die Sache des Seins*) is to be the Being *of* beings. The linguistic form of this enigmatic and multivalent genitive designates a genesis (*Genesis*), a provenance (*Herkunft*) of the pre*sent* from pre*sence* (*des Anwesenden aus dem Anwesen*). But with the unfolding of these two, the essence (*Wesen*) of this provenance remains hidden (*verborgen*). Not only is the essence of this provenance not thought out, but neither is the simple relation between pre*sence* and pre*sent* (*Anwesen und Anwesenden*). Since the dawn, it seems that pre*sence* and being-pre*sent* are each separately something. Imperceptibly, pre*sence* becomes itself a pre*sent*. ... The essence of pre*sence* (*Das Wesen des Anwesens*), and thus the difference between pre*sence* and pre*sent*, is forgotten. *The forgetting of Being is the forgetting of the difference between Being and beings.*[14]

In recalling the difference between Being and beings (the ontological difference) as the difference between presence and present, Heidegger puts forward a proposition, indeed, a group of propositions; it is not our intention here to idly or hastily 'criticize' them but rather to convey them with all their provocative force.

Let us then proceed slowly. What Heidegger wants to point out is that the difference between Being and beings, forgotten by metaphysics, has disappeared without leaving a trace. The very trace of difference has sunk from sight. If we admit that differance (is) (itself) something other than presence and absence, if it *traces*, then we are dealing with the forgetting of the difference (between Being and beings), and we now have to talk about a disappearance of the trace's trace. This is certainly what this passage from 'Der Spruch des Anaximander' seems to imply:

> The forgetting of Being is a part of the very essence of Being, and is concealed by it. The forgetting belongs so essentially to the destination of Being that the dawn of this destination begins precisely as an unconcealment of the pre*sent* in its pre*sence*. This means: the history of Being begins by the forgetting of Being, in that Being retains its essence, its difference from beings. Difference is wanting; it remains forgotten. Only what is differentiated – the present and presence (*das Anwesende und das Anwesen*) – becomes uncovered, but not *insofar as* it is differentiated. On the contrary, the matinal trace (*die frühe Spur*) of difference effaces itself from the moment that presence appears as a being-present (*das Anwesen wie ein Anwesendes erscheint*) and finds its provenance in a supreme (being)-present (*in einem höchsten Anwesenden*).[15]

The trace is not a presence but is rather the simulacrum of a presence that dislocates, displaces, and refers beyond itself. The trace has, properly speaking, no place, for effacement belongs to the very structure of the trace. Effacement must always be able to overtake the trace; otherwise it would not be a trace but an indestructible and monumental substance. In addition, and from the start, effacement constitutes it as a trace – effacement establishes the trace in a change of place and makes it disappear in its appearing, makes it issue forth from itself in its very position. The effacing of this early trace (*die frühe Spur*) of difference is therefore 'the same' as its tracing within the text of metaphysics. This metaphysical text must have retained a mark of what it lost or put in reserve, set aside. In the language of metaphysics the paradox of such a structure is the inversion of the metaphysical concept which produces the following effect: the present becomes the sign of signs, the trace of traces. It is no longer what every reference refers to in the last instance; it becomes a function in a generalized referential structure. It is a trace, and a trace of the effacement of a trace.

In this way the metaphysical text is *understood*; it is still readable, and remains to be read. It proposes *both* the monument and the mirage of the trace, the trace as simultaneously traced and effaced, simultaneously alive and dead, alive as always to simulate even life in its preserved inscription; it is a pyramid.

Thus we think through, without contradiction, or at least without granting any pertinence to such contradiction, what is perceptible and imperceptible about the trace. The 'matinal trace' of difference is lost in an irretrievable invisibility, and yet even its loss is covered, preserved, regarded, and retarded. This happens in a text, in the form of presence.

Having spoken about the effacement of the matinal trace, Heidegger can thus, in this contradiction without contradiction, consign or countersign the sealing of the trace. We read on a little further:

> The difference between Being and beings, however, can in turn be experienced as something forgotten only if it is already discovered with the presence of the present (*mit dem Anwesen des Anwesenden*) and if it is thus sealed in a trace (*so eine Spur geprägt hat*) that remains preserved (*gewahrt bleibt*) in the language which Being appropriates.[16]

Further on still, while meditating upon Anaximander's τὸ χρεών, translated as *Brauch* (sustaining use), Heidegger writes the following:

> Dispensing accord and deference (*Fug und Ruch verfügend*), our sustaining use frees the present (*das Anwesende*) in its sojourn and sets it free every time for its sojourn. But by the same token the present is equally seen to be exposed to the constant danger of hardening in the insistence (*in das blosse Beharren verhärtet*) out of its sojourning duration. In this way sustaining use (*Brauch*) remains itself and at the same time an abandonment (*Aushändigung:* handing-over) of presence (*des Anwesens*) *in den Un-fug*, to discord (disjointedness). Sustaining use joins together the dis- (*Der Brauch fügt das Un-*).[17]

And it is at the point where Heidegger determines *sustaining use* as *trace* that the question must be asked: can we, and how far can we, think of this trace and the *dis*-of differance as *Wesen des Seins*? Doesn't the *dis* of differance refer us beyond the history of Being, beyond our language as well, and beyond everything that can be named by it? Doesn't it call for – in the language of being – the necessarily violent transformation of this language by an entirely different language?

Let us be more precise here. In order to dislodge the 'trace' from its cover (and whoever believes that one tracks down some *thing*? – one tracks down tracks), let us continue reading this passage:

> The translation of τό χρεών by 'sustaining use' (*Brauch*) does not derive from cogitations of an etymologico-lexical nature. The choice of the word 'sustaining use' derives from an antecedent *translation* (*Übersetzen*) of the thought that attempts to conceive difference in the deployment of Being (*im Wesen des Seins*) toward the historical beginning of the forgetting of Being. The word 'sustaining use' is dictated to thought in the apprehension (*Erfahrung*) of the forgetting of Being. Τό χρεών properly names a trace (*Spur*) of what remains to be conceived in the word 'sustaining use,' a trace that quickly disappears (*alsbald verschwindet*) into the history of Being, in its world-historical unfolding as Western metaphysics.[18]

How do we conceive of the outside of a text? How, for example, do we conceive of what stands opposed to the text of Western metaphysics? To be sure, the 'trace that quickly disappears into the history of Being, ... as Western metaphysics,' escapes all the determinations, all the names it might receive in the metaphysical text. The trace is sheltered and thus dissimulated in these names; it does not appear in the text as the trace 'itself.' But this is because the trace itself could never itself appear as such. Heidegger also says that difference can never appear *as such:* 'Lichtung des Unterschiedes kann deshalb auch nicht bedeuten, dass der Unterschied als der Unterschied erscheint.' There is no essence of differance; not only can it not allow itself to be taken up into the *as such* of its name or its appearing, but it threatens the authority of the *as such* in general, the thing's presence in its essence. That there is no essence of differance at this point also implies that there is neither Being nor truth to the play of writing, *insofar* as it involves differance.

For us, differance remains a metaphysical name; and all the names that it receives from our language are still, so far as they are names, metaphysical. This is particularly so when they speak of determining differance as the difference between presence and present (*Anwesen/Anwesend*), but already and especially so when, in the most general way, they speak of determining differance as the difference between Being and beings.

'Older' than Being itself, our language has no name for such a differance. But we 'already know' that if it is unnamable, this is not simply provisional; it is not because our language has still not found or received this *name*, or because we would have to look for it in another language, outside the finite system of our language. It is because there is no *name* for this, not even essence or Being – not even the name 'differance,' which is not a name, which is not a pure nominal unity, and continually breaks up in a chain of different substitutions.

'There is no name for this': we read this as a truism. What is unnamable here is not some ineffable being that cannot be approached by a name; like God, for example. What is unnamable is the play that brings about the nominal effects, the relatively unitary or atomic structures we call names, or chains of substitutions for names. In these, for example, the nominal effect of 'differance' is itself involved, carried off, and reinscribed, just as the false beginning or end of a game is still part of the game, a function of the system.

What we do know, what we could know if it were simply a question of knowing, is that there never has been and never will be a unique word, a master name. This is why thinking about the letter *a* of differance is not the primary prescription, nor is it the prophetic announcement of some imminent and still unheard-of designation. There is nothing kerygmatic about this 'word' so long as we can perceive its reduction to a lower-case letter.

There will be no unique name, not even the name of Being. It must be conceived without *nostalgia*; that is, it must be conceived outside the myth of the purely maternal or paternal language belonging to the lost fatherland of thought. On the contrary, we must *affirm* it – in the sense that Nietzsche brings affirmation into play – with a certain laughter and with a certain dance.

After this laughter and dance, after this affirmation that is foreign to any dialectic, the question arises as to the other side of nostalgia, which I will call Heideggerian *hope*. I am not unaware that this term may be somewhat shocking. I venture it all the same, without excluding any of its implications, and shall relate it to what seems to me to be retained of metaphysics in 'Der Spruch des Anaximander,' namely, the quest for the proper word and the unique name. In talking about the 'first word of Being' (*das frühe Wort des Seins:* τὸ χρεών), Heidegger writes,

> The relation to the pre*sent*, unfolding its order in the very essence of pre*sence*, is unique (*ist eine einzige*). It is pre-eminently incomparable to any other relation; it belongs to the uniqueness of Being itself (*Sie gehört zur Einzigkeit des Seins selbst*). Thus, in order to name what is deployed in Being (*das Wesende des Seins*), language will have to find a single word, the unique word (*ein einziges, das einzige Wort*). There we see how hazardous is every word of thought (every thoughtful word: *denkende Wort*) that addresses itself to Being (*das dem Sein zugesprochen wird*). What is hazarded here, however, is not something impossible, because Being speaks through every language; everywhere and always.[19]

Such is the question: the marriage between speech and Being in the unique word, in the finally proper name. Such is the question that enters into the affirmation put into play by differance. The question bears (upon) each of the words in this sentence: 'Being/speaks/through every language;/every where and always/.'

Notes

This essay appeared originally in the *Bulletin de la Société française de philosophie*, LXII, No. 3 (July–September, 1968), 73–101. Derrida's remarks were delivered as a lecture at a meeting of the Société at the Sorbonne, in the Amphithéâtre Michelet, on January 27, 1968, with Jean Wahl presiding. Professor Wahl's introductory and closing remarks have not been translated. The essay was reprinted in *Théorie d'ensemble*, a collection of essays by Derrida and others, published by Editions Seuil in 1968. It is reproduced here by permission of Editions Seuil.

1   [The reader should bear in mind that 'differance,' or difference with an *a*, incorporates two significations: 'to differ' and 'to defer.' See also above, footnote 8, p. 82.—Translator.]

2   [For the term 'facilitation' (*frayage*) in Freud, cf. 'Project for a Scientific Psychology I' in *The Complete Psychological Works of Sigmund Freud*, 24 vols. (New York and London: Macmillan, 1964), I, 300, note 4 by the translator, James Strachey: 'The word "facilitation' as a rendering of the German "*Bahnung*" seems to have been introduced by Sherrington a few years after the *Project* was written. The German word, however, was already in use.' The sense that Derrida draws upon here is stronger in the French or German; that is, the opening-up or clearing-out of a pathway. In the context of the 'Project for a Scientific Psychology I,' facilitation denotes the conduction capability that results from a difference in resistance levels in the memory and perception circuits of the nervous system. Thus, lowering the resistance threshold of a contact barrier serves to 'open up' a nerve pathway and 'facilitates' the excitatory process for the circuit. Cf. also J. Derrida, *L'Ecriture et la différence*, Chap. VII, 'Freud et la scène de l'écriture' (Paris: Seuil, 1967), esp. pp. 297–305. – Translator.]

3   [On 'pyramid' and 'tomb' see J. Derrida, 'Le Puits et la pyramide' in *Hegel et la pensée moderne* (Paris: Presses Universitaires de France, 1970), esp. pp. 44–45. – Translator.]

4   Ferdinand de Saussure, *Cours de linguistique générale*, ed. C. Bally and A. Sechehaye (Paris: Payot, 1916); English translation by Wade Baskin, *Course in General Linguistics* (New York: Philosophical Library, 1959), pp. 117–18, 120.

5   *Course in General Linguistics*, p. 18.

6   [On 'supplement' see above, *Speech and Phenomena*, Chap. 7, pp. 88–104. Cf. also Derrida, *De la grammatologie* (Paris: Editions de Minuit, 1967). On '*pharmakon*' see Derrida, 'La Pharmacie de Platon,' *Tel Quel*, No. 32 (Winter, 1967), pp. 17–59; No. 33 (Spring, 1968), pp. 4–48. On 'hymen' see Derrida, 'La Double séance,' *Tel Quel*, No. 41 (Spring, 1970), pp. 3–43; No. 42 (Summer, 1970), pp. 3–45. 'La Pharmacie de Platon' and 'La Double séance' have been reprinted in a recent text of Derrida, *La Dissémination* (Paris: Editions du Seuil, 1972). – Translator.]

7   [Derrida often brackets or 'crosses out' certain key terms taken from metaphysics and logic, and in doing this, he follows Heidegger's usage in *Zur Seinsfrage*. The terms in question no longer have their full meaning, they no longer have the status of a purely signified content of expression – no longer, that is, after the deconstruction of metaphysics. Generated out of the play of differance, they still retain a vestigial trace of sense, however, a trace that cannot simply be gotten around (*incontournable*). An extensive discussion of all this is to be found in *De la grammatologie*, pp. 31–40. – Translator.]

8   Alexandre Koyré, 'Hegel à Iéna,' *Revue d'histoire et de philosophie religieuse*, XIV (1934), 420–58; reprinted in Koyré, *Etudes d'histoire de la pensée philosophique* (Paris: Armand Colin, 1961), pp. 135–73.

9   Koyré, *Etudes d'histoire*, pp. 153–54. [The quotation from Hegel (my translation) comes from 'Jenenser Logik, Metaphysik, und Naturphilosophie,' *Säm-*

tliche Werke (Leipzig: F. Meiner, 1925), XVIII, 202. Koyré reproduces the original German text on pp. 153–54, note 2. – Translator.]

10 De Saussure, *Course in General Linguistics*, p. 37.

11 G. Deleuze, *Nietzsche et la philosophie* (Paris: Presses Universitaires de France, 1970), p. 49.

12 Freud, *Complete Psychological Works*, XVIII, 10.

13 Derrida, *L'Ecriture et la différence*, pp. 369–407.

14 Martin Heidegger, *Holzwege* (Frankfurt: V. Klostermann, 1957), pp. 335–36. [All translations of quotations from *Holzwege* are mine. – Translator.]

15 *Ibid.*, p. 336.

16 *Ibid.*

17 *Ibid.*, pp. 339–40.

18 *Ibid.*, p. 340.

19 *Ibid.*, pp. 337–38.

Section 5

GENDER AND RACE

Introduction

It is difficult, in the twenty-first century, to imagine any form of cultural debate that does not explicitly address questions raised by issues of gender and race. Indeed, all the discussions staged in this Reader – of ideology, subjectivity, difference and postmodernism – inevitably involve questions both of gender and of race, and the questions of gender and race themselves pervade all areas of critical and cultural debate. In addition, it is important to acknowledge that the very categories of gender and race are not discrete domains, but are clearly overdetermined (see Althusser, Section 2.3), intersecting as they do with each other as well as with issues of sexuality, class and so on. However, given the extent and specificity of the many theoretical questions surrounding these issues, their constructions and deconstructions, we have felt it necessary to devote a separate section entirely to the concerns they raise. The seven extracts selected are intended to introduce some of the principles underlying debates about gender and race; they do not represent all that there is to those debates as a whole. Further, in order to provide a version of coherence for those debates, we have ordered the extracts so that they present initial engagements with gender (mainly through psychoanalysis), followed by a disruption of the singularity of that concept by issues of racial signification, and finally a problematization of the certainty by which the very categories of gender and race may themselves be understood to operate. Of course, such a version of coherence can only ever be arbitrary, and can, and should, be contested.

Psychoanalysis and gender

A great deal of the work on gender through the twentieth century has emerged in the wake of the psychoanalytic work of Sigmund Freud. Indeed, the signifier 'Freud' itself has often provided a kind of litmus test against which positions within the debate about theories of gender are defined. Briefly, there are those who embrace the founding principles of Freud's work and seek to develop analyses from them; there are those engaged in 'recuperative' rereadings of Freud in the interests of a politics of feminism and/or gay liberation; and there are those who define a position explicitly in resistance to the notions he advanced, usually, again, in the interests of a politics both of gender and of sexuality. Wherever we may situate ourselves within these ongoing debates, the importance of Freud's work remains.

For Freud, the psycho-sexual acquisition of gendered identity is fundamental to the entire question of identity itself, and in many ways the theories he produced represent a fairly radical departure from the biological determinism that preceded them. His notion of the polymorphously plural infant and the notion of the precariousness of repression (demanded by socially taboo desires) through the Oedipal and castration complexes (see *Standard Edition*, vol. 7: 123–245), for example, make the acquisition of gender difference not only crucial to the production of the adult subject, but also problematic to it. Since it is the characteristic of the repressed to return (usually at moments when we least expect it), a great deal of Freud's work is based upon a notion of the gendered subject as fundamentally unstable and capable of change.

However, this theorization of gender difference as a provisional effect produced through the Oedipal and castration complexes is not altogether free from a certain determination in biology. Arguably, the psycho-sexual processes that Freud describes also rely upon the attribution of meaning to visible anatomical distinctions that centre on the presence or absence of the penis, and of drives that are related to bodily instincts (see *Standard Edition*, vol. 19: 241–58). Because of these factors, the complexes that the child must go through are resolved differently (if they are resolved) for boys and for girls, and the resolution itself is based very firmly within the normalizing terrain of heterosexuality.

As with any established body of work that is widely disseminated, much within the canon of Freudian theory is contradictory and capable of varying interpretation from the cultural distance of the twenty-first century. It is perhaps this plurality of Freud's work that has led to the development of Freudian concepts within the work of contemporary theorists.

The work of Juliet Mitchell (1974) develops a theory of gendered identity that emphasizes the plurality and instabilities of the unconscious, and the repression of either the masculine or feminine capabilities of the individual subject through the social taboos and regulative norms of patriarchal society.

While this work is still grounded within the domain of psychoanalysis, the work of Jacqueline Rose (1984, 1988) and Laura Mulvey (Section 5.3) takes the Freudian framework to the analysis of cultural texts. Within Laura Mulvey's work, the Freudian equation of the masculine and the feminine with activity and passivity (both of which are aspects of the single subject) forms the basis of an analysis of the reproduction of sexual imbalance through the specifically cultural economy of visual texts. Her primary concern is not with a description of patriarchal gender distinctions, or the psychic processes that give rise to them, but with an analysis of the cultural ramifications of the textual operation of gender identification that effaces the active desires of women. Within Mulvey's analysis psychic processes are more explicitly grounded in social and textual conditions.

Écriture féminine

This impulse to material grounding is also apparent in much of the work of French feminist theorists like Hélène Cixous (Section 5.2), Luce Irigaray (1985b) and Julia Kristeva (Section 3.4). Although much of this work is itself a product of psychoanalytic theory (dependent much more upon Lacan's rereading of Freud; see Section 3.2), it also relies firmly on theories of language (Section 1.1) clearly focused upon resistance to the phallus as controlling signifier in the gendered metaphysics of Western thought. For these theorists the importance of gendered identity lies in its constitution and control in and through language – which itself is understood as the product of social and political operations of power and difference. Their model of analysis, then, is based upon language as a site of resistance to the production of gendered meanings, and to the perpetuation of heterosexually normative taboos. Cixous in particular privileges the potential bisexuality of human identity and argues (picking up on Kristeva's notion of the semiotic chora of language) for a form of writing arising from the 'feminine' body. Such a move, Cixous affirms, is revolutionary precisely because it transgresses the norms of gender difference, but also because in transgressing those norms it opens the question of identity itself to the plurality and unpredictability of the free play of the signifier.

Social construction

Still further from the site of psychoanalysis, there is a body of work concerned to theorize gender as an effect of social and cultural constructions. Much of the work of Michel Foucault (some of which we have included in Section 3, Subjectivity) provides a detailed analysis of ways in which gendered people are *discursively* constituted by forms of knowledge (of the body, sexuality, the family and so on) within specific social formations. While Foucault's analysis exposes the power relations inherent in social constructions of the subject – female and male – it also allows for the possibilities of resistance to the rigid binary categories of gendered subjectivity, which may be privileged as the norm (see, for example, *The History of Sexuality*, 1978a, and *Herculine Barbin*, 1980).

   Within the domain of critical and cultural theory, and particularly in the field of social science, the notion of the subject as the site of discursive constructions and deconstructions of gendered identity has often been central. Judith Butler's (1990) work on the social constructions of gendered subjectivity (1999) provides just one example; there has also been a proliferation of work (largely) by women focused upon the construction of gendered identity in relation to issues of race, class and sexuality (see, for example, Alvina Quintana 1990; Rosaura Sanchez 1990).

The operation of the signifier in gender and race

Moving away from concerns with theories of the construction of identity on the grounds purely of gender, a number of cultural critics have begun the work of ana- lysing cultural texts in order to show the ways in which the signifiers of gender *and* race operate to confirm and so to perpetuate social relations of power. For example, taking as his subject the controversial photographs of Robert Mapplethorpe, Kobena Mercer offers a reading of the operation of the signifier of race on the sites of both gender and sexuality. In doing so, he draws upon the psychoanalytic work of Laura Mulvey on film, but extends that discussion to address more specific issues involved in the racialized, same-sex desires of looking at art. In his terms, the look is not only gendered, but also inescapably racialized and sexualized. In this particular combi- nation, Mercer exposes the pleasure of looking (while supposedly radical – these pictures are of men rather than women, and offered as homoerotic rather than conventionally heterosexual) as confirming and perpetuating the racist stereotypes of the cultures within which they circulate.

In a similar vein, Rajeswari Sunder Rajan takes up the issue of the colonial gaze in a variety of media – newspaper reports, feminist studies, anthropology, as well as Indian national parliamentary, religious and legal debates about the values of tradition – on the deeply controversial subject of sati. Drawing on the work of Michel Foucault (see Sections 3.5 and 3.6), she offers a paradigm for reading the 'so-called third- world' not for the truths it might reveal but as a site of contest within which positions are always invested by culturally specific knowledges and relations of power.

The temporality of gender and the ambivalence of race

Finally, the work of Judith Butler and Homi K. Bhabha returns us to some fundamental questions about the taken-for-granted concepts of gender and race upon which contemporary notions of identity are founded.

For Butler, the imperative of a radical social politics that moves away from positions within definite identities is crucial. In her questioning of the assumed subject of feminist politics as simply given, she begins to reopen politics to the issues of the fictionality of identity represented in this Reader most explicitly in the sections on ideology and subjectivity above. In Butler's work, the fictionality, and thus tem- porality, of identity is not only inescapable, but also the site for the beginnings of a set of resistant practices capable of deconstructing the very metaphysics through which we come to know identity in the first place. Her work has been significant in the context of gender studies, since it marks a new direction for both theoretical understanding and political practice. In this sense, it also provides a historically specific sense of the instabilities generated by the context of AIDS (a context in which it was simply dangerous to assume that sexual practices inhered in specific categories of identity), the resurgence of masquerade in the forms of camp and drag, and the growing insistence on the ambivalence of sexualities that are mobile (neither decidedly hetero nor homo) and genders that slide (as in transsexual existence).

While the focus on these 'problems' of identity has subsequently been subsumed into an emerging paradigm of study known as 'Queer', it is important to point out that it loses the radical potential of the ideas if it simply performs the substitution of one signifier for another. Queer can mean (in the combination of signifier with an entirely different signified to that of 'gay') to unsettle, or to put out of joint, and it is this permanent process of deconstruction that defies the reassertion of a surety of identity that the work of Butler advocates.

For Homi K. Bhabha, the insistence on the precariousness and ambivalence of identity is equally important, although his focus is specifically on the radical potentials of the operation of race on the site of differance (see Derrida, Section 4). More explicitly influenced by the work of Jacques Derrida, Bhabha's concern is to establish grounds upon which the category of race can be understood not as something solid and enduring, but as an *operation* of a signifier, the meaning of which cannot be decided once and for all. Preferring to keep the signifier in a process of oscillation, Bhabha argues that it can operate to question, to deconstruct and ultimately to reveal the impossibility of the logic of Western metaphysics that invents and sustains it. However, he also warns of the dangers of taking this ambivalence to the extreme, as he believes some aspects of postmodern theory have done. By turning their back on modernity, versions of postmodernism that see the loss of the signified in the prevalence of the signifier in simulation, Bhabha argues, also turn away from the material realities of what Fanon had earlier called 'the fact of blackness'. The advocation of the ambivalence of the sign (signifier and signified) of race can be accommodated within the project of modernity, and would be more properly located there if cultural critics were not so keen to move beyond it.

Theory itself is not immune to unacknowledged gender and racial assumptions, and neither is a critical and cultural theory reader, but perhaps nothing is.

5.1

Sigmund Freud, 'On the Universal Tendency to Debasement in the Sphere of Love' (1912)

1

If the practising psychoanalyst asks himself on account of what disorder people most often come to him for help, he is bound to reply – disregarding the many forms of anxiety – that it is psychical impotence. This singular disturbance affects men of strongly libidinous[1] natures, and manifests itself in a refusal by the executive organs of sexuality to carry out the sexual act, although before and after they may show themselves to be intact and capable of performing the act, and although a strong psychical inclination to carry it out is present. The first clue to understanding his condition is obtained by the sufferer himself on making the discovery that a failure of this kind only arises when the attempt is made with certain individuals; whereas with others there is never any question of such a failure. He now becomes aware that it is some feature of the sexual object which gives rise to the inhibition of his male potency, and sometimes he reports that he has a feeling of an obstacle inside him, the sensation of a counter-will which successfully interferes with his conscious intention. However, he is unable to guess what this internal obstacle is and what feature of the sexual object brings it into operation. If he has had repeated experience of a failure of this kind, he is likely, by the familiar process of 'erroneous connection', to decide that the recollection of the first occasion evoked the disturbing anxiety-idea and so caused the failure to be repeated each time; while he derives the first occasion itself from some 'accidental' impression.

Pyschoanalytic studies of psychical impotence have already been carried out and published by several writers.[2] Every analyst can confirm the explanations provided by them from his own clinical experience. It is in fact a question of the inhibitory influence of certain psychical complexes which are withdrawn from the subject's knowledge. An incestuous fixation on mother or sister, which has never been surmounted, plays a prominent part in this pathogenic material and is its most universal content. In addition there is the influence to be considered of accidental distressing impressions connected with infantile sexual activity, and also those factors which in a general way reduce the libido that is to be directed on to the female sexual object.[3]

When striking cases of psychical impotence are exhaustively investigated by means of psychoanalysis, the following information is obtained about the psychosexual processes at work in them. Here again – as very probably in all neurotic disturbances – the foundation of the disorder is provided by an inhibition in the developmental history of the libido before it assumes the form which we take to be its normal termination. Two currents whose union is necessary to ensure a completely normal attitude in love have, in the cases we are considering, failed to combine. These two may be distinguished as the *affectionate* and the *sensual* current.

The affectionate current is the older of the two. It springs from the earliest years of childhood; it is formed on the basis of the interests of the self-preservative instinct and is directed to the members of the family and those who look after the child. From the very beginning it carries along with it contributions from the sexual instincts – components of erotic interest – which can already be seen more or less clearly even in childhood and in any event are uncovered in neurotics by psychoanalysis later on. It corresponds to *the child's primary object-choice*. We learn in this way that the sexual instincts find their first objects by attaching themselves to the valuations made by the ego-instincts, precisely in the way in which the first sexual satisfactions are experienced in attachment to the bodily functions necessary for the preservation of life.[4] The 'affection' shown by the child's parents and those who look after him, which seldom fails to betray its erotic nature ('the child is an erotic plaything'), does a very great deal to raise the contributions made by erotism to the cathexes of his ego-instincts, and to increase them to an amount which is bound to play a part in his later development, especially when certain other circumstances lend their support.

These affectionate fixations of the child persist throughout childhood, and continually carry along with them erotism, which is consequently diverted from its sexual aims. Then at the age of puberty they are joined by the powerful 'sensual' current which no longer mistakes its aims. It never fails, apparently, to follow the earlier paths and to cathect the objects of the primary infantile choice with quotas of libido that are now far stronger. Here, however, it runs up against the obstacles that have been erected in the meantime by the barrier against incest; consequently it will make efforts to pass on from these objects which are unsuitable in reality, and find a way as soon as possible to other, extraneous objects with which a real sexual life may be carried on. These new objects will still be chosen on the model (imago[5]) of the infantile ones, but in the course of time they will attract to themselves the affection that was tied to the earlier ones. A man shall leave his father and his mother – according to the biblical command – and shall cleave unto his wife; affection and sensuality are then united. The greatest intensity of sensual passion will bring with it the highest psychical valuation of the object – this being the normal overvaluation of the sexual object on the part of a man.

Two factors will decide whether this advance in the developmental path of the libido is to fail. First, there is the amount of *frustration in reality* which opposes the new object-choice and reduces its value for the person concerned. There is after all no point in embarking upon an object-choice if no choice is to be allowed at all or if there is no prospect of being able to choose anything suitable. Secondly, there is the amount of *attraction* which the infantile objects that have to be relinquished are able to exercise, and which is in proportion to the erotic cathexis attaching to them in childhood. If these two factors are sufficiently strong, the general mechanism by which the neuroses are formed comes into operation. The libido turns away from reality, is taken over by imaginative activity (the process of introversion), strengthens the images of the first sexual objects and becomes fixated to them. The obstacle raised against incest, however, compels the libido that has turned to these objects to remain in the unconscious. The masturbatory activity carried out by the sensual current, which is now part of the unconscious, makes its own contribution in strengthening this fixation. Nothing is altered in this state of affairs if the advance which has miscarried in reality is now completed in phantasy, and if in the phantasy-situations that lead to masturbatory satisfaction the original sexual objects are replaced by different ones. As a result of this substitution the phantasies become admissible to consciousness, but no progress is made in the allocation of the libido in reality. In this way it can happen that the whole of a young man's sensuality becomes tied to incestuous objects in the unconscious, or to put it another way, becomes fixated to unconscious incestuous phantasies. The result is then total impotence, which is perhaps further ensured by the simultaneous onset of an actual weakening of the organs that perform the sexual act.

Less severe conditions are required to bring about the state known specifically as psychical impotence. Here the fate of the sensual current must not be that its whole charge has to conceal itself behind the affectionate current; it must have remained sufficiently strong or uninhibited to secure a partial outlet into reality. The sexual activity of such people shows the clearest signs, however, that it has not the whole psychical driving force of the instinct behind it. It is capricious, easily disturbed, often not properly carried out, and not accompanied by much pleasure. But above all it is forced to avoid the affectionate current. A restriction has thus been placed on object-choice. The sensual current that has remained active seeks only objects which do not recall the incestuous figures forbidden to it; if someone makes an impression that might lead to a high psychical estimation of her, this impression does not find an issue in any sensual excitation but in affection which has no erotic effect. The whole sphere of love in such people remains divided in the two directions personified in art as sacred and profane (or animal) love. Where they love they do not desire and where they desire they cannot love. They seek objects which they do not need to love, in order to keep their sensuality away from the objects they love; and, in accordance with the laws of 'complexive sensitiveness'[6] and of the return of the repressed, the strange failure shown in psychical impotence makes its appearance whenever an object which has been chosen with the aim of avoiding incest recalls the prohibited object through some feature, often an inconspicuous one.

The main protective measure against such a disturbance which men have recourse to in this split in their love consists in a psychical *debasement* of the sexual object, the overvaluation that normally attaches to the sexual object being reserved for the incestuous object and its representatives. As soon as the condition of debasement is fulfilled, sensuality can be freely expressed, and important sexual capacities and a high degree of pleasure can develop. There is a further factor which contributes to this result. People in whom there has not been a proper confluence of the affectionate and the sensual currents do not usually show much refinement in their modes of behaviour in love; they have retained perverse sexual aims whose nonfulfilment is felt as a serious loss of pleasure, and whose fulfilment on the other hand seems possible only with a debased and despised sexual object.

We can now understand the motives behind the boy's phantasies mentioned in the first of these 'Contributions', which degrade the mother to the level of a prostitute. They are efforts to bridge the gulf between the two currents in love, at any rate in phantasy, and by debasing the mother to acquire her as an object of sensuality.

2

In the preceding section we have approached the study of psychical impotence from a medico-psychological angle of which the title of this paper gives no indication. It will however become clear that this introduction was required by us to provide an approach to our proper subject.

We have reduced psychical impotence to the failure of the affectionate and the sensual currents in love to combine, and this developmental inhibition has in turn been explained as being due to the influences of strong childhood fixations and of later frustration in reality through the intervention of the barrier against incest. There is one principal objection to the theory we advance; it does too much. It explains why certain people suffer from psychical impotence, but it leaves us with the apparent mystery of how others have been able to escape this disorder. Since we must recognize that all the relevant factors known to us – the strong childhood fixation, the incest-barrier and the frustration in the years of development after puberty – are to be found in practically all civilized human beings, we should be justified in expecting psychical impotence to be a universal affliction under civilization and not a disorder confined to some individuals.

It would be easy to escape from this conclusion by pointing to the quantitative factor in the causation of illness – to the greater or lesser extent of the contribution made by the various elements which determine whether a recognizable illness results or not. But although I accept this answer as correct, it is not my intention to make it a reason for rejecting the conclusion itself. On the contrary, I shall put forward the view that psychical impotence is much more widespread than is supposed, and that a certain amount of this behaviour does in fact characterize the love of civilized man.

If the concept of psychical impotence is broadened and is not restricted to failure to perform the act of coitus in circumstances where a desire to obtain pleasure is present and the genital apparatus is intact, we may in the first place add all those men who are described as psychanaesthetic: men who never fail in the act but who carry it out without getting any particular pleasure from it – a state of affairs that is more common than one would think. Psychoanalytic examination of such cases discloses the same aetiological factors as we found in psychical impotence in the narrower sense, without at first arriving at any explanation of the difference between their symptoms. An easily justifiable analogy takes one from these anaesthetic men to the immense number of frigid women; and there is no better way to describe or understand their behaviour in love than by comparing it with the more conspicuous disorder of psychical impotence in men.[7]

If however we turn our attention not to an extension of the concept of psychical impotence, but to the gradations in its symptomatology, we cannot escape the conclusion that the behaviour in love of men in the civilized world today bears the stamp altogether of psychical impotence. There are only a very few educated people in whom the two currents of affection and sensuality have become properly fused; the man almost always feels his respect for the woman acting as a restriction on his sexual activity, and only develops full potency when he is with a debased sexual object; and this in its turn is partly caused by the entrance of perverse components into his sexual aims, which he does not venture to satisfy with a woman he respects. He is assured of complete sexual pleasure only when he can devote himself unreservedly to obtaining satisfaction, which with his well-brought-up wife, for instance, he does not dare to do. This is the source of his need for a debased sexual object, a woman who is ethically inferior, to whom he need attribute no aesthetic scruples, who does not know him in his other social relations and cannot judge him in them. It is to such a woman that he prefers to devote his sexual potency, even when the whole of his affection belongs to a woman of a higher kind. It is possible, too, that the tendency so often observed in men of the highest classes of society to choose a woman of a lower class as a permanent mistress or even as a wife is nothing but a consequence of their need for a debased sexual object, to whom, psychologically, the possibility of complete satisfaction is linked.

I do not hestitate to make the two factors at work in psychical impotence in the strict sense – the factors of intense incestuous fixation in childhood and the frustration by reality in adolescence – responsible, too, for this extremely common characteristic of the love of civilized men. It sounds not only disagreeable but also paradoxical, yet it must nevertheless be said that anyone who is to be really free and happy in love must have surmounted his respect for women and have come to terms with the idea of incest with his mother or sister. Anyone who subjects himself to a serious self-examination on the subject of this requirement will be sure to find that he regards the sexual act basically as something degrading, which defiles and pollutes not only the body. The origin of this low opinion, which he will certainly not willingly acknowledge, must be looked for in the period of his youth in which the sensual current in him was already strongly developed but its satisfaction with an object outside the family was almost as completely prohibited as it was with an incestuous one.

In our civilized world women are under the influence of a similar after-effect of their upbringing, and, in addition, of their reaction to men's behaviour. It is naturally just as unfavourable for a woman if a man approaches her without his full potency as it is if his initial overvaluation of her when he is in love gives place to undervaluation after he has possessed her. In the case of women there is little sign of a need to debase their sexual object. This is no doubt connected with the absence in them as a rule of anything similar to the sexual overvaluation found in men. But their long holding back from sexuality and the lingering of their sensuality in phantasy has another important consequence for them. They are subsequently often unable to undo the connection between sensual activity and the prohibition, and prove to be psychically impotent, that is, frigid, when such activity is at last allowed them. This is the origin of the endeavour made by many women to keep even legitimate relations secret for a while; and of the capacity of other women for normal sensation as soon as the condition of prohibition is re-established by a secret love affair: unfaithful to their husband, they are able to keep a second order of faith with their lover.[8]

The condition of forbiddenness in the erotic life of women is, I think, comparable to the need on the part of men to debase their sexual object. Both are consequences of the long period of delay, which is demanded by education for cultural reasons, between sexual maturity and sexual activity. Both aim at abolishing the psychical impotence that results from the failure of affectionate and sensual impulses to coalesce. That the effect of the same causes should be so different in men and in women may perhaps be traced to another difference in the behaviour of the two sexes. Civilized women do not usually transgress the prohibition on sexual activity in the period during which they have to wait, and thus they acquire the intimate connection between prohibition and sexuality. Men usually break through this prohibition if they can satisfy the condition of debasing the object, and so they carry on this condition into their love in later life.

In view of the strenuous efforts being made in the civilized world today to reform sexual life, it will not be superfluous to give a reminder that psychoanalytic research is as remote from tendentiousness as any other kind of research. It has no other end in view than to throw light on things by tracing what is manifest back to what is hidden. It is quite satisfied if reforms make use of its findings to replace what is injurious by something more advantageous; but it cannot predict whether other institutions may not result in other, and perhaps graver, sacrifices.

3

The fact that the curb put upon love by civilization involves a universal tendency to debase sexual objects will perhaps lead us to turn our attention from the object to the instincts themselves. The damage caused by the initial frustration of sexual pleasure is seen in the fact that the freedom later given to that pleasure in marriage does not bring full satisfaction. But at the same time, if sexual freedom is unrestricted from the outset the result is no better. It can easily be shown that the psychical value of erotic needs is reduced as soon as their satisfaction becomes easy. An obstacle is required in order to heighten libido; and where natural resistances to satisfaction have not been sufficient men have at all times erected conventional ones so as to be able to enjoy love. This is true both of individuals and of nations. In times in which there were no difficulties standing in the way of sexual satisfaction, such as perhaps during the decline of the ancient civilizations, love became worthless and life empty, and strong reaction-formations were required to restore indispensable affective values. In this connection it may be claimed that the ascetic current in Christianity created psychical values for love which pagan antiquity was never able to confer on it. This current assumed its greatest importance with the ascetic monks, whose lives were almost entirely occupied with the struggle against libidinal temptation.

One's first inclination is no doubt to trace back the difficulties revealed here to universal characteristics of our organic instincts. It is no doubt also true in general that the psychical importance of an instinct rises in proportion to its frustration. Suppose a number of totally different human beings were all equally exposed to hunger. As their imperative need for food mounted, all the individual differences would disappear and in their place one would see the uniform manifestations of the one unappeased instinct. But is it also true that with the satisfaction of an instinct its psychical value always falls just as sharply? Consider, for example, the relation of a drinker to wine. Is it not true that wine always provides the drinker with the same toxic satisfaction, which in poetry has so often been compared to erotic satisfaction – a comparison acceptable from the scientific point of view as well? Has one ever heard of the drinker being obliged constantly to change his drink because he soon grows tired of keeping to the same one? On the contrary, habit constantly tightens the bond between a man and the kind of wine he drinks. Does one ever hear of a drinker who needs to go to a country where wine is dearer or drinking is prohibited, so that by introducing obstacles he can reinforce the dwindling satisfaction that he obtains? Not at all. If we listen to what our great alcoholics, such as Böcklin,[9] say about their relation to wine, it sounds like the most perfect harmony, a model of a happy marriage. Why is the relation of the lover to his sexual object so very different?

It is my belief that, however strange it may sound, we must reckon with the possibility that something in the nature of the sexual instinct itself is unfavourable to the realization of complete satisfaction. If we consider the long and difficult developmental history of the instinct, two factors immediately spring to mind which might be made responsible for this difficulty. Firstly, as a result of the diphasic onset of object-choice, and the interposition of the barrier against incest, the final object of the sexual instinct is never any longer the original object but only a surrogate for it. Psychoanalysis has shown us that when the original object of a wishful impulse has been lost as a result of repression, it is frequently represented by an endless series of substitutive objects none of which, however, brings full satisfaction. This may explain the inconstancy in object-choice, the 'craving for stimulation'[10] which is so often a feature of the love of adults.

Secondly, we know that the sexual instinct is originally divided into a great number of components – or rather, it develops out of them – some of which cannot be taken up into the instinct in its later form, but have at an earlier stage to be suppressed or put to other uses. These are above all the coprophilic instinctual components, which have proved incompatible with our aesthetic standards of culture, probably since, as a result of our adopting an erect gait, we raised our organ of smell from the ground.[11] The same is true of a large portion of the sadistic urges which are a part of erotic life. But all such developmental processes affect only the upper layers of the complex structure. The fundamental processes which produce erotic excitation remain unaltered. The excremental is all too intimately and inseparably bound up with the sexual; the position of the genitals – *inter urinas et faeces* – remains the decisive and unchangeable factor. One might say here, varying a well-known saying of the great Napoleon: 'Anatomy is destiny'.[12] The genitals themselves have not taken part in the development of the human body in the direction of beauty: they have remained animal, and thus love, too, has remained in essence just as animal as it ever was. The instincts of love are hard to educate; education of them achieves now too much, now too little. What civilization aims at making out of them seems unattainable except at the price of a sensible loss of pleasure; the persistence of the impulses that could not be made use of can be detected in sexual activity in the form of non-satisfaction.

Thus we may perhaps be forced to become reconciled to the idea that it is quite impossible to adjust the claims of the sexual instinct to the demands of civilization; that in consequence of its cultural development renunciation and suffering, as well as the danger of extinction in the remotest future, cannot be avoided by the human race. This gloomy prognosis rests, it is true, on the single conjecture that the non-satisfaction that goes with civilization is the necessary consequence of certain peculiarities which the sexual instinct has assumed under the pressure of culture. The very incapacity of the sexual instinct to yield complete satisfaction as soon as it submits to the first demands of civilization becomes the source, however, of the noblest cultural achievements which are brought into being by ever more extensive sublimation of its instinctual components. For what motive would men have for putting sexual instinctual forces to other uses if, by any distribution of those forces, they could obtain fully satisfying pleasure? They would never abandon that pleasure and they would never make any further progress. It seems, therefore, that the irreconcilable difference between the demands of the two instincts – the sexual and the egoistic – has made men capable of ever higher achievements, though subject, it is true, to a constant danger, to which, in the form of neurosis, the weaker are succumbing today.

It is not the aim of science either to frighten or to console. But I myself am quite ready to admit that such far-reaching conclusions as those I have drawn should be built on a broader foundation, and that perhaps developments in other directions may enable mankind to correct the results of the developments I have here been considering in isolation.

Notes

(Square brackets indicate editor's notes for *SE*.)

1   [*'Libidinös'*. Here 'libidinous', as contrasted with the technical 'libidinal'.]
2   Steiner (1907), Stekel (1908), Ferenczi (1908). [Freud had written a preface to Stekel's book (see *SE* v. 9, pp. 250–1).]
3   Stekel (1908, 191 ff.).
4   [The 'attachment' (or 'anaclitic') type of object-choice was discussed more fully in Freud's later paper on narcissism, *SE* v. 14.]
5   [This term was not often used by Freud, especially in his later writings. He attributed it to Jung ('Psycho-Analytic Notes', *SE* v. 12), in which passage Jung in turn says he partly chose the word from the title of a novel by the Swiss writer Carl Spitteler. The psychoanalytic journal *Imago* also owed its title to the same source, according to its co-founder, Hanns Sachs 1945, p. 63.]

6 [This term is borrowed from Jung's word-association experiments (Jung 1906).]
7 I am at the same time very willing to admit that frigidity in women is a complex subject which can also be approached from another angle. [The question is examined at length in 'The Taboo of Virginity', *SE* v. 11.]
8 [cf. 'The Taboo of Virginity'.]
9 Floerke (1902).
10 ['*Reizhunger*'. This term seems to have been introduced by Hoche and Bloch. See Freud's *Three Essays SE* v. 7.]
11 [cf. two long footnotes to Chapter IV of *Civilization and its Discontents* (*SE* v. 21), in which this idea is explored in greater detail.]
12 [This paraphrase appears again in 'The Dissolution of the Oedipus Complex' (*SE* v. 19.)]

See:
Ferenczi, S. (1908). 'Analytische Deutung und Behandlung der psychosexuellen Impotenz beim Mann', *Psychiat.-neurol. Wschr.*, 10, 298. [Trans.: The Analytic Interpretation and Treatment of Psycho-sexual Impotence', *First Contributions to Psycho-Analysis* (London, 1952), chapter 1].
Floerke, G. (1902). *Zehn Jahre mit Böcklin* (2nd ed) (Munich).
Jung, C. G. (1906). *Diagnostische Assoziationsstudien* 2 vols. (Leipzig) [Trans: *Studies in Word-Association* (London, 1918)].
Sachs, H. (1945). *Freud, Master and Friend* (Cambridge, Mass. and London).
Steiner, M. (1907). 'Die funktionelle Impotenz des Mannes und ihre Behandlung', *Wien. med. Pr.*, 48, 1535.
Stekel, W. (1908). *Nervöse Angstzustände und ihre Behandlung* (Berlin and Vienna).

5.2

Hélène Cixous, from 'Sorties' (1986)

Where is she?
Activity/Passivity
Sun/Moon
Culture/Nature
Day/Night

Father/Mother
Head/Heart
Intelligible/Palpable
Logos/Pathos.
Form, convex, step, advance, semen, progress.
Matter, concave, ground – where steps are taken, holding- and dumping-ground.
Man
Woman

    Always the same metaphor: we follow it, it carries us, beneath all its figures, wherever discourse is organized. If we read or speak, the same thread or double braid is leading us throughout literature, philosophy, criticism, centuries of representation and reflection.
Thought has always worked through opposition,
Speaking/Writing
Parole/Écriture
High/Low

    Through dual, hierarchical oppositions. Superior/Inferior. Myths, legends, books. Philosophical systems. Everywhere (where) ordering intervenes, where a law organizes what is thinkable by oppositions (dual, irreconcilable; or sublatable, dialectical). And all these pairs of oppositions are *couples*. Does that mean something? Is the fact that Logocentrism subjects thought – all concepts, codes and values – to a binary system, related to 'the' couple, man/woman?

Nature/History
Nature/Art

Nature/Mind
Passion/Action

Theory of culture, theory of society, symbolic systems in general – art, religion, family, language – it is all developed while bringing the same schemes to light. And the movement whereby each opposition is set up to make sense is the movement through which the couple is destroyed. A universal battlefield. Each time, a war is let loose. Death is always at work.

Father/son   Relations of authority, privilege, force.

The Word/Writing   Relations: opposition, conflict, sublation, return.

Master/slave   Violence. Repression.

We see that 'victory' always comes down to the same thing: things get hierarchical. Organization by hierarchy makes all conceptual organization subject to man. Male privilege, shown in the opposition between *activity* and *passivity*, which he uses to sustain himself. Traditionally, the question of sexual differance is treated by coupling it with the opposition: activity/passivity.

There are repercussions. Consulting the history of philosophy – since philosophical discourse both orders and reproduces all thought – one notices[1] that it is marked by an absolute *constant* which orders values and which is precisely this opposition, activity/passivity.

The masculine future

There are some exceptions. There have always been those uncertain, poetic persons who have not let themselves be reduced to dummies programmed by pitiless repression of the homosexual element. Men or women: beings who are complex, mobile, open. Accepting the other sex as a component makes them much richer, more various, stronger, and – to the extent that they are mobile – very fragile. It is only in this condition that we invent. Thinkers, artists, those who create new values, 'philosophers' in the mad Nietzschean manner, inventors and wreckers of concepts and forms, those who change life cannot help but be stirred by anomalies – complementary or contradictory. That doesn't mean that you have to be homosexual to create. But it does mean that there is no *invention* possible, whether it be philosophical or poetic, without there being in the inventing subject an abundance of the other, of variety: separate-people, thought-/people, whole populations issuing from the unconscious, and in each suddenly animated desert, the springing up of selves one didn't know – our women, our monsters, our jackals, our Arabs, our aliases, our frights. That there is no invention of any other I, no poetry, no fiction without a certain homosexuality (the I/play of bisexuality) acting as a crystallization of my ultrasubjectivities.[2] I is this exuberant, gay, personal matter, masculine, feminine or other where I enchants, I agonizes me. And in the concert of personalizations called I, at the same time that a certain homosexuality is repressed, symbolically, substitutively, it comes through by various signs, conduct-character, behaviour-acts. And it is even more clearly seen in writing.

Thus, what is inscribed under Jean Genet's name, in the movement of a text that divides itself, pulls itself to pieces, dismembers itself, regroups, remembers itself, is a proliferating, maternal femininity. A phantasmic meld of men, males, gentlemen, monarchs, princes, orphans, flowers, mothers, breasts gravitates about a wonderful 'sun of energy' – love, – that bombards and disintegrates these ephemeral amorous anomalies so that they can be recomposed in other bodies for new passions.

She is bisexual:

What I propose here leads directly to a reconsideration of *bisexuality*. To reassert the value of bisexuality;[3] hence to snatch it from the fate classically reserved for it in which it is conceptualized as 'neuter' because, as such, it would aim at warding off castration. Therefore, I shall distinguish between two bisexualities, two opposite ways of imagining the possibility and practice of bisexuality.

1) Bisexuality as a fantasy of a complete being, which replaces the fear of castration and veils sexual difference insofar as this is perceived as the mark of a mythical separation – the trace, therefore, of a dangerous and painful ability to be cut. Ovid's Hermaphrodite, less bisexual than asexual, not made up of two genders but of two halves. Hence, a fantasy of unity. Two within one, and not even two wholes.

2) To this bisexuality that melts together and effaces, wishing to avert castration, I oppose the *other bisexuality*, the one with which every subject, who is not shut up inside the spurious Phallocentric Performing Theater, sets up his or her erotic universe. Bisexuality – that is to say the location within oneself of the presence of both sexes, evident and insistent in different ways according to the individual, the nonexclusion of difference or of a sex, and starting with this 'permission' one gives oneself, the multiplication of the effects of desire's inscription on every part of the body and the other body.

For historical reasons, at the present time it is woman who benefits from and opens up within this bisexuality beside itself, which does not annihilate differences but cheers them on, pursues them, adds more: in a certain way *woman is bisexual* – man having been trained to aim for glorious phallic monosexuality. By insisting on the primacy of the phallus and implementing it, phallocratic ideology has produced more than one victim. As a woman, I could be obsessed by the scepter's great shadow, and they told me: adore it, that thing you don't wield.

But at the same time, man has been given the grotesque and unenviable fate of being reduced to a single idol with clay balls. And terrified of homosexuality, as Freud and his followers remark. Why does man fear *being* a woman? Why this refusal (*Ablehnung*) of femininity? The question that stumps Freud. The 'bare rock' of castration. For Freud, the repressed is not the other sex defeated by the dominant sex, as his friend Fliess (to whom Freud owes the theory of bisexuality) believed; what is repressed is leaning toward one's own sex.

Psychoanalysis is formed on the basis of woman and has repressed (not all that successfully) the femininity of masculine sexuality, and now the account it gives is hard to disprove.

We women, the derangers, know it only too well. But nothing compels us to deposit our lives in these lack-banks; to think that the subject is constituted as the last stage in a drama of bruising rehearsals; to endlessly bail out the father's religion. Because we don't desire it. We don't go round and round the supreme hole. We have no *woman's* reason to pay allegiance to the negative. What is feminine (the poets suspected it) affirms: ... and yes I said yes I will Yes, says Molly (in her rapture), carrying *Ulysses* with her in the direction of a new writing; I said yes, I will Yes.

To say that woman is somehow bisexual is an apparently paradoxical way of displacing and reviving the question of difference. And therefore of writing as 'feminine' or 'masculine.'

I will say: today, writing is woman's. That is not a provocation, it means that woman admits there is an other. In her becoming-woman, she has not erased the bisexuality latent in the girl as in the boy. Femininity and bisexuality go together, in a combination that varies according to the individual, spreading the intensity of its force differently and (depending on the moments of their history) privileging one component or another. It is much harder for man to let the other come through him. Writing is the passageway, the entrance, the exit, the dwelling place of the other in me – the other that I am and am not, that I don't know how to be, but that I feel passing, that makes me live – that tears me apart, disturbs me, changes me, who? – a feminine one, a masculine one, some? – several, some unknown, which is indeed what gives me the desire to know and from which all life soars. This peopling gives neither rest nor security, always disturbs the relationship to 'reality,' produces an uncertainty that gets in the way of the subject's socialization. It is distressing, it wears you out; and for men this permeability, this nonexclusion is a threat, something intolerable.

In the past, when carried to a rather spectacular degree, it was called 'possession.' Being possessed is not desirable for a masculine Imaginary, which would interpret it as passivity – a dangerous feminine position. It is true that a certain receptivity is 'feminine.' One can, of course, as History has always done, exploit feminine reception through alienation. A woman, by her opening up, is open to being 'possessed,' which is to say, dispossessed of herself.

But I am speaking here of femininity as keeping alive the other that is confided to her, that visits her, that she can love as other. The loving to be other, another, without its necessarily going the rout of abasing what is same, herself.

As for passivity, in excess, it is partly bound up with death. But there is a nonclosure that is not submission but confidence and comprehension; that is not an opportunity for destruction but for wonderful expansion.

Through the same opening that is her danger, she comes out of herself to go to the other, a traveler in unexplored places; she does not refuse, she approaches, not to do away with the space between, but to see it, to experience what she is not, what she is, what she can be.

Writing is working; being worked; questioning (in) the between (letting oneself be questioned) of same *and of* other without which nothing lives; undoing death's work by willing the togetherness of one-another, infinitely charged with a ceaseless exchange of one with another – not knowing one another and beginning again only from what is most distant, from self, from other, from the other within. A course that multiplies transformations by the thousands.

And that is not done without danger, without pain, without loss – of moments of self, of consciousness, of persons one has been, goes beyond, leaves. It doesn't happen without expense – of sense, time, direction.

But is that specifically feminine? It is men who have inscribed, described, theorized the paradoxical logic of an economy without reserve. This is not contradictory; it brings us back to asking about their femininity. Rare are the men able to venture onto the brink where writing, freed from law, unencumbered by moderation, exceeds phallic authority, and where the subjectivity inscribing its effects becomes feminine.

Where does difference come through in writing? If there is difference it is in the manner of spending, of valorizing the appropriated, of thinking what is not-the-same. In general, it is in the manner of thinking any 'return,' the relationship of capitalization, if this word 'return' (*rapport*) is understood in its sense of 'revenue.'

Today, still, the masculine return to the Selfsame is narrower and more restricted than femininity's. It all happens as if man were more directly threatened in his being by the nonselfsame than woman. Ordinarily, this is exactly the cultural product described by psychoanalysis: someone who still has something to lose. And in the development of desire, of exchange, he is the en-grossing party: loss and expense are stuck in the commercial deal that always turns the gift into a gift-that-takes. The gift brings in a return. Loss, at the end of a curved line, is turned into its opposite and comes back to him as profit.

But does woman escape this law of return? Can one speak of another spending? Really, there is no 'free' gift. You never give something for nothing. But all the difference lies in the why and how of the gift, in the values that the gesture of giving affirms, causes to circulate; in the type of profit the giver draws from the gift and the use to which he or she puts it. Why, how, is there this difference?

When one gives, what does one give oneself?

What does he want in return – the traditional man? And she? At first what *he* wants, whether on the level of cultural or of personal exchanges, whether it is a question of capital or of affectivity (or of love, of *jouissance*) – is that he gain more masculinity: plus-value of virility, authority, power, money, or pleasure, all of which reenforce his phallocentric narcissism at the same time. Moreover, that is what society is made for – how it is made; and men can hardly get out of it. An unenviable fate they've made for themselves. A man is always proving something; he has to 'show off,' show up the others. Masculine profit is almost always mixed up with a success that is socially defined.

How does she give? What are her dealings with saving or squandering, reserve, life, death? She too gives *for*. She too, with open hands, gives herself – pleasure, happiness, increased value, enhanced self-image. But she doesn't try to 'recover her expenses.' She is able not to return to herself, never setting down, pouring out, going everywhere to the other. She does not flee extremes; she is not the being-of-the-end (the goal), but she is how-far-being-reaches.

If there is a self proper to woman, paradoxically it is her capacity to depropriate herself without self-interest: endless body, without 'end,' without principal 'parts'; if she is a whole, it is a whole made up of parts that are wholes, not simple, partial objects but varied entirety, moving and boundless change, a cosmos where eros never stops travelling, vast astral space. She doesn't revolve around a sun that is more star than the stars.

That doesn't mean that she is undifferentiated magma; it means that she doesn't create a monarchy of her body or her desire. Let masculine sexuality gravitate around the penis, engendering this centralized body (political anatomy) under the party dictatorship. Woman does not perform on herself this regionalization that profits the couple head-sex, that only inscribes itself within frontiers. Her libido is cosmic, just as her unconscious is worldwide: her writing also can only go on and on, without ever inscribing or distinguishing contours, daring these dizzying passages in other, fleeting and passionate dwellings within him, within the hims and hers whom she inhabits just long enough to watch them, as close as possible to the unconscious from the moment they arise; to love them, as close as possible to instinctual drives, and then, further, all filled with these brief identifying hugs and kisses, she goes and goes on infinitely. She alone dares and wants to know from within where she, the one excluded, has never ceased to hear what-comes-before-language reverberating. She lets the other tongue of a thousand tongues speak – the tongue, sound without barrier or death. She refuses life nothing. Her tongue doesn't hold back but holds forth, doesn't keep in but keeps on enabling. Where the wonder of being several and turmoil is expressed, she does not protect herself against these unknown feminines; she surprises herself at seeing, being, pleasuring in her gift of changeability. I am spacious singing Flesh: onto which is grafted no one knows which I – which masculine or feminine, more or less human but above all living, because changing I.

Writing femininity transformation:

And there is a link between the economy of femininity – the open, extravagant subjectivity, that relationship to the other in which the gift doesn't calculate its influence – and the possibility of love; and a link today between this 'libido of the other' and writing.

At the present time, *defining* a feminine practice of writing is impossible with an impossibility that will continue; for this practice will never be able to be *theorized*, enclosed, coded, which does not mean it does not exist. But it will always exceed the discourse governing the phallocentric system; it takes place and will take place somewhere other than in the territories subordinated to philosophical-theoretical domination. It will not let itself think except through subjects that break automatic functions, border runners never subjugated by any authority. But one can begin to speak. Begin to point out some effects, some elements of unconscious drives, some relations of the feminine Imaginary to the Real, to writing.

What I have to say about it is also only a beginning, because right from the start these features affect me powerfully.

First I sense femininity in writing by: a privilege of *voice: writing and voice* are entwined and interwoven and writing's continuity/voice's rhythm take each other's breath away through interchanging, make the text gasp or form it out of suspenses and silences, make it lose its voice or rend it with cries.

In a way, feminine writing never stops reverberating from the wrench that the acquisition of speech, speaking out loud, is for her – 'acquisition' that is experienced more as tearing away, dizzying flight and flinging oneself, diving. Listen to woman speak in a gathering (if she is not painfully out of breath): she doesn't 'speak,' she throws her trembling body into the air, she lets herself go, she flies, she goes completely into her voice, she vitally defends the 'logic' of her discourse with her body; her flesh speaks true. She exposes herself. Really she makes what she thinks materialize carnally, she conveys meaning with her body. She *inscribes* what she is saying because she does not deny unconscious drives the unmanageable part they play in speech.

Her discourse, even when 'theoretical' or political, is never simple or linear or 'objectivized,' universalized; she involves her story in history.

Every woman has known the torture of beginning to speak aloud, heart beating as if to break, occasionally falling into loss of language, ground and language slipping out from under her, because for woman speaking – even just opening her mouth – in public is something rash, a transgression.

A double anguish, for even if she transgresses, her word almost always falls on the deaf, masculine ear, which can only hear language that speaks in the masculine.

We are not culturally accustomed to speaking, throwing signs out toward a scene, employing the suitable rhetoric. Also, it is not where we find our pleasure: indeed, one pays a certain price for the use of a discourse. The logic of communication requires an economy both of signs – of signifiers – and of subjectivity. The orator is asked to unwind a thin thread, dry and taut. We like uneasiness, questioning. There is waste in what we say. We need that waste. To write is always to make allowances for superabundance and uselessness while slashing the exchange value that keeps the spoken word on its track. That is why writing is good, letting the tongue try itself out – as one attempts a caress, taking the time a phrase or a thought needs to make oneself loved, to make oneself reverberate.

It is in writing, from woman and toward woman, and in accepting the challenge of the discourse controlled by the phallus, that woman will affirm woman somewhere other than in silence, the place reserved for her in and through the Symbolic. May she get out of booby-trapped silence! And not have the margin or the harem foisted on her as her domain!

In feminine speech, as in writing, there never stops reverberating something that, having once passed through us, having imperceptibly and deeply touched us, still has the power to affect us – song, the first music of the voice of love, which every woman keeps alive.

The Voice sings from a time before law, before the Symbolic took one's breath away and reappropriated it into language under its authority of separation. The deepest, the oldest, the loveliest Visitation. Within each woman the first, nameless love is singing.

In woman there is always, more or less, something of 'the mother' repairing and feeding, resisting separation, a force that does not let itself be cut off but that runs codes ragged. The relationship to childhood (the child she was, she is, she acts and makes and starts anew, and unties at the place where, as a same she even others herself), is no more cut off than is the relationship to the 'mother,' *as it consists of* delights and violences. Text, my body: traversed by lilting flows; listen to me, it is not a captivating, clinging 'mother'; it is the equivoice that, touching you, affects you, pushes you away from your breast to come to language, that summons *your* strength; it is the rhyth-me that laughs you; the one intimately addressed who makes all metaphors, all body(?) – bodies(?) – possible and desirable, who is no more describable than god, soul, or the Other; the part of you that puts space between yourself and pushes you to inscribe your woman's style in language. Voice: milk that could go on forever. Found again. The lost mother/bitter-lost. Eternity: is voice mixed with milk.

Not the origin: she doesn't go back there. A boy's journey is the return to the native land, the *Heimweh* Freud speaks of, the nostalgia that makes man a being who tends to come back to the point of departure to appropriate it for himself and to die there. A girl's journey is farther – to the unknown, to invent.

How come this privileged relationship with voice? Because no woman piles up as many defenses against instinctual drives as a man does. You don't prop things up, you don't brick things up the way he does, you don't withdraw from pleasure so 'prudently.' Even if phallic mystification has contaminated good relations in general, woman is never far from the 'mother' (I do not mean the role but the 'mother' as no-name and as source of goods). There is always at least a little good mother milk left in her. She writes with white ink.

Voice! That, too, is launching forth and effusion without return. Exclamation, cry, breathlessness, yell, cough, vomit, music. Voice leaves. Voice loses. She leaves. She loses. And that is how she writes, as one throws a voice – forward, into the void. She goes away, she goes forward, doesn't turn back to look at her tracks. Pays no attention to herself. Running breakneck. Contrary to the self-absorbed, masculine narcissism, making sure of its image, of being seen, of seeing itself, of assembling its glories, of pocketing itself again. The reductive look, the always divided look returning, the mirror economy; he needs to love himself. But she launches forth; she seeks to love. Moreover, this is what Valéry sensed, marking his Young Fate in search of herself with ambiguity, masculine in her jealousy of herself: 'seeing herself see herself,' the motto of all phallocentric speculation/specularization, the motto of every Teste; and feminine in the frantic descent deeper deeper to where a voice that doesn't know itself is lost in the sea's churning.

Voice-cry. Agony – the spoken 'word' exploded, blown to bits by suffering and anger, demolishing discourse: this is how she has always been heard before, ever since the time when masculine society began to push her offstage, expulsing her, plundering her. Ever since Medea, ever since Electra.

Voice: unfastening, fracas. Fire! She shoots, she shoots away. Break. From their bodies where they have been buried, shut up and at the same time forbidden to take pleasure. Women have almost everything to write about femininity: about their sexuality, that is to say, about the infinite and mobile complexity of their becoming erotic, about the lightning ignitions of such a minuscule-vast region of their body, not about destiny but about the adventure of such an urge, the voyages, crossings, advances, sudden and slow awakenings, discoveries of a formerly timid region that is just now springing up. Woman's body with a thousand and one fiery hearths, when – shattering censorship and yokes – she lets it articulate the proliferation of meanings that runs through it in every direction. It is going to take much more than language for him to make the ancient maternal tongue sound in only one groove.

We have turned away from our bodies. Shamefully we have been taught to be unaware of them, to lash them with stupid modesty; we've been tricked into a fool's bargain: each one is to love the other sex. I'll give you your body and you will give me mine. But which men give women the body that they blindly hand over to him? Why so few texts? Because there are still so few women winning back their bodies. Woman must write her body, must make up the unimpeded tongue that bursts partitions, classes, and rhetorics, orders and codes, must inundate, run through, go beyond the discourse with its last reserves, including the one of laughing off the word 'silence' that has to be said, the one that, aiming for the impossible, stops dead before the word 'impossible' and writes it as 'end.'

In body/Still more: woman is body more than man is. Because he is invited to social success, to sublimation. More body hence more writing. For a long time, still, bodily, within her body she has answered the harassment, the familial conjugal venture of domestication, the repeated attempts to castrate her. Woman, who has run her tongue ten thousand times seven times around her mouth before not speaking, either dies of it or knows her tongue and her mouth better than anyone. Now, I-woman am going to blow up the Law: a possible and inescapable explosion from now on; let it happen, right now, in language.

When '*The* Repressed' of their culture and their society come back, it is an explosive return, which is *absolutely* shattering, staggering, overturning, with a force never let loose before, on the scale of the most tremendous repressions: for at the end of the Age of the Phallus, women will have been either wiped out or heated to the highest, most violent, white-hot fire. Throughout their deafening dumb history, they have lived in dreams, embodied but still deadly silent, in silences, in voiceless rebellions.

And with what force in their fragility: 'fragility,' a vulnerability to match their matchless intensity. Women have not sublimated. Fortunately. They have saved their skins and their energy. They haven't worked at planning the impass of futureless lives. They have furiously inhabited these sumptuous bodies. Those wonderful hysterics, who subjected Freud to so many voluptuous moments too shameful to mention, bombarding his mosaic statue/law of Moses with their carnal, passionate body-words, haunting him with their inaudible thundering denunciations, were more than just naked beneath their seven veils of modesty – they were dazzling. In a single word of the body they inscribed the endless vertigo of a history loosed like an arrow from all of men's history, from biblicocapitalist society. Following these yesterday's victims of torture, who anticipate the new women, no intersubjective relationship will ever be the same. It is you, Dora, you, who cannot be tamed, the poetic body, the true 'mistress' of the Signifier. Before tomorrow your effectiveness will be seen to work – when your words will no longer be retracted, pointed against your own breast, but will write themselves against the other and against men's grammar. Men must not have that place for their own any more than they have us for their own.

If woman has always functioned 'within' man's discourse, a signifier referring always to the opposing signifier that annihilates its particular energy, puts down or stifles its very different sounds, now it is time for her to displace this 'within,' explode it, overturn it, grab it, make it hers, take it in, take it into her women's mouth, bite its tongue with her women's teeth, make up her own tongue to get inside of it. And you will see how easily she will well up, from this 'within' where she was hidden and dormant, to the lips where her foams will overflow.

It is not a question of appropriating their instruments, their concepts, their places for oneself or of wishing oneself in their position of mastery. Our knowing that there is a danger of identification does not mean we should give in. Leave that to the worriers, to masculine anxiety and its obsessional relationship to workings they must control – knowing 'how it runs' in order to 'make it run.' Not taking possession to internalize or manipulate but to shoot through and smash the walls.

Feminine strength is such that while running away with syntax, breaking the famous line (just a tiny little thread, so they say) that serves men as a substitute cord, without which they can't have any fun (*jouir*), to make sure the old mother really is always behind them watching them play phallus, she goes to the impossible where she plays the other, for love, without dying of it.

De-propriation, depersonalization, because she, exasperating, immoderate, and contradictory, destroys laws, the 'natural' order. She lifts the bar separating the present from the future, breaking the rigid law of individuation. Nietzsche, in *The Birth of Tragedy*, said that this is the privilege of divinatory, magical forces. What happens to the subject, to the personal pronoun, to its possessives when, suddenly, gaily daring her metamorphoses (because from her within – for a long time her world, she is in a pervasive relationship of desire with every being) she makes another way of knowing circulate? Another way of producing, of communicating, where each one is always far more than one, where her power of identification puts the same to rout. – And with the same traversing, dispersing gesture with which she becomes a feminine other, a masculine other, she breaks with explanation, inter-pretation, and all the authorities pinpointing localization. She forgets. She proceeds by lapse and bounds. She flies/steals.

To fly/steal is woman's gesture, to steal into language to make it fly. We have all learned flight/theft, the art with many techniques, for all the centuries we have only had access to having by stealing/flying; we have lived in a flight/theft, stealing/flying, finding the close, concealed ways-through of desire. It's not just luck if the word 'voler' volleys between the 'vol' of theft and the 'vol' of flight, pleasuring in each and routing the sense police. It is not just luck: woman partakes of bird and burglar, just as the burglar partakes of woman and bird: hesheits pass, hesheits fly by, hesheits pleasure in scrambling spatial order, disorienting it, moving furniture, things, and values around, breaking in, emptying structures, turning the selfsame, the proper upside down.

What woman has not stolen? Who has not dreamed, savored, or done the thing that jams sociality? Who has not dropped a few red herrings, mocked her way around the separating bar, inscribed what makes a difference with her body, punched holes in the system of couples and positions, and with a transgression screwed up whatever is successive, chain-linked, the fence of circumfusion?

A feminine text cannot not be more than subversive: if it writes itself it is in volcanic heaving of the old 'real' property crust. In ceaseless displacement. She must write herself because, when the time comes for her liberation, it is the invention of a *new, insurgent* writing that will allow her to put the breaks and indispensable changes into effect in her history. At first, individually, on two inseparable levels: – woman, writing herself, will go back to this body that has been worse than confiscated, a body replaced with a disturbing stranger, sick or dead, who so often is a bad influence, the cause and place of inhibitions. By censuring the body, breath and speech are censored at the same time.

To write – the act that will 'realize' the un-censored relationship of woman to her sexuality, to her woman-being giving her back access to her own forces; that will return her goods, her pleasures, her organs, her vast bodily territories kept under seal; that will tear her out of the superegoed, over-Mosesed structure where the same position of guilt is always reserved for her (guilty of everything, every time: of having desires, of not having any; of being frigid, of being 'too' hot; of not being both at once; of being too much of a mother and not enough; of nurturing and of not nurturing . . .). Write yourself: your body must make itself heard. Then the huge resources of the unconscious will burst out. Finally the inexhaustible feminine Imaginary is going to be deployed. Without gold or black dollars, our naphtha will spread values over the world, un-quoted values that will change the rules of the old game.

Notes

1   All Derrida's work traversing-detecting the history of philosophy is devoted to bringing this to light. In Plato, Hegel, and Nietzsche, the same process continues: repression, repudiation, distancing of woman; a murder that is mixed up with history as the manifestation and representation of masculine power.

2   *Prénoms de personne* [*Nobody's First Names*], Cixous, Editions du Seuil: 'Les Comtes de Hoffmann' ['Tales of Hoffmann'], pp. 112ff.

3   See *Nouvelle Revue de Psychoanalyse*, no. 7, *Bisexualité et différence des sexes* (Spring 1973).

5.3

Laura Mulvey, from 'Visual Pleasure and Narrative Cinema' (1975)

I Introduction

(a) A political use of psychoanalysis

This paper intends to use psychoanalysis to discover where and how the fascination of film is reinforced by pre-existing patterns of fascination already at work within the individual subject and the social formations that have moulded him. It takes as its starting-point the way film reflects, reveals and even plays on the straight, socially established interpretation of sexual difference which controls images, erotic ways of looking and spectacle. It is helpful to understand what the cinema has been, how its magic has worked in the past, while attempting a theory and a practice which will challenge this cinema of the past. Psychoanalytic theory is thus appropriated here as a political weapon, demonstrating the way the unconscious of patriarchal society has structured film form.

The paradox of phallocentrism in all its manifestations is that it depends on the image of the castrated women to give order and meaning to its world. An idea of woman stands as linchpin to the system: it is her lack that produces the phallus as a symbolic presence, it is her desire to make good the lack that the phallus signifies. Recent writing in *Screen* about psychoanalysis and the cinema has not sufficiently brought out the importance of the representation of the female form in a symbolic order in which, in the last resort, it speaks castration and nothing else. To summarise briefly: the function of woman in forming the patriarchal unconscious is twofold: she firstly symbolises the castration threat by her real lack of a penis and secondly thereby raises her child into the symbolic. Once this has been achieved, her meaning in the process is at an end. It does not last into the world of law and language except as a memory, which oscillates between memory of maternal plenitude and memory of lack. Both are posited on nature (or on anatomy in Freud's famous phrase). Woman's desire is subjugated to her image as bearer of the bleeding wound; she can exist only in relation to castration and cannot transcend it. She turns her child into the signifier of her own desire to possess a penis (the condition, she imagines, of entry into the symbolic). Either she must gracefully give way to the word, the name of the father and the law, or else struggle to keep her child down with her in the half-light of the imaginary. Woman then stands in patriarchal culture as a signifier for the male other, bound by a symbolic order in which man can live out his fantasies and obsessions through linguistic command by imposing them on the silent image of woman still tied to her place as bearer, not maker, of meaning.

There is an obvious interest in this analysis for feminists, a beauty in its exact rendering of the frustration experienced under the phallocentric order. It gets us nearer to the roots of our oppression, it brings closer an articulation of the problem, it faces us with the ultimate challenge: how to fight the unconscious structured like a language (formed critically at the moment of arrival of language) while still caught within the language of the patriarchy? There is no way in which we can produce an alternative out of the blue, but we can begin to make a break by examining patriarchy with the tools it provides, of which psychoanalysis is not the only but an important one. We are still separated by a great gap from important issues for the female unconscious which are scarcely relevant to phallocentric theory: the sexing of the female infant and her relationship to the symbolic, the sexually mature woman as non-mother, maternity outside the signification of the phallus, the vagina. But, at this point, psychoanalytic theory as it now stands can at least advance our understanding of the *status quo*, of the patriarchal order in which we are caught.

(b) Destruction of pleasure as a radical weapon

As an advanced representation system, the cinema poses questions about the ways the unconscious (formed by the dominant order) structures ways of seeing and pleasure in looking. Cinema has changed over the last few decades. It is no longer the monolithic system based on large capital investment exemplified at its best by Hollywood in the 1930s, 1940s and 1950s. Technological advances (16mm and so on) have changed the economic conditions of cinematic production, which can now be artisanal as well as capitalist. Thus it has been possible for an alternative cinema to develop. However self-conscious and ironic Hollywood managed to be, it always restricted itself to a formal *mise en scène* reflecting the dominant ideological concept of the cinema. The alternative cinema provides a space for the birth of a cinema which is radical in both a political and an aesthetic sense and challenges the basic assumptions of the mainstream film. This is not to reject the latter moralistically, but to highlight the ways in which its formal preoccupations reflect the psychical obsessions of the society which produced it and, further, to stress that the alternative cinema must start specifically by reacting against these obsessions and assumptions. A politically and aesthetically avant-garde cinema is now possible, but it can still only exist as a counterpoint.

The magic of the Hollywood style at its best (and of all the cinema which fell within its sphere of influence) arose, not exclusively, but in one important aspect, from its skilled and satisfying manipulation of visual pleasure. Unchallenged, mainstream film coded the erotic into the language of the dominant patriarchal order. In the highly developed Hollywood cinema it was only through these codes that the alienated subject, torn in his imaginary memory by a sense of loss, by the terror of potential lack in fantasy, came near to finding a glimpse of satisfaction: through its formal beauty and its play on his own formative obsessions. This article will discuss the interweaving of that erotic pleasure in film, its meaning and, in particular, the central place of the image of woman. It is said that analysing pleasure, or beauty, destroys it. That is the intention of this article. The satisfaction and reinforcement of the ego that represent the high point of film history hitherto must be attacked. Not in favour of a reconstructed new pleasure, which cannot exist in the abstract, nor of intellectualised unpleasure, but to make way for a total negation of the ease and plenitude of the narrative fiction film. The alternative is the thrill that comes from leaving the past behind without simply rejecting it, transcending outworn or oppressive forms, and daring to break with normal pleasurable expectations in order to conceive a new language of desire.

II Pleasure in looking/fascination with the human form

A   The cinema offers a number of possible pleasures. One is scopophilia (pleasure in looking). There are circumstances in which looking itself is a source of pleasure, just as, in the reverse formation, there is pleasure in being looked at. Originally, in his *Three Essays on Sexuality*, Freud isolated scopophilia as one of the component instincts of sexuality which exist as drives quite independently of the erotogenic zones. At this point he associated scopophilia with taking other people as objects, subjecting them to a controlling and curious gaze. His particular examples centre on the voyeuristic activities of children, their desire to see and make sure of the private and forbidden (curiosity about other people's genital and bodily functions, about the presence or absence of the penis and, retrospectively, about the primal scene). In this analysis scopophilia is essentially active. (Later, in 'Instincts and Their Vicissitudes', Freud developed his theory of scopophilia further, attaching it initially to pre-genital auto-eroticism, after which, by analogy, the pleasure of the look is transferred to others. There is a close working here of the relationship between the active instinct and its further development in a narcissistic form.) Although the instinct is modified by other factors, in particular the constitution of the ego, it continues to exist as the erotic basis for pleasure in looking at another person as object. At the extreme, it can become fixated into a perversion, producing obsessive voyeurs and Peeping Toms whose only sexual satisfaction can come from watching, in an active controlling sense, an objectified other.

At first glance, the cinema would seem to be remote from the undercover world of the surreptitious observation of an unknowing and unwilling victim. What is seen on the screen is so manifestly shown. But the mass of mainstream film, and the conventions within which it has consciously evolved, portray a hermetically sealed world which unwinds magically, indifferent to the presence of the audience, producing for them a sense of separation and playing on their voyeuristic fantasy. Moreover the extreme contrast between the darkness in the auditorium (which also isolates the spectators from one another) and the brilliance of the shifting patterns of light and shade on the screen helps to promote the illusion of voyeuristic separation. Although the film is really being shown, is there to be seen, conditions of screening and narrative conventions give the spectator an illusion of looking in on a private world. Among other things, the position of the spectators in the cinema is blatantly one of repression of their exhibitionism and projection of the repressed desire onto the performer.

B   The cinema satisfies a primordial wish for pleasurable looking, but it also goes further, developing scopophilia in its narcissistic aspect. The conventions of mainstream film focus attention on the human form. Scale, space, stories are all anthropomorphic. Here, curiosity and the wish to look intermingle with a fascination with likeness and recognition: the human face, the human body, the relationship between the human form and its surroundings, the visible presence of the person in the world. Jacques Lacan has described how the moment when a child recognises its own image in the mirror is crucial for the constitution of the ego. Several aspects of this analysis are relevant here. The mirror phase occurs at a time when children's physical ambitions outstrip their motor capacity, with the result that their recognition of themselves is joyous in that they imagine their mirror image to be more complete, more perfect than they experience in their own body. Recognition is thus overlaid with misrecognition: the image recognised is conceived as the reflected body of the self, but its misrecognition as superior projects this body outside itself as an ideal ego, the alienated subject which, reintrojected as an ego ideal, prepares the way for identification with others in the future. This mirror moment predates language for the child.

Important for this article is the fact that it is an image that constitutes the matrix of the imaginary, or recognition/misrecognition and identification, and hence of the first articulation of the I, of subjectivity. This is a moment when an older fascination with looking (at the mother's face, for an obvious example) collides with the initial inklings of self-awareness. Hence it is the birth of the long love affair/despair between image and self-image which has found such intensity of expression in film and such joyous recognition in the cinema audience. Quite apart from the extraneous similarities between screen and mirror (the framing of the human form in its surroundings, for instance), the cinema has structures of fascination strong enough to allow temporary loss of ego while simultaneously reinforcing it. The sense of forgetting the world as the ego has come to perceive it (I forgot who I am and where I was) is nostalgically reminiscent of that pre-subjective moment of image recognition. While at the same time, the cinema has distinguished itself in the production of ego ideals, through the star system for instance. Stars provide a focus or centre both to screen space and screen story where they act out a complex process of likeness and difference (the glamorous impersonates the ordinary).

C   Sections A and B have set out two contradictory aspects of the pleasurable structures of looking in the conventional cinematic situation. The first, scopophilic, arises from pleasure in using another person as an object of sexual stimulation through sight. The second, developed through narcissism and the constitution of the ego, comes from identification with the image seen. Thus, in film terms, one implies a separation of the erotic identity of the subject from the object on the screen (active scopophilia), the other demands identification of the ego with the object on the screen through the spectator's fascination with and recognition of his like. The first is a function of the sexual instincts, the second of ego libido. This dichotomy was crucial for Freud. Although he saw the two as interacting and overlaying each other, the tension between instinctual drives and self-preservation polarises in terms of pleasure. But both are formative structures, mechanisms without intrinsic meaning. In themselves they have no signification, unless attached to an idealisation. Both pursue aims in indifference to perceptual reality, and motivate eroticised phantasmagoria that affect the subject's perception of the world to make a mockery of empirical objectivity.

During its history, the cinema seems to have evolved a particular illusion of reality in which this contradiction between libido and ego has found a beautifully complementary fantasy world. In *reality* the fantasy world of the screen is subject to the law which produces it. Sexual instincts and identification processes have a meaning within the symbolic order which articulates desire. Desire, born with language, allows the possibility of transcending the instinctual and the imaginary, but its point of reference continually returns to the traumatic moment of its birth: the castration complex. Hence the look, pleasurable in form, can be threatening in content, and it is woman as representation/image that crystallises this paradox.

III Woman as image, man as bearer of the look

A   In a world ordered by sexual imbalance, pleasure in looking has been split between active/male and passive/female. The determining male gaze projects its fantasy onto the female figure, which is styled accordingly. In their traditional exhibitionist role women are simultaneously looked at and displayed, with their appearance coded for strong visual and erotic impact so that they can be said to connote *to-be-looked-at-ness*. Woman displayed as sexual object is the *leitmotif* of erotic spectacle: from pin-ups to strip-tease, from Ziegfeld to Busby Berkeley, she holds the look, and plays to and signifies male desire. Mainstream film neatly combines spectacle and narrative. (Note, however, how in the musical song-and-dance numbers interrupt the flow of the diegesis.) The presence of woman is an indispensable element of spectacle in normal narrative film, yet her visual presence tends to work against the development of a story-line, to freeze the flow of action in moments of erotic contemplation. This alien presence then has to be integrated into cohesion with the narrative. As Budd Boetticher has put it:

> What counts is what the heroine provokes, or rather what she represents. She is the one, or rather the love or fear she inspires in the hero, or else the concern he feels for her, who makes him act the way he does. In herself the woman has not the slightest importance.

(A recent tendency in narrative film has been to dispense with this problem altogether; hence the development of what Molly Haskell has called the 'buddy movie', in which the active homosexual eroticism of the central male figures can carry the story without distraction.) Traditionally, the woman displayed has functioned on two levels: as erotic object for the characters within the screen story, and as erotic object for the spectator within the auditorium, with a shifting tension between the looks on either side of the screen. For instance, the device of the show-girl allows the two looks to be unified technically without any apparent break in the diegesis. A woman performs within the narrative; the gaze of the spectator and that of the male characters in the film are neatly combined without breaking narrative verisimilitude. For a moment the sexual impact of the performing woman takes the film into a no man's land outside its own time and space. Thus Marilyn Monroe's first appearance in *The River of No Return* and Lauren Bacall's songs in *To Have and Have Not*. Similarly, conventional close-ups of legs (Dietrich, for instance) or a face (Garbo) integrate into the narrative a different mode of eroticism. One part of a fragmented body destroys the Renaissance space, the illusion of depth demanded by the narrative; it gives flatness, the quality of a cut-out or icon, rather than verisimilitude, to the screen.

B An active/passive heterosexual division of labour has similarly controlled narrative structure. According to the principles of the ruling ideology and the psychical structures that back it up, the male figure cannot bear the burden of sexual objectification. Man is reluctant to gaze at his exhibitionist like. Hence the split between spectacle and narrative supports the man's role as the active one of advancing the story, making things happen. The man controls the film fantasy and also emerges as the representative of power in a further sense: as the bearer of the look of the spectator, transferring it behind the screen to neutralise the extradiegetic tendencies represented by woman as spectacle. This is made possible through the processes set in motion by structuring the film around a main controlling figure with whom the spectator can identify. As the spectator identifies with the main male protagonist, he projects his look onto that of his like, his screen surrogate, so that the power of the male protagonist as he controls events coincides with the active power of the erotic look, both giving a satisfying sense of omnipotence. A male movie star's glamorous characteristics are thus not those of the erotic object of the gaze, but those of the more perfect, more complete, more powerful ideal ego conceived in the original moment of recognition in front of the mirror. The character in the story can make things happen and control events better than the subject/spectator, just as the image in the mirror was more in control of motor co-ordination.

In contrast to woman as icon, the active male figure (the ego ideal of the identification process) demands a three-dimensional space corresponding to that of the mirror recognition, in which the alienated subject internalised his own representation of his imaginary existence. He is a figure in a landscape. Here the function of film is to reproduce as accurately as possible the so-called natural conditions of human perception. Camera technology (as exemplified by deep focus in particular) and camera movements (determined by the action of the protagonist), combined with invisible editing (demanded by realism), all tend to blur the limits of screen space. The male protagonist is free to command the stage, a stage of spatial illusion in which he articulates the look and creates the action.[1]

C1   Sections III A and B have set out a tension between a mode of representation of woman in film and conventions surrounding the diegesis. Each is associated with a look: that of the spectator in direct scopophilic contact with the female form displayed for his enjoyment (connoting male fantasy) and that of the spectator fascinated with the image of his like set in an illusion of natural space, and through him gaining control and possession of the woman within the diegesis. (This tension and the shift from one pole to the other can structure a single text. Thus both in *Only Angels Have Wings* and in *To Have and Have Not*, the film opens with the woman as object of the combined gaze of spectator and all the male protagonists in the film. She is isolated, glamorous, on display, sexualised. But as the narrative progresses she falls in love with the main male protagonists and becomes his property, losing her outward glamorous characteristics, her generalised sexuality, her show-girl connotations; her eroticism is subjected to the male star alone. By means of identification with him, through participation in his power, the spectator can indirectly possess her too.)

But in psychoanalytic terms, the female figure poses a deeper problem. She also connotes something that the look continually circles around but disavows: her lack of a penis, implying a threat of castration and hence unpleasure. Ultimately, the meaning of woman is sexual difference, the visually ascertainable absence of the penis, the material evidence on which is based the castration complex essential for the organisation of entrance to the symbolic order and the law of the father. Thus the woman as icon, displayed for the gaze and enjoyment of men, the active controllers of the look, always threatens to evoke the anxiety it originally signified. The male unconscious has two avenues of escape from this castration anxiety: preoccupation with the re-enactment of the original trauma (investigating the woman, demystifying her mystery), counterbalanced by the devaluation, punishment or saving of the guilty object (an avenue typified by the concerns of the *film noir*); or else complete disavowal of castration by the substitution of a fetish object or turning the represented figure itself into a fetish so that it becomes reassuring rather than dangerous (hence overvaluation, the cult of the female star).

This second avenue, fetishistic scopophilia, builds up the physical beauty of the object, transforming it into something satisfying in itself. The first avenue, voyeurism, on the contrary, has associations with sadism: pleasure lies in ascertaining guilt (immediately associated with castration), asserting control and subjugating the guilty person through punishment or forgiveness. This sadistic side fits in well with narrative. Sadism demands a story, depends on making something happen, forcing a change in another person, a battle of will and strength, victory/defeat, all occurring in a linear time with a beginning and an end. Fetishistic scopophilia, on the other hand, can exist outside linear time as the erotic instinct is focused on the look alone.

IV Summary

The psychoanalytic background that has been discussed in this article is relevant to the pleasure and unpleasure offered by traditional narrative film. The scopophilic instinct (pleasure in looking at another person as an erotic object) and, in contradistinction, ego libido (forming identification processes) act as formations, mechanisms, which mould this cinema's formal attributes. The actual image of woman as (passive) raw material for the (active) gaze of man takes the argument a step further into the content and structure of representation, adding a further layer of ideological significance demanded by the patriarchal order in its favourite cinematic form – illusionistic narrative film. The argument must return again to the psychoanalytic background: women in representation can signify castration, and activate voyeuristic or fetishistic mechanisms to circumvent this threat. Although none of these interacting layers is intrinsic to film, it is only in the film form that they can reach a perfect and beautiful contradiction, thanks to the possibility in the cinema of shifting the emphasis of the look. The place of the look defines cinema, the possibility of varying it and exposing it. This is what makes cinema quite different in its voyeuristic potential from, say, striptease, theatre, shows and so on. Going far beyond highlighting a woman's to-be-looked-at-ness, cinema builds the way she is to be looked at into the spectacle itself. Playing on the tension between film as controlling the dimension of time (editing, narrative) and film as controlling the dimension of space (changes in distance, editing), cinematic codes create a gaze, a world and an object, thereby producing an illusion cut to the measure of desire. It is these cinematic codes and their relationship to formative external structures that must be broken down before mainstream film and the pleasure it provides can be challenged.

To begin with (as an ending), the voyeuristic–scopophilic look that is a crucial part of traditional filmic pleasure can itself be broken down. There are three different looks associated with cinema: that of the camera as it records the pro-filmic event, that of the audience as it watches the final product, and that of the characters at each other within the screen illusion. The conventions of narrative film deny the first two and subordinate them to the third, the conscious aim being always to eliminate intrusive camera presence and prevent a distancing awareness in the audience. Without these two absences (the material existence of the recording process, the critical reading of the spectator), fictional drama cannot achieve reality, obviousness and truth. Nevertheless, as this article has argued, the structure of looking in narrative fiction film contains a contradiction in its own premises: the female image as a castration threat constantly endangers the unity of the diegesis and bursts through the world of illusion as an intrusive, static, one-dimensional fetish. Thus the two looks materially present in time and space are obsessively subordinated to the neurotic needs of the male ego. The camera becomes the mechanism for producing an illusion of Renaissance space, flowing movements compatible with the human eye, an ideology of representation that revolves around the perception of the subject; the camera's look is disavowed in order to create a convincing world in which the spectator's surrogate can perform with verisimilitude. Simultaneously, the look of the audience is denied an intrinsic force: as soon as fetishistic representation of the female image threatens to break the spell of illusion, and the erotic image on the screen appears directly (without mediation) to the spectator, the fact of fetishisation, concealing as it does castration fear, freezes the look, fixates the spectator and prevents him from achieving any distance from the image in front of him.

This complex interaction of looks is specific to film. The first blow against the monolithic accumulation of traditional film conventions (already undertaken by radical film-makers) is to free the look of the camera into its materiality in time and space and the look of the audience into dialectics and passionate detachment. There is no doubt that this destroys the satisfaction, pleasure and privilege of the 'invisible guest', and highlights the way film has depended on voyeuristic active/passive mechanisms. Women, whose image has continually been stolen and used for this end, cannot view the decline of the traditional film form with anything much more than sentimental regret.[2]

Notes

1   There are films with a woman as main protagonist, of course. To analyse this phenomenon seriously here would take me too far afield. Pam Cook and Claire Johnston's study of *The Revolt of Mamie Stover* in Phil Hardy (ed.), *Raoul Walsh* (Edinburgh Film Festival, 1974), shows in a striking case how the strength of this female protagonist is more apparent than real.

2   This article is a reworked version of a paper given in the French Department of the University of Wisconsin, Madison, in the spring of 1973.

5.4

Kobena Mercer, from 'Reading Racial Fetishism' (1994)
Imaging the black man's sex

Robert Mapplethorpe's retrospective exhibition at the Institute for Contemporary Arts (ICA) in London during 1983 coincided with a screening of *American Pictures*, a tape-slide by Jacob Holdt, whose documentary images of the private space of poor blacks in the rural South provoked angry protest from black people in the Scala film theatre audience, who argued that they were 'pornographic.'[1] It is one thing to say that South African apartheid is 'obscene,' but to use 'pornography' in this way as a censorious term of moralistic judgment about what is only, after all, an image, is unhelpful, as it only leads to the closure, rather than a much-needed opening, of critical debate about the politics of sex and race in representation.

In a context where both antipornography feminists and the moral majorities of the New Right have politicized sexual representation, the incident highlights the structured absence of race in contemporary cultural debates on eroticism, censorship and the power of images. Moreover, the question of sexuality calls into question the static binary alternative between positive and negative images which has dominated black critiques of racial stereotypes. It was interesting, therefore, to note that no such vocal protest could be heard in the reception of Mapplethorpe's work, especially as many of his photographs involve the staging of tabooed sexual imagery usually found in that regime of representations we call pornography. Indeed for a moment the quiet enclosure of the ICA gallery was transformed into a simulacrum of a Soho sex shop as some pictures were sectioned off 'for over-18s only,' thus reconstructing the soft porn/hard porn distinctions instituted in the retail of porno-commodities.

* * *

In as much as the image-making technology of the camera is based on the mechanical reproduction of unilinear perspective, photographs primarily represent a 'look.' I therefore want to talk about Mapplethorpe's *Black Males* not as the product of the personal intentions of the individual behind the lens, but as a cultural artifact that says something about certain ways in which white people 'look' at black people and how, in this way of looking, black male sexuality is perceived as something different, excessive, Other.[2] Certainly this particular work must be set in the context of Mapplethorpe's oeuvre as a whole: through his cool and deadly gaze each found object – 'flowers, S/M, blacks'[3] – is brought under the clinical precision of his master vision, his complete control of photo-technique, and thus aestheticized to the abject status of thinghood. However, once we consider the author of these images as no more than the 'projection, in terms more or less psychological, of our way of handling texts' (Michel Foucault, 1977: 127), then what is interesting about work such as *The Black Book* is the way the text facilitates the imaginary projection of certain racial and sexual fantasies about the black male body. Whatever his personal motivations or creative pretensions, Mapplethorpe's camera-eye opens an aperture onto aspects of stereotypes – a fixed way of seeing that freezes the flux of experience – which govern the circulation of images of black men across a range of surfaces from newspapers, television and cinema to advertising, sport and pornography.

Approached as a textual system, both *Black Males* (1983) and *The Black Book* (1986) catalogue a series of perspectives, vantage points and 'takes' on the black male body. The first thing to notice – so obvious it goes without saying – is that all the men are *nude*. Each of the camera's points of view lead to a unitary vanishing point: an erotic/aesthetic objectification of black male bodies into the idealized form of a homogenous type thoroughly saturated with a totality of sexual predicates. We look through a sequence of individual, personally named, Afro-American men, but what we *see* is only their *sex* as the essential sum total of the meanings signified around blackness and maleness. It is as if, according to Mapplethorpe's line of sight: Black + Male = Erotic/Aesthetic Object. Regardless of the sexual preferences of the spectator, the connotation is that the 'essence' of black male identity lies in the domain of sexuality. Whereas the photographs of gay male S/M rituals invoke a subcultural sexuality that consists of *doing* something, black men are confined and defined in their very *being* as sexual and nothing but sexual, hence hypersexual. In pictures like 'Man in a Polyester Suit,' apart from his hands, it is the penis and the penis alone that identifies the model in the picture as a black man.

This ontological reduction is accomplished through the specific visual codes brought to bear on the construction of pictorial space. Sculpted and shaped through the conventions of the fine art nude, the image of the black male body presents the spectator with a source of erotic pleasure in the act of looking. As a generic code established across fine art traditions in Western art history, the conventional subject of the nude is the (white) female body. Substituting the socially inferior black male subject, Mapplethorpe nevertheless draws on the codes of the genre to frame his way of seeing black male bodies as abstract, beautiful 'things.' The aesthetic, and thus erotic, objectification is totalizing in effect, as all references to a social, historical or political context are ruled out of the frame. This visual codification abstracts and essentializes the black man's body into the realm of a transcendental aesthetic ideal. In this sense, the text reveals more about the desires of the hidden and invisible white male subject behind the camera, and what 'he' wants-to-see, than it does about the anonymous black men whose beautiful bodies we see depicted.

Within the dominant tradition of the female nude, patriarchal power relations are symbolized by the binary relation in which, to put it crudely, men assume the active role of the looking subject while women are passive objects to be looked at. Laura Mulvey's (1989) contribution to feminist film theory revealed the normative power and privilege of the male gaze in dominant systems of visual representation. The image of the female nude can thus be understood not so much as a representation of (hetero)sexual desire, but as a form of objectification which articulates masculine hegemony and dominance over the very apparatus of representation itself. Paintings abound with self-serving scenarios of phallocentric fantasy in which male artists paint themselves painting naked women, which, like depictions of feminine narcissism, constructs a mirror image of what the male subject wants-to-see. The fetishistic logic of mimetic representation, which makes present for the subject what is absent in the real, can thus be characterized in terms of a masculine fantasy of mastery and control over the 'objects' depicted and represented in the visual field, the fantasy of an omnipotent eye/I who sees but who is never seen.

In Mapplethorpe's case, however, the fact that both subject and object of the gaze are male sets up a tension between the active role of looking and the passive role of being looked at. This *frisson* of (homo)sexual sameness transfers erotic investment in the fantasy of mastery from gender to racial difference. Traces of this metaphorical transfer underline the highly charged libidinal investment of Mapplethorpe's gaze as it bears down on the most visible signifier of racial difference – black skin. In his analysis of the male pinup, Richard Dyer (1982) suggests that when male subjects assume the passive, 'feminized' position of being looked at, the threat or risk to traditional definitions of masculinity is counteracted by the role of certain codes and conventions, such as taught, rigid or straining bodily posture, character types and narrativized plots, all of which aim to stabilize the gender-based dichotomy of seeing/being seen.[4] Here, Mapplethorpe appropriates elements of commonplace racial stereotypes in order to regulate, organize, prop up and *fix* the process of erotic/aesthetic objectification in which the black man's flesh becomes burdened with the task of symbolizing the transgressive fantasies and desires of the white gay male subject. The glossy, shining, fetishized surface of black skin thus serves and services a white male desire to look and to enjoy the fantasy of mastery precisely through the scopic intensity that the pictures solicit.

As Homi Bhabha has suggested, 'an important feature of colonial discourse is its dependence on the concept of "fixity" in the ideological construction of otherness' (Bhabha, 1983: 18). Mass-media stereotypes of black men – as criminals, athletes, entertainers – bear witness to the contemporary repetition of such *colonial fantasy*, in that the rigid and limited grid of representations through which black male subjects become publicly visible continues to reproduce certain *idées fixes*, ideological fictions and psychic fixations, about the nature of black sexuality and the 'otherness' it is constructed to embody. As an artist, Mapplethorpe engineers a fantasy of absolute authority over the image of the black male body by appropriating the function of the stereotype to stabilize the erotic objectification of racial otherness and thereby affirm his own identity as the sovereign I/eye empowered with mastery over the abject thinghood of the Other: as if the pictures implied, Eye have the power to turn you, base and worthless creature, into a work of art. Like Medusa's look, each camera angle and photographic shot turns black male flesh to stone, fixed and frozen in space and time: enslaved as an icon in the representational space of the white male imaginary, historically at the centre of colonial fantasy.

There are two important aspects of fetishization at play here. The erasure of any social interference in the spectator's erotic enjoyment of the image not only reifies bodies but effaces the material process involved in the production of the image, thus masking the social relations of racial power entailed by the unequal and potentially exploitative exchange between the well-known, author-named artist and the unknown, interchangeable, black models. In the same way that labor is said to be 'alienated' in commodity fetishism, something similar is put into operation in the way that the proper name of each black model is taken from a person and given to a thing, as the title or caption of the photograph, an art object which is property of the artist, the owner and author of the look. And as items of exchange-value, Mapplethorpe prints fetch exorbitant prices on the international market in art photography.

The fantasmatic emphasis on mastery also underpins the specifically sexual fetishization of the Other that is evident in the visual isolation effect whereby it is only ever *one* black man who appears in the field of vision at any one time. As an imprint of a narcissistic, ego-centred, sexualizing fantasy, this is a crucial component in the process of erotic objectification, not only because it forecloses the possible representation of a collective or contextualized black male body, but because the solo frame is the precondition for a voyeuristic fantasy of unmediated and unilateral control over the other, which is the function it performs precisely in gay and straight pornography. Aestheticized as a trap for the gaze, providing pabulum on which the appetite of the imperial eye may feed, each image thus nourishes the racialized and sexualized fantasy of appropriating the Other's body as virgin territory to be penetrated and possessed by an all-powerful desire, 'to probe and explore an alien body.'[5]

Superimposing two ways of seeing – the nude which eroticizes the act of looking, and the stereotype which imposes fixity – we see in Mapplethorpe's gaze a reinscription of the fundamental *ambivalence* of colonial fantasy, oscillating between sexual idealization of the racial other and anxiety in defence of the identity of the white male ego. Stuart Hall (1982) has underlined this splitting in the 'imperial eye' by suggesting that for every threatening image of the black subject as a marauding native, menacing savage or rebellious slave, there is the comforting image of the black as docile servant, amusing clown and happy entertainer. Commenting on this bifurcation in racial representations, Hall describes it as the expression of

> both a nostalgia for an innocence lost forever to the civilized, and the threat of civilization being over-run or undermined by the recurrence of savagery, which is always lurking just below the surface; or by an untutored sexuality threatening to 'break out.' (Hall, 1982: 41)

In Mapplethorpe, we may discern three discrete camera codes through which this fundamental ambivalence is reinscribed through the process of a sexual and racial fantasy which aestheticizes the stereotype into a work of art.

The first of these, which is most self-consciously acknowledged, could be called the *sculptural* code, as it is a subset of the generic fine art nude. As Phillip pretends to put the shot, the idealized physique of a classical Greek male statue is super-imposed on that most commonplace of stereotypes, the black man as sports hero, mythologically endowed with a 'naturally' muscular physique and an essential capacity for strength, grace and machinelike perfection: well hard. As a major public arena, sport is a key site of white male ambivalence, fear and fantasy. The spectacle of black bodies triumphant in rituals of masculine competition reinforces the fixed idea that black men are 'all brawn and no brains,' and yet, because the white man is beaten at his own game – football, boxing, cricket, athletics – the Other is idolized to the point of envy. This schism is played out daily in the popular tabloid press. On the front page headlines black males become highly visible as a threat to white society, as muggers, rapists, terrorists and guerrillas: their bodies become the imago of a savage and unstoppable capacity for destruction and vio-lence. But turn to the back pages, the sports pages, and the black man's body is heroized and lionized; any hint of antagonism is contained by the paternalistic infantilization of Frank Bruno and Daley Thompson to the status of national mascots and adopted pets – they're not Other, they're OK because they're 'our boys.' The national shame of England's demise and defeat in Test Cricket at the hands of the West Indies is accompanied by the slavish admiration of Viv Richards's awesome physique – the high-speed West Indian bowler [*sic.*] is both a threat and a winner. The ambivalence cuts deep into the recess of the white male imaginary – recall those newsreel images of Hitler's reluctant handshake with Jesse Owens at the 1936 Olympics.

If Mapplethorpe's gaze is momentarily lost in admiration, it reasserts control by also 'feminizing' the black male body into a passive, decorative *objet d'art*. When Phillip is placed on a pedestal he literally becomes putty in the hands of the white male artist – like others in this code, his body becomes raw material, mere plastic matter, to be molded, sculpted and shaped into the aesthetic idealism of inert abstraction, as we see in the picture of Derrick Cross: with the tilt of the pelvis, the black man's bum becomes a Brancusi. Commenting on the differences between moving and motionless pictures, Christian Metz suggests an association linking photography, silence and death as photographs invoke a residual death effect such that, 'the person who has been photographed is dead ... dead for having been seen.'[6] Under the intense scrutiny of Mapplethorpe's cool, detached gaze it is as if each black model is made to die, if only to reincarnate their alienated essence as idealized, aesthetic objects. We are not invited to imagine what their lives, histories or experiences are like, as they are silenced as subjects in their own right, and in a sense sacrificed on the pedestal of an aesthetic ideal in order to affirm the omni-potence of the master subject, whose gaze has the power of light and death.

In counterpoint there is a supplementary code of *portraiture* which 'humanizes' the hard phallic lines of pure abstraction and focuses on the face – the 'window of the soul' – to introduce an element of realism into the scene. But any connotation of humanist expression is denied by the direct look which does not so much assert the existence of an autonomous subjectivity, but rather, like the remote, aloof, expressions of fashion models in glossy magazines, emphasizes instead maximum distance between the spectator and the unattainable object of desire. Look, but don't touch. The models' direct look to camera does not challenge the gaze of the white male artist, although it plays on the active/passive tension of seeing/being seen, because any potential disruption is contained by the subtextual work of the stereotype. Thus in one portrait the 'primitive' nature of the Negro is invoked by the profile: the face becomes an afterimage of a stereotypically 'African' tribal mask, high cheekbones and matted dreadlocks further connote wildness, danger, exotica. In another, the chiseled contours of a shaved head, honed by rivulets of sweat, summon up the criminal mug shot from the forensic files of police photography. This also recalls the anthropometric uses of photography in the colonial scene, measuring the cranium of the colonized so as to show, by the documentary evidence of photography, the inherent 'inferiority' of the Other.[7] This is overlaid with deeper ambivalence in the portrait of Terrel, whose grotesque grimace calls up the happy/sad mask of the nigger minstrel: humanized by racial pathos, the Sambo stereotype haunts the scene, evoking the black man's supposedly childlike dependency on ole Massa, which in turn fixes his social, legal and existential 'emasculation' at the hands of the white master.

Finally, two codes together – of *cropping* and *lighting* – interpenetrate the flesh and mortify it into a racial sex fetish, a juju doll from the dark side of the white man's imaginary. The body-whole is fragmented into microscopic details – chest, arms, torso, buttocks, penis – inviting a scopophilic dissection of the parts that make up the whole. Indeed, like a talisman, each part is invested with the power to evoke the 'mystique' of black male sexuality with more perfection than any empirically unified whole. The camera cuts away, like a knife, allowing the spectator to inspect the 'goods.' In such fetishistic attention to detail, tiny scars and blemishes on the surface of black skin serve only to heighten the technical perfectionism of the photographic print. The cropping and fragmentation of bodies – often decapitated, so to speak – is a salient feature of pornography, and has been seen from certain feminist positions as a form of male violence, a literal inscription of a sadistic impulse in the male gaze, whose pleasure thus consists of cutting up women's bodies into visual bits and pieces. Whether or not this view is tenable,[8] the effect of the technique here is to suggest aggression in the act of looking, but not as racial violence or racism-as-hate; on the contrary, aggression as the frustration of the ego who finds the object of his desires out of reach, inaccessible. The cropping is analogous to striptease in this sense, as the exposure of successive body parts distances the erotogenic object, making it untouchable so as to tantalize the drive to look, which reaches its aim in the denouement by which the woman's sex is unveiled. Except here the unveiling that reduces the woman from angel to whore is substituted by the unconcealing of the black man's private parts, with the penis as the forbidden totem of colonial fantasy.

Notes

'Imaging the Black Man's Sex,' first published in Jo Spence, Patricia Holland and Simon Watney, eds., *Photography/Politics Two* (London: Comedia, 1986); and 'Skin Head Sex Thing: Racial Difference and the Homoerotic Imaginary,' first published in Bad Object Choices, ed., *How Do I Look? Queer Film and Video* (Seattle: Bay

Press, 1989); this combination reprinted in Emily Apter and William Pietz, eds., *Fetishism as Cultural Discourse* (Ithaca: Cornell University Press, 1993).

1   See John Akomfrah, *City Limits* (October 10, 1983).
2   References are primarily to Robert Mapplethorpe, *Black Males* (Amsterdam: Gallerie Jurka, 1983) (with an Introduction by Edmund White); *Robert Mapplethorpe, 1970–1983* (London: Institute of Contemporary Arts, 1983) (Introduction by Allan Hollinghurst); and Robert Mapplethorpe, *The Black Book* (Munich: Schirmer/Mosel, 1986) (with an Introduction by Ntozake Shange).
3   Hollinghurst, 1983, *op. cit.*, 13.
4   See also the art historical perspective offered in Margaret Walters, *The Nude Male* (London: Paddington Press, 1978).
5   Edmund White, in Mapplethorpe, 1983, *op. cit.*, v.
6   Christian Metz, 'Photography and Fetish,' *October*, 34 (Fall 1985), 85.
7   Anthropometric uses of photography are discussed in David Green, 'Classified Subjects,' *Ten.8*, 14 (1984); and 'Veins of Resemblance: Eugenics and Photography' in *Photography/Politics Two*, *op.cit.*; and with reference to photography as surveillance, in Frank Mort, 'The Domain of the Sexual,' and John Tagg, 'Power and Photography,' *Screen Education*, 32 (Autumn 1980).
8   Rosalind Coward, 'Sexual Violence and Sexuality,' *Feminist Review*, 11 (Summer 1982), 17–22.

5.5

Rajeswari Sunder Rajan, from *Real and Imagined Women* (1993)

The subject of sati: Pain and death in the contemporary discourse on sati

I

A woman burns to death in a village in the state of Rajasthan in India. The news makes it to the front page of the *New York Times* – as had some years earlier the news that a woman had been stoned to death for adultery in a Middle East country.[1] The 'monolithic "Third World Woman"'[2] as subject instantaneously becomes an overdetermined symbol, victim not only of universal patriarchy but also of specific third world religious fundamentalism.

The stereotypical and merely sensational aspects of these 'events', isolated from their context, have tended to overwhelm not only the much greater complexity of the issues actually involved, but the equally significant protest mounted by local women's groups and other sections of the population; the continuing and persistent role of the 'west' in post-colonial gender issues; and the theoretical considerations that are of relevance to the issue of female subjectivity in general. It is some sense of these other aspects of sati in contemporary India that I attempt to communicate in the first section of this chapter. The next section explores, tentatively, how a western meditation on the subject of the body in pain may be appropriated for and contested by a specific historical and feminist project in the interests of the female subject as agent.[3] A survey of the representations of sati created upon various discursive sites – the formulations of the anti-sati legislation of 1987, the journalistic media, visual (iconic and photographic) productions, documentary films, cinema and fiction – which follows in the last section, reveals how the politics of representation crucially intersects with the procedures of subjectification of the sati in India today.

If my reading of the 'social text' of sati highlights its discursive dimension, it is because this dimension has been so crucially interwoven with the material reality of the phenomenon. (I bear in mind here the caution issued by Benita Parry: 'discourses of representation should not be confused with material realities.')[4] One index of the widespread recognition of its importance is that the new anti-sati legislation extends its scope to prohibit not only the 'commission' but also the 'glorification' of sati, a glorification achieved primarily through representations of women who commit sati. The opposition between the discursive and the 'real' has admittedly been a contentious one in feminist issues, corresponding as it does to the opposition between academic/theoretical projects on the one hand and activist interventions 'in the field' on the other; but it is not an opposition that has developed into an absolute one in the aftermath of the recent sati. A notable feature, therefore, of the recent debate on sati, a debate I recapitulate in the opening section, has been its public dimension. The fact that religious scholars, philosophers, jurists and writers have expounded their views at public meetings and conferences and interviews in the mass media and that academic historians, sociologists, psychologists and political scientists have published widely in newspapers and mass-circulation journals is indicative of the breakdown of the isolation of these spheres. In this discourse on sati one also notices the quick appropriation of academic research for interventionary purposes, and the corresponding theorizing that takes place from experiences 'in the field'.

In the analysis that follows I attempt to promote such dialectical infusion methodologically by making Elaine Scarry's subtle academic dissertation on 'the body in pain', along with popular art forms and a variety of other representations of the burning woman, converge upon the subject of sati.

II

On 4 September 1987, 18-year-old Roop Kanwar, married only seven months, died on her husband's funeral pyre in Deorala village, about two hours from Jaipur, the capital of Rajasthan. The event was reportedly witnessed by hundreds of people. The state government did not react to the news although sati is an illegal practice. The massive media interest and the concerted action of women's groups eventually led to the issue of an ordinance banning not only the commission but the glorification of sati. Nevertheless, over 300,000 people attended the *chunari mahotsav,* the function marking the thirteenth day after the sati. Huge pro-sati rallies in Jaipur protested the government's interference in the Rajputs' practice of their religious rites. The village of Deorala has now developed into a prosperous pilgrim centre. Several of those arrested after the sati have been released under political pressure, and no one has yet been convicted. In January 1988 new legislation was enacted in Parliament (The Commission of Sati (Prevention) Act, 1987) replicating the chief features of the Rajasthan State ordinance.

It was not for the first time that the government at the centre found itself under pressure both from fundamentalist forces, this time those of a large Hindu community (constituting a sizeable vote bank), and from the liberal press, women's rights groups, civil rights organizations, left political parties and world opinion to prevent the erosion of women's rights.[5] The state's commitment to secularism, interpreted as the protection of the freedom of religious practice, conflicts with another constitutional guarantee, that of the right of life (in addition to all other equal rights) to women. Compromising between its legal and liberal commitment on the one hand and political expediency on the other, it therefore in this instance passed the required legislation without actively attempting to enforce it.

Sati was prohibited by law in Bengal in 1829 by a British governor, William Bentinck. It is assumed to have declined in frequency thereafter. In post-Independence India, stray cases of sati have been reported, about forty in all, chiefly in some northern states. In the past decade, the phenomenon has seen a significant increase; a number of sati attempts have been prevented by police intervention, but four or five have been successfully carried out.

But what worries women's groups is not an epidemic of sati – sati defenders mock the triviality of the issue in terms of its numbers – but the disturbing implications of the recent phenomenon of the glorification of sati through temples and annual fairs. Rich businessmen, for the most part belonging to the Marwari community, have deified centuries-old satis by building temples to them all over Rajasthan and nearby Delhi; these centres attract thousands of devotees and rake in huge donations. Annual fairs bring prosperity to villages that have been sites of past and recent sati. As is clear, religious sanction, political complicity and economic benefits have combined to encourage a cult of sati in a climate of overall oppression of women.

The issue of sati in India today is not a simple one, but in essence it has resolved itself into a series of binary oppositions subsumed into the larger categories, 'tradition' and 'modernity'.[6] Defenders of or sympathizers with sati are purportedly on the side of 'tradition': for them sati is a venerated ritual which gains its sanction from the Vedic scriptures;[7] it is also a practice written into the history of the Rajputs and hence serves as an index of a glorious martial civilization. Belief in sati is in this view expressive of the simple and idealistic faith of India's rural masses[8] – so that the ban on sati and its celebration pits the state against the community, the colonial or westernized rulers and elites against the 'native' Indian subject.[9] The negative identity of 'modernity' – as an elite, high bourgeois and alienated 'westernization' – can be and is, by the same token, thrust upon those who take the stand of opposing sati.[10] To repudiate ancient scripture as a basis for modern practice is to invite the charge of alienation; to designate sati as crime rather than ritual, and by such designation seek to intervene through legislative prohibition, is to merely replicate the move of the colonial ruler;[11] to highlight the plight of the woman is not only to be insensitive to the identity of the Rajput community (which is defined by her act),[12] but also to be selective and hypocritical in the women's issues that one champions – and have one's bona fides questioned.[13]

It is within the problematic of 'tradition' versus 'modernity' that the opponents of sati have had to negotiate their position even as they seek to call the very terms into question. By historicizing the practice of sati, and by plotting the social, economic and political configurations of the scenario of its contemporary version, the notion of a timeless and virtually platonic sati is combated.[14] Historians conclude on the basis of regional variations in the number of satis in Bengal in the nineteenth century that the practice of sati was legitimized by local custom rather than by authoritative and invariable religious prescription.[15] The vocal and organized proponents of sati today, other investigations reveal, are not the simple rural masses, but the landed gentry and the urban business classes; the 'State' is not a nameless adversary but is made up of politicians, policemen and other functionaries deeply entrenched in regional politics; the glorification of sati through temples and fairs is a commerical reality and an entirely 'modern' phenomenon; the enactment of modern sati derives its features from popular cinema and political meetings rather than hallowed ritual.[16] When they choose to, supporters of sati may themselves claim that the issue is not the opposition between tradition and modernity, but rather 'the ironing out of the contradictions between the two'[17] – such as is displayed in the case of Roop Kanwar, a 'modern' girl in many respects, 'choosing' to commit sati in spite of her affluent background, her school education, etc. Thus the categories 'tradition' and 'modernity' are invoked and contested in a significant way in the struggle for self- and other definition between the two sides.

Nevertheless, the problematic remains insidiously coercive in framing the issue of female subjectivity. In the representations of sati in contemporary India that I shall be discussing shortly the subjectivity of the woman who commits sati remains a crucial issue; female subjectivity has in its turn hinged on the questions: Was the sati voluntary? Or was the woman forced upon the pyre? These stark alternatives were posed as an aspect of British intervention in the issue in the late eighteenth and early nineteenth centuries[18] and still retain their force when played into the series of oppositions that categorize the problematic of tradition versus modernity. For defenders of sati today all satis are voluntary, and for its opponents all of them are coerced. But when the individual woman's subjectivity is read in terms of intention, intentionality can only be a matter of conjecture and, finally, ideological conviction.

It is revealing, nevertheless, to see how transparent such intention can appear to be when read back from the initial premise that sati is suicide. In the first place there is the assertion that 'sati was never a system, it is not one now, it will not be one in the future. It is a case of an *individual decision*' (emphasis added).[19] The establishment of sati as individual decision permits the investment of the woman with the fullest integrity of free will: the analogies to the event are drawn with male heroic suicides, the religious martyr, the soldier, the ascetic monk, and the recent political activist, Gandhi or Vinobha Bhave. These equations then mark the woman as exceptional and singular.[20] Finally, a triumphantly circular argument can claim that evidence of coercion establishes only that certain satis are 'inauthentic'. The pamphlet issued by the Sati Dharam Raksha Samiti (the Committee for the Protection of the Sati Faith) in Jaipur on 15 October 1987 claimed that satis in Rajasthan have always been voluntary, unlike satis in nineteenth-century Bengal.[21] By these successive procedures of subjectification – the establishment of sati as 'individual decision', the comparison of sati-as-suicide with other socially valorized male acts of self-annihilation, the arguments that sati is the exceptional rather than the routine option exercised by the Hindu widow and that voluntarism alone bestows authenticity upon the sati – the woman who commits sati reaches the transcendent subjective state, deification.

The most thorough demystification of these procedures undertaken by anti-sati crusaders consists of the exposure of sati as murder. Their assertions that satis are coerced are not to be understood as conceding by implication that voluntary satis are therefore permissible. Coercion has been established by such evidence as the 'haste [with which sati is performed], family pressure, opiates, photographs of women imprisoned by wood and coconuts in a neck-high pyre'.[22] But even where they allow that the widow may have complied with the decision, her 'suicide' is regarded not as true 'choice' but merely as an option that is preferred to life as an ill-treated widow, or one which results from 'false consciousness' and ideological indoctrination. In any case, they have refused to grant that wanting to die is a sufficient reason to die. However, if one subscribes to a liberal ideology of the freedom of choice one must sometimes grant sati the dubious status of existential suicide. To refuse to do so is to find oneself, as feminists have done, in another bind, that of viewing the sati as inexorably a victim and thereby emptying her subjectivity of any function or agency.

The choice for the concerned feminist analyst in this predicament, if formulated as Gayatri Spivak does, as one between subject-constitution (i.e. 'she wanted to die') and object-formation (i.e. 'she must be saved from dying'), is a paralysing one.[23] Roop Kanwar is one in a succession of individual women who have emerged into the public limelight in India in the past decade, around whom issues out of all proportion to their individual stature have gathered.[24] For feminists these women cannot be regarded as mere counters in the larger play of power struggles, or as cautionary examples, as indeed they have been treated; but neither can they be aggrandized into individualistic figures of heroism or tragedy. It is in the context of this methodological crisis that the issue of conceptualizing female subjectivity as agency gains its political imperative.

Hence the necessity, as I see it, for a reconsideration of subject-status itself and of its constituents – for effecting that shift from 'concerns about the subject and consciousness to concerns about embodied subjects and personification' which Mark Seltzer has identified as a significant aspect of the contemporary discourse of 'a logistics of realism'.[25] In the case of sati, this involves shifting the emphasis from sati-as-death (murder or suicide, authentic or inauthentic) to sati-as-burning, and investigating both the subjective pain and the objective spectacle that this shift reveals.

Notes

An earlier version of this chapter was presented at a colloquium on 'Representations of Death' sponsored by the George Seferis Chair of Modern Greek Studies at Harvard University in November 1988. I am grateful to Margaret Alexiou and Margaret Higonnet for inviting me, and to the other participants for their responses. To Kamala Visweswaran, for her extended involvement in my project at every stage, and in particular for help with key theoretical portions of this chapter, I owe a special debt. Professor Sharada Jain (Women's Studies Unit, Institute of Development Studies, Jaipur) gave generously of her time and ideas when I was revising this chapter. I am also grateful to Ruth Vanita, co-editor of *Manushi*, for providing me with material on file on sati. More special debts to several other people who generously assisted me are acknowledged in the notes.

I have used 'sati' to refer, as in Hindi (and as recognized by the Oxford English Dictionary), both to 'the Hindu widow who immolates herself on the funeral pile with her husband's body', and to 'the immolation of a Hindu widow in this way'.

1   Edward Said, *Covering Islam: How the Media and the Experts Determine How We See the Rest of the World*, New York, Pantheon, 1981.

2   The phrase is Gayatri Spivak's. See 'Can the Subaltern Speak? Speculations on Widow-Sacrifice', *Wedge*, Winter/Spring 1985, pp. 120–30, esp. p. 120.

3   Elaine Scarry, *The Body in Pain: The Making and Unmaking of the World*, New York and Oxford, Oxford University Press, 1985.

4   Benita Parry, 'Problems of Current Theories of Colonial Discourse', *Oxford Literary Review* 9, 1–2, 1987, pp. 27–58, esp. p. 35.

5   The most well-known recent controversy arose out of the victory of Shahbano, a divorced Muslim woman, in the Supreme Court of India in the issue of maintenance. Her victory was followed after a year by the passage of the Muslim Women (Protection of Rights in Divorce) Act, 1986, which ruled that divorced Muslim Women would be covered by Muslim personal law and hence no longer entitled to maintenance under the common Criminal Procedure Code.

6   For a critique of this problematic, see Madhu Kishwar and Ruth Vanita, 'The Burning of Roop Kanwar', *Manushi* 42–3, September–December 1987, pp. 15–29; Sujata Patel and Krishna Kumar, 'Defenders of Sati', *Economic and Political Weekly*, 23 January 1988, pp. 129–30.

7   See Niranjan Dev Teerth, Shankaracharya (Hindu religious head) of Puri, in an interview with Anuradha Dutt, *The Illustrated Weekly of India*, 1–7 May 1988, pp. 26–9.

8   Ashis Nandy, 'The Human Factor', *The Illustrated Weekly of India*, 17–23 January 1988, pp. 20–3, esp. p. 22.

9   Inderjit Badhwar, 'Militant Defiance', *India Today*, 31 October 1987, pp. 38–41, reports a number of Rajput responses of this kind: '[Rajiv Gandhi, the Indian Prime Minister] is a parsi, married to a foreign woman, who is insulting the Hindu religion' (p. 39).

10 Nandy, 'The Human Factor'; also 'Sati in Kaliyuga', *Economic and Political Weekly*, 17 September 1988, p. 1976; Patrick Harrigan, 'Tyranny of the Elect? Bringing Bharat Mata Up to Date', *Statesman*, 5 November 1987.

11 Veena Das, 'Strange Response', *The Illustrated Weekly of India*, 28 February–5 March 1988, pp. 30–2. Das seems to suggest that the modern Indian state uses intervention in the sati issue to 'inferiorise small groups', much as the British used it to argue 'that Indians were not fit to rule themselves' (p. 32).

12 See, for instance, Kalyan Singh Kalvi, Janata Party leader, in an interview with Inderjit Badhwar, *India Today*, 31 October 1987: 'To build temples to [satis] is part of Rajput culture which believes that sati and shakti (power) are identical. ... In our culture, we worship the motherland, dharma (faith), and nari (woman). We are ready to die for any of them' (p. 41).

13 Nandy, 'The Human Factor', p. 23.

14 Kumkum Sangari and Sudesh Vaid, 'Sati in Modern India', *Economic and Political Weekly*, 1 August 1981, pp. 1284–8.

15 Lata Mani, 'Production of an Official Discourse on Sati in Early Nineteenth Century Bengal', *Economic and Political Weekly; Review of Women Studies*, 26 April 1986, pp. 32–40; also Prahlad Singh Shekhawat, 'The Culture of Sati in Rajasthan', *Manushi* 42–3, September–December 1987, pp. 30–4.

16 Kishwar and Vanita, 'The Burning of Roop Kanwar'.
17 Kumkum Sangari, 'There Is No Such Thing as Voluntary Sati', *The Times of India*, 25 October 1987.
18 Lata Mani, 'Production of an Official Discourse'.
19 Kalvi, interview.
20 The frequent argument that 'satis happen extremely rarely' (Kalvi) is intended defensively to make the point that widows are not routinely burnt. But we also realize that the spectacular value of sati would only be trivialized by its frequency – even as we are covertly reminded that power is a power to withhold death as well as to deal it.
21 Nandy also develops the distinction between authentic and inauthentic sati, in 'The Human Factor', p. 22.
22 Sangari, 'There Is No Such Thing as Voluntary Sati'.
23 Spivak, 'Can the Subaltern Speak?' p. 127.
24 Some examples are Shahbano, whose legal battle has been briefly described in n. 5; Phoolan Devi, a woman dacoit who surrendered to the police after committing a series of killings, who is now serving a sentence in jail; Vibha Mishra, an actress who was seriously burnt, but recovered, and who acquitted her arrested lover of all guilt in the burning; Indu Arora, a woman arrested for the death of her two children, who was discovered to be involved in an adulterous relationship; the three Kanpur sisters (see p. 38, n. 49).
25 Mark Seltzer, 'Statistical Persons', *Diacritics* 17, 3, Fall 1987, pp. 82–98, esp. p. 87.

5.6

Judith Butler, from *Gender Trouble* (1990)
1 Subjects of Sex/Gender/Desire

One is not born a woman, but rather becomes one.

Simone de Beauvoir

Strictly speaking, 'women' cannot be said to exist.

Julia Kristeva

Woman does not have a sex.

Luce Irigaray

The deployment of sexuality ... established this notion of sex.

Michel Foucault

The category of sex is the political category that founds society as heterosexual.

Monique Wittig

i. 'Women' as the Subject of Feminism

For the most part, feminist theory has assumed that there is some existing identity, understood through the category of women, who not only initiates feminist interests and goals within discourse, but constitutes the subject for whom political representation is pursued. But *politics* and *representation* are controversial terms. On the one hand, *representation* serves as the operative term within a political process that seeks to extend visibility and legitimacy to women as political subjects; on the other hand, representation is the normative function of a language which is said either to reveal or to distort what is assumed to be true about the category of women. For feminist theory, the development of a language that fully or adequately represents women has seemed necessary to foster the political visibility of women. This has seemed obviously important considering the pervasive cultural condition in which women's lives were either misrepresented or not represented at all.

Recently, this prevailing conception of the relation between feminist theory and politics has come under challenge from within feminist discourse. The very subject of women is no longer understood in stable or abiding terms. There is a great deal of material that not only questions the viability of 'the subject' as the ultimate candidate for representation or, indeed, liberation, but there is very little agreement after all on what it is that constitutes, or ought to constitute, the category of women. The domains of political and linguistic 'representation' set out in advance the criterion by which subjects themselves are formed, with the result that representation is extended only to what can be acknowledged as a subject. In other words, the qualifications for being a subject must first be met before representation can be extended.

Foucault points out that juridical systems of power *produce* the subjects they subsequently come to represent.[1] Juridical notions of power appear to regulate political life in purely negative terms – that is, through the limitation, prohibition, regulation, control and even 'protection' of individuals related to that political structure through the contingent and retractable operation of choice. But the subjects regulated by such structures are, by virtue of being subjected to them, formed, defined, and reproduced in accordance with the requirements of those structures. If this analysis is right, then the juridical formation of language and politics that represents women as 'the subject' of feminism is itself a discursive formation and effect of a given version of representational politics. And the feminist subject turns out to be discursively constituted by the very political system that is supposed to facilitate its emancipation. This becomes politically problematic if that system can be shown to produce gendered subjects along a differential axis of domination or to produce subjects who are presumed to be masculine. In such cases, an uncritical appeal to such a system for the emancipation of 'women' will be clearly self-defeating.

The question of 'the subject' is crucial for politics, and for feminist politics in particular, because juridical subjects are invariably produced through certain exclusionary practices that do not 'show' once the juridical structure of politics has been established. In other words, the political construction of the subject proceeds with certain legitimating and exclusionary aims, and these political operations are effectively concealed and naturalized by a political analysis that takes juridical structures as their foundation. Juridical power inevitably 'produces' what it claims merely to represent; hence, politics must be concerned with this dual function of power: the juridical and the productive. In effect, the law produces and then conceals the notion of 'a subject before the law'[2] in order to invoke that discursive formation as a naturalized foundational premise that subsequently legitimates that law's own regulatory hegemony. It is not enough to inquire into how women might become more fully represented in language and politics. Feminist critique ought also to understand how the category of 'women,' the subject of feminism, is produced and restrained by the very structures of power through which emancipation is sought.

Indeed, the question of women as the subject of feminism raises the possibility that there may not be a subject who stands 'before' the law, awaiting representation in or by the law. Perhaps the subject, as well as the invocation of a temporal 'before,' is constituted by the law as the fictive foundation of its own claim to legitimacy. The prevailing assumption of the ontological integrity of the subject before the law might be understood as the contemporary trace of the state of nature hypothesis, that foundationalist fable constitutive of the juridical structures of classical liberalism. The performative invocation of a nonhistorical 'before' becomes the foundational premise that guarantees a presocial ontology of persons who freely consent to be governed and, thereby, constitute the legitimacy of the social contract.

Apart from the foundationalist fictions that support the notion of the subject, however, there is the political problem that feminism encounters in the assumption that the term *women* denotes a common identity. Rather than a stable signifier that commands the assent of those whom it purports to describe and represent, *women*, even in the plural, has become a troublesome term, a site of contest, a cause for anxiety. As Denise Riley's title suggests, *Am I That Name?* is a question produced by the very possibility of the name's multiple significations.[3] If one 'is' a woman, that is surely not all one is; the term fails to be exhaustive, not because a pregendered 'person' transcends the specific paraphernalia of its gender, but because gender is not always constituted coherently or consistently in different historical contexts, and because gender intersects with racial, class, ethnic, sexual, and regional modalities of discursively constituted identities. As a result, it becomes impossible to separate out 'gender' from the political and cultural intersections in which it is invariably produced and maintained.

The political assumption that there must be a universal basis for feminism, one which must be found in an identity assumed to exist cross-culturally, often accompanies the notion that the oppression of women has some singular form discernible in the universal or hegemonic structure of patriarchy or masculine domination. The notion of a universal patriarchy has been widely criticized in recent years for its failure to account for the workings of gender oppression in the concrete cultural contexts in which it exists. Where those various contexts have been consulted within such theories, it has been to find 'examples' or 'illustrations' of a universal principle that is assumed from the start. That form of feminist theorizing has come under criticism for its efforts to colonize and appropriate non-Western cultures to support highly Western notions of oppression, but because they tend as well to construct a 'Third World' or even an 'Orient' in which gender oppression is subtly explained as symptomatic of an essential, non-Western barbarism. The urgency of feminism to establish a universal status for patriarchy in order to strengthen the appearance of feminism's own claims to be representative has occasionally motivated the shortcut to a categorical or fictive universality of the structure of domination, held to produce women's common subjugated experience.

Although the claim of universal patriarchy no longer enjoys the kind of credibility it once did, the notion of a generally shared conception of 'women,' the corollary to that framework, has been much more difficult to displace. Certainly, there have been plenty of debates: Is there some commonality among 'women' that preexists their oppression, or do 'women' have a bond by virtue of their oppression alone? Is there a specificity to women's cultures that is independent of their subordination by hegemonic, masculinist cultures? Are the specificity and integrity of women's cultural or linguistic practices always specified against and, hence, within the terms of some more dominant cultural formation? If there is a region of the 'specifically feminine,' one that is both differentiated from the masculine as such and recognizable in its difference by an unmarked and, hence, presumed universality of 'women'? The masculine/feminine binary constitutes not only the exclusive framework in which that specificity can be recognized, but in every other way the 'specificity' of the feminine is once again fully decontextualized and separated off analytically and politically from the constitution of class, race, ethnicity, and other axes of power relations that both constitute 'identity' and make the singular notion of identity a misnomer.[4]

My suggestion is that the presumed universality and unity of the subject of feminism is effectively undermined by the constraints of the representational discourse in which it functions. Indeed, the premature insistence on a stable subject of feminism, understood as a seamless category of women, inevitably generates multiple refusals to accept the category. These domains of exclusion reveal the coercive and regulatory consequences of that construction, even when the construction has been elaborated for emancipatory purposes. Indeed, the fragmentation within feminism and the paradoxical opposition to feminism from 'women' whom feminism claims to represent suggest the necessary limits of identity politics. The suggestion that feminism can seek wider representation for a subject that it itself constructs has the ironic consequence that feminist goals risk failure by refusing to take account of the constitutive powers of their own representational claims. This problem is not ameliorated through an appeal to the category of women for merely 'strategic' purposes, for strategies always have meanings that exceed the purposes for which they are intended. In this case, exclusion itself might qualify as such an unintended yet consequential meaning. By conforming to a requirement of representational politics that feminism articulate a stable subject, feminism thus opens itself to charges of gross misrepresentation.

Obviously, the political task is not to refuse representational politics – as if we could. The juridical structures of language and politics constitute the contemporary field of power; hence, there is no position outside this field, but only a critical genealogy of its own legitimating practices. As such, the critical point of departure is *the historical present*, as Marx put it. And the task is to formulate within this constituted frame a critique of the categories of identity that contemporary juridical structures engender, naturalize, and immobilize.

Perhaps there is an opportunity at this juncture of cultural politics, a period that some would call 'postfeminist,' to reflect from within a feminist perspective on the injunction to construct a subject of feminism. Within feminist political practice, a radical rethinking of the ontological constructions of identity appears to be necessary in order to formulate a representational politics that might revive feminism on other grounds. On the other hand, it may be time to entertain a radical critique that seeks to free feminist theory from the necessity of having to construct a single or abiding ground which is invariably contested by those identity positions or anti-identity positions that it invariably excludes. Do the exclusionary practices that ground feminist theory in a notion of 'women' as subject paradoxically undercut feminist goals to extend its claims to 'representation'?[5]

Perhaps the problem is even more serious. Is the construction of the category of women as a coherent and stable subject an unwitting regulation and reification of gender relations? And is not such a reification precisely contrary to feminist aims? To what extent does the category of women achieve stability and coherence only in the context of the heterosexual matrix?[6] If a stable notion of gender no longer proves to be the foundational premise of feminist politics, perhaps a new sort of feminist politics is now desirable to contest the very reifications of gender and identity, one that will take the variable construction of identity as both a methodological and normative prerequisite, if not a political goal.

To trace the political operations that produce and conceal what qualifies as the juridical subject of feminism is precisely the task of *a feminist genealogy* of the category of women. In the course of this effort to question 'women' as the subject of feminism, the unproblematic invocation of that category may prove to *preclude* the possibility of feminism as a representational politics. What sense does it make to extend representation to subjects who are constructed through the exclusion of those who fail to conform to unspoken normative requirements of the subject? What relations of domination and exclusion are inadvertently sustained when representation becomes the sole focus of politics? The identity of the feminist subject ought not to be the foundation of feminist politics, if the formation of the subject takes place within a field of power regularly buried through the assertion of that foundation. Perhaps, paradoxically, 'representation' will be shown to make sense for feminism only when the subject of 'women' is nowhere presumed.

Notes

1   See Michel Foucault, 'Right of Death and Power over Life,' in *The History of Sexuality, Volume I, An Introduction,* trans. Robert Hurley (New York: Vintage, 1980), originally published as *Histoire de la sexualité 1: La volonté de savoir* (Paris: Gallimard, 1978). In that final chapter, Foucault discusses the relation between the juridical and productive law. His notion of the productivity of the law is clearly derived from Nietzsche, although not identical with Nietzsche's will-to-power. The use of Foucault's notion of productive power is not meant as a simple-minded 'application' of Foucault to gender issues. As I show in chapter 3, section ii, 'Foucault, Herculine, and the Politics of Sexual Discontinuity,' the consideration of sexual difference within the terms of Foucault's own work reveals central contradictions in his theory. His view of the body also comes under criticism in the final chapter.

2   References throughout this work to a subject before the law are extrapolations of Derrida's reading of Kafka's parable 'Before the Law,' in *Kafka and the Contemporary Critical Performance: Centenary Readings,* ed. Alan Udoff (Bloomington: Indiana University Press, 1987).

3   See Denise Riley, *Am I That Name?: Feminism and the Category of 'Women' in History* (New York: Macmillan, 1988).

4   See Sandra Harding, 'The Instability of the Analytical Categories of Feminist Theory,' in *Sex and Scientific Inquiry,* eds. Sandra Harding and Jean F. O'Barr (Chicago: University of Chicago Press, 1987), pp. 283–302.

5   I am reminded of the ambiguity inherent in Nancy Cott's title, *The Grounding of Modern Feminism* (New Haven: Yale University Press, 1987). She argues that

the early twentieth-century U.S. feminist movement sought to 'ground' itself in a program that eventually 'grounded' that movement. Her historical thesis implicitly raises the question of whether uncritically accepted foundations operate like the 'return of the repressed'; based on exclusionary practices, the stable political identities that found political movements may invariably become threatened by the very instability that the foundationalist move creates.

6   I use the term *heterosexual matrix* throughout the text to designate that grid of cultural intelligibility through which bodies, genders, and desires are naturalized. I am drawing from Monique Wittig's notion of the 'heterosexual contract' and, to a lesser extent, on Adrienne Rich's notion of 'compulsory heterosexuality' to characterize a hegemonic discursive/epistemic model of gender intelligibility that assumes that for bodies to cohere and make sense there must be a stable sex expressed through a stable gender (masculine expresses male, feminine expresses female) that is oppositionally and hierarchically defined through the compulsory practice of heterosexuality.

5.7

Homi K. Bhabha, from ' "Race", Time and the Revision of Modernity' (1994)

'Dirty nigger!' Or simply, 'Look, a Negro!'

Frantz Fanon, *The Fact of Blackness*

I

Whenever these words are said in anger or in hate, whether of the Jew in that *estaminet* in Antwerp, or of the Palestinian on the West Bank, or the Zairian student eking out a wretched existence selling fake fetishes on the Left Bank; whether they are said of the body of woman or the man of colour; whether they are quasi-officially spoken in South Africa or officially prohibited in London or New York, but inscribed nevertheless in the severe staging of the statistics of educational performance and crime, visa violations, immigration irregularities; whenever 'Dirty nigger!' or, 'Look, a Negro!' is not said at all, but you can see it in a gaze, or hear it in the solecism of a still silence; whenever and wherever I am when I hear a racist, or catch his look, I am reminded of Fanon's evocatory essay 'The fact of blackness' and its unforgettable opening lines.[1]

I want to start by returning to that essay, to explore only one scene in its remarkable staging, Fanon's phenomenological performance of what it means to be *not only a nigger* but a member of the marginalized, the displaced, the diasporic. To be amongst those whose very presence is both 'overlooked' – in the double sense of social surveillance and psychic disavowal – and, at the same time, overdetermined – psychically projected, made stereotypical and symptomatic. Despite its very specific location – a Martinican subjected to the racist gaze on a street corner in Lyons – I claim a generality for Fanon's argument because he talks not simply of the historicity of the black man, as much as he writes in 'The fact of blackness' about the temporality of modernity within which the figure of the 'human' comes to be *authorized*. It is Fanon's temporality of emergence – his sense of the *belatedness of the black man* – that does not simply make the question of ontology inappropriate for black identity, but somehow *impossible* for the very understanding of humanity in the world of modernity:

> *You come too late, much too late, there will always be a world – a white world between you and us.* (My emphasis)

It is the opposition to the ontology of that white world – to its assumed hierarchical forms of rationality and universality – that Fanon turns in a performance that is iterative and interrogative – a repetition that is initiatory, instating a differential history that will not return to the power of the Same. Between *you and us* Fanon opens up an enunciative space that does not simply contradict the metaphysical ideas of progress or racism or rationality; he distantiates them by 'repeating' these ideas, makes them uncanny by displacing them in a number of culturally contradictory and discursively estranged locations.

What Fanon shows up is the liminality of those ideas – their ethnocentric margin – by revealing the *historicity* of its most universal symbol – Man. From the perspective of a postcolonial 'belatedness', Fanon disturbs the *punctum* of man as the signifying, subjectifying category of Western culture, as a unifying reference of ethical value. Fanon performs the desire of the colonized to identify with the humanistic, enlightenment ideal of Man: 'all I wanted was to be a man among other men. I wanted to come lithe and young into a world that was ours and build it together.' Then, in a catachrestic reversal he shows how, despite the pedagogies of human history, the performative discourse of the liberal West, its quotidian conversation and comments, reveal the cultural supremacy and racial typology upon which the universalism of Man is founded: 'But of course, come in, sir, there is no colour prejudice among us. . . . Quite, the Negro is a man like ourselves. . . . It is not because he is black that he is less intelligent than we are.'

Fanon uses the fact of blackness, of belatedness, to destroy the binary structure of power and identity: the imperative that 'the Black man must be Black; he must be Black in relation to the white man.' Elsewhere he has written: 'The Black man is not. [caesura] Any more than the white man' (my interpolation). Fanon's discourse of the 'human' emerges from that temporal break or caesura effected in the continuist, progressivist myth of Man. He too speaks from the signifying time-lag of cultural difference that I have been attempting to develop as a structure for the representation of subaltern and postcolonial agency. Fanon writes from that temporal caesura, the time-lag of cultural difference, in a space between the symbolization of the social and the 'sign' of its representation of subjects and agencies. Fanon destroys two time schemes in which the historicity of the human is thought. He rejects the 'belatedness' of the black man because it is only the opposite of the framing of the white man as universal, normative – *the white sky all around me*: the black man refuses to occupy the past of which the white man is the future. But Fanon also refuses the Hegelian-Marxist dialectical schema whereby the black man is part of a transcendental sublation: a minor term in a dialectic that will emerge into a more equitable universality. Fanon, I believe, suggests another time, another space.

It is a space of being that is wrought from the interruptive, interrogative, tragic experience of blackness, of discrimination, of despair. It is the apprehension of the social and psychic question of 'origin' – and its erasure – in a negative side that 'draws its worth from an almost substantive absoluteness ... [which has to be] ignorant of the essences and determinations of its being ... an absolute density ... an abolition of the ego by desire'. What may seem primordial or timeless is, I believe, a moment of a kind of 'projective past' whose history and signification I shall attempt to explore here. It is a mode of 'negativity' that makes the enunciatory present of modernity disjunctive. It opens up a time-lag at the point at which we speak of humanity through its differentiations – gender, race, class – that mark an excessive marginality of modernity. It is the enigma of this form of temporality which emerges from what Du Bois also called the 'swift and low of human doing',[2] to face Progress with some unanswerable questions, and suggest some answers of its own.

In destroying the 'ontology of man', Fanon suggests that 'there is not merely one Negro, there are *Negroes*'. This is emphatically not a postmodern celebration of pluralistic identities. As my argument will make clear, for me the project of modernity is itself rendered so contradictory and unresolved through the insertion of the 'time-lag' in which colonial and postcolonial moments emerge as sign and history, that I am sceptical of those transitions to postmodernity in Western academic writings which theorize the experience of this 'new historicity' through the appropriation of a 'Third World' metaphor; 'the First World ... in a peculiar dialectical reversal, begins to touch some features of third-world experience. ... The United States is ... the biggest third-world country because of unemployment, non-production, etc.'[3]

Fanon's sense of social contingency and indeterminacy, made from the perspective of a postcolonial time-lag, is not a celebration of fragmentation, *bricolage*, pastiche or the 'simulacrum'. It is a vision of social contradiction and cultural difference – as the disjunctive space of modernity – that is best seen in a fragment of a poem he cites towards the end of 'The fact of blackness':

> As the contradiction among the features
> creates the harmony of the face
> we proclaim the oneness of the suffering
> and the revolt.

II

The discourse of race that I am trying to develop displays the *problem of the ambivalent temporality of modernity* that is often overlooked in the more 'spatial' traditions of some aspects of postmodern theory.[4] Under the rubric 'the discourse of modernity', I do not intend to reduce a complex and diverse historical moment, with varied national genealogies and different institutional practices, into a singular shibboleth – be it the 'idea' of Reason, Historicism, Progress – for the critical convenience of postmodern literary theory. My interest in the question of modernity resides in the influential discussion generated by the work of Habermas, Foucault, Lyotard and Lefort, amongst many others, that has generated a critical discourse around historical modernity as an epistemological structure.[5] To put it succinctly, the question of ethical and cultural judgement, central to the processes of subject formation and the objectification of social knowledge, is challenged at its 'cognitivist' core. Habermas characterizes it as a form of Occidental self-understanding that enacts a cognitive reductionism in the relation of the human being to the social world:

> Ontologically the world is reduced to a world of entities *as a whole* (as the totality of objects ...); epistemologically, our relationship to that world is reduced to the capacity of know[ing] ... states of affairs ... in a purposive-rational fashion; semantically it is reduced to fact-stating discourse in which assertoric sentences are used.[6] (My emphasis)

Although this may be a stark presentation of the problem, it highlights the fact that the challenge to such a 'cognitivist' consciousness displaces the problem of truth or meaning from the disciplinary confines of epistemology – the problem of the referential as 'objectivity' reflected in that celebrated Rortyesque trope, the mirror of nature. What results could be figuratively described as a preoccupation not simply with the reflection in the glass – the idea or concept in itself – but with the frameworks of meaning as they are revealed in what Derrida has called the 'supplementary necessity of a parergon'. That is the performative, living description of the *writing* of a concept or theory, 'a relation to the history of its writing and the writing of its history also'.[7]

If we take even the most cursory view of influential postmodern perspectives, we find that there is an increasing *narrativization* of the question of social ethics and subject formation. Whether it is in the conversational procedures and 'final vocabularies' of liberal ironists like Richard Rorty, or the 'moral fictions' of Alisdair Macintyre that are the sustaining myths 'after virtue'; whether it is the *petits récits* and *phrases* that remain from the fall-out of the grand narratives of modernity in Lyotard; or the projective but ideal speech community that is rescued *within* modernity by Habermas in his concept of communicative reason that is expressed in its pragmatic logic or argument and a 'decentred' understanding of the world: what we encounter in all these accounts are proposals for what is considered to be the essential gesture of Western modernity, an 'ethics of self-construction' – or, as Mladan Dolar cogently describes it:

> What makes this attitude typical of modernity is the constant reconstruction and the reinvention of the self. ... The subject and the present it belongs to have no objective status, they have to be perpetually (re)constructed.[8]

I want to ask whether this synchronous constancy of reconstruction and reinvention of the subject does not assume a cultural temporality that may not be universalist in its epistemological moment of judgement, but may, indeed, be ethnocentric in its construction of cultural 'difference'. It is certainly true, as Robert Young argues, that the 'inscription of alterity within the self can allow for a new relation to ethics';[9] but does that *necessarily* entail the more general case argued by Dolar, that 'the persisting split [of the subject] is the condition of freedom'?

If so, how do we specify the historical conditions and theoretical configurations of 'splitting' in political situations of 'unfreedom' – in the colonial and postcolonial margins of modernity? I am persuaded that it is the catachrestic postcolonial agency of 'seizing the value-coding' – as Gayatri Spivak has argued – that opens up an interruptive time-lag in the 'progressive' myth of modernity, and enables the diasporic and the postcolonial to be represented. But this makes it all the more crucial to specify the discursive and historical temporality that interrupts the enunciative 'present' in which the self-inventions of modernity take place. And it is this 'taking place' of modernity, this insistent and incipient *spatial* metaphor in which the social relations of modernity are conceived, that introduces a temporality of the 'synchronous' in the structure of the 'splitting' of modernity. It is this 'synchronous and spatial' representation of cultural difference that must be reworked as a *framework* for cultural otherness *within* the general dialectic of doubling that postmodernism proposes. Otherwise we are likely to find ourselves beached amidst Jameson's 'cognitive mappings' of the Third World, which might work for the Bonaventura Hotel in Los Angeles, but will leave you somewhat eyeless in Gaza.[10] Or if, like Terry Eagleton, your taste is more 'other worldly' than Third World, you will find yourself somewhat dismissive of the 'real' history of the 'other' – women, foreigners, homosexuals, the natives of Ireland – on the basis 'of certain styles, values, life-experiences which can be appealed to now as a form of political critique' because 'the fundamental political question is that of demanding an equal right with others of what one might become, not of assuming some fully-fashioned identity which is merely repressed.'[11]

It is to establish a *sign of the present*, of modernity, that is not that 'now' of transparent immediacy, and to found a form of social individuation where communality is *not predicated on a transcendent becoming*, that I want to pose my questions of a contra-modernity: what is modernity in those colonial conditions where its imposition is itself the denial of historical freedom, civic autonomy and the 'ethical' choice of refashioning?

Notes

1 All citations from Fanon in the following pages come from 'The fact of blackness', in *Black Skin, White Masks*, Foreword by H. Bhabha (London: Pluto, 1986), pp. 109–40.

2 W. E. Du Bois, *The Souls of Black Folk* (New York: Signet Classics, 1982), p. 275.

3 'A conversation with Fredric Jameson', in A. Ross (ed.) *Universal Abandon: The Politics of Postmodernism* (Edinburgh: Edinburgh University Press, 1988), p. 17.

4 See my reading of Renan in Chapter 8, 'DissemiNation'.

5 Each of these writers has addressed the problem of modernity in a number of works so that selection becomes invidious. However, some of the most directly relevant are the following: J. Habermas, *The Philosophical Discourse of Modernity* (Cambridge: Polity Press, 1990), esp. chs 11 and 12; M. Foucault, *The History of Sexuality. Volume One: An Introduction* (London: Allen Lane, 1979); see also his 'The art of telling the truth', in L. D. Kritzman (ed.) *Politics, Philosophy and Culture* (New York: Routledge, 1990); J.-F. Lyotard, *The Differend* (Minneapolis: University of Minnesota Press, 1988); C. Lefort, *The Political Forms of*

Modern Society, J. B. Thomason (ed.) (Cambridge: Polity Press, 1978), especially Part II, 'History, ideology, and the social imaginary'.

6   Habermas, *The Philosophical Discourse of Modernity*, p. 311.

7   J. Derrida, *The Post Card: From Socrates to Freud and Beyond*, A. Bass (trans.) (Chicago: Chicago University Press, 1987), pp. 303–4.

8   M. Dolar, *The Legacy of the Enlightenment: Foucault and Lacan*, unpublished manuscript.

9   R. Young, *White Mythologies: Writing, History and the West* (London: Routledge, 1990), pp. 16–17. Young argues a convincing case against the Eurocentrism of historicism through his exposition of a number of 'totalizing' historical doctrines, particular in the Marxist tradition, while demonstrating at the same time that the spatializing anti-historicism of Foucault remains equally Eurocentric.

10   Cf. Young, *White Mythologies*, pp. 116–17.

11   T. Eagleton, *The Ideology of the Aesthetic* (Oxford: Blackwell, 1990), p. 414.

Section 6

POSTMODERNISM

Introduction

If it is difficult to avoid issues of gender and race in contemporary cultural criticism today, then it is equally difficult to escape discussion of postmodernism. However, while the terms 'postmodernism', 'postmodernity' and 'the postmodern condition' appear to pervade cultural debates, there is little consensus as to what such terms may signify. Indeed, the whole 'question' of postmodernism is still hotly debated.

In 1989, one cultural critic, Linda Hutcheon, ventured to suggest a definition of postmodernism that may still have value in describing some of the underlying principles of the debates that have ensued. In *The Politics of Postmodernism*, she suggested that:

> In general terms it takes the form of self-conscious, self-contradictory, self-undermining statement. It is rather like saying something whilst at the same time putting inverted commas around what is being said. The effect is to highlight, or 'highlight', and to subvert, or 'subvert', and the mode is therefore a 'knowing' and ironic – or even 'ironic' one. Postmodernism's distinctive character lies in this kind of wholesale 'nudging' commitment to doubleness or duplicity. In many ways it is an even-handed process because postmodernism ultimately manages to install and reinforce as much as undermine and subvert the conventions and presuppositions it appears to challenge.
>
> (Hutcheon 1989: 1–2)

In a sense this is the complex paradox of a mode of art, or of knowledge, that seeks to debate the present from a position within it. How do we conduct such a debate except through a continual questioning and undermining of the cultural processes of knowing, representing and debating the present? As Hutcheon's work also points out, the inevitably political dimensions of postmodernism render the debate intensely problematic but also crucially important.

In this section we have attempted to provide a sense of the most prominent positions on postmodernism and its implications, as the discussion stands today.

From the controversy and questioning inherent in that debate it would seem that two basic positions emerge: there are those who embrace the undermining and duplicitous mode that postmodernism suggests; and there are those who resist it.

For those who mourn the loss of the unifying or controlling narratives of the past, the problems with postmodernism are vast, and the objections that are raised are politically complex. At a basic level, however, those objections centre on what is perceived as the ahistorical nature of the postmodern condition. While the forms of pastiche, self-reference and the explicitly intertextual 'style' of postmodernism owe something to the mode of modernism, they do, none the less, also break with the referent of the real (history, time, art and the artist) that modernism maintained. There is no recourse, within the terms of postmodernism, to a singular 'real' history (of class or gender struggle, for example) or any singular 'real' style or art of the age. And no respect is maintained for the distinctions traditionally drawn between discrete disciplines of cultural investigation or the division within the cultural debate itself between forms of high and popular culture.

As has become apparent, the arguable 'depthlessness' that postmodernism envisages is a focus of concern across a wide political spectrum. For those of the neo-conservative right it eclipses the supposedly unifying values that structure the social order; for the liberal centre it demolishes the autonomy of individual expression; and for the Marxist left it destroys the founding platform of unified struggle, giving rise to what Fredric Jameson has called the 'problem of micropolitics' (see *Postmodernism, or the Logic of Late Capitalism* 1991). What seems to motivate all these positions is the desire to return to a grand narrative of legitimation (as Lyotard describes it; see Section 6.1). Yet the objections to postmodernism are still more complex than that. While the disparate struggles on the sites of gender, race, sex, class and differing abilities seem encouraged by the unmourned loss of a simplistic 'real' – demanding a plural micropolitics of resistance – such struggles have often resisted the incorporation of their work within the rubric of postmodernism on the grounds that its resolute undermining of the referent of the real diffuses their own very 'real' political agendas. The contradictions of postmodernism are seen to be both subversive and reconfirming of traditionally oppressive systems of thought and practice.

On the other hand, for those who would embrace the postmodern, its power lies precisely in its capacity to dissolve, or perhaps to denaturalize, the relation between the sign and its referent. The modes of pastiche and self-reflexivity which foster the objections of depthlessness are, within these terms, understood to force the realization that *all* forms of cultural production and knowledge are grounded in ideology, and that no matter how 'worthy' their motivation they can never be free of the social and political frameworks that may precede and surround them, and that they may seek to undermine. The work of Jean-François Lyotard suggests that, although postmodernism may dissolve effective theories of the agency of the subject as the source of political *action* (an objection that the work of Jameson frequently raises), it does have the advantage of denaturalizing the inevitable ideological grounding of the category of the subject as a whole, and of providing a continuing and relentless *critique* of the legitimacy of *any* form of social and ideological meaning. Against the very considerable power of Western capitalism to normalize the relation between signs and their referents, postmodernism posits the notion that the referent is an *effect* of its sign, rather than its source. From this perspective, all forms of culture and knowledge are inextricably bound up with established systems of meaning production and the discourses that operate within culture, and it is always these links that postmodernism seeks to expose.

That this strategy of exposure and critique can itself be construed as important politically is perhaps most overtly evidenced in the work of Jean Baudrillard and Slavoj Žižek on the political implications of the sustaining fictions of the 'real' within American culture (see Section 6.2) and politics (see the discussion of the Watergate affair, pp. 26–37, in *Simulations*, 1983 and of the events of 11 September 2001 in Sections 6.5 and 6.6). But it is also apparent in the work on ethics undertaken by Jacques Derrida in *The Gift of Death* (see Section 6.4) and on the relation of speculative philosophy to new developments in technological sciences, like those of artificial intelligence and robotics discussed by Lyotard in his reflections on the inhuman (see Section 6.3).

However we respond to the phenomenon of postmodern culture, thought and practice and the questions it highlights, whichever side of the debate we come down on, or even if we opt to maintain a kind of eclectic and strategic straddling of the boundaries that are now being drawn, the issues that the entire question of postmodernism raises will continue to reverberate in, and provide problems for, the discussions of culture upon which we embark.

6.1

Jean-François Lyotard, from *The Postmodern Condition* (1984)

9 Narratives of the legitimation of knowledge

We shall examine two major versions of the narrative of legitimation. One is more political, the other more philosophical; both are of great importance in modern history, in particular in the history of knowledge and its institutions.

The subject of the first of these versions is humanity as the hero of liberty. All peoples have a right to science. If the social subject is not already the subject of scientific knowledge, it is because that has been forbidden by priests and tyrants. The right to science must be reconquered. It is understandable that this narrative would be directed more toward a politics of primary education, rather than of universities and high schools.[1] The educational policy of the French Third Republic powerfully illustrates these presuppositions.

It seems that this narrative finds it necessary to de-emphasize higher education. Accordingly, the measures adopted by Napoleon regarding higher education are generally considered to have been motivated by the desire to produce the administrative and professional skills necessary for the stability of the State.[2] This overlooks the fact that in the context of the narrative of freedom, the State receives its legitimacy not from itself but from the people. So even if imperial politics designated the institutions of higher education as a breeding ground for the officers of the State and secondarily, for the managers of civil society, it did so because the nation as a whole was supposed to win its freedom through the spread of new domains of knowledge to the population, a process to be effected through agencies and professions within which those cadres would fulfill their functions. The same reasoning is a fortiori valid for the foundation of properly scientific institutions. The State resorts to the narrative of freedom every time it assumes direct control over the training of the 'people,' under the name of the 'nation,' in order to point them down the path of progress.[3]

With the second narrative of legitimation, the relation between science, the nation, and the State develops quite differently. It first appears with the founding, between 1807 and 1810, of the University of Berlin,[4] whose influence on the organization of higher education in the young countries of the world was to be considerable in the nineteenth and twentieth centuries.

At the time of the University's creation, the Prussian ministry had before it a project conceived by Fichte and counterproposals by Schleiermacher. Wilhelm von Humboldt had to decide the matter and came down on the side of Schleiermacher's more 'liberal' option.

Reading Humboldt's report, one may be tempted to reduce his entire approach to the politics of the scientific institution to the famous dictum: 'Science for its own sake.' But this would be to misunderstand the ultimate aim of his policies, which is guided by the principle of legitimation we are discussing and is very close to the one Schleiermacher elucidates in a more thorough fashion.

Humboldt does indeed declare that science obeys its own rules, that the scientific institution 'lives and continually renews itself on its own, with no constraint or determined goal whatsoever.' But he adds that the University should orient its constituent element, science, to 'the spiritual and moral training of the nation.'[5] How can this *Bildung*-effect result from the disinterested pursuit of learning? Are not the State, the nation, the whole of humanity indifferent to knowledge for its own sake? What interests them, as Humboldt admits, is not learning, but 'character and action.'

The minister's adviser thus faces a major conflict, in some ways reminiscent of the split introduced by the Kantian critique between knowing and willing: it is a conflict between a language game made of denotations answerable only to the criterion of truth, and a language game governing ethical, social, and political practice that necessarily involves decisions and obligations, in other words, utterances expected to be just rather than true and which in the final analysis lie outside the realm of scientific knowledge.

However, the unification of these two sets of discourse is indispensable to the *Bildung* aimed for by Humboldt's project, which consists not only in the acquisition of learning by individuals, but also in the training of a fully legitimated subject of knowledge and society. Humboldt therefore invokes a Spirit (what Fichte calls Life), animated by three ambitions, or better, by a single, threefold aspiration: 'that of deriving everything from an original principle' (corresponding to scientific activity), 'that of relating everything to an ideal' (governing ethical and social practice), and 'that of unifying this principle and this ideal in a single Idea' (ensuring that the scientific search for true causes always coincides with the pursuit of just ends in moral and political life). This ultimate synthesis constitutes the legitimate subject.

Humboldt adds in passing that this triple aspiration naturally inheres in the 'intellectual character of the German nation.'[6] This is a concession, but a discreet one, to the other narrative, to the idea that the subject of knowledge is the people. But in truth this idea is quite distant from the narrative of the legitimation of knowledge advanced by German idealism. The suspicion that men like Schleiermacher, Humboldt, and even Hegel harbor towards the State is an indication of this. If Schleiermacher fears the narrow nationalism, protectionism, utilitarianism, and positivism that guide the public authorities in matters of science, it is because the principle of science does not reside in those authorities, even indirectly. The subject of knowledge is not the people, but the speculative spirit. It is not embodied, as in France after the Revolution, in a State, but in a System. The language game of legitimation is not state-political, but philosophical.

The great function to be fulfilled by the universities is to 'lay open the whole body of learning and expound both the principles and the foundations of all knowledge.' For 'there is no creative scientific capacity without the speculative spirit.'[7] 'Speculation' is here the name given the discourse on the legitimation of scientific discourse. Schools are functional; the University is speculative, that is to say, philosophical.[8] Philosophy must restore unity to learning, which has been scattered into separate sciences in laboratories and in pre-university education; it can only achieve this in a language game that links the sciences together as moments in the becoming of spirit, in other words, which links them in a rational narration, or rather metanarration. Hegel's *Encyclopedia* (1817–27) attempts to realize this project of totalization, which was already present in Fichte and Schelling in the form of the idea of the System.

It is here, in the mechanism of developing a Life that is simultaneously Subject, that we see a return of narrative knowledge. There is a universal 'history' of spirit, spirit is 'life,' and 'life' is its own self-presentation and formulation in the ordered knowledge of all of its forms contained in the empirical sciences. The encyclopedia of German idealism is the narration of the '(hi)story' of this life-subject. But what it produces is a metanarrative, for the story's narrator must not be a people mired in the particular positivity of its traditional knowledge, nor even scientists taken as a whole, since they are sequestered in professional frameworks corresponding to their respective specialities.

The narrator must be a metasubject in the process of formulating both the legitimacy of the discourses of the empirical sciences and that of the direct institutions of popular cultures. This metasubject, in giving voice to their common grounding, realizes their implicit goal. It inhabits the speculative University. Positive science and the people are only crude versions of it. The only valid way for the nation-state itself to bring the people to expression is through the mediation of speculative knowledge.

It has been necessary to elucidate the philosophy that legitimated the foundation of the University of Berlin and was meant to be the motor both of its development and the development of contemporary knowledge. As I have said, many countries in the nineteenth and twentieth centuries adopted this university organization as a model for the foundation or reform of their own system of higher education, beginning with the United States.[9] But above all, this philosophy – which is far from dead, especially in university circles[10] – offers a particularly vivid representation of one solution to the problem of the legitimacy of knowledge.

Research and the spread of learning are not justified by invoking a principle of usefulness. The idea is not at all that science should serve the interests of the State and/or civil society. The humanist principle that humanity rises up in dignity and freedom through knowledge is left by the wayside. German idealism has recourse to a metaprinciple that simultaneously grounds the development of learning, of society, and of the State in the realization of the 'life' of a Subject, called 'divine Life' by Fichte and 'Life of the spirit' by Hegel. In this perspective, knowledge first finds legitimacy within itself, and it is knowledge that is entitled to say what the State and what Society are.[11] But it can only play this role by changing levels, by ceasing to be simply the positive knowledge of its referent (nature, society, the

State, etc.), becoming in addition to that the knowledge of the knowledge of the referent – that is, by becoming speculative. In the names 'Life' and 'Spirit,' knowledge names itself.

A noteworthy result of the speculative apparatus is that all of the discourses of learning about every possible referent are taken up not from the point of view of their immediate truth-value, but in terms of the value they acquire by virtue of occupying a certain place in the itinerary of Spirit or Life – or, if preferred, a certain position in the Encyclopedia recounted by speculative discourse. That discourse cites them in the process of expounding for itself what it knows, that is, in the process of self-exposition. True knowledge, in this perspective, is always indirect knowledge; it is composed of reported statements that are incorporated into the metanarrative of a subject that guarantees their legitimacy.

The same thing applies for every variety of discourse, even if it is not a discourse of learning; examples are the discourse of law and that of the State. Contemporary hermeneutic discourse[12] is born of this presupposition, which guarantees that there is meaning to know and thus confers legitimacy upon history (and especially the history of learning). Statements are treated as their own autonyms[13] and set in motion in a way that is supposed to render them mutually engendering: these are the rules of speculative language. The University, as its name indicates, is its exclusive institution.

But, as I have said, the problem of legitimacy can be solved using the other procedures as well. The difference between them should be kept in mind: today, with the status of knowledge unbalanced and its speculative unity broken, the first version of legitimacy is gaining new vigor.

According to this version, knowledge finds its validity not within itself, not in a subject that develops by actualizing its learning possibilities, but in a practical subject – humanity. The principle of the movement animating the people is not the self-legitimation of knowledge, but the self-grounding of freedom or, if preferred, its self-management. The subject is concrete, or supposedly so, and its epic is the story of its emancipation from everything that prevents it from governing itself. It is assumed that the laws it makes for itself are just, not because they conform to some outside nature, but because the legislators are, constitutionally, the very citizens who are subject to the laws. As a result, the legislator's will – the desire that the laws be just – will always coincide with the will of the citizen, who desires the law and will therefore obey it.

Clearly, this mode of legitimation through the autonomy of the will[14] gives priority to a totally different language game, which Kant called imperative and is known today as prescriptive. The important thing is not, or not only, to legitimate denotative utterances pertaining to the truth, such as 'The earth revolves around the sun,' but rather to legitimate prescriptive utterances pertaining to justice, such as 'Carthage must be destroyed' or 'The minimum wage must be set at x dollars.' In this context, the only role positive knowledge can play is to inform the practical subject about the reality within which the execution of the prescription is to be inscribed. It allows the subject to circumscribe the executable, or what it is possible to do. But the executory, what should be done, is not within the purview of positive knowledge. It is one thing for an undertaking to be possible and another for it to be just. Knowledge is no longer the subject, but in the service of the subject: its only legitimacy (though it is formidable) is the fact that it allows morality to become reality.

This introduces a relation of knowledge to society and the State which is in principle a relation of the means to the end. But scientists must cooperate only if they judge that the politics of the State, in other words the sum of its prescriptions, is just. If they feel that the civil society of which they are members is badly represented by the State, they may reject its prescriptions. This type of legitimation grants them the authority, as practical human beings, to refuse their scholarly support to a political power they judge to be unjust, in other words, not grounded in a real autonomy. They can even go so far as to use their expertise to demonstrate that such autonomy is not in fact realized in society and the State. This reintroduces the critical function of knowledge. But the fact remains that knowledge has no final legitimacy outside of serving the goals envisioned by the practical subject, the autonomous collectivity.[15]

This distribution of roles in the enterprise of legitimation is interesting from our point of view because it assumes, as against the system-subject theory, that there is no possibility that language games can be unified or totalized in any metadiscourse. Quite to the contrary, here the priority accorded prescriptive statements – uttered by the practical subject – renders them independent in principle from the statements of science, whose only remaining function is to supply this subject with information.

Two remarks:

1 It would be easy to show that Marxism has wavered between the two models of narrative legitimation I have just described. The Party takes the place of the University, the proletariat that of the people or of humanity, dialectical materialism that of speculative idealism, etc. Stalinism may be the result, with its specific relationship with the sciences: in Stalinism, the sciences only figure as citations from the metanarrative of the march towards socialism, which is the equivalent of the life of the spirit. But on the other hand Marxism can, in conformity to the second version, develop into a form of critical knowledge by declaring that socialism is nothing other than the constitution of the autonomous subject and that the only justification for the sciences is if they give the empirical subject (the proletariat) the means to emancipate itself from alienation and repression: this was, briefly, the position of the Frankfurt School.

2 The speech Heidegger gave on May 27, 1933, on becoming rector of the university of Freiburg-in-Breisgau,[16] can be read as an unfortunate episode in the history of legitimation. Here, speculative science has become the questioning of being. This questioning is the 'destiny' of the German people, dubbed an 'historico-spiritual people.' To this subject are owed the three services of labor, defense, and knowledge. The University guarantees a metaknowledge of the three services, that is to say, science. Here, as in idealism, legitimation is achieved through a metadiscourse called science, with ontological pretensions. But here the metadiscourse is questioning, not totalizing. And the University, the home of this metadiscourse, owes its knowledge to a people whose 'historic mission' is to bring that metadiscourse to fruition by working, fighting, and knowing. The calling of this

people-subject is not to emancipate humanity, but to realize its 'true world of the spirit,' which is 'the most profound power of conservation to be found within its forces of earth and blood.' This insertion of the narrative of race and work into that of the spirit as a way of legitimating knowledge and its institutions is doubly unfortunate: theoretically inconsistent, it was compelling enough to find disastrous echoes in the realm of politics.

10 Delegitimation

In contemporary society and culture – postindustrial society, postmodern culture[17] – the question of the legitimation of knowledge is formulated in different terms. The grand narrative has lost its credibility, regardless of what mode of unification it uses, regardless of whether it is a speculative narrative or a narrative of emancipation.

The decline of narrative can be seen as an effect of the blossoming of techniques and technologies since the Second World War, which has shifted emphasis from the ends of action to its means; it can also be seen as an effect of the redeployment of advanced liberal capitalism after its retreat under the protection of Keynesianism during the period 1930–60, a renewal that has eliminated the communist alternative and valorized the individual enjoyment of goods and services.

Anytime we go searching for causes in this way we are bound to be disappointed. Even if we adopted one or the other of these hypotheses, we would still have to detail the correlation between the tendencies mentioned and the decline of the unifying and legitimating power of the grand narratives of speculation and emancipation.

It is, of course, understandable that both capitalist renewal and prosperity and the disorienting upsurge of technology would have an impact on the status of knowledge. But in order to understand how contemporary science could have been susceptible to those effects long before they took place, we must first locate the seeds of 'delegitimation'[18] and nihilism that were inherent in the grand narratives of the nineteenth century.

First of all, the speculative apparatus maintains an ambiguous relation to knowledge. It shows that knowledge is only worthy of that name to the extent that it reduplicates itself ('lifts itself up,' *hebt sich auf*; is sublated) by citing its own statements in a second-level discourse (autonymy) that functions to legitimate them. This is as much as to say that, in its immediacy, denotative discourse bearing on a certain referent (a living organism, a chemical property, a physical phenomenon, etc.) does not really know what it thinks it knows. Positive science is not a form of knowledge. And speculation feeds on its suppression. The Hegelian speculative narrative thus harbors a certain skepticism toward positive learning, as Hegel himself admits.[19]

A science that has not legitimated itself is not a true science; if the discourse that was meant to legitimate it seems to belong to a prescientific form of knowledge, like a 'vulgar' narrative, it is demoted to the lowest rank, that of an ideology or instrument of power. And this always happens if the rules of the science game that discourse denounces as empirical are applied to science itself.

Take for example the speculative statement: 'A scientific statement is knowledge if and only if it can take its place in a universal process of engendering.' The question is: Is this statement knowledge as it itself defines it? Only if it can take its place in a universal process of engendering. Which it can. All it has to do is to presuppose that such a process exists (the Life of spirit) and that it is itself an expression of that process. This presupposition, in fact, is indispensable to the speculative language game. Without it, the language of legitimation would not be legitimate; it would accompany science in a nosedive into nonsense, at least if we take idealism's word for it.

But this presupposition can also be understood in a totally different sense, one which takes us in the direction of postmodern culture: we could say, in keeping with the perspective we adopted earlier, that this presupposition defines the set of rules one must accept in order to play the speculative game.[20] Such an appraisal assumes first that we accept that the 'positive' sciences represent the general mode of knowledge and second, that we understand this language to imply certain formal and axiomatic presuppositions that it must always make explicit. This is exactly what Nietzsche is doing, though with a different terminology, when he shows that 'European nihilism' resulted from the truth requirement of science being turned back against itself.[21]

There thus arises an idea of perspective that is not far removed, at least in this respect, from the idea of language games. What we have here is a process of delegitimation fueled by the demand for legitimation itself. The 'crisis' of scientific knowledge, signs of which have been accumulating since the end of the nineteenth century, is not born of a chance proliferation of sciences, itself an effect of progress in technology and the expansion of capitalism. It represents, rather, an internal erosion of the legitimacy principle of knowledge. There is erosion at work inside the speculative game, and by loosening the weave of the encyclopedic net in which each science was to find its place, it eventually sets them free.

The classical dividing lines between the various fields of science are thus called into question – disciplines disappear, overlappings occur at the borders between sciences, and from these new territories are born. The speculative hierarchy of learning gives way to an immanent and, as it were, 'flat' network of areas of inquiry, the respective frontiers of which are in constant flux. The old 'faculties' splinter into institutes and foundations of all kinds, and the universities lose their function of speculative legitimation. Stripped of the responsibility for research (which was stifled by the speculative narrative), they limit themselves to the transmission of what is judged to be established knowledge, and through didactics they guarantee the replication of teachers rather than the production of researchers. This is the state in which Nietzsche finds and condemns them.[22]

The potential for erosion intrinsic to the other legitimation procedure, the emancipation apparatus flowing from the *Aufklärung*, is no less extensive than the one at work within speculative discourse. But it touches a different aspect. Its distinguishing characteristic is that it grounds the legitimation of science and truth in the autonomy of interlocutors involved in ethical, social, and political praxis. As we have seen, there are immediate problems with this form of legitimation: the difference between a denotative statement with cognitive value and a prescriptive statement with practical value is one of relevance, therefore of competence. There is nothing to prove that if a statement describing a real situation is true, it follows that a prescriptive statement based upon it (the effect of which will necessarily be a modification of that reality) will be just.

Take, for example, a closed door. Between 'The door is closed' and 'Open the door' there is no relation of consequence as defined in propositional logic. The two statements belong to two autonomous sets of rules defining different kinds of relevance, and therefore of competence. Here, the effect of dividing reason into cognitive or theoretical reason on the one hand, and practical reason on the other, is to attack the legitimacy of the discourse of science. Not directly, but indirectly, by revealing that it is a language game with its own rules (of which the a priori conditions of knowledge in Kant provide a first glimpse) and that it has no special calling to supervise the game of praxis (nor the game of aesthetics, for that matter). The game of science is thus put on a par with the others.

If this 'delegitimation' is pursued in the slightest and if its scope is widened (as Wittgenstein does in his own way, and thinkers such as Martin Buber and Emmanuel Levinas in theirs)[23] the road is then open for an important current of postmodernity: science plays its own game; it is incapable of legitimating the other language games. The game of prescription, for example, escapes it. But above all, it is incapable of legitimating itself, as speculation assumed it could.

The social subject itself seems to dissolve in this dissemination of language games. The social bond is linguistic, but is not woven with a single thread. It is a fabric formed by the intersection of at least two (and in reality an indeterminate number) of language games, obeying different rules. Wittgenstein writes: 'Our language can be seen as an ancient city: a maze of little streets and squares, of old and new houses, and of houses with additions from various periods; and this surrounded by a multitude of new boroughs with straight regular streets and uniform houses.'[24] And to drive home that the principle of unitotality – or synthesis under the authority of a metadiscourse of knowledge – is inapplicable, he subjects the 'town' of language to the old sorites paradox by asking: 'how many houses or streets does it take before a town begins to be a town?'[25]

New languages are added to the old ones, forming suburbs of the old town: 'the symbolism of chemistry and the notation of the infinitesimal calculus.'[26] Thirty-five years later we can add to the list: machine languages, the matrices of game theory, new systems of musical notation, systems of notation for nondenotative forms of logic (temporal logics, deontic logics, modal logics), the language of the genetic code, graphs of phonological structures, and so on.

We may form a pessimistic impression of this splintering: nobody speaks all of those languages, they have no universal metalanguage, the project of the system-subject is a failure, the goal of emancipation has nothing to do with science, we are all stuck in the positivism of this or that discipline of learning, the learned scholars have turned into scientists, the diminished tasks of research have become compartmentalized and no one can master them all.[27] Speculative or humanistic philosophy is forced to relinquish its legitimation duties,[28] which explains why philosophy is facing a crisis wherever it persists in arrogating such functions and is reduced to the study of systems of logic or the history of ideas where it has been realistic enough to surrender them.[29]

Turn-of-the-century Vienna was weaned on this pessimism: not just artists such as Musil, Kraus, Hofmannsthal, Loos, Schönberg, and Broch, but also the philosophers Mach and Wittgenstein.[30] They carried awareness of and theoretical and artistic responsibility for delegitimation as far as it could be taken. We can say today that the mourning process has been completed. There is no need to start all over again. Wittgenstein's strength is that he did not opt for the positivism that was being developed by the Vienna Circle,[31] but outlined in his investigation of language games a kind of legitimation not based on performativity. That is what the postmodern world is all about. Most people have lost the nostalgia for the lost narrative. It in no way follows that they are reduced to barbarity. What saves them from it is their knowledge that legitimation can only spring from their own linguistic practice and communicational interaction. Science 'smiling into its beard' at every other belief has taught them the harsh austerity of realism.[32]

Notes

1   A trace of this politics is to be found in the French institution of a philosophy class at the end of secondary studies, and in the proposal by the Groupe de recherches sur l'enseignement de la philosophie (GREPH) to teach 'some' philosophy starting at the beginning of secondary studies: see their *Qui a peur de la philosophie?* (Paris: Flammarion, 1977), sec. 2, 'La Philosophie déclassée.' This also seems to be the orientation of the curriculum of the CEGEP's in Quebec, especially of the philosophy courses (see for example the *Cahiers de l'enseignement collégial* (1975–76) for philosophy).

2   See H. Janne, 'L'Université et les besoins de la société contemporaine,' *Cahiers de l'Association internationale des Universités* 10 (1970): 5; quoted by the Commission d'étude sur les universités. *Document de consultation* (Montréal, 1978).

3   A 'hard,' almost mystico-military expression of this can be found in Julio de Mesquita Filho, *Discorso de Paraninfo da primeiro turma de licenciados pela Faculdade de Filosofia, Ciêncas e Letras da Universidade de Saõ Paulo* (25 January 1937), and an expression of it adapted to the modern problems of Brazilian development in the *Relatorio do Grupo de Rabalho, Reforma Universitaria* (Brasilia: Ministries of Education and Culture, etc., 1968). These documents are part of a dossier on the university in Brazil, kindly sent to me by Helena C. Chamlian and Martha Ramos de Carvalho of the University of Saõ Paulo.

4   The documents are available in French thanks to Miguel Abensour and the Collège de philosophie: *Philosophes de l'Université: L'Idéalisme allemand et la question de l'université* (Paris: Payot, 1979). The collection includes texts by Schelling, Fichte, Schleiermacher, Humboldt, and Hegel.

5   'Über die innere und äussere Organisation der höheren wissenschaftlichen Anstalten in Berlin' (1810), in *Wilhelm von Humboldt* (Frankfurt, 1957), p. 126.

6   Ibid., p. 128.

7   Friedrich Schleiermacher. 'Gelegentliche Gedanken über Universitäten in deutschen Sinn, nebst einem Anhang über eine neu zu errichtende' (1808), in E. Spranger, ed., *Fichte, Schleiermacher, Steffens über das Wesen der Universität* (Leipzig, 1910), p. 126ff.

8   'The teaching of philosophy is generally recognized to be the basis of all university activity' (ibid., p. 128).

9   Alain Touraine has analyzed the contradictions involved in this transplantation in *Université et société aux Etats-Unis* (Paris: Seuil, 1972), pp. 32–40 [Eng. trans. *The Academic System in American Society* (New York: McGraw-Hill, 1974)].

10 It is present even in the conclusions of Robert Nisbet, *The Degradation of the Academic Dogma. The University in America, 1945–70* (London: Heinemann, 1971). The author is a professor at the University of California, Riverside.

11 See G. W. F. Hegel, *Philosophie des Rechts* (1821) [Eng. trans. T. M. Knox, *Hegel's Philosophy of Right* (Oxford: Oxford University Press, 1967)].

12 See Paul Ricoeur, *Le Conflit des interprétations. Essais d'herméneutique* (Paris: Seuil, 1969) [Eng. trans. Don Ihde, *The Conflict of Interpretations* (Evanston, Ill.: Northwestern University Press, 1974)]; Hans Georg Gadamer, *Wahrheit und Methode* 2nd ed. (Tübingen: Mohr. 1965) [Eng. trans. Garrett Barden and John Cumming, *Truth and Method* (New York: Seabury Press, 1975)].

13 Take two statements: 1) 'The moon has risen'; 2) 'The statement /The moon has risen/ is a denotative statement'. The syntagm /The moon has risen/ in statement 2 is said to be the autonym of statement 1. See Josette Rey-Debove, *Le Métalangage* (Paris: Le Robert, 1978), pt. 4.

14 Its principle is Kantian, at least in matters of transcendental ethics – see the *Critique of Practical Reason*. When it comes to politics and empirical ethics, Kant is prudent: since no one can identify himself with the transcendental normative subject, it is theoretically more exact to compromise with the existing authorities. See for example, 'Antwort an der Frage: "Was ist 'Aufklärung'?"' (1784) [Eng. trans. Lewis White Beck, in *Critique of Practical Reason and Other Writings in Moral Philosophy* (Chicago: Chicago University Press, 1949)].

15 See Kant, 'Antwort', Jürgen Habermas, *Strukturwande! der Öffentlichkeit* (Frankfurt: Luchterhand, 1962). The principle of *Öffentlichkeit* ('public' or 'publicity' in the sense of 'making public a private correspondence' or 'public debate') guided the action of many groups of scientists at the end of the 1960s, especially the group 'Survivre' (France), the group 'Scientists and Engineers for Social and Political Action' (USA), and the group 'British Society for Social Responsibility in Science.'

16 A French translation of this text by G. Granel can be found in *Phi*, supplement to the *Annales de l'université de Toulouse – Le Mirail* (Toulouse: January 1977).

17 See note 1. Certain scientific aspects of postmodernism are inventoried by Ihab Hassan in 'Culture, Indeterminacy, and Immanence: Margins of the (Postmodern) Age,' *Humanities in Society* 1 (1978): 51–85.

18 Claus Mueller uses the expression 'a process of delegitimation' in *The Politics of Communication* (New York: Oxford University Press, 1973), p. 164.

19 'Road of doubt ... road of despair ... skepticism,' writes Hegel in the preface

to the *Phenomenology of Spirit* to describe the effect of the speculative drive on natural knowledge.

20 For fear of encumbering this account, I have postponed until a later study the exposition of this group of rules. [See 'Analyzing Speculative Discourse as Language-Game,' *The Oxford Literary Review* 4, no. 3 (1981): 59–67.]

21 Nietzsche, 'Der europäische Nihilismus' (MS. N VII 3); 'der Nihilism, ein normaler Zustand' (MS. W II 1); 'Kritik der Nihilism' (MS. W VII 3); 'Zum Plane' (MS. W II 1), in *Nietzshes Werke kritische Gesamtausgabe*, vol. 7, pts. 1 and 2 (1887–89) (Berlin: De Gruyter, 1970). These texts have been the object of a commentary by K. Ryjik, *Nietzsche, le manuscrit de Lenzer Heide* (typescript, Département de philosophie, Université de Paris VIII [Vincennes]).

22 'On the future of our educational institutions,' in *Complete Works* (note 35), vol. 3.

23 Martin Buber, *Ich und Du* (Berlin: Schocken Verlag, 1922) [Eng. trans. Ronald G. Smith, *I and Thou* (New York: Charles Scribner's Sons, 1937)], and *Dialogisches Leben* (Zürich: Müller, 1947); Emmanuel Levinas, *Totalité et Infinité* (La Haye: Nijhoff, 1961) [Eng. trans. Alphonso Lingis, *Totality and Infinity: An Essay on Exteriority* (Pittsburgh: Duquesne University Press, 1969)], and 'Martin Buber und die Erkenntnis theorie' (1958), in *Philosophen des 20. Jahrhunderts* (Stuttgart: Kohlhammer, 1963) [Fr. trans. 'Martin Buber et la théorie de la connaissance', in *Noms Propres* (Montpellier: Fata Morgana, 1976)].

24 *Philosophical Investigations*, sec. 18, p. 8.

25 Ibid.

26 Ibid.

27 See for example, 'La taylorisation de la recherche,' in (*Auto*) *critique de la science* (note 26), pp. 291–93. And especially D. J. de Solla Price, *Little Science, Big Science* (New York: Columbia University Press, 1963), who emphasizes the split between a small number of highly productive researchers (evaluated in terms of publication) and a large mass of researchers with low productivity. The number of the latter grows as the square of the former, so that the number of high productivity researchers only really increases every twenty years. Price concludes that science considered as a social entity is 'undemocratic' (p. 59) and that 'the eminent scientist' is a hundred years ahead of 'the minimal one' (p. 56).

28 See J. T. Desanti, 'Sur le rapport traditionnel des sciences et de la philosophie,' in *La Philosophie silencieuse, ou critique des philosophies de la science* (Paris: Seuil, 1975).

29 The reclassification of academic philosophy as one of the human sciences in this respect has a significance far beyond simply professional concerns. I do not think that philosophy as legitimation is condemned to disappear, but it is possible that it will not be able to carry out this work, or at least advance it, without revising its ties to the university institution. See on this matter the preamble to the *Projet d'un institut polytechnique de philosophie* (typescript, Département de philosophie, Université de Paris VIII [Vincennes], 1979).

30 See Allan Janik and Stephan Toulmin, *Wittgenstein's Vienna* (New York: Simon

& Schuster, 1973), and J. Piel, ed., 'Vienne début d'un siècle,' *Critique*, 339–40 (1975).

31 See Jürgen Habermas, 'Dogmatismus, Vernunft unt Entscheidung – Zu Theorie und Praxis in der verwissenschaftlichen Zivilisation' (1963), in *Theorie und Praxis* [*Theory and Practice*, abr. ed. of 4th German ed., trans. John Viertel (Boston: Beacon Press, 1971)].

32 'Science Smiling into its Beard' is the title of chap. 72, vol. 1 of Musil's *The Man Without Qualities*. Cited and discussed by J. Bouveresse, 'La Problématique du sujet' (note 54).

6.2

Jean Baudrillard, from *Simulations* (1983)

The simulacrum is never that which conceals the truth – it is the truth which conceals that there is none.
The simulacrum is true.

Ecclesiastes

If we were able to take as the finest allegory of simulation the Borges tale where the cartographers of the Empire draw up a map so detailed that it ends up exactly covering the territory (but where the decline of the Empire sees this map become frayed and finally ruined, a few shreds still discernible in the deserts – the metaphysical beauty of this ruined abstraction, bearing witness to an Imperial pride and rotting like a carcass, returning to the substance of the soil, rather as an aging double ends up being confused with the real thing) – then this fable has come full circle for us, and now has nothing but the discrete charm of second-order simulacra.[1]

Abstraction today is no longer that of the map, the double, the mirror or the concept. Simulation is no longer that of a territory, a referential being or a substance. It is the generation by models of a real without origin or reality: a hyperreal. The territory no longer precedes the map, nor survives it. Henceforth, it is the map that precedes the territory – PRECESSION OF SIMULACRA – it is the map that engenders the territory and if we were to revive the fable today, it would be the territory whose shreds are slowly rotting across the map. It is the real, and not the map, whose vestiges subsist here and there, in the deserts which are no longer those of the Empire, but our own. *The desert of the real itself.*

In fact, even inverted, the fable is useless. Perhaps only the allegory of the Empire remains. For it is with the same Imperialism that present-day simulators try to make the real, all the real, coincide with their simulation models. But it is no longer a question of either maps or territory. Something has disappeared: the sovereign difference between them that was the abstraction's charm. For it is the difference which forms the poetry of the map and the charm of the territory, the magic of the concept and the charm of the real. This representational imaginary, which both culminates in and is engulfed by the cartographer's mad project of an ideal coextensivity between the map and the territory, disappears with simulation – whose operation is nuclear and genetic, and no longer specular and discursive. With it goes all of metaphysics. No more mirror of being and appearances, of the real and its concept. No more imaginary coextensivity: rather, genetic miniaturisation is the dimension of simulation. The real is produced from miniaturised units, from matrices, memory banks and command models – and with these it can be reproduced an indefinite number of times. It no longer has to be rational, since it is no longer measured against some ideal or negative instance. It is nothing more than operational. In fact, since it is no longer enveloped by an imaginary, it is no longer real at all. It is a hyperreal, the product of an irradiating synthesis of combinatory models in a hyperspace without atmosphere.

In this passage to a space whose curvature is no longer that of the real, nor of truth, the age of simulation thus begins with a liquidation of all referentials – worse: by their artificial resurrection in systems of signs, a more ductile material than meaning, in that it lends itself to all systems of equivalence, all binary oppositions and all combinatory algebra. It is no longer a question of imitation, nor of reduplication, nor even of parody. It is rather a question of substituting signs of the real for the real itself, that is, an operation to deter every real process by its operational double, a metastable, programmatic, perfect descriptive machine which provides all the signs of the real and short-circuits all its vicissitudes. Never again will the real have to be produced – this is the vital function of the model in a system of death, or rather of anticipated resurrection which no longer leaves any chance even in the event of death. A hyperreal henceforth sheltered from the imaginary, and from any distinction between the real and the imaginary, leaving room only for the orbital recurrence of models and the simulated generation of difference.

Hyperreal and imaginary

Disneyland is a perfect model of all the entangled orders of simulation. To begin with it is a play of illusions and phantasms: Pirates, the Frontier, Future World, etc. This imaginary world is supposed to be what makes the operation successful. But what draws the crowds is undoubtedly much more the social microcosm, the miniaturised and *religious* revelling in real America, in its delights and drawbacks. You park outside, queue up inside, and are totally abandoned at the exit. In this imaginary world the only phantasmagoria is in the inherent warmth and affection of the crowd, and in that sufficiently excessive number of gadgets used there to specifically maintain the multitudinous affect. The contrast with the absolute solitude of the parking lot – a veritable concentration camp – is total. Or rather: inside, a whole range of gadgets magnetise the crowd into direct flows – outside, solitude is directed onto a single gadget: the automobile. By an extraordinary coincidence (one that undoubtedly belongs to the peculiar enchantment of this universe), this deep-frozen infantile world happens to have been conceived and realised by a man who is himself now cryogenised: Walt Disney, who awaits his resurrection at minus 180 degrees centigrade.

The objective profile of America, then, may be traced throughout Disneyland, even down to the morphology of individuals and the crowd. All its values are exalted here, in miniature and comic strip form. Embalmed and pacified. Whence the possibility of an ideological analysis of Disneyland (L. Marin does it well in *Utopies, jeux d'espaces*): digest of the American way of life, panegyric to American values, idealised transposition of a contradictory reality. To be sure. But this conceals something else, and that 'ideological' blanket exactly serves to cover over a *third-order simulation*: Disneyland is there to conceal the fact that it is the 'real' country, all of 'real' America, which *is* Disneyland (just as prisons are there to conceal the fact that it is the social in its entirety, in its banal omnipresence, which is carceral). Disneyland is presented as imaginary in order to make us believe that the rest is real, when in fact all of Los Angeles and the America surrounding it are no longer real, but of the order of the hyperreal and of simulation. It is no longer a question of a false representation of reality (ideology), but of concealing the fact that the real is no longer real, and thus of saving the reality principle.

The Disneyland imaginary is neither true nor false; it is a deterrence machine set up in order to rejuvenate in reverse the fiction of the real. Whence the debility, the infantile degeneration of this imaginary. It is meant to be an infantile world, in order to make us believe that the adults are elsewhere, in the 'real' world, and to conceal the fact that real childishness is everywhere, particularly amongst those adults who go there to act the child in order to foster illusions as to their real childishness.

Moreover, Disneyland is not the only one. Enchanted Village, Magic Mountain, Marine World: Los Angeles is encircled by these 'imaginary stations' which feed reality, reality-energy, to a town whose mystery is precisely that it is nothing more than a network of endless, unreal circulation – a town of fabulous proportions, but without space or dimensions. As much as electrical and nuclear power stations, as much as film studios, this town, which is nothing more than an immense script and a perpetual motion picture, needs this old imaginary made up of childhood signals and faked phantasms for its sympathetic nervous system.

Note

1   Cf. J. Baudrillard, *L'échange symbolique et la mort* ('L'ordre des simulacres') (Paris: Gallimard, 1975).

6.3

Jean-François Lyotard, from *The Inhuman* (1991)

You philosophers ask questions without answers, questions that have to remain unanswered to deserve being called philosophical.

* * *

While we talk, the sun is getting older. It will explode in 4.5 billion years. It's just a little beyond the halfway point of its expected lifetime. It's like a man in his early forties with a life expectancy of eighty. With the sun's death your insoluble questions will be done with too. It's possible they'll stay unanswered right up to the end, flawlessly formulated, though now both grounds for raising such questions as well as the place to do this will no longer exist. You explain: it's impossible to think an end, pure and simple, of anything at all, since the end's a limit and to think it you have to be on both sides of that limit. So what's finished or finite has to be perpetuated in our thought if it's to be thought of as finished. Now this is true of limits belonging to thought. But after the sun's death there won't be a thought to know that its death took place.

That, in my view, is the sole serious question to face humanity today. In comparison everything else seems insignificant. Wars, conflicts, political tension, shifts in opinion, philosophical debates, even passions – everything's dead already if this infinite reserve from which you now draw energy to defer answers, if in short thought as quest, dies out with the sun. Maybe death isn't the word. But the inevitable explosion to come, the one that's always forgotten in your intellectual ploys, can be seen in a certain way as coming before the fact to render these ploys posthumous – make them futile. I'm talking about what's X'd out of your writings – matter. Matter taken as an arrangement of energy created, destroyed and recreated over and over again, endlessly. On the corpuscular and/or cosmic scale I mean. I am not talking about the familiar, reassuring terrestrial world or the reassuring transcendent immanence of thought to its objects, analogous to the way the eye transcends what's visible or *habitus* its *situs*. In 4.5 billion years there will arrive the demise of your phenomenology and your utopian politics, and there'll be no one there to toll the death knell or hear it. It will be too late to understand that your passionate, endless questioning always depended on a 'life of the mind' that will have been nothing else than a covert form of earthly life. A form of life that was spiritual because human, human because earthly – coming from the earth of the most living of living things. Thought borrows a horizon and orientation, the limitless limit and the end without end it assumes, from the corporeal, sensory, emotional and cognitive experience of a quite sophisticated but definitely earthly existence – to which it's indebted as well.

With the disappearance of earth, thought will have stopped – leaving that disappearance absolutely unthought of. It's the horizon itself that will be abolished and, with its disappearance, your transcendence in immanence as well. If, as a limit, death really is what escapes and is deferred and as a result what thought has to deal with, right from the beginning – this death is still only the life of our minds. But the death of the sun is a death of mind, because it is the death of death as the life of the mind. There's no sublation or deferral if nothing survives. This annihilation is totally different from the one you harangue us about talking about 'our' death, a death that is part of the fate of living creatures who think. Annihilation in any case is too subjective. It will involve a change in the condition of matter: that is, in the form that energies take. This change is enough to render null and void your anticipation of a world after the explosion. Political science-fiction novels depict the cold desert of our human world after nuclear war. The solar explosion won't be due to human war. It won't leave behind it a devastated human world, dehumanized, but with none the less at least a single survivor, someone to tell the story of what's left, write it down. Dehumanized still implies human – a dead human, but conceivable: because dead in human terms, still capable of being sublated in thought. But in what remains after the solar explosion, there won't be any humanness, there won't be living creatures, there won't be intelligent, sensitive, sentient earthlings to bear witness to it, since they and their earthly horizon will have been consumed.

Assume that the ground, Husserl's *Ur-Erde*, will vanish into clouds of heat and matter. Considered as matter, the earth isn't at all originary since it's subject to changes in its condition – changes from further away or closer, changes coming from matter and energy and from the laws governing Earth's transformation. The *Erde* is an arrangement of matter/energy. This arrangement is transitory – lasting a few billion years more or less. Lunar years. Not a long time considered on a cosmic scale. The sun, our earth and your thought will have been no more than a spasmodic state of energy, an instant of established order, a smile on the surface of matter in a remote corner of the cosmos. You, the unbelievers, you're really believers: you believe much too much in that smile, in the complicity of things and thought, in the purposefulness of all things! Like everyone else, you will end up victims of the stabilized relationships of order in that remote corner. You'll have been seduced and deceived by what you call nature, by a congruence of mind and things. Claudel called this a '*co-naissance*', and Merleau-Ponty spoke of the chiasmus of the eye and the horizon, a fluid in which mind floats. The solar explosion, the mere thought of that explosion, should awaken you from this euphoria. Look here: you try to think of the event in its *quod*, in the advent of 'it so happens that' before any quiddity, don't you? Well, you'll grant the explosion of the sun is the *quod* itself, no subsequent assignment being possible. Of that death alone, Epicurus ought to have said what he says about death – that I have nothing to do with it, since if it's present, I'm not, and if I'm present, it's not. Human death is included in the life of human mind. Solar death implies an irreparably exclusive disjunction between death and thought: if there's death, then there's no thought. Negation without remainder. No self to make sense of it. Pure event. Disaster. All the events and disasters we're familiar with and try to think of will end up as no more than pale simulacra.

Now this event is ineluctable. So either you don't concern yourself with it – and remain in the life of the mind and in earthly phenomenality. Like Epicurus you say 'As long as it's not here, I am, and I continue philosophizing in the cozy lap of the complicity between man and nature.' But still with this glum afterthought: *après moi le déluge*. The deluge of matter. You'll grant there's a significant point of divergence between our thinking and the classical and modern thought of Western civilization: the obvious fact of there being no nature, but only the material monster of *D'Alembert's Dream*, the *chôra* of the *Timaeus*. Once we were considered able to converse with Nature. Matter asks no questions, expects no answers of us. It ignores us. It made us the way it made all bodies – by chance and according to its laws.

Or else you try to anticipate the disaster and fend it off with means belonging to that category – means that are those of the laws of the transformation of energy. You decide to accept the challenge of the extremely likely annihilation of a solar order and an order of your own thought. And then the only job left you is quite clear – it's been underway for some time – the job of simulating conditions of life and thought to make thinking remain materially possible after the change in the condition of matter that's the disaster. This and this alone is what's at stake today in technical and scientific research in every field from dietetics, neurophysiology, genetics and tissue synthesis to particle physics, astrophysics, electronics, information science and nuclear physics. Whatever the immediate stakes might appear to be: health, war, production, communication. For the benefit of humankind, as the saying goes.

6.4

Jacques Derrida, from *The Gift of Death* (1995)

In the exemplary form of its absolute coherence, Hegel's philosophy represents the irrefutable demand for manifestation, phenomenalization, and unveiling; thus, it is thought, it represents the request for truth that inspires philosophy and ethics in their most powerful forms. There are no final secrets for philosophy, ethics, or politics. The manifest is given priority over the hidden or the secret, universal generality is superior to the individual; no irreducible secret that can be legally justified (*fondé en droit* says the French translation of Kierkegaard) – and thus the instance of the law has to be added to those of philosophy and ethics; nothing hidden, no absolutely legitimate secret. But the paradox of faith is that interiority remains 'incommensurable with exteriority' (69). No manifestation can consist in rendering the interior exterior or show what is hidden. The knight of faith can neither communicate to nor be understood by anyone, she can't help the other at all (71). The absolute duty that obligates her with respect to God cannot have the form of generality that is called duty. If I obey in my duty towards God (which is my absolute duty) *only in terms of duty*, I am not fulfilling my relation to God. In order to fulfill my duty towards God, I must not act *out of duty*, by means of that form of generality that can always be mediated and communicated and that is called duty. The absolute duty that binds me to God himself, in faith, must function beyond and against any duty I have. 'The duty becomes duty by being traced back to God, but in the duty itself I do not enter into relation to God' (68). Kant explains that to act morally is to act 'out of duty' and not only 'by conforming to duty.' Kierkegaard sees acting 'out of duty,' in the universalizable sense of the law, as a dereliction of one's absolute duty. It is in this sense that absolute duty (towards God and in the singularity of faith) implies a sort of gift or sacrifice that functions beyond both debt and duty, beyond duty as a form of debt. This is the dimension that provides for a 'gift of death' which, beyond human responsibility, beyond the universal concept of duty, is a response to absolute duty.

In the order of human generality, a duty of hate is implied. Kierkegaard quotes Luke 14:26: ' "If any one comes to me and does not hate his own father and mother and his wife and children and brothers and sisters, yes, and even his own life, he cannot be my disciple".' Recognizing that 'this is a hard saying' (72), Kierkegaard nevertheless upholds the necessity for it. He refines its rigor without seeking to make it less shocking or paradoxical. But Abraham's hatred for the ethical and thus for his own (family, friends, neighbors, nation, but at the outside humanity as a whole, his own kind or species) must remain an absolute source of pain. If I put to death or grant death to what I hate it is not a sacrifice. I must sacrifice what I love. I must come to hate what I love, in the same moment, at the instant of granting death. I must hate and betray my own, that is to say offer them the gift of death by means of the sacrifice, not insofar as I hate them, that would be too easy, but insofar as I love them. I must hate them insofar as I love them. Hate wouldn't be hate if it only hated the hateful, that would be too easy. It must hate and betray what is most lovable. Hate cannot be hate, it can only be the sacrifice of love to love. It is not a matter of hating, betraying by one's breach of trust, or offering the gift of death to what one doesn't love.

But is this heretical and paradoxical knight of faith Jewish, Christian, or Judeo-Christian-Islamic? The sacrifice of Isaac belongs to what one might just dare to call the common treasure, the terrifying secret of the *mysterium tremendum* that is a property of all three so-called religions of the Book, the religions of the races of Abraham. This rigor, and the exaggerated demands it entails, compel the knight of faith to say and do things that will appear (and must even be) atrocious. They will necessarily revolt those who profess allegiance to morality in general, to Judeo-Christian-Islamic morality, or to the religion of love in general. But as Patočka will say, perhaps Christianity has not yet thought through its own essence, any more than it has thought through the irrefutable events through which Judaism, Christianity, and Islam have come to pass. One cannot ignore or erase the sacrifice of Isaac recounted in Genesis, nor that recounted in the Gospel of Luke. It has to be taken into account, which is what Kierkegaard proposes. Abraham comes to hate those closest to him by keeping silent, he comes to hate his only beloved son by consenting to put him to death [*lui donner la mort*]. He hates them not out of hatred, of course, but out of love. He doesn't hate them any less for all that, on the contrary. Abraham must love his son absolutely to come to the point where he will grant him death, to commit what ethics would call hatred and murder.

How does one hate one's own? Kierkegaard rejects the common distinction between love and hate; he finds it egotistical and without interest. He reinterprets it as a paradox. God wouldn't have asked Abraham to put Isaac to death, that is, to make a gift of death as a sacrificial offering to himself, to God, unless Abraham had an absolute, unique, and incommensurable love for his son:

> for it is indeed this love for Isaac that makes his act a sacrifice by its paradoxical contrast to his love for God. But the distress and the anxiety in the paradox is that he, humanly speaking, is thoroughly incapable of making himself understandable. Only *in the instant* when his act is in absolute contradiction to his feelings, only then does he sacrifice Isaac, but the reality of his act is that by which he belongs to the universal, and there he is and remains a murderer. (74, translation modified – DW)

I have emphasized the word *instant:* 'the instant of decision is madness,' Kierkegaard says elsewhere. The paradox cannot be grasped in time and through mediation, that is to say in language and through reason. Like the gift and 'the gift of death,' it remains irreducible to presence or to presentation, it demands a temporality of the instant without ever constituting a present. If it can be said, it belongs to an atemporal temporality, to a duration that cannot be grasped: something one can neither stabilize, establish, grasp [*prendre*], apprehend, or comprehend. Understanding, common sense, and reason cannot seize [*begreifen*], conceive, understand, or mediate it; neither can they negate or deny it, implicate it in the work of negation, make it work: in the act of *giving death*, sacrifice suspends both the work of negation and work itself, perhaps even the work of mourning. The tragic hero enters into mourning. Abraham, on the other hand, is neither a man of mourning nor a tragic hero.

In order to assume his absolute responsibility with respect to absolute duty, to put his faith in God to work, or to the test, he must also in reality remain a hateful murderer, for he consents to put to death. In both general and abstract terms, the absoluteness of duty, of responsibility, and of obligation certainly demands that one transgress ethical duty, although in betraying it one belongs to it and at the same time recognizes it. The contradiction and the paradox must be endured *in the instant itself*. The two duties must contradict one another, one must subordinate (incorporate, repress) the other. Abraham must assume absolute responsibility for sacrificing his son by sacrificing ethics, but in order for there to be a sacrifice, the ethical must retain all its value; the love for his son must remain intact, and the order of human duty must continue to insist on its rights.

The account of Isaac's sacrifice can be read as a narrative development of the paradox constituting the concept of duty and absolute responsibility. This concept puts us into relation (but without relating to it, in a double secret) with the absolute other, with the absolute singularity of the other, whose name here is God. Whether one believes the biblical story or not, whether one gives it credence, doubts it, or transposes it, it could still be said that there is a moral to this story, even if we take it to be a fable (but taking it to be a fable still amounts to losing it to philosophical or poetic generality; it means that it loses the quality of a historic event). The moral of the fable would be morality itself, at the point where morality brings into play the gift of the death that is so given. The absolutes of duty and of responsibility presume that one denounce, refute, and transcend, at the same time, all duty, all responsibility, and every human law. It calls for a betrayal of everything that manifests itself within the order of universal generality, and everything that manifests itself in general, the very order and essence of manifestation; namely, the essence itself, the essence in general to the extent that it is inseparable from presence and from manifestation. Absolute duty demands that one behave in an irresponsible manner (by means of treachery or betrayal), while still recognizing, confirming, and reaffirming the very thing one sacrifices, namely, the order of human ethics and responsibility. In a word, ethics must be sacrificed in the name of duty. It is a duty not to respect, out of duty, ethical duty. One must behave not only in an ethical or responsible manner, but in a nonethical, nonresponsible manner, and one must do that *in the name of* duty, of an infinite duty, *in the name of* absolute duty. And this name which must always be singular is here none other than the name of God as completely other, the nameless name of God, the unpronounceable name of God as other to which I am bound by an absolute, unconditional obligation, by an incomparable, nonnegotiable duty. The other as absolute other, namely, God, must remain transcendent, hidden, secret, jealous of the love, requests, and commands that he gives and that he asks to be kept secret. Secrecy is essential to the exercise of this absolute responsibility as sacrificial responsibility.

In terms of the moral of morality, let us here insist upon what is too often forgotten by the moralizing moralists and good consciences who preach to us with assurance every morning and every week, in newspapers and magazines, on the radio and on television, about the sense of ethical or political responsibility. Philosophers who don't write ethics are failing in their duty, one often hears, and the first duty of the philosopher is to think about ethics, to add a chapter on ethics to each of his or her books and, in order to do that, to come back to Kant as often as possible. What the knights of good conscience don't realize, is that 'the sacrifice of Isaac' illustrates – if that is the word in the case of such a nocturnal mystery – the most common and everyday experience of responsibility. The story is no doubt monstrous, outrageous, barely conceivable: a father is ready to put to death his beloved son, his irreplaceable loved one, and that because the Other, the great Other asks him or orders him without giving the slightest explanation. An infanticide father who hides what he is going to do from his son and from his family without knowing why, what could be more abominable, what mystery could be more frightful (*tremendum*) vis-à-vis love, humanity, the family, or morality?

6.5

Jean Baudrillard, from *The Spirit of Terrorism* (2002)

In all these vicissitudes, what stays with us, above all else, is the sight of the images. This impact of the images, and their fascination, are necessarily what we retain, since images are, whether we like it or not, our primal scene. And, at the same time as they have radicalized the world situation, the events in New York can also be said to have radicalized the relation of the image to reality. Whereas we were dealing before with an uninterrupted profusion of banal images and a seamless flow of sham events, the terrorist act in New York has resuscitated both images and events.

Among the other weapons of the system which they turned round against it, the terrorists exploited the 'real time' of images, their instantaneous worldwide transmission, just as they exploited stock-market speculation, electronic information and air traffic. The role of images is highly ambiguous. For, at the same time as they exalt the event, they also take it hostage. They serve to multiply it to infinity and, at the same time, they are a diversion and a neutralization (this was already the case with the events of 1968). The image consumes the event, in the sense that it absorbs it and offers it for consumption. Admittedly, it gives it unprecedented impact, but impact as image-event.

How do things stand with the real event, then, if reality is everywhere infiltrated by images, virtuality and fiction? In the present case, we thought we had seen (perhaps with a certain relief) a resurgence of the real, and of the violence of the real, in an allegedly virtual universe. 'There's an end to all your talk about the virtual – this is something real!' Similarly, it was possible to see this as a resurrection of history beyond its proclaimed end. But does reality actually outstrip fiction? If it seems to do so, this is because it has absorbed fiction's energy, and has itself become fiction. We might almost say that reality is jealous of fiction, that the real is jealous of the image. ... It is a kind of duel between them, a contest to see which can be the most unimaginable.

The collapse of the World Trade Center towers is unimaginable, but that is not enough to make it a real event. An excess of violence is not enough to open on to reality. For reality is a principle, and it is this principle that is lost. Reality and fiction are inextricable, and the fascination with the attack is primarily a fascination

with the image (both its exultatory and its catastrophic consequences are themselves largely imaginary).

In this case, then, the real is superadded to the image like a bonus of terror, like
an additional *frisson*: not only is it terrifying, but, what is more, it is real. Rather than
the violence of the real being there first, and the *frisson* of the image being added to
it, the image is there first, and the *frisson* of the real is added. Something like an
additional fiction, a fiction surpassing fiction. Ballard (after Borges) talked like this
of reinventing the real as the ultimate and most redoubtable fiction.

The terrorist violence here is not, then, a blowback of reality, any more than it
is a blowback of history. It is not 'real'. In a sense, it is worse: it is symbolic.
Violence in itself may be perfectly banal and inoffensive. Only symbolic violence is
generative of singularity. And in this singular event, in this Manhattan disaster
movie, the twentieth century's two elements of mass fascination are combined: the
white magic of the cinema and the black magic of terrorism; the white light of the
image and the black light of terrorism.

We try retrospectively to impose some kind of meaning on it, to find some kind
of interpretation. But there is none. And it is the radicality of the spectacle, the
brutality of the spectacle, which alone is original and irreducible. The spectacle of
terrorism forces the terrorism of spectacle upon us. And, against this immoral
fascination (even if it unleashes a universal moral reaction), the political order can
do nothing. This is *our* theatre of cruelty, the only one we have left – extraordinary
in that it unites the most extreme degree of the spectacular and the highest level of
challenge. ... It is at one and the same time the dazzling micromodel of a kernel of
real violence with the maximum possible echo – hence the purest form of spectacle
– and a sacrificial model mounting the purest symbolic form of defiance to the
historical and political order.

We would forgive them any massacre if it had a meaning, if it could be interpreted as historical violence – this is the moral axiom of good violence. We would
pardon them any violence if it were not given media exposure ('terrorism would be
nothing without the media'). But this is all illusion. There is no 'good' use of the
media; the media are part of the event, they are part of the terror, and they work in
both directions.

The repression of terrorism spirals around as unpredictably as the terrorist act
itself. No one knows where it will stop, or what turnabouts there may yet be. There
is no possible distinction, at the level of images and information, between the
spectacular and the symbolic, no possible distinction between the 'crime' and the
crackdown. And it is this uncontrollable unleashing of reversibility that is terrorism's true victory. A victory that is visible in the subterranean ramifications and
infiltrations of the event – not just in the direct economic, political, financial slump
in the whole of the system – and the resulting moral and psychological downturn –
but in the slump in the value-system, in the whole ideology of freedom, of free
circulation, and so on, on which the Western world prided itself, and on which it
drew to exert its hold over the rest of the world.

To the point that the idea of freedom, a new and recent idea, is already fading
from minds and mores, and liberal globalization is coming about in precisely the
opposite form – a police-state globalization, a total control, a terror based on 'law-

and-order' measures. Deregulation ends up in a maximum of constraints and restrictions, akin to those of a fundamentalist society.

A fall-off in production, consumption, speculation and growth (but certainly not in corruption!): it is as though the global system were making a strategic fall-back, carrying out a painful revision of its values – in defensive reaction, as it would seem, to the impact of terrorism, but responding, deep down, to its secret injunctions: enforced regulation as a product of absolute disorder, but a regulation it imposes on itself – internalizing, as it were, its own defeat.

Another aspect of the terrorists' victory is that all other forms of violence and the destabilization of order work in its favour. Internet terrorism, biological ter-rorism, the terrorism of anthrax and rumour – all are ascribed to Bin Laden. He might even claim natural catastrophes as his own. All the forms of disorganization and perverse circulation operate to his advantage. The very structure of generalized world trade works in favour of impossible exchange. It is like an 'automatic writing' of terrorism, constantly refuelled by the involuntary terrorism of news and infor-mation. With all the panic consequences which ensue; if, in the current anthrax scare,[1] the hysteria spreads spontaneously by instantaneous crystallization, like a chemical solution at the mere contact of a molecule, this is because the whole system has reached a critical mass which makes it vulnerable to any aggression.

There is no remedy for this extreme situation, and war is certainly not a solution, since it merely offers a rehash of the past, with the same deluge of military forces, bogus information, senseless bombardment, emotive and deceitful lan-guage, technological deployment and brainwashing. Like the Gulf War: a non-event, an event that does not really take place.

And this indeed is its *raison-d'être*: to substitute, for a real and formidable, unique and unforeseeable event, a repetitive, rehashed pseudo-event. The terrorist attack corresponded to a precedence of the event over all interpretative models; whereas this mindlessly military, technological war corresponds, conversely, to the model's precedence over the event, and hence to a conflict over phoney stakes, to a situation of 'no contest'. War as continuation of the absence of politics by other means.

Note

1   This text was written in October 2001 and published in *Le Monde* on November 3 2001.

6.6

Slavoj Žižek, from *Welcome to the Desert of the Real* (2002)

On today's market, we find a whole series of products deprived of their malignant properties: coffee without caffeine, cream without fat, beer without alcohol. . . . And the list goes on: what about virtual sex as sex without sex, the Colin Powell doctrine of warfare with no casualties (on our side, of course) as warfare without warfare, the contemporary redefinition of politics as the art of expert administration, that is, as politics without politics, up to today's tolerant liberal multiculturalism as an experience of the Other deprived of its Otherness (the idealized Other who dances fascinating dances and has an ecologically sound holistic approach to reality, while practices like wife beating remain out of sight . . .)? Virtual Reality simply generalizes this procedure of offering a product deprived of its substance: it provides reality itself deprived of its substance, of the hard resistant kernel of the Real – just as decaffeinated coffee smells and tastes like real coffee without being real coffee, Virtual Reality is experienced as reality without being so. What happens at the end of this process of virtualization, however, is that we begin to experience 'real reality' itself as a virtual entity. For the great majority of the public, the WTC explosions were events on the TV screen, and when we watched the oft-repeated shot of frightened people running towards the camera ahead of the giant cloud of dust from the collapsing tower, was not the framing of the shot itself reminiscent of spectacular shots in catastrophe movies, a special effect which outdid all others, since – as Jeremy Bentham knew – reality is the best appearance of itself?

And was not the attack on the World Trade Center with regard to Hollywood catastrophe movies like snuff pornography versus ordinary sado-masochistic porno movies? This is the element of truth in Karl-Heinz Stockhausen's provocative statement that the planes hitting the WTC towers was the ultimate work of art: we can perceive the collapse of the WTC towers as the climactic conclusion of twentieth-century art's 'passion for the Real' – the 'terrorists' themselves did not do it primarily to provoke real material damage, but *for the spectacular effect of it*. When, days after September 11 2001, our gaze was transfixed by the images of the plane hitting one of the WTC towers, we were all forced to experience what the 'compulsion to repeat' and *jouissance* beyond the pleasure principle are: we wanted to see it again and again; the same shots were repeated *ad nauseam*, and the uncanny satisfaction we got from it was *jouissance* at its purest. It was when we watched the two WTC towers collapsing on the TV screen, that it became possible to experience the falsity of 'reality TV shows': even if these shows are 'for real', people still act in them – they simply play themselves. The standard disclaimer in a novel ('Characters in this text are fictional, any resemblance to real-life characters is purely accidental') also holds for participants in reality soaps: what we see there are fictional characters, even if they play themselves for real.

The authentic twentieth-century passion for penetrating the Real Thing (ultimately, the destructive Void) through the cobweb of semblances which constitutes our reality thus culminates in the thrill of the Real as the ultimate 'effect', sought after from digitalized special effects, through reality TV and amateur pornography, up to snuff movies. Snuff movies which deliver the 'real thing' are perhaps the ultimate truth of Virtual Reality. There is an intimate connection between the virtualization of reality and the emergence of an infinite and infinitized bodily pain, much stronger than the usual one: do not biogenetics and Virtual Reality combined open up new 'enhanced' possibilities of *torture*, new and unheard-of horizons of extending our ability to endure pain (through widening our sensory capacity to sustain pain, through inventing new forms of inflicting it)? Perhaps the ultimate Sadeian image of an 'undead' victim of torture who can bear endless pain without having the escape into death at his or her disposal is also waiting to become reality.

The ultimate American paranoiac fantasy is that of an individual living in a small idyllic Californian city, a consumerist paradise, who suddenly starts to suspect that the world he is living in is a fake, a spectacle staged to convince him that he is living in a real world, while all the people around him are in fact actors and extras in a gigantic show. The most recent example of this is Peter Weir's *The Truman Show* (1998), with Jim Carrey playing the small-town clerk who gradually discovers the truth that he is the hero of a permanent twenty-four-hour TV show: his home town is in fact a gigantic studio set, with cameras following him everywhere. Among its predecessors, it is worth mentioning Phillip K. Dick's *Time out of Joint* (1959), in which the hero, living a modest daily life in a small idyllic Californian city in the late 1950s, gradually discovers that the whole town is a fake staged to keep him satisfied. ... The underlying experience of *Time out of Joint* and of *The Truman Show* is that the late-capitalist consumerist Californian paradise is, in its very hyperreality, in a way *unreal*, substanceless, deprived of material inertia. And the same 'derealization' of the horror went on after the WTC collapse: while the number of victims – 3,000 – is repeated all the time, it is surprising how little of the actual carnage we see – no dismembered bodies, no blood, no desperate faces of dying people ... in clear contrast to reporting on Third World catastrophes, where the whole point is to produce a scoop of some gruesome detail: Somalis dying of hunger, raped Bosnian women, men with their throats cut. These shots are always accompanied by an advance warning that 'some of the images you will see are extremely graphic and may upset children' – a warning which we never heard in the reports on the WTC collapse. Is this not yet further proof of how, even in this tragic moment, the distance which separates Us from Them, from their reality, is maintained: the real horror happens *there*, not *here*?[1]

So it is not only that Hollywood stages a semblance of real life deprived of the weight and inertia of materiality – in late-capitalist consumerist society, 'real social life' itself somehow acquires the features of a staged fake, with our neighbours behaving in 'real' life like stage actors and extras. . . . Again, the ultimate truth of the capitalist utilitarian despiritualized universe is the dematerialization of 'real life' itself, its reversal into a spectral show. Among others, Christopher Isherwood gave expression to this unreality of American daily life, exemplified in the motel room: 'American motels are unreal! . . . They are deliberately designed to be unreal. . . . The Europeans hate us because we've retired to live inside our advertisements, like hermits going into caves to contemplate.' Peter Sloterdijk's notion of the 'sphere' is literally realized here, as the gigantic metal sphere that envelops and isolates the whole city. Years ago, a series of science-fiction films like *Zardoz* or *Logan's Run* forecast today's postmodern predicament by extending this fantasy to the community itself: the isolated group living an aseptic life in a secluded area longs for the experience of the real world of material decay. Is not the endlessly repeated shot of the plane approaching and hitting the second WTC tower the real-life version of the famous scene from Hitchcock's *Birds*, superbly analysed by Raymond Bellour, in which Melanie approaches the Bodega Bay pier after crossing the bay in a little boat? When, as she approaches the wharf, she waves to her (future) lover, a single bird (first perceived as an indistinguishable dark blot) unexpectedly enters the frame from above right, and hits her on the head.[2] Was not the plane which hit the WTC tower literally the ultimate Hitchcockian blot, the anamorphic stain which denaturalized the idyllic well-known New York landscape?

The Wachowski brothers' hit *Matrix* (1999) brought this logic to its climax: the material reality we all experience and see around us is a virtual one, generated and co-ordinated by a gigantic mega-computer to which we are all attached; when the hero (played by Keanu Reeves) awakens into 'real reality', he sees a desolate landscape littered with burnt-out ruins – what remains of Chicago after a global war. The resistance leader, Morpheus, utters the ironic greeting: 'Welcome to the desert of the real.' Was it not something of a similar order that took place in New York on September 11? Its citizens were introduced to the 'desert of the real' – for us, corrupted by Hollywood, the landscape and the shots of the collapsing towers could not but be reminiscent of the most breathtaking scenes in big catastrophe productions.

When we hear how the attacks were a totally unexpected shock, how the unimaginable Impossible happened, we should recall the other defining catastrophe from the beginning of the twentieth century, the sinking of the *Titanic*: this, also, was a shock, but the space for it had already been prepared in ideological fantasizing, since the *Titanic* was the symbol of the might of nineteenth-century industrial civilization. Does not the same hold also for these attacks? Not only were the media bombarding us all the time with talk about the terrorist threat; this threat was also obviously libidinally invested – just remember the series of movies from *Escape from New York* to *Independence Day*. That is the rationale of the often-mentioned association of the attacks with Hollywood disaster movies: the unthinkable which happened was the object of fantasy, so that, in a way, America got what it fantasized about, and that was the biggest surprise. The ultimate twist in this link between Hollywood and the 'war against terrorism' occurred when the Pentagon decided to solicit the help of Hollywood: at the beginning of October 2001, the press reported that a group of Hollywood scenarists and directors, specialists in catastrophe movies, had been established at the instigation of the Pentagon, with the aim of imagining possible scenarios for terrorist attacks and how to fight them. And this interaction seemed to be ongoing: at the beginning of November 2001, there was a series of meetings between White House advisers and senior Hollywood executives with the aim of co-ordinating the war effort and establishing how Hollywood could help in the 'war against terrorism' by getting the right ideological message across not only to Americans, but also to the Hollywood public around the globe – the ultimate empirical proof that Hollywood does in fact function as an 'ideological state apparatus'.

We should therefore invert the standard reading according to which the WTC explosions were the intrusion of the Real which shattered our illusory Sphere: quite the reverse – it was before the WTC collapse that we lived in our reality, perceiving Third World horrors as something which was not actually part of our social reality, as something which existed (for us) as a spectral apparition on the (TV) screen – and what happened on September 11 was that this fantasmatic screen apparition entered our reality. It is not that reality entered our image: the image entered and shattered our reality (i.e. the symbolic coordinates which determine what we experience as reality). The fact that, after September 11, the openings of many 'blockbuster' movies with scenes which bear a resemblance to the WTC collapse (tall buildings on fire or under attack, terrorist acts ...) were postponed (or the films were even shelved) should thus be read as the 'repression' of the fantasmatic background responsible for the impact of the WTC collapse. Of course, the point is not to play a pseudo-postmodern game of reducing the WTC collapse to just another media spectacle, reading it as a catastrophe version of the snuff porno movies; the question we should have asked ourselves as we stared at the TV screens on September 11 is simply: *Where have we already seen the same thing over and over again?*

Notes

1   Another case of ideological censorship: when firefighters' widows were interviewed on CNN, most of them gave the expected performance: tears, prayers ... all except one who, without a tear, said that she does not pray for her dead husband, because she knows that prayer will not bring him back. Asked if she dreams of revenge, she calmly said that that would be a true betrayal of her husband: had he survived, he would have insisted that the worst thing to do is to succumb to the urge to retaliate ... there is no need to add that this clip was shown only once, then disappeared from the repetitions of the same interviews.

2   See Chapter 3 of Raymond Bellour, *The Analysis of Film*, Bloomington: Indiana University Press 2000.

Summaries

1.1 Ferdinand de Saussure, from *Course in General Linguistics* (trans. Wade Baskin, London: Peter Owen Ltd, 1974, pp. 111–19, 120–1; first published 1916)

While common sense seems to tell us that words reflect a reality outside language and are basically names for *things*, Saussurean linguistics dispenses with this view to show that language is an internally self-sufficient system, consisting of values. Prior to Saussure the study of language had been mainly *diachronic*: that is, an analysis of its changing forms across history. Saussure distinguishes his area of concern as *synchronic*, considering how a language works at a given moment as a rule-governed system. In order to do this, he makes two further crucial distinctions: between *langue* and *parole*, between *signifier* and *signified*. What anyone actually says, their writing or utterance, is termed *parole* but the system of a particular language allowing someone to generate a meaningful utterance, according to rules for word formation and sentence structure, constitutes its *langue*. On this basis Saussure argues that the common-sense notion of 'words' needs to be broken down and divided into signifier and signified (a distinction as old as classical rhetoric).

While the signifier consists of the sounds used by a particular language, arranged one after another in a temporal order, the signifieds are the concepts or meanings assigned to any conventional unit of sound. If we hear two people speaking in a language we don't know, we can pick up some of its signifiers but don't have access to the signified meanings that go with them. When signifier and signified are joined together they make up a sign. Out of the whole range of noises possible for the human voice a particular language draws on certain selected sounds to make up signifiers, the smallest unit used being a *phoneme*. But phonemes, as subsequent work has confirmed, are in themselves wholly arbitrary, defined only by their opposition or difference from one another, as /c/ in Modern English is contrasted with /b/. Signified meanings, similarly, are specified not by their relation to the real but in their relation to each other, their internal differences.

For these reasons Saussure claims that the relation between signifier and signified is by nature arbitrary (since no two languages use exactly the same sounds to act as phonemes) and that it is only because of the social convention operating for a particular language that a given string of phonemes (such as /c/a/t/) is agreed to mean a certain furry mammal, while /b/a/t/ in contrast can work to mean a flying mammal (and something you hit something with). It is crucial to his influence that in all of this Saussure steps aside from the question of the relation between the verbal sign ('word') and the referent (or real object). And it provides support for his account to note that signs work perfectly well although their referent may be very hard to define (such as the word 'if') or doesn't exist in reality at all (for example, 'dragon').

1.2 Roland Barthes, 'The Great Family of Man' from *Mythologies* (trans. Annette Lavers, London: Random House, 1993, pp. 100–3; first published 1957)

Between 1954 and 1956 Roland Barthes set himself the task of writing a short piece each month on a current aspect of French popular culture, attacking with all the satiric zest of a Parisian intellectual (and man of the left) the sacred objects of the French petit-bourgeoisie: Persil soap-powder advertising, the design of the latest Citroën, publicity for Garbo's face. He recognizes that the enormous growth and dissemination of the media – especially television – since 1950 pose new problems for critical analysis, particularly of the visual media. To this he brings two theoretical weapons, Saussure's account of the sign (see Section 1.1) and the Marxist conception of ideology (see Sections 2.1 and 2.2). To the concepts of signifier and signified Barthes adds the insights of the Danish linguist Louis Hjelmslev, who had argued that a discursive mode – a style, use of a national or regional language, even a physiognomy – operated with a 'connotative semiotic' to yield a meaning over and above the signs of which it consisted (see Hjelmslev 1961: 114–18). Taking the cover of a popular French weekly magazine, Barthes argues that if the dots and colours of the photograph constitute the signifier and the image of the young black man saluting the national flag makes up the signified, this completed sign acts as a *new* signifier for another, hidden signified ('that France is a great empire' etc.).

In the essay reprinted here, Barthes considers the connotative value of an exhibition of photographs in Paris entitled 'The Great Family of Man' in order to show how the discourse of humanism, guaranteed by God, is at work at the very heart of French bourgeois culture. In doing so, he lays bare the ideological significance of the obviousness of the concept of humanity upon which the exhibition relies (particular, yet universal) and highlights the colonial implications of such a phenomenon. In denaturalizing what seems most natural and soothing about the photographs, Barthes ultimately reminds us of the 'real' history at work in their margins. The history, that is, of a difference founded upon struggle and discrimination.

1.3 Pierre Macherey, from *A Theory of Literary Production* (trans. Geoffrey Wall, London: Taylor and Francis, 1978, pp. 82–95; first published in Paris in 1966)

Tradition tells us that the object of criticism is to explain and interpret, to make explicit that which is implicit, to fill in the gaps and to expand upon the partial explanations provided by the text in order to make it whole and complete. What Macherey performs in *A Theory of Literary Production* is a critical analysis of this traditional assumption – a deconstruction of its terms – and in that process he advocates an alternative 'symptomatic' reading practice: a reading practice, that is, founded upon a search for the contradictions, discontinuities and omissions that are displayed within a literary work but of which it cannot speak. The project of such a practice is *not* to smooth over or to make up for the problems that the work embodies, but to expose them, to submit them to a process of questioning, and in so doing to produce a 'real' knowledge of the conditions of literary production, ideology and finally history.

For Macherey, the meaning of a literary work is not contained simply in what it says, but is produced in a relationship between that which it says and that which it *cannot* say. The work is divided – split between the spoken and the unspoken, both of which are necessary components of its conditions of existence. This split is formed as the result of a further division – between the ideological project of the work and the constraints imposed upon that project by the conventions of its existence within specifically literary form. What is produced from this conflict is what Macherey calls (borrowing the concept from Freud) the unconscious of the work. This unconscious constitutes an absence at the work's centre, which, as Macherey argues, is what gives it 'life'. It constitutes the radical otherness of the work, containing that which is repressed – cast into the margins – in order that the conscious project may be fulfilled. As with the repressed that inhabits the unconscious of Freudian theory, however, the continual marginalization of the repressed of the text can never be guaranteed. The repressed can return or, at least within Macherey's terms, can be *made* to return by the efforts of a reading practice that privileges contradiction and omission. Through the practice of such a privileging the text can be made to turn upon itself, to perform a critique of its own terms and values, and ultimately to reveal within itself evidence not only of its own conditions of production but also of the limits of ideological representation, and of history as the history of struggle for the production and control of meaning.

1.4 Umberto Eco, from 'The Narrative Structure in Fleming' (from *The Role of the Reader*, Indianapolis: Indiana University Press, 1984, pp. 144–8; first published 1966)

Given the enormous success of the Bond novels (and now films) Umberto Eco sets out in this essay an analysis of what he calls the 'narrating machine' in order to understand its appeal to, and therefore pleasure for, the reader. In doing so, he maps out the structural devices of the first of the novels (*Casino Royale*), which, he argues, established the formula from which the rest were to emerge. Like a game of chess, the game that is Bond is always played out within the parameters of certain rules, and each of the pieces – Bond, Villain, M – moves within those rules according to the possibilities already laid out for them. In the process of identifying those structures, and by the analogy of the game, Eco is able to argue that the pleasure of the novels for the reader lies in watching the particulars of each of the narratives unfold within a structure of rules or possibilities that is reassuringly constant.

It is this constant that, for Eco, is ultimately conservative, in that its pleasure simply reconfirms the reader in a position of comfortable stability, producing a form of redundancy by narrating precisely the already known. Nothing in the reading relation produced by the structuring machine of the narration challenges us to think beyond the bounds of what we always already knew was most obvious about both ourselves and the cultures we inhabit. And, in this sense, the very structure of the text is, in and of itself, ideological. It is not the *content* of the Bond novels that alone produces the ideological positions offered by the text, but the *method* of constructing the contents into a narrative. Ultimately, this creates what Eco calls an 'escape machine geared for the entertainment of the masses'.

1.5 Colin MacCabe, from 'Realism and the Cinema: Notes on Some Brechtian Theses' (from *Theoretical Essays*, Manchester: Manchester University Press, 1985, pp. 34–9; first published in *Screen* in 1974)

MacCabe's essay appeared first in a special number of the English film journal, *Screen*, concerned with Brecht and the possibility of radical cinema. Earlier in the twentieth century the logician Alfred Tarski had distinguished between what is said in a sentence of a language – how a language is *used* – and a higher order or meta-language in which that object language is mentioned or discussed. Drawing both on Roland Barthes's account of the five codes of a text (see *S/Z* 1975) and on Althusser's analysis of ideology (see Section 2.3), MacCabe argues that realism in novels, films and other texts should be understood not in terms of a *reflection* of reality but as an effect by which discourse positions its reader. Gathered together, the different discourses of a realist text are categorized into a hierarchy between object language and meta-language. Corresponding to the empiricist view that knowledge can be obtained directly through experience, realism invites its reader to 'look through' the meta-language and so 'see' as if directly what is represented in the object language (speech, character, narrated event). Thus the signifiers of the text become effaced as the reader accedes 'transparently' to the signified.

(The term 'classic realism' is used to isolate a type by distinguishing it from more controversial versions (Dickens, Dostoevsky); and the illustration by the contrast between direct and indirect speech is just that, an illustration. 'Dominant specularity', a concept borrowed from Lacan's analysis of the mirror stage (see Section 3.2), refers to a position in which the subject is secured the apparent coherence and plenitude of the Imaginary, as it were outside and looking in.)

2.1 Karl Marx, 'Preface' to *A Contribution to the Critique of Political Economy* (from Karl Marx and Friedrich Engels, *Selected Works*, London: Lawrence and Wishart, 1950, 2 vols, vol. 1, pp. 328–9)

A passage of writing contested by commentary as much as anything in the Bible, Marx's account of how the economic base determines the social and ideological superstructure of society may perhaps best be read with the opening disclaimer firmly in mind ('the general result at which I arrived' etc.).

Across history one form of political economy has been transformed into another: from primitive communism (hunter-gatherers) to the Asiatic mode of production (slavery), the economies of ancient Greece and Rome to feudalism. Characterizing an epoch, a mode of production consists of both *forces* (technology together with forms of organizing labour, such as the factory system) and *relations* (forms of property ownership). Transition occurs when development of the productive forces comes into conflict with the relations of production, enabling a new, previously subordinate class to emerge as the dominant class for the next epoch. A classical example would be the emergence of the merchant class of feudalism as the bourgeois class with the development of market forces in the capitalist mode of production; and this will happen again when the proletariat, whose interests are not class-bound but universal, take over ownership of the forces of production, so inaugurating communism and bringing to an end what Marx calls 'prehistory'. Intimately related to the 'shape' of society, the mode of production or economic base can also be seen to determine the legal and political superstructure of each epoch, as well as its ideology. Thus, against the conventional view that individuals think up ideas out of thin air, Marx argues that people's ideas are determined according to who they are and where they are in society. It may be noted, however, that, as well as a deterministic account of ideology, Marx also envisages it as having its own force and autonomy as the 'ideological forms' in which people become conscious of social conflict and fight it out.

2.2 Karl Marx and Friedrich Engels, from *The German Ideology* (from Karl Marx and Friedrich Engels, *Collected Works*, London: Lawrence and Wishart, 1975, vol. 4, pp. 59–61)

In the years after Hegel died (from cholera) in 1832 a group of 'Young' or 'Left' Hegelians began to turn Hegel's demand for a better world against itself, particularly by arguing that in religious belief people alienate themselves by imagining their own energies as belonging to God. Marx and Engels reply to Ludwig Feuerbach and the others in great detail at the level of content, but also by treating these contemporary German ideas as a symptom and reading them as ideology; that is, as the interests of a class expressed in the form of ideas. As such, ideology works by re-presenting local and sectarian interests as universal and necessary, so exercising power not merely when a subordinate class is dominated but because the class holding such ideas is confirmed in its sense of itself.

2.3 Louis Althusser, from 'Ideology and Ideological State Apparatuses (Notes towards an Investigation)' (*Lenin and Philosophy*, trans. Ben Brewster, London: Verso, 1971, pp. 136–8, 152–3, 153–6, 159–64, 168–70; first published 1970)

Why, when political freedom is there to be taken, do people not grab it? That is the question Althusser confronts in the year after the failure of the French revolution of

1968. His answer is twofold: that the state has penetrated more deeply into everyday life than ever before; that ideology operates in us not simply as a set of conscious opinions but at an unconscious level by making us who we are, constructing us to think we are free (and so don't need to change anything). From Marx, Althusser derives the principle that an economic system must not only produce material but also reproduce the means of production (machines, factory buildings etc.), especially by reproducing labour power. By this he means people willing to accept their assigned position in the productive process. From Gramsci, he borrows the concept of hegemony, which recognizes that a ruling bloc wins obedience not only through force (and Repressive State Apparatuses) but also by seeking consent (through the Ideological State Apparatuses (ISAs)).

What the ISAs work on is the subject, taking babies (the merely physical human being, which Althusser terms 'concrete individuals') and transforming them into thinking beings, able to go off on their own five or six years later and answer 'Here' when the teacher calls out their names in school. For this Althusser turns to psychoanalysis, to Freud's account of how the I, not innate, has to be developed in the process of a split between conscious and unconscious, and to Lacan's analysis of the mirror stage (see Section 3.2). When Althusser writes of subjects as living out an 'imaginary' relationship to their real conditions of existence, he is using Lacan's account of how the ego is set up within the order of the Imaginary as distinct from the Real. And in borrowing from French legal discourse the term *interpellation* to describe the way ideology transforms individuals into subjects he is referring to at least three things: (a) parents hailing their children ('Who's a good little boy, then?'); (b) the way any society imposes rules on its members through the functioning of what Freud called the superego; (c) the model of religious vocation, as when Samuel hears God calling his name and is instructed to answer, 'Speak, for thy servant heareth' (I Samuel 3: 1–14). In each of these kinds of relation the individual subject recognizes/ misrecognizes itself reflected in an Absolute Subject and accepts the situation as natural.

2.4 Simone de Beauvoir, from *The Second Sex* (trans. and ed. H. M. Parshley, New York: Random House Inc., 1953, pp. 14–18)

For Simone de Beauvoir, ideology boils down to language – where language is conceived as the structure through which conceptual thought is produced (see Saussure, Section 1.1). Within Western metaphysics, she argues, language structures thought through a series of dualities – nature/culture, body/mind, white/black – so that concepts arise not by virtue of anything intrinsic to themselves but in relationships of difference to one another. And it is within this frame that she considers the question 'what is woman?'

'Woman', she argues, has come to be constituted as 'sex', in terms of her body (her organs, her gender) but also as the sexual object of men, in her perceived ability to be objectified, possessed and finally mastered. As 'sex', woman is also, therefore, secondary to man – 'the second sex' – precisely because woman, in this conceptual duality of thought, constitutes the lack against which man can constitute himself.

Drawing on Hegel, de Beauvoir explains that this secondary position is further legitimated through the constitution of man as absolute – in this case, the absolute *human* subject, free of the cultural constraints of gender – against which woman is construed as object – not human but *woman*, subject to sex and gender. In this sense, woman is only possible conceptually in her difference to, or estrangement from, that absolute. Woman is, therefore, always Other.

However, for Hegel, thought is not determined once and for all as a set of eternal truths. Indeed, it is constantly subject to a dialectical process through which the internal contradictions of any assertion (Thesis: Man) are revealed by the constitution of what is in excess of it (Antithesis: Woman) and can thereby be reformulated in a steady march towards a more perfect Ideal.

It is not clear whether de Beauvoir has in mind the Hegelian dialectic in all its specificities here, but she does conclude that the power relation apparent in the duality man/woman is not inevitable.

(This notion of woman as socially constructed is taken up again in the work of Cixous (see Section 5.2) and Butler (see Section 5.6) and marks the beginning of a theoretical move away from the terrain of class as embodiment of ideology, to the assertion of differences of race, gender, sexuality etc.)

2.5 Edward Said, from *Orientalism* (London: Pantheon, 1985, pp. 201–4, 226–31)

What Edward Said explores in *Orientalism* is the set of representations – categories, images and classifications – that have produced the Orient as an object of (largely) Western understanding, the Orient supposedly being all that is not Europe. The Orient, he argues, is less a force of nature than a fact of cultural production. It is not a given reality that exists simply to be described or distorted, but is *produced* within the domain of Orientalism: a domain, that is, which has 'Orientalized' the Orient by producing a variety of knowledges of it, and, as a result, has come to exercise power over it in the process by which an active Western subject *knows* and *masters* a passive Eastern object. *Orientalism* is in effect, then, a demonstration of the inseparable relationship between representation and reality. It documents the ways in which the former governs and dominates the latter; and it exposes the relations of power inherent in systems of representation that, to a large extent, protest their innocence under the guise of scholarship.

In order to do this, Said draws specifically upon Foucault's notion of discourse as a system of regulation (see Section 3.5). Understood as a discourse, Orientalism becomes a way of structuring, regulating and placing the Orient through the production of a series of minutely detailed knowledges of it. These knowledges are drawn from fields as diverse as geography, science, culture, travel and war, and are so carefully detailed that they have come to invest almost every possible layer of life. What occurs in the process of the production of these knowledges is the whole fictioning of a culture, or cultural meanings, which is regulated in such minute ways that it comes, eventually, to be regarded as 'natural'. Indeed, over the long period of time in which the Orient has been the object of Western interest, such knowledges have become authoritative versions of it. The originally explicit political forces and activities that motivated the production of these knowledges have been relegated to the margins of history, and the discourse of Orientalism itself has been elided with a simple cultural 'truth', so that what the Orient 'really' is becomes forgotten.

The interests served by the discourse of Orientalism are clear. The relationship between the West and its object of knowledge is fundamentally a relationship of power and domination. Yet the implications of the Orientalization of the Orient extend also to the West. If we can say that the Orient exists (largely) as a fiction, then it is possible also to assert that it is a fiction necessary to the construction of an opposing fiction – that of the West. Just as Lacan had proposed that the identity of the human individual is produced in a dialectic between the subject and the Other (see Section 3.2), so Said suggests that the identity of the West is produced in its own dialectical relationship to the Orient. For Said, the meaning of both the Orient and the West is not inherent in either, but is constructed in a relationship of difference between the two. The Orientalization of the Orient, then, is useful to the West in as much as it defines that which the West is *not* – what Said calls its 'deepest and most recurring [image] of the Other'. Within these terms, the category of the 'White Man' (Said uses the masculine form throughout) is, like that of the 'Oriental', a product of discursive construction. Deeply felt and experienced as natural, it is, none the less, an existence that is, to a very large and very political extent, a fiction of culture.

2.6 Homi K. Bhabha, from 'The "Other" Question' (*Screen*, vol. 24, no. 6 (1983), pp. 18–21, 22–5, 30, 32–4)

Bhabha's essay continues to focus on the question of ideology in relation to the difference of race. The task he sets himself is to identify the *process* of subjectification made plausible through the operation of stereotypical discourse. The point of the project is to 'clear a space for the other'. In this, he departs significantly from the works of both Fanon (see Section 3.3) and Said (see Section 2.5), which precede him and to which he is indebted.

For Bhabha, any account of the meaning of oppression and discrimination is limited if it does not simultaneously address the question of identity as both determined and resistant in culture. While *Orientalism* provides an important critique of the fantasy structure of the Occident's dominance of the Orient, Bhabha points out that this is destined always to replicate the structures of originary power if it does not address the dynamics of conflict, which, he argues, must always be an effect of the relation between the master and slave. The colonial subject, he argues, is constructed in a 'repertoire of conflictual positions' that render him, or indeed her, the site of *both* fixity and fantasy in a process that cannot be anything other than uneven, divided, incomplete and, therefore, potentially disruptive of the effect of colonial power. In this sense, Bhabha suggests that the effort of orientalizing must always fail.

However, Bhabha takes this opportunity to warn that any representation of 'otherness' is also fraught with the possibilities of appropriation. He takes deconstruction (in the mode of Derrida; see Section 4.1) to task for appropriating the place of 'the other' as a figure of excess in the metaphysics of the West for the purposes of undoing it. This, he argues, performs a double displacement: it is both the appropriation of the other, and the marginalization of the other by implicitly fixing it as singular, tangible, different.

Can we escape this? Perhaps. One step towards avoiding the repetition of the ideological structures of colonial discourse is, for Bhabha, to recognize the site of the other as a 'mixed economy' of perverse and ambivalent collusions among a variety of positions inscribed in race, but also gender, sexuality, class and so on: a site, that is, where a variety of ever changing claims on the colonial blend and clash. Of course, we would also need a theoretical framework that allowed for such plurality and that privileged as its object not simply the insistence upon the particularities of a single identity but also the ambivalent contradictions, and in the end the very impossibility of identity as something whole and apparent to itself.

2.7 Slavoj Žižek, from *The Sublime Object of Ideology* (London and New York: Verso, 1989, pp. 47–51)

Is ideology best understood as a set of ideas that can be transcended by political or cultural awareness, or is its operation so fundamental to the constitution of our unconscious that even when we think we have observed and resisted it, we continue in its thrall? For Žižek, crucially, the latter is certainly the case, and as a model for resistant practice, ideology is fundamentally flawed. It is flawed, moreover, since it takes no account of desire.

Here Žižek invokes Lacan (see Section 3.2) in order to confront the centrality of desire to the very operation of ideology itself. Like Althusser (see Section 2.3) he argues that the classical Marxist model of ideology is only a partial account since there is within it always the possibility of stepping outside of it. For Althusser, we have argued, ideology has no inside or outside, but so saturates thought that it constitutes the very conditions upon which the inside and the outside are themselves founded. However, if Althusser can be said to inflect Marx with Lacan, Žižek confronts the two head-on. From a Lacanian perspective, he argues, ideology designates 'a totality set on effacing the traces of its own impossibility' and, as such, can only be disrupted at the level of the unconscious.

Two important questions arise from this: (a) how is this, theoretically, the case; and (b) what are the material implications of such an assertion for a radical contemporary egalitarian politics?

In the first instance, Žižek's notion of ideology seems to stem from a parallel drawn between what he terms 'ideological fantasy' (what masks the illusion that structures our real) and the 'fantasy of self' (the illusion that masks identity as lack in order to produce an effect of stability for the ego). This parallel, it would seem, puts Žižek's notion of ideology firmly within the terrain of the Lacanian imaginary – what masks, through fantasy, the existence of the real and the symbolic so that we may gain a sense of ourselves as fully functioning and commanding subjects. Ideology is fantasy in as much as its operation guarantees our sense of ourselves as functioning, rational, thoughtful and coherent beings. But, as always, fantasy is tricky. And here Žižek invokes Lacan's analysis of the dream, wherein the dream embodies desire as the relation of being to lack (*manque à être*; see Section 3.2). Here the subject is nothing more than an effect of a collective illusion, or 'ideological dream'. And, as such, our only hope of breaking that dream is to 'confront the Real of our desire'.

For Žižek, this would mean understanding racism, totalitarianism and anti-Semitism as both an effect of our unconscious desire (arising from it) *and* an attempt to preserve the imaginary of our identity as ideological subjects through the manipulation of that effect in order to mask the very impossibility of subjectivity itself. In this way, we would understand the operation of ideology as deeply insidious and, therefore, difficult to transcend – since our very sense of ourselves depends upon it.

Presumably, we resist the operation of ideology by resisting the structures through which our identity is made possible. Quite what that resistance might look like, or who might be prepared to effect it, is, I guess, still to be seen. In the meantime, as an analysis of anti-Semitism, and how most effectively to resist it, this is at least a provocative intervention.

3.1 Sigmund Freud, from *Beyond the Pleasure Principle* (from *The Standard Edition of the Psychological Works of Sigmund Freud*, vol. XVIII, trans. James Strachey, London: Random House, 1993, pp. 283–7)

The First World War in Europe produced what has now become a reasonably infamous phenomenon. Thousands of soldiers returned from the front line suffering a degree of trauma known colloquially as shell shock. One of the manifestations of this was a rather desperate reiteration of the traumatic event that had harmed them – sometimes in persistent nightmares, sometimes in the obsessive repetition of certain actions in a waking state. These manifestations were unsettling to Freud because he had previously advanced a theory of human subjectivity in which it seemed reasonable to argue that the id of human identity (the unconscious) is governed by what he called the 'pleasure principle'. That is, it seeks pleasure and avoids unpleasure. But the actions of these soldiers led him to re-evaluate this principle in order to account for something that clearly lay beyond it. And so, in 1920, he began an account of what leads the subject to remember and to repeat an event they experience as unpleasurable to the point of trauma.

For Freud, the obsession with unpleasure starts in the early stages of life when the infant must find a way of coming to terms with loss. His argument, via his observations of his young grandson's invention for himself of the fort/da game, is that the boy repeats the initial distressing experience of his mother's disappearance by 'staging the disappearance of objects within his reach'. This connects with loss in two ways: (a) it acts as a conduit for anger, as in the declaration 'Go to the fwont!', which signifies the meaning of the absence of the father, an absence that clearly the child does not regret; and (b) it can be mastered by the child in the enactment of a fantasy of control. Playing the fort/da game shifts the originary loss (of the mother) on to an object that can be retrieved at will, thus affording the child the illusion of mastery or control in a situation that, otherwise, is experienced as the trauma of lack.

This account points us towards one of the founding principles of a post-structuralist account of the subject: that identity both arises and is constituted on the grounds of loss. This is a loss, moreover, that can never be overcome except in and through the fantasy of mastery, which in its turn can never quite deliver the promise it holds out.

3.2 Jacques Lacan, 'The Mirror Stage as Formative of the Function of the I as Revealed in Psychoanalytic Experience' (from *Écrits: A Selection*, trans. Alan Sheridan, London: Taylor and Francis, 1977, pp. 1–7; originally a lecture delivered at the Sixteenth International Congress of Psychoanalysis in Zurich on 17 July 1949)

'Who am I?' This seemingly reasonable question hides what it presupposes – that I am an identifiable speaking subject knowing language and so able to ask questions like this. How did I get to *be able* to do that in the first place? In 'The Mirror Stage' Lacan outlines an answer that has had revolutionary implications. For against Descartes's account of the I as a *Cogito* ('I think therefore I am') in which my identity and my being are at one, Lacan argues that the I depends on what is other than itself; the I is therefore an effect socially – discursively – constructed.

For Lacan, 'I am a hole surrounded by something': the human subject originates not in presence and identity but in a lack or absence, which Lacan terms *manque à être*; we define ourselves as human in the impossible task of phantasizing ourselves as complete, desiring (and thinking we find) a plenitude that will make good that originary lack. Of this wider process of attempted self-identification the mirror stage, affecting babies between 6 and 18 months, is both a matrix and a compelling example.

During the 1920s and 1930s work in biology and psychology had drawn attention to the importance of sight and mimicry among animals. What Lacan stresses is the radically different effect that a mirror has on a human baby – unlike a dog or a pigeon he (Lacan treats the subject throughout as masculine) greets the reflected (or specular) image with jubilation as his likeness. Why? The act of looking in a mirror encompasses two possibilities: (a) it is an optical effect producing an image of the face the wrong way round and much smaller; (b) I can say 'It's me'. The identity in the mirror is an external effect, which I assume is me. For Lacan, my identity is a likeness reflected back from everyone else (the other) (beginning, as it were with the parent who 'hails' the baby into language – 'Who's a good little girl, then?' etc.). My identity is not something I recognize because that would suppose I was *already there* able to do the recognizing (contrast Althusser's view, Section 2.3): my identity comes about in a dialectic between the subject and the other (a subject's ego is 'that which is reflected of his [sic] form in his objects'; Lacan 1977a: 194). Unreal, fictional, having an 'alienating destination' (like the asymptotic curve of a graph, which will never actually coincide with an axis), this kind of I, achieved in exchange with the other, is the only one I can ever have.

Since my identity is not a recognition but a *misrecognition* (*méconnaissance*) why am I driven to seek it? Although in fact when I am born I am only a tiny part of reality, I don't know that (and 'I' am not yet there to know it anyway). At a point when the experience of the infant (Latin: *infans*, not speaking) consists largely of forms of *imago* (unconscious prototypical figures as theorized by Jung), but when the baby can move around, perhaps with a baby-walker, bumping into things, then the inner world (*Innenwelt*) and the world around (*Umwelt*) begin to become separated for it. Now lack expresses itself when the toddler experiences reality through a phantasy of 'the body in pieces' (*le corps morcelé*), and so it is captivated by the coherent form (*Gestalt*) promised to it by the mirror and the ideal of the body as an imaginary unity. (And why lack? Lacan follows biological thinking in referring to the human species as being born too soon.)

In the I, as in the specular image, the subject seems perfectly to master its own lack. But the apparent solidity and permanence of the ego must be constantly maintained against all that risks making it come to pieces. As Freud noted that in dreams a building may mean the dreamer, so Lacan suggests that the I is like a fortress, which must constantly defend itself through denial (*Verneinung*) of every-thing that threatens to undo it. But then everything does. The I, then, is a paranoiac structure, likely to release aggression against whatever reminds it of its own unreality. (Here Lacan also draws on the work of Freud's daughter, Anna, especially *The Ego and the Mechanisms of Defence* (1937); he also refers to Roger Caillois, the French literary critic and sociologist of religion.)

3.3 Frantz Fanon, from 'The Fact of Blackness' (from *Black Skin/White Masks*, trans. Charles Markmann, New York: Grove Atlantic, 1991, pp. 109–12; first published in Paris in 1951)

What happens to the illusion of self in our encounter with an openly aggressive other? This is the question Fanon asks in his analysis of the colonial subject. In the intro-duction to *Black Skin/White Masks* Fanon states that 'The Negro is not. Any more than the white man.' The condition of subjectivity, then, is merely the illusion of presence constituted in the imaginary – the assumption of an *image* of wholeness in which we may, however temporally, believe. That image, however, is precarious, since it depends upon two things: both the demand and the desire to *be* for an other. Language (or, any social mode of representation) calls us into identity within a system of relational differences founded primarily between the 'I' (which we believe con-stitutes us, but which in fact pre-exists us and, moreover, consists of nothing but a relational difference to other signifiers in the chain of meaning within which 'we' operate; see Lacan, Section 3.2) and all that is not 'I'. To take up the position of the 'I' in language, then, is to be called by the other (in this case, meaning) into a constitution of self which grants the illusion of 'being there'. In order to maintain that illusion, we must be recognized by the other in a process in which we constantly desire the affirmation of our presence in the gaze of the other.

Stated like this, identity becomes a baldly precarious business. It is what psy-choanalysis has called a paranoid structure that maintains the illusion of its meaning only in the continual process of defending itself against all that would threaten its undoing.

Such is the condition of the psyche – the very space of 'Man' – as psychoanalysis sees it. And it is this concept of subjectivity that underlies the framework through which Fanon seeks to address the question of the colonial constitution of the Black Man. He is, however, ambivalent about the answer. He writes, variously, that 'the black man is not a man', and that 'my Negro consciousness does not hold itself out as lack. It *is*.' He hovers, therefore, between the notion that identity – *all* identity – is simply an illusion masking a fundamental lack, and the possibility that the potentially endless absence of being (in this case, of the black man) can be arrested in something like a 'Negro consciousness'.

In the course of this extract, one can see why. Migrating from the Antilles to Europe, the black man is caught in the gaze of an other that explicitly threatens the fantasy of the self as human, as man, as collectively 'there'. The insistent repetition of 'Look, mama, a Negro' performs a double alienation from being for the subject, who becomes an object, in a web of historically and materially constituted differ-ence.

There is, of course, a certain amount of fear and anxiety in the gaze ('I'm frigh-tened') but for Fanon, the possibility of subjective undoing is here only a one-way street. The black man, he argues, must be black in relation to the white man, but he denounces as false any claim that the reverse must also be possible. For Fanon, the play of difference that such an assertion might begin is arrested by history. What he calls the 'metaphysics' of the black man is divided in a way which that of the white man is not. In the colonial encounter, the black man is constituted in two frames of reference: a humanist metaphysics, in which Man is simply Man, undifferentiated and unalienated; and a colonial history, in which the black man is dehumanized by the colonial power of myth-making. In the colonial encounter the black man is not only fixed by the white man's gaze but also, and simultaneously, annihilated by it.

In order not to fall apart, the black man must constitute for himself an alternative, resistant, fantasy of self – not the eternal truth of a humanism that excludes him, but a belief in negritude, which, dialectically, refuses lack.

3.4 Julia Kristeva, from 'The System and the Speaking Subject' (London: *Times Literary Supplement*, 12 October 1973, pp. 1249–50)

'The system and the speaking subject' posits a psycho-linguistic theory of the pro-duction of the subject in and through language. Focusing upon language as a sig-nifying *process*, including transgressions as well as confirmations of the law of the symbolic, the essay moves away from the notion of the stable subject as master of the system. It posits, instead, a notion of an unstable subject precariously produced upon the site of a tension between elements of language that confirm the rules of the system and at the same time threaten to undermine its existence as such. As a theory of the subject, then, the essay depends upon a theory of language that makes several departures from those which precede it.

Kristeva begins by offering an overview of what she calls the field of semiology from her own critical perspective of the revolutionary potential it offers or denies. The problem with semiology from this perspective is its reliance upon the notion of language as a system or structure. In order for signification to take place, the continuum of possible sounds (semiotic chora) must, like the subject of psychoanalysis, be divided, ordered and arranged. This splitting of sounds enables their arrangement into 'significant' and 'insignificant' sounds – those which have meaning, and those which do not. Sounds which have meaning are subject to the law that governs language: they obey a specific set of rules and structures of grammar, and as such are homogeneous. Those which do not are repressed and exist only as a kind of rhythmical (yet also threatening) presence within symbolic language. The splitting of the continuum is what Kristeva calls the 'thetic' (or static) stage of language. Since it is the semiotic that offers the potential to disrupt the symbolic, any analysis that focuses exclusively upon this thetic, or structuring, stage of language is, within Kristeva's terms, inadequate. It excludes the disruptive dimension of language in favour of the structure of the system, and so also excludes the implication of language as a process centred upon the speaking subject.

Since the linguistic theory she outlines cannot encompass the disruptive elements of language Kristeva seeks to privilege, she advances in place of it her own critical framework – that of 'semanalysis'. Semanalysis focuses upon language as process, which involves the acceptance of the symbolic law for the purposes of 'renovating' it. In order to do this, Kristeva draws upon the work of Freud, which theorizes the splitting of the subject (between conscious and unconscious), and that of Hegel and Marx, which theorizes the government of the subject in and through a series of social codes. In this way, Kristeva conceives of language as something that is much more than simply a system. Linguistic practice – language spoken by people – becomes both a drive-governed phenomenon and a social space. As such, it concerns the individual but is implicated at the same time in the constitution of the individual within the social order. Concerned with the possibilities of disrupting that order, Kristeva turns to the work of Lacan (see Section 3.2).

She displaces Lacan's distinction between the Imaginary and the Symbolic into a distinction between the semiotic and the symbolic. While the symbolic stands for the law under which language operates, the semiotic refers to all the disruptive elements present within the signifying process: non-linguistic sounds, moments of meaninglessness and even silences. The symbolic and the semiotic exist inevitably together. What Kristeva calls the 'phenotext' (language that obeys the rules of communication and presupposes a subject of speech as well as a subject that is addressed) exists in opposition to what she calls the 'genotext' (deviations that form a relative and shifting trajectory not restricted to two poles of communication between two fully formed subjects). Within the phenotext the presence of the genotext can always be traced, and it is the interaction between the two that constitutes the signifying process – what makes signification and subjectivity possible. Produced through the interaction between these two terms, the subject is caught in a paradox – a position that is at once both subversive and confirming, and that subsequently produces the subject as unstable, unfixed and ultimately, like language itself, very much in process.

(Melanie Klein (1882–1960), whom Kristeva refers to, was a British psycho-analyst concerned especially to understand the objects phantasized by the pre-Oedipal infant.)

3.5 Michel Foucault, from *Discipline and Punish: The Birth of the Prison* (trans. Alan Sheridan, London: Penguin, 1977, pp. 195–203, 205, 215–17; first published in Paris in 1975)

Contemporary society is, as Foucault contends, a disciplinary society. It functions most effectively, therefore, not through the exertion of force, but through an incite-ment to regulation. It works by dividing and individualizing the communal group – investing everyone within that group with a distinct sense of place, function and attribution. It operates according to a double mode, that of binary division and branding: between individuals who are mad/sane, abnormal/normal, sick/healthy and so on. It is efficient precisely because it produces people who *subject themselves* to its terms, who regulate their own individual 'self' and, therefore, regulate the body of society as a whole. It is not, Foucault insists, that the 'beautiful totality of the indi-vidual is amputated, repressed [or] altered' by the social order, but that the individual is carefully fabricated within it. What this extract traces, then, is a history of specific historical events and circumstances that gave rise to this 'careful fabrication'. In order to do this Foucault focuses upon two particular historical events: the organization of the city brought about by the plague at the end of the seventeenth century, and the design of Jeremy Bentham's 'panopticon', which revolutionized the prison system in the nineteenth century.

The environment produced by the coming of the plague represents a significant event in the organization of the community along individual lines. Operating a tech-nique of strict spatial partitioning, it ensured that each individual was assigned to a place and fixed within it. All the inhabitants of the plague-ridden city were compelled to speak the 'truth' of their own condition and with it the 'truth' of their own existence. Against the plague, discipline brought into play a specific form of power, which involved the confinement of individuals, but also their training as individuals. Through the process of continual regulation and constant divisions between sickness and health, each individual was subjected to a whole series of techniques for surveillance, assessment, supervision and correction, producing in effect the 'Utopia' of the per-fectly governed city.

Bentham's design of the panopticon in the nineteenth century represents the consolidation of this technique of power and constitutes the architectural develop-ment of its effectiveness. Basically it consists of a central watchtower surrounded by a series of individual cells, cut off from each other but constantly and wholly visible from the central tower. The central tower can be seen from the cells, but the presence of an observer within that tower can never be verified. The subsequent effect of the panoptic arrangement is what Foucault calls the 'automatic functioning of power'. It creates within the individual a sense of being continually watched regardless of whether or not they actually are, so that, after a period of time, individuals come to regulate their own behaviour. They become caught in a power situation of which they are themselves the bearers, and the actual exercise of discipline itself becomes unnecessary. 'A real subjection is born mechanically from a fictitious relation.' While he focuses here upon two specific institutions, Foucault is quick to insist that each has more general implications for the functioning of society as a whole. The panopticon is not just a building, but a 'mechanism of power reduced to its ideal form'; a mechanism of power, that is, which can now be diffused. It is no longer necessarily operated by a central repressive apparatus, but invested within each individual, who in turn assumes responsibility for his or her own subjection. At work in every institution – from the family to the madhouse – it is a mechanism of power that invests every layer of the human mind and body, and through which a whole type of individual and of society emerges.

(Jeremy Bentham was a British utilitarian philosopher, 1748–1832.)

3.6 Michel Foucault, from *The History of Sexuality, Volume One: An Introduction* (trans. Robert Hurley, London: Penguin, 1978, pp. 64–73; first published in Paris in 1976)

Is sexuality spontaneous and rational or is it socially constructed? Is sexuality best understood as the site upon which the subject is produced simply through the process of repression, or, more insidiously, through an incitement to the inscription of the individual within positive forms of pleasure? These are the questions posed by *The History of Sexuality*. In return, Foucault offers no concrete solutions but posits instead the hypothesis that the techniques of power that govern the individual function most effectively when they are concealed, or rather when they are disguised as friendly forces. He takes as the focus of his investigation the production of the subject through the discourses of sex that emerged in the nineteenth century, and that, he implies, continue to control the constitution of the subject in the present day. The hypothesis, then, is that power operates with regard to sex not simply by forbidding desire or refusing to recognize it, but by putting into circulation a whole mechanism by which 'true' discourses of sex are continually produced. This mechanism, within the nineteenth century, is what Foucault calls 'scientia sexualis', or the production of a specific form of knowledge of the individual, and a will to self-knowledge by the individual, through the scientific discourse of sex. It is Foucault's hypothesis that sex has come to function as an important means of producing and regulating the subject not by virtue of anything inherent in sex itself, but by virtue of the tactics of power inherent in the discourse of science.

For Foucault, these tactics of power gravitate around the procedures of confession. Originally a Christian rite of penance for the attrition of sin, the confession has increasingly come to function as a means of producing the truth of the individual through the articulation of the deepest secrets of their most private pleasures. Although the confession came to speak of sex, however, it was, by itself, inadequate to the analysis of 'human nature'. The pleasures of which the subject spoke had also to be inscribed within an ordered system of knowledge, a way of attributing meaning to that which was spoken (but not necessarily understood), so that science became an effective means of producing and governing the human subject. It accorded to sex, and to a proliferation of sexual pleasures to which individuals were then referred by the discourse of science, the status of truth. Scientia sexualis demands of sex that it speaks its truth, but also that it tells us our truth or, rather, 'the deeply buried truth of that truth about ourselves which we think we possess in our immediate conscious-ness'. Confession is no longer a test, but a 'sign' – revealing the very core of the meaning of our existence.

Operating in this way, the revelation of truth comes to function not simply as the effect of a power that constrains the individual, but as the ultimate act of individual liberation. Scientia sexualis, then, is seen to produce a truth that belongs not to power, but to freedom.

3.7 Roland Barthes, from *The Pleasure of the Text* (trans. Richard Miller, New York: Hill and Wang, 1975, pp. 9–17)

Although Barthes's distinction between text of pleasure and text of bliss seems descriptively plausible and has entered critical currency, it rests on a theoretical basis that he leaves largely implicit, a basis that is essentially Lacanian (see Section 3.2). Lacan works with an ontological distinction between the Real, the Symbolic and the Imaginary. The real remains outside discourse, since Lacan denies that human subjects can experience the real except as it is constructed in and by sym-bolization; the symbolic consists of the intersubjective order of representation and the signifier; in the imaginary the subject wins a sense of identity, meaning and presence for itself from the signifier (so in the example of the mirror phase, the mirror and the subject's body are real, the reflection in the mirror is symbolic, while the identity misrecognized in the reflection is imaginary). Lacan reserves the term *jouissance* for the possibility that the subject may encounter the real without med-iation. Far from being pleasant, such an encounter is much more likely to be terrible, a trauma like shell shock (in his book of that name published in 1920 Freud starts off his attempt to understand what is beyond the pleasure principle by discussing First World War traumas; see Freud, *Standard Edition*, vol. 18). In French *jouissance*, as well as meaning legal possession (enjoying a right), suggests orgasm and is hardly translatable ('bliss' misses the violence of what is at stake). Lacan treats sexual climax as like trauma because more than anything else it can simulate the fulfilment of desire in the real.

Thus the text of bliss for Barthes works by tearing a hole in signification so that the real, the body, comes through; or rather the *effect* of that, since the real cannot be felt except as it is symbolized (hence Barthes writes not of the real body but of 'the body of the text'). In contrast to this loss, pleasure derives from imaginary presence, all the ways in which the I knows, intends and masters meaning in what is after all only the organization of the signifier. It is important to stress that bliss and pleasure, although generally corresponding to realist versus modernist texts, are states of subjectivity and relative to each other. Barthes supposes that the reader of the realist text typically skips bits and introduces gaps so as to deflect pleasure towards bliss.

Finally, of course, Barthes picks up the ideas of Bertolt Brecht in finding a political contrast between the text that confirms and the text that undermines conventional meaning by introducing difference into what appears to be unified and the same as itself.

(Barthes also enjoys his own play with language: *tmesis* means separating parts of a word by introducing a word into it (e.g. 'what things soever'), though it is used loosely here for the process of missing bits of text; *asyndeton* means omitting conjunctions; *speleology* is the study of caves; and a *phalanstery* was a utopian community of no more than 1800 persons as envisaged by the French socialist François Fourier; for phenotext (versus genotext) see Kristeva (Section 3.4).)

4.1 Jacques Derrida, 'Differance' (from *Speech and Phenomena and Other Essays on Husserl's Theory of Signs*, trans. David B. Allison, Evanston, IL: Northwestern University Press, 1973, pp. 129–60)

The essay was first given as a lecture before the Société français de philosophie at the Amphithéâtre Michelet on 27 January 1968 and, under the title 'La Différance', published simultaneously in the *Bulletin de la société français de la philosophie*, vol. 60, no. 3, July/September 1968, pp. 73–101, and in *Theorie d'ensemble* (Paris: du Seuil, 1968; collection Tel Quel), along with contributions by members of the Tel Quel group, including Barthes, Kristeva and Philip Sollers; in *Marges de la philosophie*, published in 1972, it is also entitled 'La différance'.

5.1 Sigmund Freud, 'On the Universal Tendency to Debasement in the Sphere of Love (Contributions to the Psychology of Love II)' (trans. Alan Tyson, from *Standard Edition*, ed. James Strachey, London: Hogarth Press, 1957, vol. 11, pp. 177–90. Freud wrote three 'Contributions to the Psychology of Love': 'A Special Type of Object Choice Made by Men' (1910); this second; and a third on 'The Taboo of Virginity' (1917))

If, as Juliet Mitchell (1974: xv) argues in *Psychoanalysis and Feminism*, 'psychoanalysis is not a recommendation *for* a patriarchal society, but an analysis *of* one', then Freud's psychoanalysis might well be wrong about femininity, yet right about masculinity. That problem is immediately signalled by the title of this essay, for, although the tendency is said to be universal, the essay is almost exclusively concerned with men (a situation not much mitigated even if we blame the translator for turning the German *Allgemeinste* or 'general' into the English 'universal').

'All women are whores except my mother, who is a saint', says an old Italian proverb (quoted in Truffaut's film *The Bride Wore Black*). It is precisely this contradictory masculine attitude expressing itself in a ferociously imposed double standard that Freud in this essay seeks to exhibit and understand, a feature that would have been strikingly apparent to him in a Vienna where so many middle-class men lived one life with their wives and another with one of the huge number of prostitutes making a living in the city. In one respect Freud's answer is disarmingly simple if his theory of the Oedipus complex makes sense. For Freud, 'the finding of an object is in fact a refinding of it' (*Standard Edition*, vol. 7, p. 222); and so a man's sexual drive originates with his first love, his mother, but in response to the prohibition on incest becomes transformed into desire for another adult woman. It is difficult but necessary for men to separate the feeling for the other adult woman from the feeling for the mother on which it is modelled, and this leads to a polarizing of ideas of women between the overvalued Madonna figure who is loved and the undervalued Whore figure who is desired.

As the essay suggests, women are also subject to the same problem of psychical impotence expressing itself in frigidity, but much less so, for reasons Freud discusses elsewhere (notably in his two essays on 'Female Sexuality' (1931, *Standard Edition*, vol. 21) and 'Feminine Sexuality' (1933, *Standard Edition*, vol. 22)). While both the little girl and little boy take the mother as their first object, the girl moves (if she does) to the father and then to the other adult man, but the boy moves (if he does) *directly* from the mother to the other woman. For him the proximity of the two (and so the problem) is much more acute.

Freud also begins to explore reasons why sexual desire cannot be satisfied, beginning by noting that the original object must be represented by 'an endless series of substitutive objects', suggesting that human culture may be incompatible with the satisfaction of sexual drive, and then turning to history to develop this theme. Not only does the polarization of masculine desire have a clear cultural and historical expression in the instituted forms of Eros versus Agape, love 'sacred' and 'profane', but further Freud speculates that Courtly Love, developed under the influence of Christianity, was needed to give a value to the sexual relation unknown in antiquity.

(Psychoanalysis works with a technical vocabulary. The word 'object' has a formal sense as a thing or person that is the object of a drive and so caught up in forms of phantasy (in this respect an object is mainly symbolic). 'Libido' is the reservoir of psychic energy that becomes divided between ego and sexual instincts (or drive) and channelled into various kinds of investment or 'cathexis'. Drive that remains stuck with an earlier object is said to be 'fixated'. An 'imago' is an unconscious prototypical figure (see also p. 82); in a 'reaction-formation' an attitude occurs diametrically opposed to a repressed wish; 'sublimation' is the process in which sexual drive is taken up in relation to the ego and so directed towards another aim. The view that 'we are born between the piss and the shit' (*inter urinas et faeces nascimur*) is not Freud but St Augustine.)

5.2 Hélène Cixous, 'Sorties: Out and Out: Attacks/Ways Out/Forays' (from *The Newly Born Woman* by Hélène Cixous and Catherine Clement, trans. Betsy Wing, Manchester: Manchester University Press and Minneapolis: University of Minnesota Press, 1986, pp. 63–4, 83–9, 91–7; first published in Paris in 1975)

Cixous's writing is, in and of itself, a call to action, revolution and transgression. Privileging contradiction, silence and the sliding of the signifier, she operates within theoretical structures only to subvert them. Her primary concern is to undermine the logocentrism (the idea that meaning is fully present in the word) and phallocentrism (the privileging of the phallus as the ultimate signifier) inherent in Western philosophical discourse. She posits instead a notion of the feminine as a positive source of energy, instability and diversity, capable of subverting that which has traditionally worked to oppress and to silence women. To do this, Cixous draws upon the work of established theorists (Derrida, Kristeva and Lacan) but always with the traces of escape from their terms carefully woven into the fabric of her own text.

For Cixous the subject 'woman' is the product of linguistic difference, the effect of a hierarchical structuring of thought (activity/passivity, Culture/Nature and so on), all of which comes down, she suspects, to the ultimate coupling of man/woman. As long as we remain stuck within these binary oppositions, victory always comes down to the same thing: the 'glorious phallic monosexuality' of male privilege. What Cixous seeks, then, are ways out (sorties) from the rigid structures that place woman in a gendered and heterosexually determined relationship of difference to man.

In order to do this she revives a notion of bisexuality – not as the fantasy of a complete being that replaces the fear of castration, but as the location within the 'self' of a split, an unstable division between contradictory elements that simply coexist. The effect of this division is mobility – a constantly shifting self whose meaning may at moments be fixed but that contains within it the possibility always of moving on, accepting rather than repressing the other of the 'I', within discourse. While psychoanalysis has traditionally denied the femininity of masculine sexuality – theorizing the construction of both upon the terms of loss and fear of loss – Cixous sees no reason why that must be so. 'Nothing compels us', she asserts, 'to deposit our lives in these lack-banks' (see Lacan, Section 3.2). She argues, instead, for the celebration of difference and anomaly, the 'springing up of selves we didn't know', and the 'I/play of bisexuality', which circumvents the closure of meaning through differance (see Section 4).

It is, however, more likely to be women who are capable of maintaining the play of difference that Cixous's notion of bisexuality demands; and it is, for historical reasons, also women who are most likely to benefit from the transgressions of the patriarchal order that it performs. Paradoxically, if there is a self-proper to woman it is her capacity to 'depropriate' herself without self-interest, and it is this capacity for depropriation that holds possibilities for the future. This capacity is linked explicitly to the female body and female desire. While masculine sexuality is centred upon the penis, female sexuality is multiply diverse – not constrained to a single signifier but spread throughout the body and capable at any moment of performing an 'explosive return'. If the constitution of the masculine depends upon the rigid binaries that structure language and thought, and is wholly susceptible to the repression of that which transgresses those binaries, the feminine still reverberates with the instabilities of that which 'comes-before-language': that is, precisely all of the libidinal drives and rhythmical flows of the pre-Oedipal stage (see Kristeva's notion of the disruptive presence of the semiotic within the symbolic, in Section 3.4).

There is, then, a link between the economy of femininity that Cixous describes and the act of writing as transformation and creation. The call to action which she sounds is the call to feminine writing (*écriture féminine*) – a form of writing that works upon difference and plurality. Woman must, Cixous asserts, write her body. She must produce texts that destroy the closure of binary oppositions and celebrate instead the pleasures (*jouissance*; see Section 3.7) of open-ended textuality; texts that, like the female erotic, cannot be defined or theorized, enclosed or coded, texts that will 'blow up' the patriarchal law of language itself, challenging the law of the symbolic by ceaselessly displacing the system of couples and positions by which it fixes the subject 'woman'.

Although feminine writing is most obviously linked to the body, it is not exclusively the property of woman. To claim it as such would indeed be to return us to the arena of binary oppositions Cixous seeks to destroy. Feminine writing is, instead, that which displays the libidinal femininity of transgression and diversity, and as such can theoretically be located in works produced by writers of either sex.

5.3 Laura Mulvey, from 'Visual Pleasure and Narrative Cinema' (*Screen*, vol. 16, no. 3, Autumn 1975, pp. 6–14, 17–18)

Juliet Mitchell in *Psychoanalysis and Feminism* (1974) drew fresh attention to Freud's 1931 account of female sexuality (see *Standard Edition*, vol. 21: 221–43). Since both little girls and little boys are equally active in seeking the mother during the pre-Oedipal phallic stage, what needs to be explained, Mitchell argues, is how women's activity and drive may be turned towards a passive aim, unconsciously internalizing patriarchy. In a well known footnote added to *Three Essays on the Theory of Sexuality* of 1915, Freud denied that sexuality was simply 'biological' or 'sociological', proposing that 'masculine' and 'feminine' were equally attributes of a single subject, equivalent to 'active' and 'passive' (*Standard Edition*, vol. 7: 218–19). Mulvey analyses the reproduction of sexual imbalance by a visual regime that extends well beyond Hollywood (into magazine photography and advertising, for instance).

This works through the superimposition of a series of binaries: narcissism/desire, looking/being looked at, active/passive, masculine/feminine. Psychoanalysis distinguishes between self-love and love for the other (narcissism or 'ego libido' and desire or 'sexual instinct'). In Hollywood cinema men are invited to identify with a male protagonist in looking at and desiring women as objects, while women identify with the female figures passively looked at. Women's own desire – and identification with an active figure – becomes effaced. In the typical Hollywood narrative women's otherness is mastered either through sadistic aggression or by being fetishized (in his essay on 'Fetishism' Freud argues that this is an essentially male response to the threat imputed to women if they are seen to lack the phallus, the fetish being a phantasy object erected in place of the lack, which is disavowed, see *Standard Edition*, vol. 21: 147–57).

Mulvey's essay has provoked a small library of feminist scholarship (see her own subsequent essay on the female viewer, 1989; Cowie 1984; de Lauretis 1984; Doane 1987; Modleski 1988). (The 'Name of the Father' is the signifier in whose virtue, Lacan argues, patriarchy instates lack; 'scopophilia' (*Schaulust*) means simply 'visual pleasure'; for the 'mirror phase', see Lacan (Section 3.2); the *diegesis* of a film is all that is represented in its narrative.)

5.4 Kobena Mercer, from 'Reading Racial Fetishism: The Photographs of Robert Mapplethorpe' (from *Welcome to the Jungle: New Positions in Black Cultural Studies*, New York and London: Routledge, 1994, pp. 171–83)

While there has been a great deal of work on the objectification of women in the visual regimes of popular culture (art, cinema and advertising), little attention has been paid to the imaging of men – especially black men – in relation to sex. This essay provides the grounds on which such an analysis may be performed.

Drawing on the work of the feminist theorist Laura Mulvey (see Section 5.3), Mercer's reading of Mapplethorpe's photographs of black men maps a metaphorical transfer of the erotic investment of woman as 'sex', and its subsequent fetishistic fantasy of mastery for men, on to the ground of racial difference. In this way, he is able to read Mapplethorpe's work as the 'imagining of the black man's sex' through racial and sexual fantasies about black men that persist in contemporary culture. What he locates in the photographic scene are three codes (modes of looking), which, he argues, serve to aestheticize the stereotype of the black man as sexual object (to be both desired and feared) in the work of art.

The first of these codes Mercer calls the *sculptural* code, already inherent in a fine art tradition, where the body becomes an unconscious prototypical figure. The body of the beautiful black man is overvalued, 'idealized to the point of envy'. While this produces a certain degree of ambivalence in the look, Mercer argues that this is arrested in Mapplethorpe's images through the feminization of the black male body, casting it into the position of a passive, rather than active, object.

The second code, which, Mercer argues, supplements the first, he calls the code of *portraiture*. Here he identifies the gaze as it is seemingly returned by the object of the image in the fantasy pleasure of looking and being looked at. However, once again, any potential ambivalence generated in this structuring of the gaze is recuperated through the subtextual work of the stereotype of the black male as 'primitive', 'tribal', as it recalls the bank of forensic images of the black man as criminal (in the mug shot, for example, used to supplement the claim that it is black men who commit crime). Here the black man is simply confirmed in his status as a dangerous inferior, at whom it is perfectly possible simply to look.

The third code is really the fusion of two – *cropping* and *lighting* – where the body of the black man is phantasmatically fragmented, cut down into fetishized pieces, never displayed as a whole, and at the same time, lit in such a way as to emphasize the unmistakable blackness of his skin. Here Mercer argues that, while the blackness of the man's skin emphasizes his otherness to the white man's gaze, the fetishization of his body parts recuperates the threat that otherness might suggest in an aggressive act of mastery. The fear of the other engendered by the very process of looking is, then, allayed. In this way, the ego (of the white male viewer) can be protected from the fear of its own undoing just as it is in the fetishized image of woman in main-stream cinema as Mulvey describes it.

As these three techniques coalesce in the images produced by Mapplethorpe, then, the image of the black man emerges as safely erotic, since the pleasure of the text, formally and hence ideologically, is generated from and acts to confirm the aggression and hatred of racism already well entrenched in the culture as a whole.

5.5 **Rajeswari Sunder Rajan**, from 'The Subject of Sati: Pain and Death in the Contemporary Discourse on Sati' (from *Real and Imagined Women: Gender, Culture and Postcolonialism*, London and New York: Routledge, 1993, pp. 15–19)

'What does woman want?' This is a question famously asked by Freud. For Rajan, it is difficult to answer because woman is so deeply entrenched in representation – both politically and culturally – that she has become the site of a kind of intellectual power struggle. For the so-called 'Third World Woman' this is particularly problematic, since, as a figure (or sign) of woman, her meaning would seem to depend upon her ideological value. For Western feminism she is all too easily the victim of patriarchy generally, and of a fanatical kind of traditionalism in her particular Third World context. Torn between the colonizing discourses of tradition and modernity, the Third World woman is reduced to passive object. Whether she can ever be other than this is the question implicitly posed here.

The point of the analysis is not to fix the truth of woman by judging one discursive construction to be more authentic or useful than another, but to display woman as a discursive space that is 'multiple, contingent and frequently contradictory'. However, it is clear in the analysis of sati that arises from this that Western liberal notions of woman in general, and of Third World Woman in particular, are opened to scrutiny and to some extent also to challenge. If we cannot say what the woman wants in this instance of self-immolation, then we can at least say how her subjectivity is constructed in the discourses that compete to define her.

That images of oppression and brutality come so easily to mind in the Western imagination of the Indian woman who immolates herself on the funeral pyre is in this account an index of the West's imbrication in the Orientalist project outlined by Said (see Section 2.5). Martyrdom is not simply the province of an Eastern fundamentalism, but also has a long tradition in the Christianity of the West. Who, or what, after all is Joan of Arc? Is she a willing victim of tradition, a passive object of patriarchal control or an icon of resistance who chooses to die? That we can think such a figure differently in the West says nothing either of woman or of what she might want, but instead speaks clearly of her discursive positioning and its subsequent cultural and ideological implications. This is never, in Rajan's analysis, to say that sati is either morally or ethically 'right' (or wrong for that matter), but to say that its meaning is conflictual and complex, produced not in truth but on the sites of, and for, political contestation. In its speculative willingness to think differently about issues of freedom and intent in relation to the practice of sati by Indian women, Rajan's analysis constantly reminds us of the perils of forgetting that identity itself is always in flux.

5.6 Judith Butler, from *Gender Trouble: Feminism and the Subversion of Identity* (New York and London: Routledge, 1990, pp. 1–5)

In her analysis of 'woman' as the 'subject' of feminism, Judith Butler rigorously exploits the play in the concept of the subject between two of its possible meanings: subject of (arising from) and subject to (constrained by). Within this play she locates the impossibility of woman as an independent point of origin for representation, arguing instead that woman emerges only as an effect of discourse. In the political terms of feminism, this means that the subject woman is constituted as an effect of the very discourse that seeks, ironically, to represent her. She is, in other words, both constituted as a subject within its terms and subsequently constrained by those terms in the process of being constituted. Paradoxically, feminism produces the very subject on behalf of which it purports to speak.

This is not a new idea. As Butler herself points out, the presumed universality of the category of 'woman' within feminism has been challenged over the many years it has been in use. It has been rejected on the basis of the exclusions it sets up: black women, lesbians, working-class women and the transgendered have all critiqued the notion of woman as given on the grounds of its refusal of difference. For Judith Butler, however, it is not simply a question of making the category more inclusive in order to sustain a politics of identity in which woman can be more variously understood. For her, the problem lies more insidiously with the very category of woman itself.

Drawing on the earlier work of Michel Foucault (see Section 3.6), Butler argues that a progressive gender politics would be concerned not as much with authenticating the subject woman, as with tracing a genealogy of the terms and conditions of the discursive constitution of woman. The questions asked then would not be 'what is woman' or 'what does she want', but how has woman been understood to 'be' and what are the terms and consequences of those understandings? This would show not only that woman has always been an unstable and transient category, an effect of social and political mores, but also that as a category, she is simply an effect of the knowledges within which she can be fabricated at any particular moment in time.

That woman is an effect and not an origin of discourse in this way is, for Butler, an ontological fact that does not need to be ignored. We don't have to authenticate a politics of resistance to contemporary possibilities for gender on the basis of something that is simply real, or true, and certainly not on the basis of something that is eternally 'there'. The ontological impossibility of woman does not stop us interceding in undemocratic constitutions of woman (however we might define them), it simply prevents us from fixing them for all time. In this way, the subject woman is never foreclosed, it remains fluid and open to new possibilities in the future, which we cannot even yet imagine in this moment of our present.

5.7 Homi K. Bhabha, from ' "Race", Time and the Revision of Modernity' (in *The Location of Culture*, London and New York: Routledge, 1994, pp. 236–41)

In his conclusion to *The Location of Culture*, Homi Bhabha resists the temporal rush towards the realization of the moment of our present in an ideal of postmodernism, since for him its uncritical depthlessness simply reproduces the ethnocentrism of the Enlightenment project it is meant to replace. Race, he argues, disappears in the destruction of the grand narratives associated with the modernity we are supposed to have outlived, and with it the grounds upon which a colonial subject may speak or act.

   While there is, of course, a certain conception of modernity that has entailed a notion of temporal progress upon which the contemporary urge to postmodernism trades, this does not, according to Bhabha, have to be so. Modernism is not exclusively confined to a notion of history as a dialectical progress from the dark ages past to the enlightened ages of the future in which man, as a central and universalizing figure, is held to be both the source and subject of change. Modernity has, in fact, embodied much more of a confusion of time and of categories than such a view would allow, and it is in attending to this aspect of the modern (rather than abandoning its project altogether) that we may produce a space of understanding in which the real material substance of difference can be respected and understood.

   For this so-called 'revision' of modernity, Bhabha returns us to the work of Fanon (see Section 3.3). Fanon's account of difference in his essay 'The Fact of Blackness' is important to Bhabha for at least two reasons: first, it reminds us that racism is still a material presence in our contemporary world; second, it opens up, or displays, what he calls a 'lag of time' in the signifying project of modernity. More than this, if properly understood, Fanon's suggested attention to this lag of time will destroy the binary structures of power and identity that postmodernism simply attempts to forget in its emphasis on the surfaces of performance or simulation. This, for Bhabha, would be a properly modern move.

   This potential to destroy the ontology of man, the humanist ideal of man as the subject of Enlightenment thinking, comes about for Bhabha in what he calls the 'belated' insistence of the black man. When Fanon speaks, it is from a position both inside and outside of modernity. He enters the stage of the humanist ideal, but disrupts its logic through his insistence on difference. He is not man, but a *black* man. This can be recuperated by a notion of progress which says that the white man is the originary subject of Enlightenment thinking, and the black man a derivative and inferior other, but only if we ignore the gap that it opens up. This is a gap that is indispensable to Bhabha, since it is the inevitable gap of any process of signification. It is the lag of time between the enunciation (of the ideal) and the enounced (the manifestation of that ideal). Since the two are neither identical nor simultaneous, a space is generated within which the terms of the ideal itself may be undone. Fanon, in this sense, speaks in a space between symbolization (of the social fact) and the sign of its representatives (the subjects and agents of that fact). The insistence of difference here calls the substance of the ideal into question. Difference, then, as an insistent presence rather than a forgotten absence, can destabilize the very categories of the ideal we believe we know. Man, as ontological entity in this scenario, is not merely enriched to include difference, nor abandoned in its incapacity to recognize it, but destroyed by the logic of its own impossibility.

(Bhabha's argument relies on a number of complex terms peculiar to deconstruction. Caesura indicates a break or a pause; catachrestic, the misappropriation of a word or phrase. In the work of Gayatri Spivak, upon which Bhabha draws, catachresis is the misuse of categories (woman, essential etc.) in order to signify something in excess of their original meaning; sublation refers to the repression or removal of something; a parergon indicates something surplus to the work, like the frame in painting, which stands by the work of art; a supplement is something that can be added to, or substituted for, something but that in the process calls the something into question. W. E. B. Du Bois, to whom Bhabha refers in this essay, was an American black rights campaigner in the late nineteenth and early twentieth centuries. With Booker T. Washington, he helped to found the National Association for the Advancement of Colored People.)

6.1 Jean-François Lyotard, from *The Postmodern Condition: A Report on Knowledge* (trans. Geoff Bennington and Brian Massumi, Manchester: Manchester University Press and Minneapolis: Minnesota University Press, 1984, pp. 31–41; first published in Paris in 1979)

For Jean-François Lyotard the condition of postmodern culture is intimately related to the condition of knowledge within the post-industrial world. Within the analysis he offers here, the postmodern condition itself is characterized by the delegitimation of knowledge: the breakdown of the single and overriding narrative (meta, or grand, narrative) which has served to guarantee the truth, or use-value, of knowledge throughout history. He takes as the focus of his analysis the status of science, and traces the principles by which it has been legitimated.

There are, Lyotard argues, two major versions of narrative legitimation: the political and the philosophical. Within the political narrative legitimation depends upon the rhetoric of 'freedom' and emancipation of 'the people', and science assumes the status of a 'means to an end'. All people have the right to scientific knowledge, and if their liberation is to be achieved, that right to knowledge must be fulfilled. According to this version scientific knowledge finds its legitimation not in itself, but in the practical subject – humanity – and in recourse to the freedom of will of that subject. Science is legitimated, then, by its use-value, the belief in the grand narrative principle of justice, humanity and emancipation. (Lyotard draws on Wittgenstein's argument that all knowledge comes about on the basis of variable 'language games'; see Wittgenstein 1967: 5ff.)

Within the philosophical narrative, on the other hand, the legitimation of science depends upon the principle, or what Lyotard calls the 'metaprinciple', of 'speculation'. Within these terms, scientific knowledge first finds its legitimation within itself, not as a means to an end, but more as an end in itself. It is never wholly an end in itself, however, since it depends also upon a notion of what Lyotard calls the 'Spirit of the Nation' and the 'Life of the Spirit'. For Lyotard, this mode of legitimation demands a different kind of language game – the utilization of prescriptive statements of justice, but of declarative statements of authenticity, or truth.

Within contemporary post-industrial society and postmodern culture, however, the grounds upon which the question of the legitimation of knowledge is formulated have shifted. The grand narrative (of humanity or science), regardless of its legitimation through the narratives of either emancipation or speculation, has lost its credibility. While related to developments in technology and the technological control of information (the whole 'technoscience' of advanced capitalism), the delegitimation that Lyotard traces is the culmination of the 'problem of legitimation' inherent in the language games of the history of the legitimation of knowledge itself. As Lyotard asks succinctly in *The Postmodern Condition*, 'What proof is there that my proof is true?' (p. 24).

Founded upon a notion that knowledge is really only knowledge when it is capable of reduplicating itself by citing its own statements in a second order of discourse, which then functions to legitimate them, science can never, ultimately, guarantee itself as anything more than an act of faith. Science, in other words, plays only its own games. It can neither guarantee nor control the languages of other discourses or forms of knowledge. As a result, a variety of fields of knowledges and narratives proliferate, and the notion of a universal (unifying) meta-language is lost.

For Jean-François Lyotard, then, the postmodern condition is the condition of a culture in which the grand narrative has collapsed, leaving culture itself as the site of a patchwork of smaller, diverse and fragmented narratives with no single unifying guarantee outside of themselves.

6.2 Jean Baudrillard, from *Simulations* (trans. Paul Foss, Paul Patton and Philip Beitchman, New York: Semiotext(e), 1983, pp. 1–4, 23–6; first published in Paris in 1975)

Disneyland *is* the real America: a frightening thought, or the confirmation of deep-seated Anglo/European suspicions? For Jean Baudrillard, perhaps, the answer would be both, although Europe itself could never be vindicated, since within his terms America is by no means exclusive in its foundation of a society through the process of simulation. For Baudrillard the importance of the answer lies in its analysis of the condition of postmodernity.

This condition is generated by what Baudrillard calls 'the age of simulation', or the 'third order' of simulation in a long history stretching from feudal times to the present day. Breaking with the belief in a fixed hierarchy of signs that were simply construed as the real – the belief that signs could *exchange* for meaning, and that something could guarantee that exchange (usually God in medieval times) – the first order of signification constructed reality through the process of representation (the production of signs that sought to imitate the real, to reflect it). In the second order – what the German Marxist Walter Benjamin (1973) has called 'the age of mechanical reproduction' – signification came to function through the process of reproduction of 'original' representations (signs which referred to signs which, in turn, referred to reality).

While the first and second orders maintain a notion of connection between representation and the real, for the third order of what Baudrillard calls 'simulation' such a connection is no longer valid. We now participate in, and are constructed through, a system of signs that devour representation, signs that no longer refer to something outside themselves – a presence whose absence they mark – but serve to mask the absence of any exterior, or basic, reality (see Lyotard, Section 6.1). When the real is no longer what it used to be, nostalgia proliferates in the form of myths of origin and signs of reality, simulation.

In the postmodern world of simulations, what Baudrillard calls the 'representational imaginary' (the imaginary relation between the real and its representation) is dissolved. In its place springs forth a world of 'hyperreality', a world of self-referential signs (see Derrida, Section 4) engendering a reality more real than any shreds of a memory of the real itself.

In this extract he takes as one illustrative example the American phenomenon of Disneyland. The Disneyland imaginary constitutes neither the real America nor an unreal version of it, but functions instead as imaginary in order to maintain the fiction that the America outside of Disneyland is real. Disneyland functions, then, in the same way that prisons function in a disciplinary society: to conceal the fact that society *as a whole* is carceral (see Foucault, Section 3.5). Disneyland functions as an imaginary simulation to conceal the fact that America *as a whole* is itself a series of simulations.

6.3 Jean-François Lyotard, from *The Inhuman* (trans. Geoffrey Bennington and Rachel Bowlby, Cambridge: Polity Press, 1991, pp. 8–12; first published in Paris in 1988)

One of the major concerns of much of Lyotard's work since 1968 has been to engage the limits of a certain kind of speculative philosophy on the grounds of its own lack: that is, in its concern to show the infinity of thought (the end without end) it fails to account for the complexities of matter through which, for him at least, thought itself is born. In his account of the explosion of the sun in 4.5 billion years' time, Lyotard finds what he calls the 'pure event', which will finally and irreconcilably display the utopian limits of this kind of thinking.

In 4.5 billion years the sun will explode. This will be inescapable and will be the event to end all events. It will constitute the pure event: that is, negation without remainder, rendering the condition of our future that of absolute nothingness. At present, we are unprepared for this, since the condition of our contemporary philosophy and science is characterized by two systems of thinking, each of which is rendered inadequate by the prospect of the event itself. In response to this prospect, Lyotard argues there are currently two possibilities: we can ignore it and continue along the lines of speculative thought we are comfortable in, or we can attempt to fend it off by creating an alternative that might transcend, or survive, it. Each, however, is, in and of itself, inadequate to the task of survival. Thought as pure speculation without an account of matter can never adequately capture the essence of existence as intelligent thought. Neither can the current techno-science of matter, without an account of speculative thought, be adequate for the complexities of existence in these terms. Herein lie both Lyotard's question and his answer to it. 'Can thought go on without a body?' *No.* Thought and body (matter) are inextricable to one another. One simply cannot exist without the other.

Thought, perceived as extricable from matter, or the body, is simply an effect of systems of logic. While it is systematic (arising from the system of language as pure difference), it also prioritizes the notion of a remainder; that which is always in excess of the desire for the closure (the finiteness) of the system itself. However, this remainder is always and only ever an effect of the system of differences from which it arises. It takes no account, in other words, of the phenomenon of matter in its realization of a theory of thought. Lyotard's problematization of this conception is twofold: (a) the deluge of matter that will be the explosion of the sun will cancel out the possibility of this idea of thought as pure speculation. There will be nothing beyond the explosion to survive, and so to think, the event. We simply will not possess the means to think it, and (b) that deluge of matter will, in turn, expose the limits of speculative thinking in its ending of thought by the death of matter. The end of matter will then expose the impossibility of thought in its final demonstration of the mutual dependency of the two. But, of course, at the time of the explosion of the sun, it will be too late for humanity to do anything about this.

Hope, if there is to be such, can only be invested in the philosophical move towards the embodiment of thought. That the body matters so much to Lyotard in this account is evidence of his long project to expose the lack of deconstruction (see Derrida, Section 4.1) through the remainder of matter in the account of subjectivity provided by psychoanalysis. For psychoanalysis, the material body gives rise to thought (it motivates it) in a fundamental way. The material body suffers. It suffers because of the division between the satisfaction of desires and the taboo which forbids that. In the space of the unconscious, all that is repressed of material being (via social taboos) lurks as a permanent instability for thought (as meaning); in other words, that which perpetually threatens the undoing of meaning in the remainder of being. In suffering, desire is born, and with desire, thought is made possible. Without it, thought is mere speculation. Mere speculation must be made uncomfortable by the reminder of material being. Otherwise, all is lost.

6.4 Jacques Derrida, from *The Gift of Death* (trans. David Wills, Chicago and London: The University of Chicago Press, 1995, pp. 63–7; first published in Paris in 1992)

For Derrida, one of the most insistent questions of our time is the meaning of moral and ethical responsibility. How can we act, if at all, with absolute responsibility, morality and ethics? What are justice, duty and responsibility, and how can they be manifest in human actions? What might it mean to say that one may act morally or ethically without self-interest? Does an understanding of concepts such as morality and ethics fundamentally militate against the possibilities of an action being moral or ethical? Here, in *The Gift of Death*, Derrida locates these questions at the heart of his own reading of Western religion and philosophy, asking what is involved in the act of giving and of giving death. However, the two acts may not be distinguishable, or may resonate each in the other. In French, to give (*donner*) plays across two possibilities: 'to give' and 'to put to death'. As the analysis of responsibility unfolds, then, it may seem that the act of giving that Derrida has in mind here involves an irreducible paradox. To give can only be ethical if the act of giving destroys the gift itself.

The fable of Isaac, with which this extract is concerned, serves as one example of the paradox that Derrida locates at the heart of concepts such as duty and responsibility – a paradox perhaps most easily filtered through some of his earlier writings on the notion of the gift. In *Given Time* (1992b), Derrida reads the concept of giving as an event invested with self-interest. No matter how one gives to the other, he argues, there is always an element of return for the self. One cannot give without in turn being confirmed by the act of giving and therefore benefiting in some way from it. Thus, the gift becomes an aporia (a moment in which oppositions are held in suspension without resolution). This aporia is later reinscribed by Derrida within the concept of justice, where, he argues, if justice is to be possible, it must constitute an act of giving without return. In these terms, justice is conceived as 'gift without exchange' (see Cornell *et al.* 1992 (eds) *Deconstruction and the Possibility of Justice*). In the fable of Isaac, in order to fulfil an obligation to the other (in this case, God), Abraham must give without any possibility of return, and without recourse to the rational or that which might justify the act in reason. The moment of such an act, of course, can only be fleeting – it happens, if it happens at all, in the absolute instance of its enactment. It happens outside of the passage of time, which might allow for the logic of both language and reason to transform it into something other than the gift without exchange.

And here we are returned to the concept of justice, or the paradox of acting morally and ethically without self-interest (or, for that matter, without the interest of a system of logic that says this is moral, this is not). To act ethically is to act with absolute responsibility to the other where, outside of religion, the other is always a point beyond metaphysics, a point of absoluteness above all empirical systems of justice, law and so on. For Derrida, justice can only be, if it can be at all, a point of irreconcilable disjuncture between self and other. It must happen in an instant, without the passage of time, for in the time it takes to make a decision to act morally or with responsibility, the act itself becomes meaningful in terms of the self. As such, it is not the gift as Derrida would have it. What this implies is that no one can act ethically on the basis of a reasoned system of ethics, since the passage of time involved in the enactment of a reasonable decision will always contradict the very project (the aim, or intention to act ethically) from which it comes. To be ethical thus paradoxically means not being ethical, not knowing the ethical in ethical terms. In the same terms, and by recourse to Derrida's original analogy, in order to act ethically (with absolute responsibility not to law but to the absoluteness of the other) I must always enact the sacrifice of Abraham. The impossibility of actually doing so perhaps suggests that whenever we invoke ethics as a guarantee of the justness of an action, we cease to act ethically at all.

(The essay by Patočka referred to by Derrida in this extract appears in *Heretical Essays on the Philosophy of History*. Jan Patočka was a Czech philosopher who, with others, spoke out for the Charta 77 human rights declaration of 1977. As the translator's notes to Derrida's *The Gift of Death* remind us, Patočka died from a brain haemorrhage, after eleven hours of police interrogation, on 13 March 1977. The fable of Isaac referred to throughout this extract appears in Genesis 22: 1–19.)

6.5 Jean Baudrillard, from *The Spirit of Terrorism* (London and New York: Verso, 2002, pp. 26–34)

What constitutes the real of the events of 11 September 2001? It is probably safe to assert that the truth of the event (if such there can be) is impossible to realize, despite the proliferation of truth claims made on its behalf. For Baudrillard, this event is interesting for the further speculation it lends to one of his overriding concerns: the relation of signification to the real. For him, our contemporary society is marked by the loss of any notion of the real as the primacy of the signifier penetrates and consumes it. And, in the events of 11 September, he sees nothing to contradict this.

For Baudrillard, whatever took place in New York that day can never be anything more than an effect of the operation of signification through which it was realized. The real-time communication of the global network of news ensured that what we witnessed was the image in all its purity, expunged of a content that might be said to be real. Indeed, in the proliferation of the image, the impossibility of the real was merely restated. This is not to be mourned, however, since it is in this very realization of the real as 'redoubtable fiction' that, Baudrillard argues, the radical potentiality of the event may lie. There is, he asserts, no possible response to the symbolism of the event that does not involve the undoing of all that sustains the fiction that is what America now calls 'the free world'.

In this reading, the global war on terrorism evoked by the events of 11 September is, in return for the event, merely an empty gesture, since it serves only to reconfirm the absence of the concepts of justice, freedom and democracy at the heart of the world order they are intended to signify. Where, we might ask, are justice and democracy in the destruction of Afghanistan, the holding of prisoners without charge in Guantánamo Bay and the deployment of weapons of mass destruction in Iraq in an effort to rid the world of weapons of mass destruction and the terror they supposedly wield? As a gesture, this war on terrorism is empty, because it fails quite spectacularly to signify the rightness of American actions over and against those of its 'other'. It fails to signify because it is only a partial sign: the signifier (war on terror) with no referent in a signified (America is free of terror, and is therefore rightly the guardian of world order, since it always acts justly and democratically). What America insists it can achieve, then, has already been lost to it, since it merely repeats that which it decries.

What this analysis draws attention to is the impossibility of exchange in the circulation of the symbolic. Since America's war on terror is mere rhetoric, the signifier without the signified, it is unconvincing and openly contradictory. It simply cannot be exchanged for the actions of those involved in the destruction of the twin towers of the World Trade Center. Hence, for Baudrillard, there is no effective response to the events of 11 September. Conventional warfare, in its claim to materiality, does nothing to diffuse the power of the symbolic. It is merely, as Baudrillard concludes, the 'continuation of politics by other means'.

6.6 Slavoj Žižek, from *Welcome to the Desert of the Real* (London and New York: Verso, 2002, pp. 10–17)

For Slavoj Žižek, the power of the event that was 11 September 2001 lies not in the material devastation it wrought, but in the *spectacular* effect of it. In his reading, this event has shattered the meaning of all other events, by engaging the real of our world in the thoroughly postmodern terms of its own constitution. In this sense, like Baudrillard (see Section 6.5), Žižek argues that the event marks a constitutive difference of engagement, one that it is singularly difficult to understand or to respond to except in its own terms.

In some ways, the *spectacular* effect of the event was obvious from the start. The destruction of the World Trade Center not only hit hard at the power base of global capital, but also symbolically disrupted the idealism of its image as a monolith nestled into the skyline of New York. What was hit that day was also an image, an image of a benign America projected through the signifier of the Manhattan skyline and the countless movies in which that signifier stands in for the permanence both of America's might and of its heart. For Žižek that signifier was, like so many of the products of late capitalism, a symbolization devoid of the hard kernel of its real: like a decaffeinated coffee, it still smelt and tasted like the real, but with its substance removed so as not to contaminate, or to threaten, 'us'. And therein lies the power of the event. In the immediacy of the circulation of the images of destruction we were confronted by the primacy of a singular and privileged signifier allowing us to glimpse the lack behind every other we have ever experienced. It was not that we came face to face with the real that day, but that we met its lack. What we experienced was the absence of the real as anything other than the signifiers that both constitute and devour it.

That this was uniquely traumatic is evidenced for Žižek in the operation of the images that circulated of the event, and in the persistent and anxious iteration of two images in particular: of people running towards the camera with a cloud of dust about to engulf them, and of the second plane looming large overhead seconds before it hit the second tower. There is something uncanny about these images. While we have seen them so many times before in the aesthetic of Hollywood cinema, there was, none the less, something strange about their familiarity. We did not expect the ease with which the derealization of the real in the symbolic could be effected. And, while we constantly awaited the arrival of the real, it never came. It is not, Žižek claims, that 'reality entered our image' that day, but that 'the image entered and shattered our reality (i.e. the symbolic coordinates which determine what we experience as reality)'.

In a world of hyperreal simulations (the primacy of the symbolic) the real can no longer be realized except as the extreme vulnerability of signification. There is no remainder of the signifier in such a world, merely the vague and inaccessible reminiscence of something that is lost.

Biographical notes

Dates are for first publication; English translations are listed in the Bibliography.

Louis Althusser   French Marxist philosopher (born Algeria 1918, died 1989). *For Marx*, 1965; *Reading Capital*, with Etienne Balibar, 1968; *Lenin and Philosophy*, 1971.

Roland Barthes   French literary critic and semiotician (1915–80); Professor of Semiology at the College de France from 1976. *Mythologies*, 1957; *Elements of Semiology*, 1964; *S/Z*, 1970; *The Pleasure of the Text*, 1973; *A Lover's Discourse: Fragments*, 1977.

Jean Baudrillard   French writer and critic (born 1929); from 1966 to 1987 taught Sociology at the University of Nanterre. *For a Critique of the Political Economy of the Sign*, 1972; *Forget Foucault*, 1977; *The Perfect Crime*, 1996; *The Vital Illusion*, 2000; *Impossible Exchange*, 2001; *The Spirit of Terrorism*, 2002.

Simone de Beauvoir   French existentialist writer, novelist and social essayist (1908–86). *The Ethics of Ambiguity*, 1947; *L'Envitee*, 1943; *The Second Sex*, 1949.

Homi K. Bhabha   Born in Bombay, 1949; Professor of Humanities at the University of Chicago. *Nation and Narration*, 1990; *The Location of Culture*, 1994.

Judith Butler   Maxine Elliot Professor in the Departments of Rhetoric and Comparative Literature at the University of California, Berkeley (born 1956). *Gender Trouble*, 1990; *Bodies That Matter*, 1993; *The Psychic Life of Power*, 1997; *Excitable Speech*, 1997; with Ernesto Laclau and Slavoj Žižek, *Antigone's Claim*, 2000.

Hélène Cixous   French feminist writer, born in Algeria in 1937; Professor of English Literature at the University of Vincennes. *The Exile of James Joyce*, 1968;

'The laugh of the Medusa', 1975; *The Newly Born Woman*, with Catherine Clement, 1975.

Jacques Derrida French philosopher, born in Algeria in 1930; teaches philosophy at the Ecole Normale Superieure in Paris. *'Speech and Phenomena' and Other Essays on Husserl's Theory of Signs*, 1967; *Of Grammatology*, 1967; *Writing and Difference*, 1967; *Dissemination*, 1972; *Margins of Philosophy*, 1972; *The Post Card from Socrates to Freud and Beyond*, 1980; *Given Time*, 1992; *Spectres of Marx*, 1994; *The Gift of Death*, 1992.

Umberto Eco Italian literary critic, novelist and essayist (born 1932); President of the Scoula Supériore di Studi Umanistici at the University of Bologna. *The Name of the Rose*, 1978; *The Role of the Reader*, 1984; *Travels in Hyperreality*, 1987.

Friedrich Engels German co-author with Karl Marx (1820–95); ran a business in Manchester after exile. *The Condition of the Working Class in England in 1844* (1845) (see Marx and Engels, *Collected Works*).

Frantz Fanon Born in 1925 in the French colony of Martinique, died in 1961; psychoanalyst, postcolonial writer and political revolutionary, working actively for the liberation of Algeria; Head of Psychiatry at the Blida-Joinville Hospital, he also spent some time as Ambassador to Ghana for the Provisional Algerian Government. *Black Skin/White Masks*, 1952; *The Wretched of the Earth*, 1961.

Michel Foucault French philosopher and historian of ideas (1926–84); Professor of History and Systems of Thought at the College de France. *Madness and Civilisation*, 1961; *The Order of Things*, 1966; *The Archaeology of Knowledge*, 1969; *Discipline and Punish: The Birth of the Prison*, 1975; *History of Sexuality*, vols 1, 2 and 3, 1976 and 1984.

Sigmund Freud German founder of psychoanalysis (1856–1939); fled from Nazism to London, 1938. *The Interpretation of Dreams* (1900) (see *Standard Edition*).

Antonio Gramsci Born in Sardinia 1891, died 1937; worked for Italian Communist Party and was imprisoned by Mussolini in 1926. *Prison Notebooks*, 1971.

Martin Heidegger German philosopher (1889–1976); 1929, Chair of Philosophy at Freiburg in succession to Edmund Husserl (below); made Rector of the University under the Nazis, 1934 but resigned in 1935; removed from Chair in 1945 on charge that he had served the interests of the Nazi movement. *Being and Time*, 1927; *An Introduction to Metaphysics*, lecture 1935, published 1953 (see *Basic Writings*, 1978).

Edmund Husserl German philosopher (1859–1938); Professor at University of Freiburg, 1916; developed phenomenology, project for producing an analysis of the contents of consciousness, while suspending (or 'bracketing') the question of the relation between consciousness and the real. *Ideas*, 1913; *Logical Investigations*, 1922 (written 1900–1); *Cartesian Meditations*, 1929.

Julia Kristeva   French feminist writer, literary critic and psychoanalyst; born Bulgaria, 1941; Professor at the University of Paris VII. *Revolution in Poetic Language*, 1974; *Desire in Language*, 1979; 'Women's time', 1981; *Strangers to Ourselves*, 1994; *Crisis of the European Subject*, 2000; *Revolt, She Said*, 2001.

Jacques Lacan   French psychoanalyst (1901–81); his weekly seminars, which started in 1953, were attended, especially during the 1960s, by (among others) Althusser, Barthes, Derrida and Kristeva. *The Four Fundamental Concepts of Psychoanalysis*, seminar 1964–5, published 1953; *Écrits*, 1977; see also *The Language of the Self*, 1953; *Feminine Sexuality*, 1982; *The Ego in Freud's Theory*, 1991; *The Psychoses*, 1993; his complete works, over 20 volumes of the 'Seminaires', is being prepared by Jacques-Alain Miller and gradually published in English.

Emmanuel Levinas   Philosopher, born in Lithuania in 1906; attended lectures given by Husserl at Freiburg, 1928–9; director of the École Normale Israélite Orientale, Paris, 1946; Professor of Philosophy at the Sorbonne, 1973; Levinas rejects any philosophical rationalizing in favour of a sense of experience open to the Other (see Hand 1989). *Time and the Other*, originally lectures, 1946–7, 1979; *Totality and Infinity*, 1961.

Claude Lévi-Strauss   Belgian anthropologist, born 1908; Chair of Social Anthropology at the Collège de France, 1958; his work tended to show that binary oppositions were basic to human thought; *Structural Anthropology*, 1958; *The Savage Mind*, 1962.

Georg Lukács   Hungarian Marxist philosopher and literary critic (1885–1971); *History and Class Consciousness*, 1923; *The Historical Novel*, 1937; *The Meaning of Contemporary Realism*, 1958.

Jean-François Lyotard   French philosopher (1924–98); Professor at the University of Paris VIII, 1972–87; *The Postmodern Condition*, 1979; *The Differend*, 1983; with Jean-Loup Thebaud, *Just Gaming*, 1979; *The Inhuman*, 1991; *Postmodern Fables*, 1997.

Colin MacCabe   English literary critic, born 1951; Professor at University of Pittsburgh, he is also Head of Research at the British Film Institute. *James Joyce and the Revolution of the Word*, 1978; *Theoretical Essays*, 1985.

Pierre Macherey   French literary critic, born 1938; member of the French Communist Party and colleague of Louis Althusser; Professor of Philosophy at the University of Lille III. *A Theory of Literary Production*, 1966; with Étienne Balibar,

'On literature as ideological form', 1974 (see Young 1981); *The Object of Literature*, 1990; *In a Materialist Way*, 1998.

Karl Marx   German political economist (1818–83); exiled to London in 1849. *Capital*, 1867 (see *Collected Works*).

Kobena Mercer   British cultural critic. *Black Film, British Cinema*, 1987; *Welcome to the Jungle*, 1994; *Isaac Julien*, 2001.

Laura Mulvey   British film maker and feminist critic, born 1941. 'Riddles of The Sphinx', 1977; 'Amy', 1980; *Visual and Other Pleasures*, 1989.

Rajeswari Sunder Rajan   Teaches English at the University of Delhi. *Real and Imagined Women*, 1993; *The Scandal of the State*, 2003.

Edward Said   Palestinian literary critic, born Jerusalem 1935, died New York, 2003; member of the Palestine National Council; went to the United States in the late 1950s; Parr Professor of English and Comparative Literature at Columbia University. *Orientalism*, 1978; *The Question of Palestine*, 1979; *The World, the Text, and the Critic*, 1983; *Culture and Imperialism*, 1994; *Covering Islam*, 1997.

Ferdinand de Saussure   Swiss linguist (1857–1913); professor at the University of Geneva, 1891; three series of lectures on general linguistics (1907, 1908–9, 1910–11) were collated by Charles Bally and Albert Sechahaye and published after his death as the *Course of General Linguistics*, 1916.

Slavoj Žižek   Slovenian philosopher and cultural critic, born 1949; Professor at the Institute for Sociology, Ljubljana, and at the European Graduate School. He is also founder and president of the Society for Theoretical Psychoanalysis, Ljubljana. *Sublime Object of Ideology*, 1989; *The Ticklish Subject*, 1999; *The Art of the Ridiculous Sublime*, 2000; *Welcome to the Desert of the Real*, 2002.

Bibliography

Althusser, Louis (1969) *For Marx*, trans. Ben Brewster. London: New Left Books (first published 1965).

Althusser, Louis (1971) *Lenin and Philosophy*, trans. Ben Brewster. London: New Left Books.

Althusser, Louis (1976) *Essays in Self-Criticism*. London: New Left Books.

Althusser, Louis and Balibar, Étienne (1970) *Reading Capital*, trans. Ben Brewster. London: New Left Books (first published 1968).

Arnold, Matthew (1960) *Culture and Anarchy*. Cambridge: Cambridge University Press (first published 1867).

Beauvoir, Simone de (1953) *The Second Sex*, trans. H. M. Parshley. New York: Random House.

Beauvoir, Simone de (2000) *Ethics of Ambiguity*. Sacramento, CA: Citadel Press.

Barthes, Roland (1967) *Elements of Semiology*, trans. Annette Lavers and Colin Smith. London: Jonathan Cape (first published 1964).

Barthes, Roland (1972) *Mythologies*, trans. Annette Lavers. London: Jonathan Cape.

Barthes, Roland (1975a) *S/Z*, trans. Richard Miller. London: Jonathan Cape (first published 1970).

Barthes, Roland (1975b) *The Pleasure of the Text*, trans. Richard Miller. London: Jonathan Cape.

Barthes, Roland (1978) *A Lover's Discourse: Fragments*, trans. Richard Howard. New York: Farrar, Straus and Giroux (first published 1977).

Baudrillard, Jean (1975) *The Mirror of Production*, trans. Mark Poster. St Louis, MO: Telos Press (first published 1973).

Baudrillard, Jean (1981) *For a Critique of the Political Economy of the Sign*, trans. Charles Levin. St Louis, MO: Telos Press (first published 1972).

Baudrillard, Jean (1983) *Simulations*, trans. Paul Foss *et al.* New York: Semiotext(e) (first published 1975).

Baudrillard, Jean (1987) *Forget Foucault*, trans. Sylvere Lautringer. New York: Semiotext(e) (first published 1977).

Baudrillard, Jean (1996) *The Perfect Crime*, trans. Chris Turner. London: Verso.

Baudrillard, Jean (2001a) *Impossible Exchange*, trans. Chris Turner. London: Verso.

Baudrillard, Jean (2001b) *The Vital Illusion*, ed. Julia Witwer. New York: Columbia University Press.

Baudrillard, Jean (2002) *The Spirit of Terrorism*, trans. Chris Turner. London and New York: Verso.

Belsey, Catherine (1985) *The Subject of Tragedy*. London: Routledge.

Belsey, Catherine (1994) *Desire: Love Stories in Western Culture*. Oxford: Blackwell.

Belsey, Catherine (2002) *Critical Practice*. London: Routledge.

Belsey, Catherine (2002) *Poststructuralism: A Very Short Introduction*. Oxford: Oxford University Press.

Belsey, Catherine and Jane Moore (eds) (1997) *The Feminist Reader: Essays in Gender and the Politics of Literary Criticism*. London: Palgrave Macmillan.

Benjamin, Walter (1973) "The work of man in the age of mechanical reproduction," in *Illuminations*, trans. Harry Zohn. London: Fontana/Collins.

Bennett, Tony (1979) *Formalism and Marxism*. London: Methuen.

Bhabha, Homi K. (1983) "The 'other' question", *Screen*, 24(6).

Bhabha, Homi K. (ed.) (1990) *Nation and Narration*. London: Routledge.

Bhabha, Homi K. (1994) *The Location of Culture*. London: Routledge.

Botting, Fred (1999) *Sex, Machines and Navels: Fiction, Fantasy and History in the Future Present*. Manchester: Manchester University Press.

Botting, Fred and Wilson, Scott (2001a) *Bataille*. London: Palgrave Macmillan.

Botting, Fred and Wilson, Scott (2001b) *The Tarantinian Ethics*. London: Sage.

Bristow, Joseph (1997) *Sexuality*. London: Routledge.

Burgin, Victor (1986) *The End of Art Theory: Criticism and Post-modernity*. Atlantic Highlands, NJ: Humanities Press International.

Butler, Judith (1990) *Gender Trouble: Feminism and the Subversion of Identity*. New York and London: Routledge.

Butler, Judith (1993) *Bodies that Matter: On the Discursive Limits of 'Sex'*. New York and London: Routledge.

Butler, Judith (1997a) *Excitable Speech: Contemporary Scenes of Politics*. New York and London: Routledge.

Butler, Judith (1997b) *The Psychic Life of Power: Theories in Subjection*. Palo Alto, CA: Stanford University Press.

Butler, Judith, Laclau, Ernesto and Žižek, Slavoj (2000) *Antigone's Claim: Kinship between Life and Death*. New York: Columbia University Press.

Cixous, Hélène (1972) *The Exile of James Joyce*, trans. Sally Purcell. New York: David Lewis (first published 1968).

Cixous, Hélène (1976) "The laugh of the Medusa", trans. Keith Cohen and Linda Cohen, *Signs*, 1 (Summer): 875–99 (first published 1975).

Cixous, Hélène (1981) "Castration or decapitation?", trans. Annette Kuhn, *Signs*, 7(1): 41–55 (first published 1976).

Cixous, Hélène and Clement, Catherine (1986) *The Newly Born Woman*, trans. Betsy Wing. Manchester: Manchester University Press (first published 1975).

Cornell, Drucilla, Rosenfeld, Michel and Gray Carlson, David (eds) (1992) *Deconstruction and the Possibility of Justice*. New York: Routledge.

Cowie, Elizabeth (1984) "Fantasia", *m/f*, 9: 71–105.

Debord, Guy (1983) *Society of the Spectacle*. Detroit: Black & Red (first published 1976).

de Lauretis, Teresa (1984) *Alice Doesn't: Feminism, Semiotics, Cinema*. Bloomington, IL: Indiana University Press.

Derrida, Jacques (1972) "La double seance", in *La dissemination*. Paris: Seuil.

Derrida, Jacques (1973a) *'Speech and Phenomena' and Other Essays on Husserl's Theory of Signs*, trans. D. B. Allison. Evanston, IL: Northwestern University Press (first published 1967).

Derrida, Jacques (1973b) "Avoir l'oreille de la philosophie", in L. Finas, S. Kofman, R. Lapone and J. M. Rey (eds), *Écarts: Quatre essais a propos de Jacques Derrida*. Paris: Fayard.

Derrida, Jacques (1976) *Of Grammatology*, trans. Gayatri Chakravorty Spivak. London: Johns Hopkins University Press (first published 1967).

Derrida, Jacques (1978) *Writing and Difference*, trans. Alan Bass. London: Routledge & Kegan Paul (first published 1967).

Derrida, Jacques (1979) *Spurs: Nietzsche's Styles*, trans. Barbara Harlow. Chicago, IL: University of Chicago Press (first published 1972).

Derrida, Jacques (1981) *Dissemination*, trans. Barbara Johnson. London: Athlone Press (first published 1972).

Derrida, Jacques (1982) *Margins of Philosophy*, trans. Alan Bass. Brighton: Harvester.

Derrida, Jacques (1987a) *Positions*, trans. Alan Bass. London: Athlone.

Derrida, Jacques (1987b) *The Post Card: From Socrates to Freud and Beyond*, trans. Alan Bass. Chicago: Chicago University Press (first published 1980).

Derrida, Jacques (1992a) *The Gift of Death*, trans. David Wills. Chicago, IL: University of Chicago Press.

Derrida, Jacques (1992b) *Given Time: 1. Counterfeit Money*, trans. Peggy Kamuf. Chicago, IL: University of Chicago Press.

Derrida, Jacques (1992c) "Force of law: the 'mystical foundation of authority' ", in Drucilla Cornell, Michel Rosenfeld and David Gray Carlson (eds) *Deconstruction and the Possibility of Justice*. New York: Routledge.

Derrida, Jacques (1994) *Spectres of Marx: The State of the Debt, the Work of Mourning and the New International*, trans. Peggy Kamuf. New York: Routledge.

Doane, Mary Ann (1987) *The Desire to Desire: The Woman's Film of the 1940s*. London: Macmillan.

Dyer, Richard (1982) "Don't look now – the male pin-up", *Screen*, 23(3/4).

Eagleton, Terry (1983) *Literary Theory: An Introduction*. Oxford: Blackwell.

Eagleton, Terry (1991) *Ideology: An Introduction*. London: Verso.

Eagleton, Terry (1996) *The Illusions of Postmodernism*. Oxford: Blackwell.

Eagleton, Terry (2000) *The Idea of Culture*. Oxford: Blackwell.

Eagleton, Terry (2002) *Marxism and Literary Criticism*. London: Routledge.

Easthope, Antony (1983) *Poetry as Discourse*. London: Routledge.

Easthope, Antony (1986) *What a Man's Gotta Do: The Masculine Myth in Popular Culture*. London: Paladin.

Easthope, Antony (1991a) *British Poststructuralism Since 1968*. London: Routledge.

Easthope, Antony (1991b) *Literary into Cultural Studies*. London: Routledge.

Easthope, Antony (1999) *The Unconscious*. London: Routledge.

Easthope, Antony (2001) *Privileging Difference*, ed. Catherine Belsey. London: Palgrave Macmillan.

Eco, Umberto (1978) *The Name of the Rose*, trans. William Weaver. London: Vintage.

Eco, Umberto (1984) *The Role of the Reader: Explorations in The Semiotics of Texts*. Bloomington, IL, University of Indiana Press.

Eco, Umberto (1987) *Travels in Hyperreality*. London: Picador.

Fanon, Frantz (1967) *The Wretched of The Earth*, trans. Constance Farrington. London: Penguin.

Fanon, Frantz (1986) *Black Skin/White Masks*, trans. Charles Lam Markmann. London: Pluto.

Foucault, Michel (1970) *The Order of Things*, trans. A. M. Sheridan. London: Tavistock (first published 1966).

Foucault, Michel (1971) *Madness and Civilisation: A History of Insanity in the Age of Reason*, trans. Richard Howard. London: Tavistock (first published 1961).

Foucault, Michel (1972) *The Archaeology of Knowledge*, trans. A. M. Sheridan Smith. New York: Pantheon (first published 1969).

Foucault, Michel (1977) *Discipline and Punish*, trans. A. M. Sheridan. London: Alien Lane (first published 1975).

Foucault, Michel (1978a) *Introduction: The History of Sexuality, vol. 1*, trans. Robert Hurley. London: Penguin Books (first published 1976).

Foucault, Michel (1978b) *I, Pierre Riviere*, trans. Frank Jellinek. London: Peregrine (first published 1973).

Foucault, Michel (1980) *Herculine Barbin*, trans. Richard McDougall. Brighton: Harvester Press (first published 1978).

Foucault, Michel (1985) *The Use of Pleasure: The History of Sexuality, vol. 2*, trans. Robert Hurley. London: Penguin Books (first published 1984).

Foucault, Michel (1986) *The Care of The Self: The History of Sexuality, vol. 3*, trans. Robert Hurley. London: Penguin Books (first published 1984).

Freud, Anna (1937) *The Ego and the Mechanisms of Defence*. London: Hogarth.

Freud, Sigmund (1953–76) *Standard Edition*, trans. James Strachey, 22 vols. London: Hogarth Press in association with the Institute of Psycho-Analysis.

Gilroy, Paul (1990) *There Ain't No Black in the Union Jack: The Cultural Politics of Race and Nation*. London: Routledge.

Gilroy, Paul (1993) *The Black Atlantic: Modernity and Double Consciousness*. London and New York: Verso.

Glover, David and Kaplan, Cora (2000) *Genders*. London: Routledge.

Gramsci, Antonio (1971) *Selections from the Prison Notebooks*, trans. Quintin Hoare and Geoffrey Nowell-Smith. London: Lawrence & Wishart.

Hall, Stuart (1980) "Cultural studies: two paradigms", *Media, Culture and Society*, 2: 57–72.

Hall, Stuart (1982) "The whites of their eyes: racist ideologies and the media", in George Bridges and Rosalind Brunt (eds) *Silver Linings: Some Strategies for the Eighties*. London: Lawrence & Wishart.

Hamilton, Paul (2003) *Historicism*. London: Routledge.

Hand, Sean (ed.) (1989) *The Levinas Reader*. Oxford: Blackwell.

Hawkes, David (1996) *Ideology*. London: Routledge.

Hawkes, Terry (1977) *Structuralism and Semiotics*. London: Methuen.

Hegel, Georg Wilhelm Friedrich (1942) *Philosophy of Right*, trans. T. M. Knox. Oxford: Clarendon Press.

Heidegger, Martin (1959) *An Introduction to Metaphysics*, trans. Ralph Manheim. New Haven, CT: Yale University Press (first published 1953).

Heidegger, Martin (1962) *Being and Time*, trans. John Macquarrie and Edward Robinson. Oxford: Blackwell (first published 1927).

Heidegger, Martin (1978) *Basic Writings: From 'Being and Time', 1927, to 'The Task of Thinking', 1964*, ed. D. F. Krell. London: Routledge & Kegan Paul.

Hjelmslev, Louis (1961) *Prolegomena to a Theory of Language*, trans. F. J. Whitfield. Madison, WI: University of Wisconsin Press (first published 1843).

Husserl, Edmund (1960) *Cartesian Mediations: An Introduction to Phenomenology*, trans. D. Cairns. The Hague: Nijhoff (first published 1929).

Husserl, Edmund (1970) *Logical Investigations*, trans. J. N. Findlay. London: Routledge & Kegan Paul (first published 1922).

Husserl, Edmund (1983) *Ideas Pertaining to a Pure Phenomenology and to a Phenomenological Philosophy, First Book*, trans. F. Kersten. The Hague: Nijhoff (first published 1913).

Hutcheon, Linda (1989) *The Politics of Postmodernism*. London and New York: Routledge.

Irigaray, Luce (1985a) *Speculum of the Other Woman*, trans. Gillian Gill. Ithaca, NY: Cornell University Press (first published 1974).

Irigaray, Luce (1985b) *This Sex which Is Not One*, trans. Catherine Porter. Ithaca, NY: Cornell University Press (first published 1977).

Jameson, Fredric (1971) *Marxism and Form*. Princeton, NJ: Princeton University Press.

Jameson, Fredric (1972) *The Prison-house of Language*. Princeton, NJ: Princeton University Press.

Jameson, Fredric (1981) *The Political Unconscious*. London: Methuen.

Jameson, Fredric (1991) *Postmodernism, or the Logic of Late Capitalism*. Durham, NC: Duke University Press.

Jencks, Charles (1977) *The Language of Postmodern Architecture*. London: Academy.

Kristeva, Julia (1973) "The system and the speaking subject", *Times Literary Supplement*, 12 October: 1249–50.

Kristeva, Julia (1980) *Desire in Language*, trans. Thomas Gora, Alice Jardine and Leon S. Roudiez. Oxford: Basil Blackwell (first published 1979).

Kristeva, Julia (1981) "Women's time", trans. Alice Jardine and Harry Blake, *Signs*, 7(1): 13–35.

Kristeva, Julia (1984) *Revolution in Poetic Language*, trans. Margaret Wailer. New York: Columbia University Press (first published 1974).

Kristeva, Julia (1991) *Strangers to Ourselves*, trans. Leon Roudiez. Brighton: Harvester Wheatsheaf.

Kristeva, Julia (2000) *Crisis of the European Subject*. Baltimore, MD: The Other Press.

Kristeva, Julia (2001) *Revolt She Said*. New York: Semiotext(e)/Foreign Agents Series.

Lacan, Jacques (1976) *The Language of the Self*, trans. Anthony Wilden. Baltimore, MD: Johns Hopkins University Press (first published 1953).

Lacan, Jacques (1977a) *The Four Fundamental Concepts of Psychoanalysis*, trans. Alan Sheridan. London: Hogarth (first published 1973).

Lacan, Jacques (1977b) *Écrits: A Selection*, trans. Alan Sheridan. London: Tavistock.

Lacan, Jacques (1982) *Feminine Sexuality*, trans. Jacqueline Rose. London: Macmillan.

Lapsley, Robert and Westlake, Michael (1988) *Film Theory: An Introduction*. Manchester: Manchester University Press.

Levinas, Emmanuel (1969) *Totality and Infinity: An Essay on Exteriority*, trans. Alphonso Lingis. Pittsburgh, PA: Duquesne University Press.

Levinas, Emmanuel (1987) *Time and the Other*, trans. Richard Cohen. Pittsburgh, PA: Duquesne University Press (first published 1979).

Lévi-Strauss, Claude (1963) *Structural Anthropology*, trans. C. Jacobson and B. G. Schoepf. New York: Basic Books (first published 1958).

Lévi-Strauss, Claude (1966) *The Savage Mind*. London: Weidenfeld & Nicholson (first published 1962).

Loomba, Ania (1998) *Colonialism/Postcolonialism*. London: Routledge.

Lukács, Georg (1962) *The Historical Novel*, trans. Hannah and Stanley Mitchell. London: Merlin (first published 1937).

Lukács, Georg (1963) *The Meaning of Contemporary Realism*, trans. John and Necke Mander. London: Merlin (first published 1958).

Lukács, Georg (1971) *History and Class Consciousness*, trans. Rodney Livingstone. London: Lawrence & Wishart (first published 1923).

Lyotard, Jean-François (1983) *The Differend*, trans. G. van den Abbele. Minneapolis: University of Minnesota Press.

Lyotard, Jean-François (1984) *The Postmodern Condition*, trans. Geoff Bennington and Brian Massumi. Manchester: Manchester University Press (first published 1979).

Lyotard, Jean-François (1991) *The Inhuman: Reflections on Time*, trans. Geoffrey Bennington and Rachel Bowlby. Cambridge: Polity Press.

Lyotard, Jean-François (1997) *Postmodern Fables*, trans. Georges van den Abeele. Minneapolis: University of Minnesota Press.

Lyotard, Jean-François and Thébaud, Jean-Loup (1985) *Just Gaming*, trans. Wlad Godzich. Minneapolis: University of Minnesota Press (first published 1979).

MacCabe, Colin (1978) *James Joyce and the Revolution of the Word*. London: Macmillan.

MacCabe, Colin (1985) *Theoretical Essays*. Manchester: Manchester University Press.

McHale, Brian (1987) *Postmodernist Fiction*. London and New York: Methuen.

Macherey, Pierre (1978) *A Theory of Literary Production*, trans. Geoffrey Wall. London: Routledge & Kegan Paul (first published 1966).

Macherey, Pierre (1990) *The Object of Literature*, trans. David Macey. Cambridge: Cambridge University Press.

Macherey, Pierre and Balibar, Étienne (1981) "On literature as ideological form", in Robert Young (ed.) *Untying the Text*. London: Routledge & Kegan Paul.

Macherey, Pierre (1998) *In a Materialist Way: Selected Essays*, trans. Ted Stolze, ed. Warren Montag. London: Verso.

Marx, Karl (1970) *Capital*. London: Lawrence & Wishart (first published 1867).

Marx, Karl and Engels, Friedrich (1950) *Selected Works*, two volumes. London: Lawrence & Wishart.

Marx, Karl and Engels, Friedrich (1975) *Collected Works*, 44 volumes. London: Lawrence & Wishart.

Mercer, Kobena (ed.) (1987) *Black Film, British Cinema*. London: Institute of Contemporary Arts.

Mercer, Kobena (1994) *Welcome to the Jungle: New Positions in Black Cultural Studies*. New York and London: Routledge.

Mercer, Kobena (2001) *Isaac Julien*. London: Ellipses.

Mills, Sara (2000) *Discourse*. London: Routledge.

Mitchell, Juliet (1974) *Psychoanalysis and Feminism*. London: Allen Lane.

Modleski, Tania (1988) *The Women who Knew too Much: Hitchcock and Feminist Theory*. New York: Methuen.

Morgan, Robert P. (1977) "On the analysis of recent music", *Critical Inquiry*, 4(1): 33–53.

Mulhern, Francis (2000) *Culture/Metaculture*. London: Routledge.

Mulvey, Laura (1989) *Visual and Other Pleasures*. London: Macmillan.

Nietzsche, Friedrich Wilhelm (1974) *The Gay Science*, trans. Walter Kaufmann. New York: Vintage Books (first published 1882).

Norris, Christopher (1987) *Derrida*. London: Fontana.

Norris, Christopher (1998) *What's Wrong with Postmodernism: Critical Theory and the Ends of Philosophy*. Brighton: Harvester Wheatsheaf.

Norris, Christopher (2002) *Deconstruction: Theory and Practice*. London: Routledge.

Norris, Christopher and Roden, David (eds) (2002) *Jacques Derrida*, four volume set. London: Sage.

Quintana, Alvina (1990) "Politics, representation and the emergence of a Chicana/o aesthetic", *Cultural Studies*, 4(3): 257–63.

Rajan, Rajeswari Sunder (1992) *The Lie of the Land: English Literary Studies in India*. New Delhi: Oxford University Press.

Rajan, Rajeswari Sunder (1993) *Real and Imagined Women: Gender, Culture and Postcolonialism*. London and New York: Routledge.

Rajan, Rajeswari Sunder (2003) *The Scandal of the State*. Durham, NC: Duke University Press.

Richter, Hans (1965) *Dada: Art and Anti-Art*. London: Thames & Hudson.

Riviere, Joan (1929) "Womanliness as a masquerade", *International Journal of Psychoanalysis*, 10: 303–13.

Rose, Jacqueline (1984) *The Case of Peter Pan*. London: Macmillan.

Rose, Jacqueline (1988) *Sexuality in the Field of Vision*. London: Verso.

Said, Edward (1979) *The Question of Palestine*. New York: Times Books.

Said, Edward (1983) *The World, the Text, and the Critic*. Cambridge: Cambridge University Press.

Said, Edward (1985) *Orientalism*. New York: Random House (first published 1978).

Said, Edward (1994) *Culture and Imperialism*. London: Vintage.

Said, Edward (1997) *Covering Islam: How the Media and the Experts Determine How We See the Rest of the World*. London: Vintage.

Sanchez, Rosaura (1990) "Ethnicity, ideology and academia", *Cultural Studies*, 4(3): 294–302.

Saussure, Ferdinand de (1974) *Course in General Linguistics*, trans. Wade Baskin. London: Fontana.

Spivak, Gayatri Chakravorty (1983) "Displacement and the discourse of woman", in Mark Krupnick (ed.) *Displacement: Derrida and After*. Bloomington, IL: Indiana University Press: 169–90.

Spivak, Gayatri Chakravorty (1987) *In Other Worlds: Essays in Cultural Politics*. New York: Methuen.

Spivak, Gayatri Chakravorty (1990) *The Post-Colonial Critic*, ed. Sarah Harasym. London: Routledge.

Trachtenberg, Stanley (ed.) (1985) *The Postmodern Moment*. Westport, CT: Greenwood Press.

Tzara, Tristan (1931) "Memoirs of Dadaism", in Edmund Wilson, *Axel's Castle*. New York: Charles Scribner's Sons.

Virilio, Paul (2002) *Ground Zero*, trans. Chris Turner. London: Verso.

Voloshinov, V. N. (1973) *Marxism and the Philosophy of Language*, trans. Ladislav Matejka and I. R. Titunik. New York and London: Seminar Press (first published 1929).

Williams, Raymond (1958) *Culture and Society, 1780–1950*. London: Chatto & Windus.

Williams, Raymond (1961) *The Long Revolution*. London: Chatto & Windus.

Williams, Raymond (1973) *The Country and the City*. London: Chatto & Windus.

Williams, Raymond (1976) *Keywords*. London: HarperCollins.

Williams, Raymond (1977) *Marxism and Literature*. London: Oxford University Press.

Wilson, Scott (1995) *Cultural Materialism: Theory and Practice*. Oxford: Blackwell.

Wittgenstein, L. J. J. (1967) *Philosophical Investigations*, 3rd edn, trans. G. E. M. Anscombe. Oxford: Blackwell (first published 1953).

Young, Robert (ed.) (1981) *Untying the Text*. London: Routledge & Kegan Paul.

Young, Robert J. C. (1990) *White Mythologies: Writing, History and the West*. London: Routledge.

Young, Robert J. C. (1994) *Colonial Desire: Hybridity in Theory, Culture and Race*. London: Routledge.

Young, Robert J. C. (1996) *Torn Halves: Political Conflict in Literary and Cultural Theory*. Manchester: Manchester University Press.

Žižek, Slavoj (1989) *The Sublime Object of Ideology*. London and New York: Verso.

Žižek, Slavoj (1999) *The Ticklish Subject*. London: Verso.

Žižek, Slavoj (2000) *The Art of the Ridiculous Sublime*. Seattle, WA: University of Washington Press.

Žižek, Slavoj (2002) *Welcome to the Desert of the Real*. London and New York: Verso.

Index

References in italics refer to entries in the Summaries and Biographical notes